THE PARABLES

THE PARABLES

Jewish Tradition and Christian Interpretation

BRAD H. YOUNG

B
BakerAcademic
a division of Baker Publishing Group
Grand Rapids, Michigan

Published by Baker Academic
a division of Baker Publishing Group
P.O. Box 6287, Grand Rapids, MI 49516-6287
www.bakeracademic.com

Baker Academic edition published 2012
ISBN 978-0-8010-4820-3

Previously published in 1998 by Hendrickson Publishers

Printed and bound by CPI Group (UK) Ltd, Croydon, CR0 4YY

The Library of Congress has cataloged the original edition as follows:
Young, Brad.
The parables: Jewish tradition and Christian interpretation / Brad H. Young.
p. cm.
Includes bibliographical references and indexes.
ISBN 1-56563-244-3
1. Jesus Christ—Parables. 2. Bible. O.T.—Parables. 3. Parables in rabbinical literature. 4. Jesus Christ—Jewishness. I. Title.
BT375.2.Y67 1988
226.8′06—dc21 98-17098

This book is dedicated in loving memory to
Dr. Robert L. Lindsey of Jerusalem, who contributed so
much to my life and to my understanding of the teachings
of Jesus. His linguistic research, synoptic discoveries,
and love for the country of Israel and her peoples
have been a rich source of inspiration for me.

Table of Contents

PART V:
The Disciple's Call: A Life of Learning and Doing

PART VI:
Torah Learning and God's Reign

Foreword

This great new book by Brad H. Young is a decisive step in the right direction. Like his previous books, this innovative work on the parables shows that Jesus is both a foundation of the Christian faith and at the same time an integral part of Second Temple period Judaism. Jewish thought is not—as is often claimed—merely a background for Jesus but is in reality the original context and natural framework of his message.

Few people have recognized this basic fact, not only because of inveterate Christian inhibitions but also because it is a very rare case that a NT scholar can break the language barrier and move freely in the Hebrew and Aramaic sources of early Judaism proficiently, as Young is able to do. Similarly, Jewish scholars often do not use their advantage in this area of research and sometimes cannot move freely in the Christian material because even they are not always free from their own inherited inhibitions. All who are involved in the study of Judaism, however, as well as everyone seeking a better understanding of Jesus, will be challenged by Young's creative and solid research. Very often the NT, and especially the Synoptic Gospels, elucidate other Jewish sources. This function of the Gospels is similar to that of the Dead Sea Scrolls in contemporary Jewish research.

The parables of Jesus are a part of a broader problem. If one has not become acquainted thoroughly with the other thousands of rabbinic parables, one may have the erroneous impression that Jesus invented this literary form. When one has learned from the rabbinic parables, one is compelled to ask how far the parables of Jesus are the expression of his own specific message and how far he has accepted common Jewish theology and incorporated it in his own message. A similar question arises when one hears other portions of the words of Jesus. For instance, how far is the Lord's Prayer typically Christian, and how far does it belong organically to the world of Judaism? Or, to put it another way, what is the melodious sound of Jesus' instrument in the Jewish orchestra that was playing a dramatic symphony during his time?

Two other vital questions remain. They are similar but not identical. The first involves the stream of ancient Judaism to which Jesus belongs, and the second regards his own self-awareness. Jesus surely does not belong to the Zealot movement. He is not an Essene or a Sadducee. The parables are at home exclusively in rabbinic Judaism. They are a typical form of teachings that characterize thought patterns near to the Pharisees. Some parables were invented by the rabbis to serve exegetical purposes. Others focus more on higher theological concerns of daily living. The parables not invented for biblical exegesis explain human dependence upon God and the essence of the divine nature. They promote rabbinic ethics and moral conduct. As an effective vehicle of communication, the rabbinic parable brings the people nearer to the Jewish humane approach of relating to other people. The parables inspire and challenge the people with a fresh awareness of God's character. How can a person comprehend God and his ways? The rabbinic parables often represent the new sensitivity flowing out of the lenient and compassionate school of Hillel. Because Jesus belonged to this kind of Jewish ethics, he liked to use parables to achieve his purpose. The rabbinic parables have the same aim as Jesus himself.

In fact, it is difficult to determine when Jesus is expressing an opinion in his parables that would conflict with other contemporary Jewish teachers. For one example, the content of Jesus' parables emphasizes, more than other rabbinic parables, his opinion that the sinners are equal with the righteous. In fact, the sinners are more highly valued before God than those who are proud of their own goodness. This seems to be the message of one parable so significant for Jesus, the Laborers in the Vineyard (Matt 20:1–16). Unlike a rabbinic parallel, where the same salary is paid to all the laborers because the latecomers produce the same amount of work as those who started early, in Jesus' parable the owner of the vineyard pays all the laborers the same wage regardless of job performance. He wants to be good to all, without any distinctions. While God accepts the sinner in rabbinic parables as well, Jesus more than some other teachers seems to emphasize divine favor given to the outcast.

It is easier to answer the second question, namely, how far do Jesus' parables express his own high self-awareness (about which I have no doubt)? Jesus' person is less present in his parables than many suppose. In the parable of the Sower (Luke 8:4–8, 11–18 and parallels), for instance, the content does not, as far as I can see, express the idea that the sower in the parable must be identified with Jesus himself. As I understand it, there is only one parable in which Jesus speaks about his sonship and his future tragedy. This is the parable of the Wicked Tenants (Luke 20:9–19 and parallels). Here Jesus identifies himself with the only beloved son and prophet, foreseeing his own imminent death. As in the parable of the Laborers in the Vineyard (Matt 20:1–16), Jesus transforms existing rabbinic parabolic teaching. At the end of the rabbinic version the son becomes the heir. In Jesus' parable the son is killed.

This new book by Brad H. Young is a wonderful aid to a real understanding of Jesus' theology and ethics as embedded in his parables. With scholarly precision, Young explores Jesus' ethics and theology in comparison with early Jewish teachings. The parallel Jewish material helps to interpret correctly Jesus' message. Without Young's painstaking research it would not be possible for Christian readers to have access to the pertinent Jewish sources, which are mostly unknown to the common intelligent reader. It is today indispensable to learn about the Jewish side of Jesus in order to understand our changing world and to find the right way to overcome the present crisis. We all are indebted to Young for his pioneering work.

DAVID FLUSSER
PROFESSOR EMERITUS OF SECOND TEMPLE PERIOD
JUDAISM AND EARLY CHRISTIANITY
HEBREW UNIVERSITY
JERUSALEM

Acknowledgments

Many friends and colleagues have contributed much to the research and writing of *The Parables: Jewish Tradition and Christian Interpretation.* As the book is being prepared for publication, my heart is filled with gratitude to so many who worked diligently with me on this project.

First I must thank Joseph Frankovic. Joseph devoted much time and energy to reading the entire manuscript carefully. He not only made important editorial suggestions but also strengthened the text by finding additional sources from his own independent research. His sensitivity to the sometimes fragile relationship between the church and the synagogue has guided his fine efforts. His doctoral work at Jewish Theological Seminary as well as his graduate studies at Oral Roberts University have prepared him to be a bridge builder between the Christian and Jewish communities through academic achievement and educational excellence. He is an outstanding scholar who will continue to make a meaningful contribution to research. I deeply appreciate his efforts on behalf of the present book, which is much improved because of his editorial assistance and scholarly acumen.

Words cannot express my deep feelings of appreciation to Prof. David Flusser of the Hebrew University. Prof. Flusser is a genius who is incredibly gifted in textual analysis. I count it the supreme privilege and joy of my life to have been able to work with him during my doctoral studies at the Hebrew University and to serve as his research assistant and editor. I am grateful that he agreed to write the prolegomenon to this book. He has given me fresh insight into the parables, and I treasure the years we have been able to work together in exploring the interrelationships among the Synoptic Gospels, linguistic analysis, and comparative study of Jewish and Christian texts. Without him this book would have been impossible. He has been a constant source of inspiration, assistance, and direction. I value his suggestions, which improved the manuscript decisively.

The book is dedicated to the memory of Dr. Robert L. Lindsey, who passed away on May 31, 1995. Dr. Lindsey was one of my closest friends. From him I have learned much about the life and teachings of Jesus. He was kind enough to review the chapter on the parable of the Sower. Since at that time he had lost the feeling in his fingers and was unable to type, he dictated a long letter of response to his beloved wife, Margaret, and sent it to me. His insights have been crucial in the research and writing of this book. I admired Dr. Lindsey not only for his fine scholarship but also because he was such a *mensch*, who lived his life in selfless service to others. His life has touched so many people, from the orphans he raised at Baptist Village to the congregation he pastored in Jerusalem. His brilliant mind and original thought will continue to challenge some of the "assured results" of NT scholarship in the years ahead. His academic work reminds us that the evidence is always of greater value than the conclusions.

Prof. Shmuel Safrai helped me with a number of difficult questions. His creative and intuitive approach to rabbinic studies has assisted greatly. Many of the guiding principles he gave to me, as one of the advisors on my doctoral thesis, have helped in the formation of this book, and I have appreciated his willingness to discuss with me, in the years after my studies in Jerusalem, textual issues relating to the parables. Dr. Steven Notley read portions of the text and offered valuable suggestions. Dr. Notley's knowledge of the historical geography of the Holy Land as well as his textual study of the Synoptic Gospels have assisted me. Mark Hall gave freely of his time as an editor, reading much of the text and suggesting important revisions. I would be remiss if, at this point, I neglected to acknowledge with gratitude Founder/ Chancellor Oral Roberts and the strong platform he and Oral Roberts University have provided for the pursuit and exploration of the scholarly issues surrounding Christian and Jewish theology. He has both personally and academically promoted improved relationships and active dialogue among Christians and Jews, providing a receptive arena for understanding the words of Jesus, appreciating the Jewish people and esteeming their faith. Moreover, I have benefited greatly from my interaction with my colleagues at the university, Dr. Howard Ervin, Dr. Tom Mathew, Dr. Robert Mansfield, Dr. Jerry Horner and Dr. Trevor Grizzle.

Dr. Roy Blizzard and his lovely wife, Gloria, have given strong encouragement. Dr. Blizzard's love for Hebrew and dedication to understanding the words of Jesus have inspired many students. Dr. Tom Benediktson of Tulsa University assisted me in dealing with some questions relating to Latin grammar and translation.

My family, and especially my son, Matthew David (named after Prof. David Flusser), have been understanding and helpful. My mother and father, Claudeen and Sen. John W. Young, have stood with me, strongly supporting the effort. I happily mention some very special friends who have shown interest in the work and given firm support: Rabbi Marc Boone Fitzermann, Dr. Burton Visotzky, Rabbi David Wolpe, Rabbi Leon Klenicki, Joseph

Puder, Roni Wexler, Ken and Lenore Mullican, Clarence and Pat Wagoner, Sheila Mudd, Dr. Marvin Wilson, Margaret Lindsey, Patrick Alexander, Dr. Ron Mosley, Dr. Mike and Ruby Butchko, David Bivin, Dwight Pryor, Dr. Peter Tomson, Francisco Munoz, Steven Schmidt, Robert Morris, Jack Poirier, and Pat Young. My special thanks to Gayle Brazil for preparing the index. A number of the advisory board members of the Gospel Research Foundation must be mentioned for their support. Tim Eckblad, Barry Chambliss, Jimmy White, and John Mark Young have strengthened the work through their help and encouragement. David Reed helped with editing and proofreading the manuscript. Students in my classes have asked meaningful questions concerning Jesus and the Gospels, and I have benefited from their inquisitive minds and fresh perspectives.

Many friends and colleagues have given of their time and effort to improve the present work. I have valued their kind assistance, recognizing my own limitations. While it is impossible to mention everyone who has made a contribution to this book, I have deeply appreciated all, especially my students, who have helped me understand the parables of Jesus. The parables merit our careful attention and very best efforts of interpretation. We will never even begin to understand Jesus of the Gospels apart from his parables. I feel a great debt to so many fine scholars, inquisitive students, and personal friends who have forced me to examine more carefully the rich Jewish heritage of Jesus and the cultural backdrop of the Gospel parables.

Part 1

The Historical Development and the Theological Significance of Parables in Judaism and Christianity

1 Introduction: Gospel and Rabbinic Parables

PARABLES

The reality of God is revealed in the word-pictures of a parable. Jesus and the rabbis of old taught about God by using concrete illustrations that reach the heart through the imagination. They challenged the mind on the highest intellectual level by using simple stories that made common sense out of the complexities of religious faith and human experience. On the one hand, in finite terms God is beyond human comprehension, but on the other, his infinite majesty may be captured in vivid stories of daily life.

The Hebrew parable, mashal (משל), has a wide range of meanings. The word is stretched from its basic meaning of similarity or resemblance to cover any type of illustration, from a proverbial saying to a fictitious story. It may refer to a proverb, riddle, anecdote, fable, or allegory. A mashal defines the unknown by using what is known. The mashal begins where the listener is, but then pushes beyond into a new realm of discovery. The rabbinic parable illustrates its point by redescribing, in drama, the nature of God and human responses to his love.

The Greek parable, *parabolē* (παραβολή), refers to what is cast alongside. The dramatic image of a story illustration is thrown out as a comparison of the reality of the source with its fictional representation in words. It may refer to a saying or story example. The idea of resemblance is not quite as pronounced in the Greek word *parabolē* as it is in the Hebrew term *mashal*, but both terms show a likeness between the images of an illustration and the object being portrayed. The Jesus of the Synoptic Gospels loves to use miniature plays to communicate his message. The word-picture of the parable creates a drama that redescribes in clear terms the reality being illustrated. The resemblance between the reality and the illustration makes an instructive comparison.

The genre of story parables, however, seems to be independent of the terms selected to designate them. Jesus and the rabbis of old created these illustrations, and their stories became known as parables. Jewish teachers seem to have developed the classic form of the parable from their religious heritage and cultural experience. The method of teaching developed first, then the term parable (mashal or *parabolē*) was used to describe the story illustrations that resulted. In this book we will pursue an inductive study of the parables, as mini-dramas designed to teach a message by illustrating a resemblance between the source of the word-picture and its redescription in metaphor. Moreover, we will look at the background of the story in Jewish culture and religion, as A. M. Hunter has already suggested in his fine, popular book on the parables: "The word itself, *parabole*, is of course Greek, and means a comparison or analogy. Aristotle discusses it in his *Rhetoric*. But the antecedents of Christ's parable must be sought not in Hellas but in Israel; not in the Greek orators but in the Old Testament prophets and the Jewish Fathers."[1]

The way the parables speak about God is deeply rooted in the historical and cultural background of the Hebrew Bible. The rich imagery used to describe God is similar to that of the Bible. The differences between the East and the West have been perceptively brought out by John Donahue when he describes biblical statements about God:

> Biblical statements about God and God's actions in the world are expressed in a language of images that moves in the rhythmic cadences of Hebrew poetry. God is not simply powerful but one who "kills and brings to life; he brings down to sheol and raises up" (1 Sam. 2:6). God does not simply free a people but leads them out of a house of bondage "with a mighty hand and an outstretched arm" (Deut. 5:15). The Hebrew Bible images a God who lays the foundations of the earth and shuts in the sea with doors (Job 38:4, 8), who seeks an unfaithful people with the longing of a rejected lover (Hosea 2) and remembers a people with a mother's love (Isa. 49:14–15). The biblical God speaks through images that touch hidden depths of human experience and cover the whole gamut of human emotion.[2]

Parables are like that. God's redemptive work is redefined in vivid images of strength and force. The Eastern mind tended to conceive of God in dynamic metaphors; God is known through his mighty acts. Parables describe God in similar images. This type of language is appropriate for the later rabbinic *meshalim* (parables). Jesus knew well this medium of communication. Hunter boldly asserts, "Doubtless it was in the synagogue that Jesus first heard men

---

[1] A. M. Hunter, *Interpreting the Parables* (London: SCM, 1972) 8. Hunter surely knew Jeremias's theory, discussed below, that Jesus invented parabolic teaching. Hunter rightly rejected it.

[2] John R. Donahue, *The Gospel in Parable, Metaphor, Narrative, and Theology in the Synoptic Gospels* (Philadelphia: Fortress, 1988) 1.

talking in parables."[3] Jesus used the parable to drive home his message about God and God's relationship to every human being. Each person has supreme value for the parable teacher of the Gospels. The stress on human relationships emerges from the interaction among the stock characters within the drama of the Gospel parables.

The Gospel parables of Jesus, moreover, are full of everyday ordinariness along with a God-consciousness. The unexpected usually enters into the drama with a surprise action by one of the leading characters or an unanticipated change of events. The stage of daily life becomes the scene for viewing the world from God's perspective. By putting God and his ways on open display for all to ponder, the parables create a new dimension. God enters the world of humanity with the challenge of religious conviction and corresponding action. The listener catches a glimpse of the divine character and the spiritual realities of life. Parables use rich imagery of language to catch the listener unaware. At first it all seems so familiar, and then a shift develops in the plot of the story. The ordinariness of the parable is transformed by a surprising twist. A consciousness of God and his way of viewing the world enters the commonplace scene to communicate the divine message. The familiar setting of the parable allows each person to understand God's will. The local color of the story is changed for a special purpose. This storytelling methodology is present in both rabbinic and Gospel parables. They share many common motifs and literary types in this dynamic process, which demands interaction from every listener.

Parables are a shadow of the substance. The physical reality of the parable reveals the natural affinity between the world in which we live and the spiritual dimension. The theological presuppositions of the parables undergird the descriptive elements of a dramatic presentation. The drama comes alive in meaning because of the theological significance of the parables.

In the creative genius of the parable teacher's imagination, the listener is catching glimpses of the divine character. The shadow is an inexact representation of the substance. But in the shadow one discovers a clear outline of many features of the reality. In many ways, God is the ultimate reality, providing the substance for the shadow in the word-pictures of a parable. In fact, the old root word behind the Hebrew term mashal refers to shadow. In one early Semitic proverb, the king is the shadow or resemblance of God, and a common person is the likeness of the royal ruler. J. Heintz has stressed this point in his discussion of this ancient saying that compares the king to God. Heintz believes that the comparison (mashal) is based on an earlier tradition. The comparison itself is made in an official address to the king Asarhaddon or Assurbanipal between 680 and 627 B.C.E.[4] It has far-reaching ramifications for the meaning of parables in ancient Semitic thought.

---

[3] Hunter, *Parables*, 8.

[4] J. G. Heintz, "Royal Traits and Messianic Figures: A Thematic and Iconographical Approach (Mesopotamian Elements)," *The Messiah* (ed. J. Charlesworth; Minneapolis:

> As it is said, "The [human] king is the shadow of the god, and man [the human being] is the shadow of the [human] king." Thus the king himself is the perfect resemblance of the god![5] (=LAS, no. 145)

The word for parable is instructive here as highlighting the likeness between divine majesty and human royalty. The human king is the "perfect resemblance" or the shadow of the god. Heintz observes, "This important text, though difficult to interpret, presents the interesting citation of an archaic proverb very relevant to the theme that qualifies the king as 'the image of god.'"[6] Rabbinic and Gospel parables first and foremost tell us about God. They are stamped with the image of God, who is the substance of the shadow. Through comparative language, they teach the listener about the divine character by showing what God is like. The listener moves from what is known in his or her experience unto the unknowable in human understanding. God is like a generous householder or a compassionate father. The likeness of the parable is the shadow of the object.

"Above all else," says David Stern, one of the foremost authorities on rabbinic parables, "the mashal represents the greatest effort to imagine God in all Rabbinic literature."[7] The rabbis talked about God in parables. The creative process of conceptual thought brings life to simple stories about kings, householders, or fathers who resemble some aspect of God's character. How can one imagine what God almighty is like? In Stern's eyes, rabbinic parables constitute the strongest effort to reveal his nature. Community leaders and old rabbis tried to communicate the divine character and sought to comprehend God's will by telling stories about daily living. They recognized the affinity between the natural realm and the ways of God. So it is with Jesus and his Jewish parables.

Augsburg Fortress, 1992) 52–66. Cf. also S. Loewenstamm, "Chaviv Adam Shnivra Betzelem," *Tarbiz* 27 (1957–1958): 1–2; and "Beloved Is Man in That He Was Created in the Image," in *Comparative Studies in Biblical and Ancient Oriental Literature* (Vluyn: Neukirchener, 1980) 48–50.

[5]Heintz, "Royal Traits," 62.

[6]Ibid.

[7]David Stern, *Parables in Midrash: Narrative and Exegesis in Rabbinic Literature* (Cambridge: Harvard University Press, 1991) 93. Stern perceptively observes,

> The one character in the mashal who is never a type or stock character is the king; he is the only character consistently to possess a personality—or personalities, since he can change utterly from one mashal to another—and this distinction among characters may stand, from a theological perspective, as an emblem of God's profound difference from all else in the universe. For our concerns, however, the more pressing question is the nature of God's character, the precise personality of His characterization as king. The image of God as king—ubiquitous in the Bible, and common in other ancient Near Eastern literatures—is distinct in the mashal in that the king here is a genuine character.

PARABLES AS GOSPEL

One-third of the recorded sayings of Jesus in the Synoptic Gospels are in parables. If we do not understand the parables, we miss what may be known about the historical Jesus. One must understand parables to know Jesus. But the approaches advanced to study the Gospel parables are in conflict with one another. In this study we will seek to find common ground among the positive elements of the various approaches that have been advanced to understand the teachings of Jesus. The historical and critical method is the starting point. Recent advances in textual study, archaeology, Greek studies, epigraphy, literary analysis, folklore, the Dead Sea Scrolls research, rabbinic thought, and Jewish religious movements have provided fresh insights into the parabolic instruction of the Gospels.[8] After all, Jesus was a Jew, and his parables represent a form of Judaism from his time.

The Semitisms of the Synoptic Gospels reveal the rich heritage of Jews and Judaism during the days when the temple was a reality. The Greek elements of the texts, however, also show the editorial process and the reinterpretation of the parables for a new setting beyond the ministry of Jesus within the life of the early church. The Christian interpretation of the parables at the close of the first and the beginning of the second centuries infused new meaning into the Gospels. While the parables have a message that transcends time, the reinterpretation of the illustrations in a new context often has distorted the authentic meaning. Far-fetched allegories and teachings directly opposed to Jesus and his Judaism have undermined the force of the parabolic messages that the original audiences heard. Because every interpreter of the parables is limited by time and place as well as by a different religious and cultural orientation, historical research promises to discover more about Jesus and his methods of teaching. Jesus' Jewish culture and his devotion to Torah open up much of the deeper meaning of the parables for us. Ancient Judaism is the backdrop for Jesus and his parables.

The Gospels make one thing clear: Jesus is fond of teaching in parables. Moreover, the stories of God and people that Jesus used to illustrate his message called for a decision from everyone who listened. Parables are works of art in the discipline of communication. In fact, Jesus' parables are prime examples of Jewish haggadah.

Parables as Haggadah

First and foremost, both the parables of Jesus and the parables of the rabbis must be studied as Jewish haggadah. Haggadah, or storytelling with

[8] See, e.g., the important work of P. W. van der Horst, *Ancient Jewish Epitaphs* (Kampen, Netherlands: Pharos, 1991), which covers a long-neglected area of study, Jewish funerary epigraphy. His valuable analysis has pointed out the pervasive use of Greek in much inscriptional evidence.

a message, has its own dynamic within the parameters of religious and ethical teaching. Often designed to be entertaining or even captivating, the haggadah proclaims a powerful message that usually demands a decision. A good story can drive home the point better than a sermon. Often an earthy illustration says so much more than a lofty homily. But haggadah is more than entertaining stories because it serves a higher purpose, centering on God's way among people whom he loves. After all, the focus of haggadah is to understand the divine nature. Regarding the purpose of haggadah, the rabbis teach us, "If your desire is to know Him who spoke and the world came into being, then study Haggadah and from this study you will know Him who spoke the world into being and you will cleave to His ways."[9] One who seeks to know God must listen to the stories from haggadah and learn its message. Such illumination precedes obedience. The haggadah makes a path for the earnest student who loves God and seeks his ways.

Of course, haggadah embraces a much wider genre of Jewish literature than parables. Generally speaking, whatever is not halakah (legal lore) or midrash (Bible exposition) may be called haggadah. Haggadah is found in abundance in midrash as well as in some halakic texts. Haggadah bridged the gap between the common people and the highly educated. By focusing on the heart and the imagination, haggadah reaches people on all levels, from the learned to the untutored, in the ways of Torah. The Jewish theologian Abraham Joshua Heschel proclaimed the distinctives of haggadah in comparison with halakah in this way: "Halacha deals with subjects that can be expressed literally; agada introduces us to a realm which lies beyond the range of expression. Halacha teaches us how to participate in the eternal drama. Halacha gives knowledge; agada gives us aspiration. Halacha gives us the norms for action; agada, the vision of the ends of living."[10] In Heschel's thinking, haggadah inspires the people while halakah deals more with details. Both disciplines of study have significant roles, but haggadah captures the heart through the imagination. It reaches out and takes hold of the spiritual qualities of the human heart. It reveals God's presence in personal experience. The world of haggadah often soared high above to reach ordinary people below. It communicated God's love in a meaningful way to the most erudite scholar as well as to the common folk.

---

[9] *Sifre Deut.* 49 (*Sifre Devarim*, ed. L. Finkelstein [New York: Jewish Theological Seminary, 1969] 115). The saying, attributed to the dorshe hagadot, is: דורשי הגדות אומרים רצונך להכיר את מי שאמר והיה העולם למוד הגדה שמתוך כך אתה מכיר את מי שאמר והיה העולם ומדבק בדרכיו.

[10] Abraham Joshua Heschel, *God in Search of Man: A Philosophy of Judaism* (New York: Farrar, Straus and Giroux, 1976) 336–37. Heschel also explains the relationship of haggadah and halakah thus: "Agada deals with man's ineffable relations to God, to other men, and to the world. Halacha deals with details, with each commandment separately; agada with the whole of life, with the totality of religious life."

A fine example of haggadah is found in the story of R. Eleazer's encounter with the exceedingly ugly man. Unlike the exceedingly ugly man, who probably had labored menially throughout the day, R. Eleazer had the privilege of devoting himself entirely to the study of Torah. His master was R. Meir, and perhaps R. Eleazer and his beloved teacher had spent the day learning the deeper things of God.

The Rabbi and the Exceedingly Ugly Man

> On one occasion Rabbi Eleazer son of Rabbi Simeon was coming from Migdal Gedor, from the house of his teacher. He was riding leisurely on his donkey by the riverside and was feeling happy and elated because he had studied much Torah. There he chanced to meet an exceedingly ugly man who greeted him, "Peace be upon you, rabbi." He, however, did not return his greeting but instead said to him, "*Raca* ['Empty one' or 'Good for nothing'] how ugly you are! Is everyone in your town as ugly as you are?" The man replied; "I do not know, but go and tell the craftsman who made me, 'How ugly is the vessel which you have made.'" When R. Eleazer realized that he had sinned he dismounted from the donkey and prostrated himself before the man and said to him, "I submit myself to you, forgive me!"[11]

Rabbi Eleazar could not hold his tongue. When he encountered the exceedingly ugly man, all he could think about was that ugliness. When he made his stinging insult, he failed to see each person as created in the image of God. The ugly man, on the other hand, perhaps because of life experience, had come to realize the deeper significance of the story of creation—every human being, attractive or otherwise, has the divine image superimposed. Each person is crafted according to plan by the master designer. In the world of haggadah, one discovers the healthy tension between a scholar and an unlearned man. In this case, the lofty scholar, who had the privilege of studying all day, crossed paths with the ignorant day laborer. The scholar rides a donkey. The ugly man walks. The scholar's opportunities in education and superior financial standing far exceed that of the day laborer, who had to work hard to survive. But who has greater wisdom?

The incident described teaches more about the love of others who are created in the divine image than exhortations from the pulpits of churches or synagogues. The haggadah reaches the heart and challenges the mind. It inspires the people to see God's image—even in the face of another human being with a wretched, uncomely appearance. The intellect grasps the meaning of the biblical text. But haggadah penetrates the heart with the message that every human being is created in the image of God. According to the

[11] b. *Taan.* 20a–b, *Abot R. Nat.*, version A, ch. 41 (*Aboth de Rabbi Nathan*, ed. S. Schechter [Vienna: Lippe, 1887] 66a); *Der. Er. Rab.* 4:1 (*Masekhtot Derekh Eretz*, ed. M. Higger [2 vols.; Jerusalem: Makor, 1970] 1:166 vol. 1; *Pirke Ben Azzai* 2:1). See also ch. 15 of my *Jesus the Jewish Theologian* (Peabody Mass.: Hendrickson, 1995), 163–70.

exceedingly ugly man, a parable-like comparison may be made between a human craftsman who forms a vessel and the divine creator who formed each person out of the dust. The story illustrates, moreover, the deep Jewish roots of Jesus' teachings on love. Like Jesus, many streams of thought in ancient Judaism stressed loving the outcast. Many Jewish teachers from the period would have strongly embraced the commandment of Jesus, "But I say to you, Love your enemies."[12]

In Judaism, haggadah inspires esteem for others by calling to remembrance God and each person who is created in his image. Haggadah infuses life into the written word. The Bible simply describes the story of creation. Haggadah reveals the ones created in God's image in the nameless faces of all humanity. Moreover, anyone who kills another has murdered an entire world and diminished the divine image. Causing one soul to perish from Israel, the rabbis warn, is like wiping out an entire nation.[13] An earthly king stamps every coin with his image, and all the coins look exactly alike. Not so in regard to God himself! The rabbis teach, "the King of kings, the Holy One, blessed be he, has stamped every human being with the likeness of the first human and there is not a single individual who looks the same as another."[14] Perhaps these theological concepts serve as a background for the saying of Jesus, "Then render to Caesar the things that are Caesar's, and to God the things that are God's."[15] After all, not only is Caesar's image stamped on coins that he has minted; the divine image of the King of kings is stamped upon each person. Jesus was calling upon the people to give everything to God, the Creator of every human being.

Parable lore reveals the divine character in the physical world. Haggadah illustrates the ways of God. For the rabbis, every human being is like God, because of the creation story. They teach about creation in haggadah in order to expand the mind and reach the soul. Parables are filled with the likeness of God in metaphoric language describing everyday life. One must be trained to see the likeness of God in the parables. Rabbi Meir develops this theme in a remarkable parable, in which he draws a direct correspondence between God and a human being hanged upon a cross.

---

[12] Matt 5:44. See also David Flusser, "A New Sensitivity in Judaism and the Christian Message," in his *Judaism and the Origins of Christianity* (Jerusalem: Magnes, 1988) 469–89.

[13] Compare m. *Sanh.* 4:5.

[14] See m. *Sanh.* 4:5 (cf. *Mishnah*, ed. C. Albeck [6 vols.; Jerusalem: Bialik Institute, 1978] 4:182; English trans. in Herbert Danby, *The Mishnah* [New York: Oxford University Press, 1977] 388) and parallels.

[15] Luke 20:25; Matt 22:21, and Mark 12:17. Cf. also the saying of Hillel in *Lev. Rab.* 34:3. Hillel had a high self-awareness, esteeming himself as being created in God's likeness. In Hillel's eyes, even taking a bath should be considered a meritorious deed in God's service, because an earthly king hires laborers to wash and care for his statues.

Identical Twins

Rabbi Meir used to say, "Why does the Scripture teach, '... for a hanged man is accursed by God' [Deut 21:33]? The matter may be compared to two brothers who were identical twins. One was the king of the entire world and the other one went out and joined a band of robbers. Eventually they caught the one who was a robber. They crucified him upon a cross. Each one who passed by exclaimed, 'That one being crucified looks just like the king!' Thus it was said, '... for a hanged man is accursed by God.'"[16]

This amazing parable compares God and every human being to the king of all the world and a wicked criminal. The crucified one in this parable almost seems like Jesus.[17] In much of Christian theology, he alone is like God in that he could be called an identical twin. In R. Meir's creative thought and interpretation of Deut 21:23, "for a hanged man is accursed by God," however, even a criminal may be considered a divine twin because every person is created in God's image. The parable calls upon the listener to ponder in amazement. A human being, even someone quite unlike God, living a life doing wrong, such as a robber, may still be compared to God's identical twin. As Jewish haggadah, the parable reveals the divine nature in startling metaphoric description based upon common human experience.

All parables fall within the realm of haggadah, even though haggadah encompasses much more than parables. The rabbinic parable describes the relationship between God and his people. The theological significance, as Jakob Petuchowski has convincingly argued, must be fully appreciated.[18] Sometimes parables illustrate the message of Torah through dynamic redescription. But they go beyond exegesis. Often rabbinic parables portray the divine nature in the theater of life. Drama becomes an effective mode of communication. The unknown God is revealed in what is known by human experiences of life.

The unpretentious setting as well as the straightforward approach of most parables has led some to criticize their simplicity. Perhaps the popular nature of these stories also contributed to the degrading of their significance. In the one midrash, the rabbis warn against undermining the importance of the parables: "Let not the parable be lightly esteemed in your eyes, because

---

[16] See t. *Sanh.* 9:7 (*Tosefta*, ed. M. Zuckermandel [Jerusalem: Wahrmann, 1937] 429). I appreciate the insight of David Flusser, who observed the significance of this illustration for the study of parables. Cf. J. Neusner, trans., *The Tosefta* (New York: KTAV, 1981) 227–28.

[17] The possibility that R. Meir had Jesus in mind when he told the parable should not be dismissed completely, though it seems somewhat unlikely. In all events, the Jewish parable does portray images that are related to Christian thought.

[18] Jakob Petuchowski, "The Theological Significance of the Parable in Rabbinic Literature and the New Testament," *Christian News from Israel* 23 (1972–1973) 76–86.

by means of the parable, a person can master the words of Torah."[19] The parables provided a way for the people to understand Torah. In rabbinic lore, Solomon used parables for illustrations. They were "handles" for the Torah.[20] The parables made the message lucid and practical. They, like a guideline that a person has devised in order to find his or her way through a huge palace with many chambers, provide a path through the intricacies of the Torah. Parables illuminate and clarify the meaning of the sacred text.

While Torah does teach halakah, and haggadah does illustrate God's will, at times halakah and haggadah compete with one another as different methods of interpreting Jewish faith and practice. Two rabbis are teaching in the same town. One teaches haggadah, and the other treats supposedly more serious issues relating only to halakah. The people abandon the one who delves deeply into the details of legal matters in order to hear the words of Torah expounded in thought-provoking illustrations. Rabbi Chaya b. Abba, who does not believe that anything takes a second place to halakah, is offended by the popular success of his colleague R. Abbahu, who captures the attention of the common people through his haggadic lore. The halakic mind clashes with the spirit of the haggadist. In an open conflict, R. Chaya b. Abba attacks R. Abbahu, who makes his defense by telling a parable!

Halakah and Haggadah

> R. Abbahu answered him: "I will tell you a parable. To what may the matter be compared? It may be compared to two men. One of them was selling precious stones and the other various kinds of small ware. To whom do the people rush? Is it not to the seller of various kinds of small ware?"[21]

By comparing haggadah to various kinds of small ware and halakah to precious stones, R. Abbahu makes his concession to R. Chaya b. Abba. He does not dispute the quintessential importance of halakah, but he does argue that haggadah has a popular appeal because it is within the grasp of the common folk. Everyone enjoys the dynamic force of a good illustration. For R. Abbahu, a parable settles the dispute. The Talmud illustrates the friction between two competing methods of study, the one that promotes halakah and the other haggadah. They are related, but haggadah inspires the people and enables them to understand complex issues.

Who can argue with the truth conveyed clearly in the words of a dynamic parable? The only way to refute a parable is with another parable. The rabbis debate conflicting viewpoints with similar-sounding parables. One parable may be used to prove a point, and then a second will be used to prove the

---

[19] See *Song Rab.* 1.1.8; cf. also Shimshon Donski, *Midrash Rabbah Sir Hashirim* (Tel Aviv: Dvir, 1980) 6.

[20] Ibid. See Donski's edition, אל יהי המשל הזה קל בעיניך שעל ידי המשל הזה אדם יכול לעמוד בדברי תורה.

[21] b. *Sota* 40a and parallels.

exactly opposite opinion. The schools of Shammai and Hillel disputed with one another over the essence of the creation narrative in the Bible. Were the heavens created before the earth, or was the earth created before the heavens? The biblical text is somewhat ambiguous on the subject. But, as in most cases involving the many disputes between the schools of Shammai and Hillel, the disciples of Hillel seem to present more convincing arguments. This state of affairs may be attributed in part to the fact that the followers of Hillel became the caretakers of the Jewish tradition because their views gained prevalence in subsequent history.

The Heaven and the Earth

> "The heaven and the earth" [Gen 1:1]. The School of Shammai say: The heaven was created first. However the School of Hillel maintain: The earth was created first. In support of their view, the School of Shammai say, "It may be compared to a king who first made a throne and then his footstool, for it is written, 'The heaven is my throne and the earth is my footstool' [Isa 66:1]." The School of Hillel maintain, in support of their view, "It may be compared to a king who builds a palace. Only after he built the lower story did he build the upper story, for it is written, 'In the day that the LORD God made earth and heaven' [Gen 2:4]."[22]

Both positions may be supported from the biblical text. According to Gen 1:1, the heavens preceded the earth, whereas Gen 2:4 says that the earth was made first. The issue may be resolved through a parable. The parable of the school of Shammai, however, is like the parable produced by the school of Hillel. The same parable may be revised and used to support a very different argument.

The imprecise world of haggadah is not so far removed from the realities of life. The illusion created by a picture is not the same as the reality. Each parable is a work of art that may produce different responses. The interpreter should allow the context and the artist to guide him or her in seeking the proper response. Contradictions and inconsistencies characterize religious philosophy and the practical experience of the faithful. The parables make sense out of the complexities of life even when they reflect inherent inconsistencies themselves.

A parable is an artistic representation. It is a picture of life. Dramatic portrayals within parables are the common characteristics of both rabbinic and Gospel texts. Since the parables are a genre within different types of literary works, or a genre within other genres, comparative study is crucial for a proper understanding of both Gospel and rabbinic parables. The parables of Jesus and those of the rabbis have much in common. As haggadah they tell a story about God and invite their listeners to cleave to his ways.

---

[22] See *Gen. Rab.* 1:15 (ed. Albeck, 1:13); *Midr. Sam.* 28b.

The parables are designed to portray a reality. In a world of metaphorical redescription, the reality behind the parable is dramatized in word-pictures. One must carefully consider the relationship between the picture and the reality while recognizing that the metaphor and the object are not one and the same. The parables give only a pictorial representation. We discover points of contact between the reality being portrayed and the picture. But the picture is not the reality. In some ways, these points resemble feathers that guide an arrow. A parable of haggadah may have multiple points of comparison between the picture and the reality, but it has one purpose. The multiple points of comparison are like the feathers aligned with the shaft of an arrow when it is aimed at a target. Because of the feathers the arrow flies steadily toward a specific destination in the same way that a parable is told to make one point.[23] It communicates a single message, which usually requires a decision. A forceful illustration makes it difficult to ignore the call for an immediate reaction. The parable is designed to elicit a response, a decision.

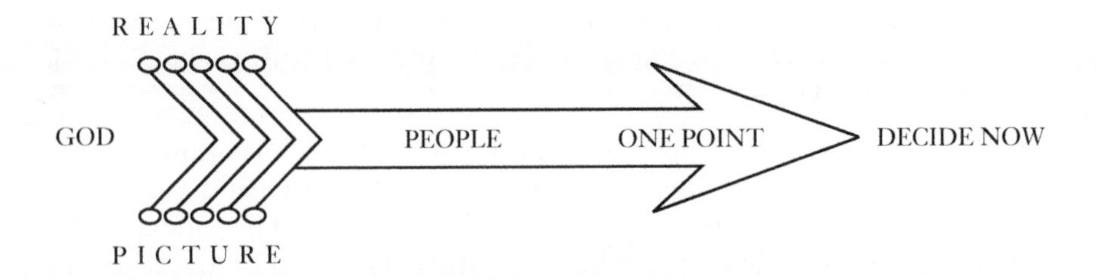

The parables of Jewish haggadah present a spiritual reality in pictures. They begin with God and involve people. They communicate one message and urge a decision. So while a parable teacher may intend more than one point of comparison between the picture and the reality it illustrates, the drama leads in one direction to communicate a single message. The parables enable the listener to see things the way God sees them. They see human beings

[23] See Hunter, *Parables*, 10: "A parable usually has only one *tertium;* an allegory may have a dozen. In other words, the allegory is a kind of 'description in code,' and, if it is to be fully understood, it must be deciphered point by point, feature by feature. On the other hand, in the parable there is one chief point of likeness between the story and the meaning, and the details simply help to make the story realistic and so serve the central thrust of the parable—like feathers which wing the arrow." As illustrated by my diagram, I believe that a parable may have multiple points of comparison between the picture and the reality. Each point of comparison, however, should be clearly made by either the storyteller or the context of the parable. Creating allegory will distort the single message of the illustration. An oriental parable teacher could not be restricted to the rule of one *tertium*. The interpreter must listen to the parable teacher's story and examine the context.

from God's point of view and challenge the listener to respond to his eternal message. They take the abstract world of spiritual values and enable the audience to visualize them in concrete terms.

PARABLES AS FOLKLORE

Rabbinic and Gospel parables are authentic representations of folk culture. The themes of the stories reveal a people's rich cultural heritage. Royal and aristocratic families are viewed through the eyes of the common folk. Agricultural laborers fill the dramatic scenes of the stories. The plots, which often involve the rich and their money or the landowners and their work forces, are derived from the situations of daily life. They may even contain depictions of high-society weddings. Parables excite attention through the human characteristics of vice and virtue. They are filled with both evil and good while they make use of a fascinating cast of villains and heroes. These stories are fond of contrast, exaggeration, intrigue, and surprise. Money, power, greed as well as generosity, humility, and compassion generate the interest of the listener. Attention-attracting stories communicate the truths of God and the spiritual values of religious life. Humor is also prominent in many folklore traditions. Though much humor is culturally conditioned, the situation comedy of some stories is still apparent.

The Amoraic sage R. Berechiah tells a parable concerning the fat man and the little donkey. The dry wit of the story transcends its cultural setting.

The Donkey and the Fat Man

> R. Berechiah told a parable of a fat man riding on an donkey. The fat man was wondering "When can I get off the donkey?" The donkey was wondering "When will he get off me?" When the time came for the fat man to get off, I do not know which one was more glad.[24]

Originally the story was designed to explain a paradox in the biblical account of the exodus. After the struggle to convince Pharaoh to let the people go, the Egyptians were relieved to see the Israelites leave and the pestilences that had afflicted Egypt cease. The paradox is that both the Egyptians and the Israelites were happy. How may one grasp the irony of the situation? Who was more happy, the Egyptians or the Israelites? The matter may be compared to a fat man riding on a little donkey. The element of folk humor is still felt in the comedy of the situation. It is a folktale that has been used to illustrate a biblical text.

---

[24]*Midr. Pss.* 114:1; 105:11 (Yalkut); see also the discussion of humor by H. K. McArthur and R. M. Johnston, *They Also Taught in Parables* (Grand Rapids: Zondervan, 1990) 129. See the English translation by W. Braude, *The Midrash on Psalms* (2 vols.; New Haven: Yale University Press, 1958) 2:215.

Parables resemble folk stories drawn from a shared cultural experience. In some ways, they have common features with a prevalent form of folklore known as the fable. While some Gospel sayings allude to fable lore and some rabbinic anecdotes are clear replicas of fables, most parables should be placed in an entirely different category. A closer look at the parables shows their distinctive qualities, even though the same Hebrew term, mashal, may designate either parable or fable. Because animals with human characteristics play leading roles in the fable, sometimes a distinction in Hebrew has been made by referring to fables as *mishle shualim*, "fox comparisons," and parables as *meshalim*, "comparisons" or "likenesses." The Jewish people were acquainted with fable lore. Their culture did not escape the pervasive influence of Hellenism.

One of the eminent authorities on fables, H. Schwarzbaum, defines a fable as "a fictitious tale told for the purpose of communicating a certain idea, or a truth of some kind, metaphorically."[25] Like parables, fables make use of metaphorical word-pictures to convey a message about the reality behind the illustration. Concerning the purpose of a fable, Schwarzbaum stresses, "the exclusive object of fable is generally to instruct, and particularly to teach some lesson, to enforce a precept, to convey a definite idea or philosophical concept, to illustrate some principle of conduct." For Schwarzbaum, fables teach a message "through the transparent analogy of actions of gods, heroes, men, animals, and even inanimate objects often furnished by the fabulist with human traits and emotions."[26] Leading fable authority Edwin Ben Perry follows Theon, the second-century C.E. author who described fable in the Aesopic sense of the definition λόγος ψευδὴς εἰκονίζων ἀλήθειαν, "a fictitious story picturing truth."[27] As a recognized scholar of Aesop's fables, Perry finds much merit in Theon's approach. "This is a perfect and complete definition provided we understand the range of what is included under the terms λόγος (story) and ἀλήθειαν (truth)."[28] In studying the relationship between the illustration and the message, Perry focuses attention on the fable itself. "The 'story' may be contained in no more than a single short sentence, or it may be much longer, or include some dialogue; but it must be told in the past tense, as stories normally are, and it must purport to be a particular action or series of actions, or an utterance, that took place once upon a time through the agency of particular characters."[29]

---

[25] Haim Schwarzbaum, *The Mishle Shualim (Fox Fables) of Rabbi Berechiah Ha-Nakdan: A Study in Comparative Folklore and Fable Lore* (Kiron, Israel: Institute for Jewish and Arab Folklore Research, 1979) i.

[26] Ibid.

[27] *Babrius and Phaedrus,* ed. and trans. Ben Edwin Perry (LCL; Cambridge: Harvard University Press, 1965; repr., 1984) xix–xx; see Theon, *Progymnasmata,* ch. 3.

[28] *Babrius and Phaedrus,* ed. Perry, xix–xx.

[29] Ibid.

The cultural setting and the teaching context make a significant difference in the interpretation of a fable. Consider the similarities and differences between Aesop's fable of "The Middle-Aged Man with Two Mistresses" and the rabbinic parallel about "The Man with Two Wives." Aesop's version in Babrius explores the meaning of a man's relationship with women, while the rabbis have their minds on the study of Torah. They deal with the issues surrounding haggadah and halakah. The fable has been recycled in the Jewish literature and given an entirely new meaning. On the other hand, Aesop's version deals with the precarious position of a man involved with two mistresses, one older and the other younger.

The Middle-Aged Man with Two Mistresses

> A man already in middle age was still spending his time on love affairs and carousals. He wasn't young any more, nor was he as yet an old man, but the white hairs on his head were mixed up in confusion with the black. He was making love to two women, one young, and the other old. The young woman wanted him to look like a young lover, the old one like one of her own age. Accordingly, on every occasion the mistress who was in the prime of her life plucked out such of his hairs as she found to be turning white, and the old woman plucked out the black ones. This went on until each of them presented the other with a baldpated lover by the pulling out of his hair. [Aesop told this fable in order to show how pitiable a man is who falls into the hands of women. Women are like the sea, which smiles and lures men onto its sparkling surface, then snuffs them out.][30]

The humorous story is full of life and probably circulated widely. In Babrius, a moral that betrays a strong prejudice against women is attached to the story.[31] The moral could just as easily have referred to the whimsical character of a middle-aged man who is unfaithful to his lover as to the biased portrayal of a woman who entices a man and then destroys him. For that matter, the lesson drawn from the story would more aptly have illustrated the folly of a middle-aged man flirting with different women.

The rabbis take the story out of its worldly context of a man with two lovers and employ the same anecdote to illustrate methods of Bible study. The problem of one who studies halakah without haggadah is like a man with two wives. Rabbi Ammi and R. Assi were exchanging words of Torah with R. Isaac. One wished to hear homiletical aspects of the biblical text while the other kept interrupting R. Isaac because he desired to learn halakic matters. They both interrupted to the point that their enthusiasm prevented R. Isaac from teaching Torah. One method of study might be neglected at the expense of the other. The scholar must embrace all disciplines of Torah learning.

---

[30] Babrius, Fable 22 (ibid., 32); Phaedrus, Fable 2.2 (p. 235).

[31] The moral is missing in Phaedrus's version.

The Man with Two Wives

> When R. Ammi and R. Assi were sitting before R. Isaac the Smith, one of them said to him: "Will the Master please tell us some legal points?" While the other said: "Will the Master please give us some homiletical instruction?" When he commenced a homiletical [haggadic] discourse he was prevented by the one, and when he commenced a legal discourse he was prevented by the other. He therefore said to them: I will tell you a parable: To what is this like? To a man who has had two wives, one young and the other old. The young one used to pluck out his white hair, whereas the old one used to pluck out his black hair. He thus finally remained bald on both sides.[32]

For the rabbis, the humorous story of satisfying two lovers is a clear illustration of the proper method of Bible study. Learning halakah without homiletical application will leave the scholar bald on both sides. The immediate predicament of R. Isaac is that he cannot teach Torah at all because one colleague plucks out his haggadic hairs while the other is plucking his halakic ones. Rabbi Isaac is an accomplished scholar who can discourse in either halakah or haggadah, while R. Ammi and R. Assi are confined to one or the other approach. The new reality behind the word-picture is taken out of the cultural experiences of the Jewish people, where Torah learning is central.

While the rabbis had contact with the world of fable lore, they reinterpreted the meaning of the stories for their own purposes. The fable of the heron who removes a bone stuck in the lion's throat is used by R. Joshua ben Chananyah to avert a revolt against Rome. Hadrian had disappointed the people of Israel. The Roman Senate had promised that they could rebuild the temple. Then Hadrian changed the order. After the destruction of the temple, much discontent prevailed among the people. The second revolt in the days of Bar Kochba make this fact clear. Sufficient provocation by the Roman authorities could have sparked a Jewish revolt. The Romans broke faith by rescinding the order to rebuild the temple. The rabbis wanted to preserve the peace. They selected a scholar of Scripture, Joshua ben Chananyah, to pacify the strong popular unrest that could result in war. Joshua ben Chananyah preserved peace by telling the people a fable.

The people would have been entertained by the wit and comedy of a heron helping a lion. The solemn warning is, of course, quite frightening. The lion is so powerful that he can do anything he wants. No one can argue with the lion. Neither should the people entertain thoughts of challenging Roman military might.

---

[32] b. *B. Kam.* 60b (I. Epstein, ed., *The Babylonian Talmud* [35 vols.; London: Soncino, 1935–1978] 350); see also the fine discussion by Schwarzbaum, *Fox Fables*, ii–iii. Also of interest here is the language. Aramaic is used to tell the story of the context, in which the rabbis argue over haggadah and halakah. The parable of the Man with Two Wives, however, is told in Hebrew.

The Heron and the Lion

> Thereupon [the Sages] decided: Let a wise man go and pacify the congregation. Then let R. Joshua b. Chananyah go, as he is a master of Scripture. So he went and harangued them: "A wild lion killed [an animal], and a bone stuck in his throat. Thereupon he proclaimed: 'I will reward anyone who removes it.' An Egyptian heron, which has a long beak, came and pulled it out and demanded his reward. 'Go,' he replied, 'you will be able to boast that you entered the lion's mouth in peace and came out in peace' [unscathed]. Even so, Let us be satisfied that we entered into dealings with this people in peace and have emerged in peace."[33]

By way of contrast, the cultural context in Aesop is completely unrelated to the issues confronting the Jewish people during the days of R. Joshua ben Chananyah. Nonetheless such an application is entirely suitable for this story about the weak heron and a fierce wolf, which is replaced by the lion in the rabbinic version of the story. The people of antiquity were largely naturalists at heart because of their contact with the wonders of wildlife. Their innate fascination with the animal kingdom produced a ready audience for fable lore. The animals' behavior and interrelationships mirrored those of people. People studied animals to learn about themselves. They could identify with the heron's fear of the wolf.

Dr. Heron's Fee

> Once a wolf had a bone lodged in his throat. He promised a heron that he would give a suitable fee if the latter would let his neck down inside and draw out the bone, thus providing a remedy for his suffering. The heron drew out the bone and forthwith demanded his pay. The wolf grinned at him, baring his sharp teeth, and said: "It's enough pay for your medical services to have taken your neck out of a wolf's mouth safe and sound."
>
> You'll get no good in return for giving aid to scoundrels, and you'll do well not to suffer some injury yourself in the process.[34]

Fables were widely used in antiquity.[35] In the Hebrew Bible, illustrations such as Jotham's fable of the bramble and Jehoash's fable of the thistle are dynamic expressions of Near Eastern culture.[36] The Greek and Latin collections of Babrius and Phaedrus have preserved many colorful tales, which have entertained audiences for centuries. Sadly, many other fables probably were lost in the transmission of oral cultures. The same would be true of rabbinic parables.

---

[33] *Gen. Rab.* 64:10 (ed. Albeck, 2:712; Epstein, 580). In genre, the story is a clear example of fable, which makes use of animals with human characteristics. Unlike all rabbinic parables, this fable is told in Aramaic. See also Schwarzbaum, *Fox Fables,* ix–x.

[34] Babrius, Fable 94 (*Babrius and Phaedrus,* ed. Perry, 114); Phaedrus, Fable 1.8 p. 200).

[35] See the discussion by Schwarzbaum, *Fox Fables,* i–lv.

[36] Judg 9:8–15; 2 Kgs 14:8–14.

Jesus, too, shows a knowledge of fable lore. As David Flusser has demonstrated, Jesus recalled the rich imagery of the fable of "The Oak and the Reed" when he described John the Baptist. He asked the people, "What did you go out into the wilderness to behold? A reed shaken by the wind?"[37] Which is more powerful, the reed or the oak? The first response is a majestic oak. But in a storm with violent gusts, the oak is broken while the reed is merely shaken.[38] In such a storm, the flexible reed proves stronger than the mighty oak. John the Baptist was broken because of his prophetic call. He was unwilling to compromise his message. Those who occupy kings' palaces, however, are finely attired politicians who blow with the wind, this direction and that, according to the expediency of the moment. The satire of the fable has political implications. But Jesus applies the imagery to John, who is a prophet. He is no reed shaken by the wind.

In addition, Jesus seems to have been acquainted with a version of the fable of "The Fisherman with the Flute." The fisherman invites the fish to hear the tune of his flute and dance. But as the fisherman plays the flute, the fish refuse to dance. When he catches them in the net, however, then they dance. Jesus speaks about the generation that did not dance to the music. They did not realize that the time had come. He warns them concerning their failure to heed the prophetic message of John the Baptist. He satirizes their behavior: "They are like children sitting in the market place and calling to one another, 'We piped to you, and you did not dance; we wailed, and you did not weep.' "[39] In the fable of "The Fisherman with the Flute," the fish ignore the music of the flute. They are free and arrogant. After they are caught in the net, by way of contrast, the fish dance as they squirm this way and that without hearing the fisherman's tune. "Dance now without any music" the fisherman tells the fish; "it would have been better for you to have danced some time ago when I was supplying music for the dance."[40] As Flusser has demonstrated, the saying of Jesus is an echo of some version of this fable, which was widely circulated.[41] The people should have listened to John the Baptist and responded to his prophetic appeal. Though John and Jesus had different approaches to ministry—one came eating and drinking with outcasts, and the other withdrew from society—both were prophets. As

---

[37] Matt 11:7; Luke 7:24.

[38] Babrius, Fable 36, "The Oak and the Reed," (*Babrius and Phaedrus*, ed. Perry, 51). Cf. Fable 64, "The Fir Tree and the Bramble" (pp. 80–81). The fir tree, though more beautiful than the bramble, is in danger of being cut down. It concludes with the moral "Every distinguished man not only has greater fame than lesser men but he also undergoes greater dangers." See the insightful discussion and analysis of David Flusser, *Die rabbinischen Gleichnisse und der Gleichniserzähler Jesus* (Bern: Peter Lang, 1981) 52, 153.

[39] Luke 7:32; Matt 11:16–17.

[40] See Babrius, Fable 9, "The Fisherman with the Flute" (*Babrius and Phaedrus*, ed. Perry, 14–17). The example is discussed by Flusser, *Gleichnisse*, 153–54. Compare also the words of Eccl 3:4, ". . . a time to dance."

[41] Flusser, *Gleichnisse*, 153–54.

a prophet, John the Baptist is like the fisherman who played his flute. Many did not respond. At the final judgment, they will dance.

On the one hand, fable lore penetrated oriental society, Hebrew thought, and Jewish culture. On the other hand, Gospel parables and their rabbinic counterparts are different from fables. Gospel and rabbinic parables have their own distinctive characteristics. While fables tend to employ animals and plants as leading characters who behave like humans, parables prefer real people from everyday life. Parables portray a realistic setting, where people are people and animals are animals. So the storytelling technique of parable lore, as we encounter it in the Gospels, as well as in rabbinic literature, is distinctive in its own right. Often the fable contains numerous points of comparison in an allegorical representation of truth. In contrast, the parable is less allegorical and more dynamic. The stock characters of parables, such as king, servant, steward, son, or prince, are selected for theological or exegetical reasons. Points of comparison flow toward one point. The parable teaches one message and urges a decision. But the major difference between fables and parables involves the reality behind the illustration. The fables are more anthropological, whereas parables are more theological. Parables tend to be theocentric. Without God, Gospel and rabbinic parables lose their central focus.

In interpreting the message of Jesus and the rabbis, the reality behind their parables is crucial. They imaged God through metaphor and personal experience. The one God of the Hebrew Bible and the Jewish people's encounter with history has shaped the creation of a genre of illustrations that pushes beyond the parameters of fable lore. The essential difference between fables and parables is God. The parables of Jesus and the rabbis are filled with the awe of God. Many times they address some aspect of Torah, but they are not concerned primarily with exegesis. They preach love for the God of Israel and the Israel of God.

Parables should not be removed from the ethnic culture of the people who heard and enjoyed them. The ethnicity of parable lore, as well as the concept of God in Hebrew thought, make the parables unique. Jesus told stories to his own people. He knew their language. He was a part of Jewish culture. Even though many rabbinic parables come from a later period as expressions of Jewish folklore and religious thought, they reveal the heart and imagination of a people. They should be studied side by side with the Gospel texts. As the recognized folklore scholar Valdimir Propp has demonstrated, the tales of folk literature tell the story of a people. The study of their ethnic experience as well as their religious orientation is essential. One should seek the ethnicity of the parable in religious belief and folk culture. Propp observes, "The earliest forms of material culture and social organization are the object of ethnography. Therefore, historical folklore, which attempts to discover the origin of its phenomena, rests upon ethnography. There cannot be a materialist study of folklore independent of ethnography."[42] Gospel and rabbinic parables are the cultural heritage of a historical people.

The Greek fable had another point of reference. In contrast to the Hebrew concept of God, one may consider the worldview of the tale surrounding the cattle driver seeking the aid of one god or another to recover his ox. In the humorous fable "Better to Lose the Ox Than Catch the Thief" the cattle driver seeks the help of the nymphs by making a vow to offer an animal sacrifice if they will only help him find his lost bull. (Gods and goddesses who are influenced by human promises of gifts fill the conceptual world of Greek folk culture.)

Better to Lose the Ox Than Catch the Thief

> A cattle-driver in a remote part of the forest was searching for a horned bull that he had lost. He made a vow to the mountain-roaming nymphs that he would offer up to them a lamb in sacrifice if he should catch the thief. Coming over a ridge, he caught sight of his fine bull being feasted upon by a lion. Then the unlucky fellow vowed that he would bring an ox to the sacrifice if he succeeded in getting away from the thief.
>
> From this we may well learn not to pray the gods for something ill-considered, moved by a grief brought on us temporarily.[43]

How vastly different is the Hebrew concept of God during the Second Temple period, which is echoed in Gospel and rabbinic parables! The cattle driver who tries to recover his bull is willing to sacrifice a lamb to the gods in order to find the thief. When the thief turns out to be a lion that attacks him, he raises the offer to an ox—probably his most prized possession—if he can only escape with his life.

The view of God in the parable of the Prodigal Son is remarkably different. He is a compassionate father who lovingly reaches out to his sons. The king in rabbinic parables images the majesty and glory of the almighty God. Often the parables dramatize the Jewish people's encounter of the divine presence through the reality of human experience. In word-pictures, parables metaphorically redescribe the nature of God through the lens of this encounter. The whole process is a fruit of Second Temple period Judaism and the cultural experience of the Jewish people. Their folk culture and religion have indelibly impacted the development of parable teaching. Theological belief rooted in the teachings of Torah finds expression in word-pictures and dramatic scenes from real life.

The conceptual world and theological framework of Gospel and rabbinic parables are different from fables, even though some of the storytelling elements of folklore are the same. The theology of the rabbis markedly

---

[42] V. Propp, *Theory and History of Folklore* (Minneapolis: University of Minnesota Press, 1985) 9.

[43] Babrius, Fable 23 (*Babrius and Phaedrus*, ed. Perry, 35).

departs from the thought of the fable teachers. It is the reality behind the metaphoric representation that determines the development of a parable. Faith in the one God of Israel is what separates the parables from fables. Parables preach love for the God of Israel and urge the people to make a decision to follow the teachings of Torah. The awe and reverence of God is the major objective.

Jesus is very much a part of this world. His parables portray a cultural reality within the heritage of his people. The folklore of the Jewish people is a stream flowing through the stories and anecdotes, which often are used to illustrate the teachings of the Bible or the oral law. Sometimes the rabbinic parables are more involved with biblical illustration than with theological inquiry. A parabolic example may redescribe the biblical story through drama. Many rabbinic parables would be classified as illustrations designed for Bible exposition, while others are more homiletical. They may seek higher theological ground in the classic form of teaching. They may capture the moment of oral communication more fully. Hillel tells his disciples that he is going to perform an important religious duty. They ask him what is the commandment he is going to do. They probably thought that he was going to visit a sick person or give charity to a needy individual. But Hillel tells them that he is going to the bathhouse. They are shocked. Does taking a bath constitute the performing of a mitzvah? Hillel tells them a story. A king hires a laborer to wash his statuary. If a human king pays his laborer to care for his statue, how much more value is a person created in the image of God worthy of care! The one washing oneself must acknowledge the divine presence and recognize that personal esteem in simple actions such as taking a bath are fulfilling God's commandments as much as other religious duties. The parabolic example is not a direct explanation of the Torah's text. It catches the attention of the listener and communicates a message on a higher level than intellectual assent. This type of rabbinic illustration shares much in common with the teachings of Jesus.

The interpreter must learn to listen for the elements of folklore and culture when reading the sacred texts of Judaism and Christianity. The parable teaches more by intuition than by precept. The message is caught rather than learned. Jewish folklore and early rabbinic parables awaken the inner spirituality of the listener rather than challenge the intellect in the purely cognitive realm. This is especially true of the classic form of parable so characteristic of the Gospels and early Jewish teachings.

At least six foundational features are discovered in this classic form of the story parable. While minor deviations from this classic form are fairly common, these six components were the building blocks used by popular teachers who illustrated their messages about God and inter-personal relationships through parables. A master parable teacher creatively built the illustration using a basic model or paradigm. The model emerged during the process of active discourse and oral instruction. Later these elements became more standardized in the compilation of written tradition and the editing of manuscripts. These foundational building blocks, however, reveal the artistry and creativity of original thinkers who sought to communicate the deeper meaning of religious faith effectively. They should be studied inductively, in an effort to grasp the full impact of effective communication. As Jewish haggadah, they reveal sophisticated storytelling technique and an imaginative method of teaching spiritual truth. In the classic form, the listener is led on the path for change. Learning is change. Discovery leads to action.

SIX COMPONENTS OF THE CLASSIC FORM

1. Prolegomenon. The prolegomenon may be a single word, such as "To" or "Parable." The standard phrase, "A parable, to what may the matter be compared? To a . . . ," became the accepted form to introduce a parable. Often in the Gospel texts Jesus introduces a parable by saying, "The kingdom of God is like . . ." It is probable that these introductory formulas became more standardized in the written form of the parables. In the oral form, such introductions were brief.[44] The prolegomenon serves to prepare the audience. It builds anticipation for a parable.

2. Introduction of the cast. The characters of the parable are crucial for the plot and final outcome of the story. The parable of the Prodigal Son begins by saying, "A man had two sons." The father and his two sons are important for the story, even though the traditional Christian interpretation has focused on the first part of the drama, which involves the resolution of the conflict concerning the prodigal son. The elder brother, however, is also one of the man's two sons. The careful interpreter will always pay close attention to every actor in the drama.

3. Plot of the story. At this juncture the drama begins. What is the story about? The listener is orientated to the dramatic movements of the plot. The listener begins to participate in the action by identifying with the characters. The story line is driven by the development of the parable's plot and the motivation of its characters.

4. Conflict. The classic form of parable often introduces a major conflict. It may be a family crisis, such as in the parable of the Prodigal Son. It may be connected to the relationship between the master of an estate and his servants or a very wealthy person and the poor outcasts of the community. The conflict focuses on the major problem and begs for a solution.

5. Conflict resolution. The parable will lead the listener on a path toward a resolution of the conflict. The audience actively participates in the process. Conflict resolution invites listener involvement with the plot of the drama. Sometimes the parable is left without a clear resolution and invites the

[44] See Robert L. Lindsey and E. dos Santos, *A Comparative Greek Concordance of the Synoptic Gospels* (3 vols.; Jerusalem: Baptist House, 1985–1989), s.v. "parable."

audience to decide the matter. Usually, however, the parable leads the listener to an early resolution of the conflict and illustrates the resemblance between the fiction of the parable and the reality of life.

6. Call to decision and/or application. In the Gospels, Jesus often calls the listener to a point of decision. But both Gospel and rabbinic parables frequently make an application for life. The rabbis will use the word *kakh*, "thus *it is also with* . . ." They apply the parable to daily living or illustrate the purpose of the story. The classic form of rabbinic parables, as with so much Jewish haggadah, speaks to the heart and the imagination of the people and calls for a response. The call to decision and/or application is the major turning point of the parable. Here the storyteller is describing the significance of his or her tale and explaining the central theme.

While the interpreter should be aware of these six features of the classic form of story parable, one will encounter many deviations from these foundational components. Sometimes the story is streamlined. On occasion the classic form will be expanded. Usually the deviations will occur in the plot, conflict, and resolution of the conflict stages of development.

The parable of the Prodigal Son, for instance, introduces a new plot and a major conflict with the elder brother. As an illustration, the classic form has been expanded. The audience has been set up for the deviation from the beginning. The parable has prepared the stage for a surprise already in the introduction of the cast, which mentioned a man and his two sons. In a similar way, the Gospel parable of the Unmerciful Servant introduces a second mini-drama. A major conflict is resolved when the king forgives his first servant of an enormous debt. This is like the prodigal who returns home and is received by his compassionate father. But the stories do not end there. Second conflicts are introduced. The prodigal has a brother, and the servant who received mercy is called upon to show mercy to his colleague. The second mini-drama becomes the primary focus of the parable teller. In these examples the classic form of the parable has been artistically expanded for more dramatic impact.

Other examples of deviation abbreviate the form, such as the parable of the Mustard Seed and Leaven. Here the process of nature is dramatized to show a resemblance to the kingdom of heaven. The features of the classic form, which involve conflict and resolution of conflict, have been streamlined and replaced with the action of leaven in the dough or the growth of a mustard seed. The rabbis used parables frequently in exposition of biblical texts. In these exegetical parables, the scenes of the Bible are reenacted in the drama of a parable. Expositional parables are closely linked to the text of Scripture. But exposition of Torah is not the only type of rabbinic parable. The earliest form was rooted more in life experience than in exegesis. This earlier classic form of rabbinic mashal does not have a direct link to the Torah. Rather, this type of parable teaches the listener how to fulfill God's will more through intuition than by exegesis. The people grasp the higher meaning of Torah intuitively in the realm of haggadah rather than intellectually in the domain of halakic analysis. This type of rabbinic parable is more like those of the Gospels. They lead to action by demanding a decision. Decisive action is needed for the urgency of the situation.

In all events, deviations from the classic form may be discerned in the study of parable lore. But the foundation of parable teaching is based on a model that developed from the popular oral teachings of respected religious leaders and Bible expositors. Jesus heard this type of teaching in his youth. The Jewish theology of his parables is the essence of the reality behind the metaphor. He is reaching for the higher significance of Torah as he teaches its practical application. Like rabbinic parables, his message catches the listener and motivates that person to make a decision. The urgency of the time requires immediate action. Hence parables infused fresh life into the religious experience of the people by showing the resemblance between the spiritual world beyond and human existence below. Jewish spirituality must be lived in daily experience.

PARABLES AS THEOLOGY

In 1972 Petuchowski challenged parable scholars with the intriguing observation that many Gospel and rabbinic parables preach the same theology.[45] The theological outlook of these parables is identical, even though they are derived from two diverse religious traditions. Flusser, moreover, has shown the strong theological solidarity between ancient Judaism and nascent Christianity. In a major foundational study, Flusser elucidated the new sensitivity in Jewish religious thought during the Second Temple period.[46] During this time a fresh intensity for Jewish piety focused greater attention on love rather than fear, stressing a much more intentional approach to the teachings: "Love the Lord your God" and "your neighbor as yourself." The message of the parables communicates the force of this new sensitivity in ancient Judaism, which powerfully influenced the teachings of Jesus.

Perhaps more than any other scholar, Flusser has pioneered a comprehensive methodology for the study of the Gospel parables that reveals their theological foundation in ancient Judaism through synoptic analysis, comparative study, and linguistic research. Now Stern has called upon us to recognize that the rabbinic parable is the supreme attempt, in all of Jewish literature, to imagine what God is like.[47] The theological significance of the parables, however, has not always received the attention that it merits. The comparative study of rabbinic and Gospel parables, moreover, reveals a strong, shared identity. Hence the theological meaning of the parables of Jesus should be sought in the synagogue rather than the church. Jesus is a

[45] Petuchowski, "Significance."

[46] Flusser, *Origins*, 469–89.

[47] Stern, *Parables in Midrash*, 93–97.

teacher of Torah. He focuses on the meaning of the kingdom of heaven with an unprecedented vigor. As a religious teacher, he is a theologian whose theology is rooted in Torah, in true Judaism, as one who knew and experienced his personal faith within the community. Perhaps he should be called a Jewish theologian, a magnetic preacher who would certainly be better understood in the synagogues of the first century than in the churches of today.

The Jewishness of Jesus is related to faith in the one God of Israel. Too often faith in Jesus completely overshadows the faith of Jesus. The religion focused on Jesus as the object of belief overwhelms the deep convictions of Jesus. He was a religious Jew in the context of first-century Israel. He piously practiced his beliefs in pious devotion. He preached from the Torah and the prophets, not from the Epistles of the Apostle Paul. Jesus was consumed with a message of God's compassion, which he discovered in the prayers of the synagogue and the readings of the Torah portion, rather than the hymns of the church and the NT lectionary. G. E. Lessing, during the period of the Enlightenment, struggled with this issue.[48] Religious faith in Jesus should never obscure Jewish belief and practice during the time in which he lived.

The Gospel records provide insight into the practices of the Jewish people during the Second Temple period. Even if the final compilation of the Synoptics was after the destruction of Jerusalem—an issue that continues to be discussed and debated—the sources behind the Gospels demonstrate the high historical value of the texts for the study of Jewish practices during the Second Temple period. In fact, one must seriously entertain another pertinent question: can ancient Judaism be understood apart from the Jesus of the Gospels? The examination of the wide diversity in Judaism of the Second Temple period cannot exclude the Gospel records. In truth, these sacred documents of the NT faith contain valuable evidence that can enrich greatly the study of early Jewish belief and practice. Not only must Judaism see the value of studying the Gospel records; Christianity must see also the value of studying the Jewish writings. New Testament scholars and the church must face bravely the uneasy question, "Can Jesus be understood apart from Judaism?" Christian scholars must study the sacred literature of the Jewish people. On the other hand, talmudic scholars and the synagogue will ask the question, "Can the study of the Gospel texts illuminate the history and the culture of the Jewish people from the days of the temple before it was destroyed by the Romans?"

The parting of the ways between the church and the synagogue and the mutual self-definition of faith communities have not always encouraged honest academic inquiry into the common heritage that made each community distinctive. The Holocaust, the founding of the state of Israel, and the

[48] See Gotthold Lessing, *Lessing's Theological Writings*, ed. and trans. Henry Chadwick (Stanford: Stanford University Press, 1956) 106.

recent discoveries of scrolls, as well as scholarly research, make it possible to reexamine the origins of Christianity in the light of ancient Judaism and to achieve a sharper and more objective picture of Christian beginnings and the common Jewish heritage that blossomed into two distinctive expressions of faith in the one God. The scholarly investigation of Christian origins and Jewish thought of the Second Temple period could be compared to someone who was given the task of remarrying a divorced couple. The church and the synagogue have parted ways in an ugly divorce, involving grave misunderstandings and tortuous injuries. After the divorce attorneys of history have completed their work and the judge has determined the final settlement, careful and informed study of the marriage relationship will be a sensitive undertaking for all parties involved. Serious parable study must be informed of the hard realities of Jewish and Christian self-definition.

Nonetheless, the task of understanding Jesus in the context of Jewish life is a precious goal that demands the dedication of careful and objective scholarly scrutiny. Jesus was a theologian. His theology was based on the rich Jewish traditions of Scripture, doctrine, belief, and practice. He was a Jewish teacher who lived in a specific setting. He was not educated in a Christian seminary. He never studied systematic theology. Jesus did not learn about God by going to church. He never recited the Apostles' Creed nor heard a Christian sermon, yet he was a theologian. But the ramifications of his theological approach to God and humankind, with its origin in the synagogue and not the church, have seldom been recognized by scholars.[49] The study of the life and teachings of Jesus has suffered from a series of weaknesses. In this study four disciplines of research will be employed to enlighten the examination of Jesus and his parabolic instruction. When combined, they provide fresh vistas for exploration of the world of the parables.

1. Textual analysis. One must carefully study the interrelationships among the Synoptic Gospels in order to distinguish between the core message of Jesus and the Christian interpretation of his teachings.

2. Linguistic examination. The Semitisms of the Synoptic Gospels demand a careful study of the language of the text. Often the key to understanding the Greek of the Synoptics is to translate the text into [Mishnaic]

---

[49] While the historical issues are more complex than choosing Hellenism or Judaism, A. J. Heschel insightfully described a problem: "The process of dejudaization within the church paved the way for abandonment of origins and alienation from the core of its message. The vital issue for the church is to decide whether to look for roots in Judaism and consider itself an extension of Judaism or to look for roots in pagan Hellenism and consider itself as an antithesis to Judaism. The spiritual alienation from Israel is most forcefully expressed in the teaching of Marcion, who affirmed the contrariety and abrupt discontinuity between the God of the Hebrew Bible and the God whom Jesus had come to reveal" ("Protestant Renewal: A Jewish View," in *Jewish Perspectives on Christianity* [ed. F. Rothschild; New York: Crossroad, 1990] 302).

Hebrew, using the best linguistic tools available for careful reconstruction of the language of the *Vorlage* (underlying text) of the Gospels.[50]

3. Parallel sources. The relevant religious sources must be carefully studied in order to appreciate Jesus and the various interpretations of his teachings within the crosscultural environment of the Gospels. A rich blend of Hellenism and Judaism flourished during the period. Jesus should be placed believably in the context of Second Temple period Judaism. Archaeology, the Dead Sea Scrolls, recent investigations in the study of the Pseudepigrapha and the Apocrypha, Hellenistic Judaism, rich resources of Greek, Hebrew, and Aramaic epigraphy, as well as Greek religious and philosophical thought must be studied. The discipline of research most commonly neglected, however, seems to be the scientific examination of rabbinic thought and literature. As Heschel has reminded us, the birth of Jesus is Bethlehem rather than Athens; he was at home among the people of Israel.[51] In all events, the study of Jewish thought in talmudic texts so often provides the richest insight into the parables of the Gospels. All sources must be scientifically examined and critically evaluated.

4. Theological reflection. The theology of Jesus has deep roots in contemporary Jewish sources. The Judaism of Jesus should be studied as the foundation of the church's Christianity. One cannot understand Jesus without an appreciation of the original context of Second Temple Judaism.

TREASURES NEW AND OLD

The parabolic method of the Synoptic Gospels invited a blending of the old and the new. In Matt 13:52 the words of Jesus concerning parables describe the process: "And he said to them, 'Therefore every scribe who has been trained for the kingdom of heaven is like a householder who brings out of his treasure what is new and what is old."[52] When viewed in the context of the Second Temple period, the Gospel parables are imbued with old and new. According to a saying attributed to Hillel, anyone who does not add to

---

[50] Probably the consensus of scholars today would look for an Aramaic *Vorlage* of the Gospel tradition or even an Aramaic-speaking Christian community. I am convinced that the parables of Jesus are derived from a Hebrew source that has been translated into Greek and adapted for the Gospel text. In any case, almost all agree that the Semitic flavor of the Gospels is of great importance for understanding the historical Jesus. See also my book, *Jesus and His Jewish Parables*, 40–42.

[51] Heschel asks, "What is the pedigree of the Christian Gospel? These are the words with which the New Testament begins: 'The book of the genealogy of Jesus Christ, the son of David, the son of Abraham' (Matt. 1:1; see also 1 Cor. 10:1–3; 1 Pet. 1:10ff.). Yet the powerful fascination with the world of Hellenism has led many minds to look for the origins of the Christian message in the world of Hellas. How odd of God not to have placed the cradle of Jesus in Delphi, or at least in Athens?" ("Protestant Renewal," 303).

[52] Cf. Flusser, *Origins*, xii.

one's learning through new and innovative creativity should be killed.[53] One adds to the old as one captures the essence of Torah and passes the message on to subsequent generations. The parables embrace the old world of Jewish learning by making new out of the earlier traditions. The new, however, is not a rejection of the old but rather a renewal and reapplication that blends together a powerful combination of ancient themes and fresh ideas.

Such a process makes the message of Torah relevant. This dynamic breathes fresh life into the old message, which actualizes Torah in experience. It does not replace or cancel Torah but renews its essence through revalidation and reinterpretation. The primary objective of Jewish learning is to realize the purpose of Torah in the fear of God. Each generation must embrace the old and the new. Through this innovative process a parabolic illustration creates a new story that infuses life into the old by adding to what has been learned.

The ancient Torah inspired fresh analysis and creative interpretation. Householders, day laborers, thieves, bandits, judges, widows, shepherds, farmers, priests, Levites, embezzlers, as well as kings and queens, princes and princesses, rich and poor, ordinary men and women, young and old—taking the stage of rabbinic and Gospel parables, they capture the imagination of the original audience. Most of the new stories are combinations of the old.[54] The possibilities for original plots and innovative story lines drawn from a treasure store of stock characters and folklore settings are limitless.

In fact, the parables of Jesus in the Synoptic Gospels have striking similarities to the parables in rabbinic literature. The relationship between Jesus' parables and those of rabbinic literature merits intensive investigation. As Flusser has shown, embarking on a new approach of comparative study with scientific method promises significant results.[55] Comparatively study-

---

[53] *Abot* 1:13. Compare also the saying of Ben Bag Bag in *Abot* 3:25.

[54] Unfortunately, many of the old school would have embraced without question the view expressed by Siegfried Goebel, *The Parables of Jesus* (Edinburgh: T. & T. Clark, 1894) 13: "To me, the supposition that certain leading forms and phrases in several parables of Christ passed over into Rabbinical tradition without consciousness of their origin, seems best to correspond to the mutual relations of the parables in question." Today more would embrace what Pinchas Lapide noted about the Jewish parallels to the Sermon on the Mount: "For the fact that the plaster, the cement, and all the building stones come from Jewish quarries in no way diminishes the greatness of the architect who has used these raw materials to design and erect his own moral code. After all, Beethoven did not invent a single new note to compose the Ninth Symphony, his immortal masterpiece" (*Sermon on the Mount* [New York: Orbis, 1986] 10). It is not a question of who copied whom but how we can understand both. Compare also I. Abrahams, *Studies in Pharisaism and the Gospels* (1917; repr. New York: KTAV, 1967) 90–107. Abrahams observes (p. 91), "There must have been a large Jewish stock of fables and parables floating about long before they were set down in writing."

[55] See especially Flusser, *Gleichnisse.*

ing rabbinic and Gospel parables enhances our understanding of both these religious traditions so sacred to both Christians and Jews.

When the parables of Jesus are studied as a genre within the Gospels and the rabbinic parables are examined within their literary context, a number of significant facts emerge. First, the texts of the Gospel parables contain remarkable Semitisms in the Greek texts preserved by the church. Second, the rabbinic parables are always written in Hebrew, even if on occasion Aramaic words or phrases occur. Third, parables in their concise story form are unknown outside the Gospels and rabbinic literature.[56] This classic form, so characteristic of the Gospels and a large category of rabbinic parables, shows the close relationship between Jesus and other Jewish teachers.[57] Indeed, most of the rabbinic parables known to us are dated after the Gospel texts, although some of these sources are roughly contemporary with or earlier than the Synoptics. Because of a later date or difficulty in accurate dating, some have claimed that responsible scholars should ignore evidence drawn from rabbinic texts. In the comparative study of folklore, however, diachronic as well as synchronic analysis is often employed to comprehend a people and their culture. If one views rabbinic parables as echoes of Jewish culture, folklore tradition, and theology, that person would be irresponsible to ignore their evidence for the Gospel texts.[58] Which is more responsible scholarship, to ignore evidence or to explore the meaning and the message of Judaism in all its rich diversity over the centuries?[59] A careful analysis of all the evidence is a more productive methodology.

---

[56] See my *Jesus and His Jewish Parables* (Mahwah, N.J.: Paulist, 1989), where I have discussed in greater detail the question relating to the study of the parables as a genre within a genre (pp. 55–128, 236) and the very critical question concerning the original language of the parables of the Gospels (40–42).

[57] This point has been stressed to me by Shmuel Safrai of the Hebrew University (private communication). Peter J. Tomson observes that Paul did not use Jewish parables (*Paul and the Jewish Law* [Assen: Van Gorcum, 1990] 31). See Tomson's important discussion, "Judaism and Hellenism," in his chapter on Paul's historical background, 31–33.

[58] For a sensitive analysis of Jewish life and cultural experience in the first century, see especially S. Safrai's studies in S. Safrai, M. Stern, D. Flusser, and W. C. van Unnik, eds., *The Jewish People in the First Century* (Amsterdam: Van Gorcum, 1974): "Home and Family," 2:728–92; "Religion in Everyday Life," 2:793–833; "The Temple," 2:865–907; "The Synagogue," 2:908–43; "Education and the Study of Torah," 2:945–70.

[59] Here it must be noted that there is sometimes little agreement among talmudic scholars regarding issues of higher criticism. While J. N. Epstein may not agree with the dating of rabbinic texts by S. Lieberman, care should be taken to consider each argument, and each text must be studied individually. In regard to comparative study of NT and rabbinic literature, E. P. Sanders has discussed the problem. On the one hand, "the rabbinic compilations . . . are later than our period," but on the other hand, "they certainly contain older material. Scholars of all schools accept attributions to a named Pharisee or rabbi as being fairly reliable: a rule attributed to Shammai probably reflects his view."

The parables constitute a genre with its own independent characteristics. They should be studied as examples of a unique form within oral tradition and written texts.[60] When one divorces the Gospel parables from their parallels in rabbinic literature, the form and the structure of the texts as well as their theological message will reflect the arbitrary biases of the interpreter. In this book the genre of parables as a didactic technique will be studied to shed light on the deeper theological significance of Gospel and rabbinic parables.

Needless to say, the synoptic problem and questions relating to the scientific study of rabbinic literature are of vital importance. Samuel Sandmel has warned against the dangers of "parallelomania," when scholars go mad searching for far-fetched parallels between Jewish and Christian texts.[61] Indeed, without a careful analysis of the original settings of both the rabbinic and the Gospel parables the messages of the texts inevitably will be compromised.[62] The parable as a genre within each individual literary context must be weighed wisely and circumspectly in the light of all available evidence. Since the work of Dibelius, scholars have recognized that a form may be adapted by different literatures to achieve diverse purposes.[63] The fine work of Clemens Thoma and Simon Lauer has shown the similar structure and teaching technique of some rabbinic parables and those of the Gospels.[64] Thoma and Lauer, stressing the original context of the rabbinic parables, have helped us capture the essence of the sages' teachings. Henry Fischel has taught us the relationship between rabbinic literature and Greco-Roman philosophy.[65] Hellenism impacted Judaism,

---

See E. P. Sanders, *Judaism: Practice and Belief, 63 BCE–66 CE* (London: SCM, 1992) 10. In NT studies, sayings of Papias that appear in the fourth-century work of Eusebius are often dated to 130 C.E. Eusebius is quoting Papias. In a similar way, many sayings in talmudic literature preserve earlier traditions. Hillel is quoted at Yavne, and we may with caution accept many of these attributions. The rabbis took care to preserve a teaching in the name of the authority who taught it.

[60] See also the fine studies in Clemens Thoma and Michael Wyschogrod, eds., *Parable and Story in Judaism and Christianity* (Mahwah, N.J.: Paulist, 1989).

[61] See Samuel Sandmel, "Parallelomania," *JBL* 81 (1962): 1–13.

[62] As Clemens Thoma has noted: "There are many unresolved questions and several deficiencies in contemporary research concerning rabbinic parables. For example, many scholars deplore the fact that the study of the rabbinic parable takes place in the shadow of midrashic research and, even more so, in that of Christian and Jewish ideological presuppositions. Also, a very selective, short-sighted and apologetic comparison between rabbinic parables and the parables of Jesus is an example of unprofessional and overly ideological communication" ("Literary and Theological Aspects of the Rabbinic Parables," in Thoma and Wyschogrod, *Parable and Story*, 26. I have treated this sensitive area of comparative study in my *Jewish Parables*, 55–128, 236–81.

[63] See Martin Dibelius, *From Tradition to Gospel* (ET; New York: Scribner, 1934).

[64] See C. Thoma and S. Lauer, *Die Gleichnisse der Rabbinen* (Bern: Peter Lang, 1986).

[65] Henry A. Fischel, *Rabbinic Literature and Greco-Roman Philosophy* (Leiden: Brill, 1973). See especially his discussion of *Chreia*, pp. 78–89.

but Hellenistic influence should not be treated as a complete conquest. The rich Hebrew compilations of the Tannaitic literature, the Hebrew Dead Sea Scrolls, as well as the many works of the Apocrypha and the Pseudepigrapha that were translated from Semitic originals demonstrate a thriving culture that remained focused on the God of the Bible while incorporating other philosophical and religious traditions into a strong faith. Martin Hengel has shown the meaning of Hellenistic Judaism.[66] The works of Saul Lieberman and Menahem Stern have made lasting contributions to understanding the original historical environment of first-century Israel.[67] The parables reveal this fascinating cultural diversity.

The parable is a flexible medium of communication that gave itself to serve different masters. Considering the possible applications of the parable, one is surprised that the parable was not employed in other oral or literary teachings. The fact that Jesus and the rabbis exclusively employ parables in this classic form strongly suggests a close relationship between the teachings attributed to Jesus in the Gospels and the instruction of Israel's sages. As will be seen in the following chapters, not only do the rabbinic parables and those of the Gospels have a common structure, similarities in motifs, parallel themes, identical forms, and like plots; they also frequently betray the same theological message.[68]

PURPOSE OF PARABLES

The purpose of the parables in the Gospels and in rabbinic literature was to instruct. Jesus' parables illustrate and teach, despite the argument of a number of scholars that they were designed to conceal his message from the people. The comparative study of the parable as a genre proves that the force behind the parable was designed to drive home a point. The parable is always

[66] See the comprehensive survey and in-depth analysis of Martin Hengel, *Judaism and Hellenism* (ET; London: SCM, 1974).

[67] See especially the incomparable work of Saul Lieberman, *Hellenism in Jewish Palestine* (New York: Jewish Theological Seminary, 1962); his *Greek in Jewish Palestine* (New York: Feldheim, 1965); and his collected Hebrew writings, *Mechkarim Betorat Eretz Yisrael* (Jerusalem: Magnes, 1991). Lieberman examined the question in an important article, "How Much Greek in Jewish Palestine?" reprinted in *Texts and Studies* (New York: KTAV, 1974) 216–34. See the rich insights and careful analysis of the evidence by M. Stern, "The Greek and Latin Literary Sources," in Safrai, et al., *Jewish People*, 2:18–36; and the fine collection of his Hebrew articles published posthumously (after Stern's tragic and untimely death by the hands of terrorists in Jerusalem), *Mechkarim Betoldot Yisrael Beyame Bayit Sheni* (Jerusalem: Yad Izhak Ben Zvi, 1991). The historical situation has been lucidly described by Elias Bickerman, *The Jews in the Greek Age* (New York: Jewish Theological Seminary, 1988).

[68] See the very important study of Petuchowski, "Significance"; as well as "A Panel Discussion of the Parable," *Christian News from Israel* 23 (1973): 144–45.

related to its original context. Sometimes the context has been lost in the transmission of the tradition, and thereby the original meaning of the parable may become more difficult to understand. Nevertheless, the intended function of the parable was to communicate a message.[69]

The purpose of the parable is closely related to its context. At first parables were oral stories told to illustrate and communicate. Being told before live audiences, they were intended to entertain and challenge the listener by urging a response. This classic form is often presented in the Gospels. Flusser has demonstrated conclusively that the earlier classic form of the parable was adapted and used for exegetical purposes.[70] The classic form of parabolic instruction is well attested in the Gospels. Powerful themes are illustrated in mini-dramas portrayed in popular oral teaching with wide appeal and with carefully constructed plots, each with a single purpose. The exact same classic form appears in rabbinic literature. A parable could be employed for a variety of occasions. The same parable might be used to illustrate diverse themes in different contexts.

The Gospels portray Jesus as an itinerant teacher who taught in parables. As Jesus travels from place to place, he sits down in a boat to teach the people, or upon a mountain, or on the plain. He also appears sitting in the temple giving instruction. His disciples ask him questions, and he gives his response. As Adolf Büchler noted over eighty years ago, numerous examples from rabbinic literature describe similar circumstances.[71] The rabbis frequently taught their followers in the open air of the great outdoors. As a teacher told a parable, the setting of the mini-drama may have been seen by the listeners somewhere around them. The open fields of harvest or the fishermen's nets around the Sea of Galilee may have been the actual background for the presentation of some Gospel and rabbinic parables. The point was further emphasized in the study of parables and agricultural life made by A. Feldman.[72] The parable lore of rabbinic literature is rich in vivid word-pictures based on the rural setting of country life.

---

[69] See especially the Hebrew article on the parables of Jesus and rabbinic parables by David Flusser in his *Yahadut Umekorot Hanatzrut* (Tel Aviv: Sifriyat Poalim, 1979) 150–209. Also see the recent popular study by D. de la Maisonneuve, "Parables of Jesus and Rabbinic Parables," *Sidic* 19 (1987): 8–15, where Maisonneuve argues cogently for an understanding of the parables that recognizes their instructional purpose.

[70] See especially Flusser's "Ursprung und Vorgeschichte der jüdischen Gleichnisse," in *Gleichnisse,* 141–60. See also the discussion in my *Jewish Parables,* 38, 105–9. Cf. also C. Thoma, "Prolegomena zu einer Übersetzung und Kommentierung der rabbinischen Gleichnisse," *TZ* (1982): 518–31, and Thoma and Lauer, *Gleichnisse.*

[71] See A. Büchler, "Learning and Teaching in the Open Air in Palestine," *JQR* 4 (1914): 485ff. For parallels to the peripatetic teachers such as the Cynics see F. Gerald Downing, *Cynics and Christian Origins* (Edinburgh: T. & T. Clark, 1992).

[72] A. Feldman, *The Parables and Similes of the Rabbis, Agricultural and Pastoral* (Cambridge: Cambridge University Press, 1927).

The Talmud explains that Johanan ben Zachai sat in the shadow of the temple and taught his disciples.[73] Instruction in the open air was characteristic of early rabbinic teachings. Moreover, the teacher probably used parables regularly to communicate his message effectively. The Tannaitic midrash *ʾAbot de Rabbi Nathan* relates the story of what happened when Johanan ben Zachai's disciples came to comfort him after his son had died. Their beloved master was now a bereaved father. Perhaps quite significantly, R. Eleazer b. Arach uses a parabolic illustration to accomplish his task. Though the precise date of this episode in rabbinic literature cannot be determined with certainty, the episode suggests that the parable was already a known form of instruction at this early period.

The Object of Value

> R. Eleazar entered and sat down before him. He said to him, "I will tell you a parable: To what may the matter be compared? To a man with whom the king deposited an object of value. Every single day the man would weep and cry out, saying: 'Woe unto me! When will I be free [of the responsibility] of this trust in peace?' You too, master, you had a son? He studied the Torah, the Prophets, the Holy Writings, he studied mishnah, halachot, agadot, and he departed from the world without sin. And you should be comforted when you have returned your trust unimpaired." Rabban Johanan said to him: "Rabbi Eleazar, my son, you have comforted me the way men should give comfort!"[74]

---

[73] See b. *Pesach* 27a; and cf. the discussion of Abraham Heschel concerning the importance of haggadah in the teaching of the Tannaim in general and in the instruction of Johanan b. Zachai in particular, in A. Heschel, *Torah Men Hashamayim* (New York: Soncino, 1962) X–XI. Heschel demonstrates the importance of haggadah and its relationship to halakah. See *Tanchuma* (*Midrash Tanchuma*, ed. S. Buber [Wilna: Wittwa & Gebrüder Romm, 1885]), Lech Lackah 10, where Johanan b. Zachai is remembered for sitting and teaching his disciples the Torah portion with haggadah and Mishnah, as well as the passage in *Abot R. Nat.*, version B, ch. 28, where Johanan b. Zachai is described: "he studied every section of the Torah; he studied Scripture and Targum, *halachah* and *aggadah*, (arcane) speech and parable" (cf. A. Saldarini, *The Fathers according to Rabbi Nathan* [Leiden: Brill, 1975] 166 n. 5). Cf. A. Hyman, *Toldot Tannaim Veamoraim* (3 vols.; Jerusalem: Boys Town, 1964) 2:674–81. See also the words of Eleazer ben Shamua in *Abot R. Nat.*, version A, ch. 28.

[74] *Abot R. Nat.*, version A, ch. 14. For a discussion of the context of this parable and its relationship to R. Johanan b. Zachai's disciples, see L. Finkelstein, *Mevo Lemesechtot Avot Veavot Derabbi Natan* (New York: Jewish Theological Seminary, 1950) 42–44. Finkelstein suggests that the prominence given to Eleazar ben Arach in spite of the fact that he abandoned the sages indicates that an early date must be assigned to the tradition. See also the parallels to the context in *Abot* 2 and in *Abot R. Nat.*, version B, ch. 29, where the parable itself does not appear. David Flusser has called my attention to a close parallel to this idea in *The Sentences of Pseudo-Phocylides*, l. 106: "For the spirit is a loan from God to mortals, and his image." (See the fine critical edition by P. W. van der Horst, *The Sentences of Pseudo-Phocylides* [Leiden: Brill, 1978] 94–95, for the text and especially the important notes on pp. 189–90, where van der Horst discusses the parallels to this idea

The occasion of the parable is the consolation of Johanan ben Zachai by his most esteemed disciple.[75] When the other disciples have failed, R. Eleazar uses a parable to comfort his master. Johanan must view his pain from another perspective. By depicting the loss of his son in a nonthreatening manner, R. Eleazer helped his master to understand life, death, and the divine purpose in another light. In the context, the other disciples tried to comfort their master by citing specific cases from the Bible that describe parents who lost their children. These examples only intensified his pain because they reminded him of someone else's grief. The parable gave comfort to R. Johanan. It redefined the reality of the life situation. The parable helped R. Johanan to view the loss of his son from another, less painful vantage point. It redescribed his experience from the perspective of faith in God. The text also provides a good example of how parabolic teaching appears in rabbinic literature in diverse contexts.

The reality of the parable is discovered in its metaphoric redefinition of the facts.[76] By telling a story about a king who had given a valuable trust requiring arduous care, the parable reminded Johanan ben Zachai of God, the trust of Johanan's son and his own challenging parental obligations, as well as his personal fulfillment in seeing the accomplishments of his child. The parable redefines the reality of the situation. It is not an allegory. But it is not free from code words that form a sequence to teach a single point.[77] They are feathers that guide the arrow to make a specific point.

The fact that a story parable appears here in a text that describes a conversation between R. Johanan ben Zachai and one of his five disciples, as well as the observation that another parable is attributed to R. Johanan ben Zachai in the Talmud, is of significance.[78] The text of ʾ*Abot de Rabbi Nathan* preserves many early traditions.[79] Nothing in these texts indicates that

---

in Jewish Hellenistic texts and their relationship to the OT motif from Gen 1:26–27.) See also A. Marmorstein, "Das Motiv vom veruntreuten Depositum in der jüdischen Volkskunde," *MGWJ* 78 (1934): 183–95. The well-known idea that the spirit is a loan from God was developed into a story parable. Marmorstein's very important study examines the cultural and linguistic issues of the text. I am grateful to David Flusser for his insight concerning this rabbinic parable.

[75] Ibid.

[76] See some of the suggestions of Paul Ricoeur, "Biblical Hermeneutics," *Semeia* 4 (1975): 75. A recent discussion of Ricoeur's work has appeared in a study of the parable of the Wicked Husbandmen by David Stern, "Jesus' Parables from the Perspective of Rabbinic Literature: The Example of the Wicked Husbandmen," in Thoma and Wyschogrod, *Parable and Story*, 42–80. See also my treatment of the parable of the Wicked Husbandmen in *Parables*, 282–316.

[77] See Young, *Jewish Parables*, 103–9.

[78] b. *Shabb.* 153a; cf. *Semachot Derabbi Chiya* 2:1; and see my *Jewish Parables*, 103–4, 178–79. See also Flusser, *Gleichnisse*, 41–43 and 170–71.

[79] See Finkelstein, *Mavo Lemesechtot*, xxxii–xxxiii. Judah Goldin has arrived at similar conclusions. See *The Fathers according to Rabbi Nathan* (New York: Schocken, 1974) xxi.

parables were an entirely new method of teaching. In fact, the parabolic teaching attributed to Jesus in the Gospels would suggest otherwise.[80] Jesus seems to be using a popular method of teaching that is also reflected in the later rabbinic literature. Whether these story parables originated with the authors to whom they are ascribed is difficult to know with absolute certainty. As reminiscences of later disciples, they would represent the character of teaching contemporary with the great spiritual leaders of an earlier age. While less-than-meticulous historians of antiquity have been known to introduce anachronisms into their interpretations of past events, in regard to parabolic teaching the early evidence of the Gospels indicates that rabbinic parables frequently preserve a form of religious instruction that flourished during the Second Temple period. The parables of the Gospels appear as remnants of early Jewish parabolic teaching. Assigning all rabbinic parables to a later time, therefore, is embarking on a highly subjective and questionable enterprise. Surely Jewish parabolic teaching developed long before the destruction of the temple.

Joachim Jeremias, perhaps the most influential parable scholar of our time, held firm his opinion that Jesus was the first parable teacher.[81] Now this approach has been seriously challenged, and one can hardly defend it objectively. Though the evidence is fragmentary, Jesus is much more likely to have used a method of teaching that was already practiced by other Jewish sages during the period. It was his genius and masterful use of the medium that popularized his teaching. As has been seen, probably one-third of all the recorded words of Jesus in the Synoptic Gospels are uttered in parables.[82] Indeed, parables seem to characterize the method of Jesus' instruction,

---

See also his article, "The Two Versions of Abot de-Rabbi Nathan," *HUCA* 19 (1945): 97–120. There is little reason to doubt that the work is basically Tannaitic. Cf. also H. L. Strack, *Einleitung in Talmud und Midrasch* (rev. G. Stemberger; Munich: C. H. Beck, 1981) 215–17.

[80] The Gospels should be viewed as preserving the early teaching methods of the Jewish people in the first century.

[81] J. Jeremias, *Parables of Jesus* (trans. S. H. Hooke; London: SCM, 1972) 12. Jeremias claims, "Jesus' parables are something entirely new." Jeremias longed to discover incomparable originality in Jesus, which tended to make an unwarranted break between Jesus and his people. Earlier materials from the Second Temple period are surely contained in rabbinic literature. Cf. also Louis Finkelstein, who has even claimed that some sections of rabbinic literature are derived from preexilic and exilic times: "Like the bricks and stones of ancient palaces, these words of the Prophets were incorporated into later structures" (*New Light from the Prophets* [New York: Basic, 1969] 1).

[82] Although NT scholars may not agree on the exact number of parables, certainly the amount of dominical parabolic teachings in the Gospels is considerable. Cf. R. H. Stein, *Introduction to the Parables of Jesus* (Philadelphia: Westminster, 1981) 22–26; and see B. B. Scott's list in *Hear Then the Parable: A Commentary on the Parables of Jesus* (Minneapolis: Fortress, 1989) 460. See also the list of Gospel parables according to Jeremias, *Parables of Jesus*, 247–48.

drawing old and new from his treasure store. A strong personality and a captivating religious genius emerges from the core of the parabolic teaching in the Gospels—a quality that does not characterize the later church's redaction of Christian tradition. Though often misunderstood, the parables promise to teach us much about Jesus and his original environment.

CONCLUSIONS

The parabolic teachings of Jesus and the parables contained in rabbinic literature form a specialized genre. The study of parables as a literary genre merits careful examination in itself. The similarities between Gospel and rabbinic parables point to a common background. The common motifs and plots of these mini-dramas are drawn from a rich repository of parable lore. The conceptual world and points of reference within the story parables are shared in both the Gospel and the Jewish traditions. The study of rabbinic parables is not complete without consideration of the Gospel texts. Neither is the examination of the Gospel parables possible without careful study of the parables of talmudic literature. The parables are also a genre. Common themes and shared motifs must be examined in light of similar plots in other story parables.

The identity of thought and the theological significance of the message of the parables, providing a means to understand God and to view humanity, suggest a shared environment. The theological solidarity between Jesus and the Jewish sages too often has been minimized in parable study. The differences will never be appreciated until the full impact of the unity of the theological thought of Jesus and his contemporaries is realized. While the parables serve multifaceted functions in diverse literary contexts, they effectively communicate the deep spiritual values of religious faith. In reality these metaphoric story illustrations possess the ability to transcend religious philosophies and to break into the everyday lives of the listeners. They challenge and illuminate the audience's concept of the divine character, as well as each person's individual relationship and responsibility to others. A study of the rich legacy of Gospel and rabbinic parables indicates not only that these illustrations often succeed in their task but also that they provide a communal bond between nascent Christianity and ancient Judaism. In this work the parables of Jesus will be explored in light of their Christian interpretations and Jewish tradition.

Part 2

Jewish Prayer and the Parables of Jesus

2 *The Contemptible Friend and the Corrupt Judge*

FOCUS

Modern scholarship has struggled with the meaning of these two partner parables (Luke 11:5–8; 18:1–8). As a result, many perplexing questions have emerged concerning these illustrations, which on the surface do not appear to be difficult. Do the parables teach preparedness for the Last Judgment? Do they teach constancy in prayer? Should they be studied together or separately? Is it possible that they were taught on the same occasion? What is the main theme of the parables? While many scholars have viewed the parables as teaching about prayer in daily life, others have argued for an eschatological interpretation. Sometimes the meaning of the end times overshadows all other approaches, and the emphasis on a life of prayer in the personal piety of the Jewish people is eclipsed.

At the outset, it should be stated that these parables are very closely related to one another, not only in the word-pictures that they use in humorous mini-dramas but also in the one major theme that emerges from the plots of both stories. Jesus often used dual parables to drive home a point. Quite probably these two parables were told on the same occasion to make his message clear. At least in the earliest sources of the Gospel record, strong evidence supports the use of partner illustrations that reinforce each other in parallel sayings and parables. In addition, one should note a possible danger of reading too much end-time theology into the plots of these humorous stories. A preoccupation with eschatology, which pervades many current studies on the parables, quite often loses sight of the obvious practical interpretation of the texts in the context of first-century Judaism. To some degree, the redaction of the Gospel narratives contributes to the misunderstanding. Nonetheless one must always be very attentive to the setting in life—Jewish theology—of Jesus and of the message of the parables. The early Jewish sources on prayer and tenacity provide rich background for these dramatic stories of village life. As situation comedies from first-century Jewish life, they convey a powerful message of God and his ways with his people.

PARABLES AND PRAYER

The problem with prayer is God. Heschel has made it clear that the supreme barrier one faces during prayer is not the words or the liturgy but rather the way one understands the nature of God. In order to challenge one's concept of God, Jesus employed humorous story parables to make his listeners redefine their view of God's character. The parables traditionally known as the Importunate Friend and the Unjust Judge are twin parables that use exaggerated character reversal. The parables role-play with the divine image. By exaggerated characterizations of action unlike God, they make the listeners understand the divine nature. Perhaps it would be preferable to rename them the Contemptible Friend and the Corrupt Judge. The exaggerated behavior of the person who refused to help a friend in need and the judge who did not care about a helpless widow is reversed in the divine character. Yet when it came to prayer, the disciples prayed as if God were like an untrustworthy friend or an evil judge, unconcerned about their needs. The parables challenge one's concept of God while they teach expectancy in prayer.

In this case, the exaggerated role reversal of the parables employs the Jewish principle of the light and the weighty *(kal vechomer)*. On the light *(kal)* side, if a person will respond to the persistent demands of a friend or if a corrupt judge will be moved to act on behalf of a widow only because of her constant annoying complaints, how much more on the weighty *(chomer)* side will God answer the prayers of his people? The rabbis in the early tannaitic literature customarily used this principle of interpretation by saying *al achat kamah vekamah* (על אחת כמה וכמה), "how much more," at the transition point between the light side of the argument and the weighty. The cartoonlike images of the friend and the judge may be known in human behavior, but it is absurd to suggest, within the context of the Jewish view of God, that God would behave in such a manner. The Lord is merciful and full of grace. God is the opposite of a bad friend or a corrupt judge. Jesus is teaching about prayer by illustrating the divine character. God is a good friend. He is a righteous judge. As a friend he is trustworthy and as a judge he is fair. God is unlike human beings, who in their weaknesses are consumed by their self-interests and show little concern for other people.

By giving a comical characterization of what God is not like, Jesus teaches his listeners what God is like. God is one's good and trusted friend. He is a righteous and conscientious judge who helps those who are in need.

The parables deal with the core of the problem of prayer. They describe the divine nature by opposites.

TRENDS IN SCHOLARSHIP

Two streams of thought in current studies of these twin parables have focused on the problem of the main theme of the stories.[1] Do they deal with prayer, or are they designed to make an entirely different point? In modern interpretation, two basic approaches have won favor. First, Jeremias has emphasized the eschatological approach.[2] Second, Bailey has discussed the parable of the Importunate Friend's cultural setting and has concluded that the main theme of the parable is "avoidance of shame" in the honor-and-shame society of the Middle East.[3] Both of these widely accepted approaches have missed the main point of these partner parables. Here it is worthwhile to study the texts in light of their Jewish background in order to discover the application of these texts in the context of Jesus' teachings and first-century Judaism.

---

[1] See especially the fine discussion by Flusser, *Gleichnisse*, 85ff. Flusser has noted the conflict between the eschatological tone at the end of the parable of the Unjust Judge and the emphasis on prayer. He has argued for the theme of persistent prayer as the subject of the stories while he has broken new ground on the proper hermeneutic for rabbinic and Gospel parables. B. B. Scott has commented on the current literature on the parables (*Hear*, 86–92, 175–88). For the most part, Scott goes along with Bailey when he concludes (p. 91), "In Who is a Friend? the end is achieved through an appeal not to friendship but to shamelessness." The approach outlined by Flusser is much more productive because he has observed the emphasis on prayer in daily Jewish life. As Flusser has shown in his examination of the redaction of Luke's text, the evangelist has properly understood the theme of prayer.

[2] See Jeremias, *Parables of Jesus*,, 146–60. He views the parables within the theme of the "Great Assurance" before the "Imminence of Catastrophe." The importance of prayer is secondary to the original form of the parable, which was distorted by Luke's expansion (p. 105).

[3] See K. E. Bailey, *Poet and Peasant* (Grand Rapids: Eerdmans, 1976) 119–41. Bailey writes, "In summary, the parable of the Friend at Midnight is seen to be an Oriental story of a man who knows his request in the night will be honored even by a neighbor who does not like him. The key to the parable is the definition of the word ἀναίδεια. This word took on the meaning of 'persistence.' It is here more appropriately translated 'avoidance of shame,' a positive quality" (p. 133). In Bailey's argument, the avoidance of shame is a positive quality in the Middle Eastern culture, which would be appropriate to God in the teachings of Jesus. Sensitivity to culture is a positive contribution of Bailey's work. Unfortunately, he seldom makes note of the great transformation of culture that occurred in the Middle East with the rise of Islam and the vast differences between Jewish thought in the classical rabbinic sources and modern Arab culture. No doubt Jesus was much closer to the Pharisees than to Lebanese peasants.

Jeremias writes, "While the contrast-parables express the confidence of Jesus in the face of doubt concerning his mission, the parables of the Judge and the Friend are intended to imbue the disciples with the certainty that God will deliver them from the coming tribulation."[4] He shifts the focus of the parables from prayer to the "coming tribulation," which fits in well with his general approach to the parables, emphasizing the "eschatological crisis" as the original context. While it is true that either the picture of going before a judge or the conclusion of the parable in the Gospel[5] (Luke 18:18: "When the Son of man comes, will he find faith on earth?") may suggest the end-time judgment, one must listen carefully to the storyteller to catch the main point. The widow is not being judged in the courtroom. She goes to receive justice in her case against her adversary. For the end-time theme one would expect the judge to pass judgment on her. The reference to faith (πίστις) in this saying and the mention of the "persistence" (ἀναίδεια)[6] of the widow in the parallel illustration, as well as the progression of the action in the plots of the two stories, suggest another message that is closer to the cultural heritage of Jesus in the first century.

The primary focus of the parables can be understood only by careful examination of the words of Jesus in the Gospel texts and by an in-depth study of their setting. When care is taken to consider the Hebrew character of the sayings of Jesus as well as parallel texts in early Jewish literature, the main point of the parables' message will emerge from the side issues that can obscure the clear purpose of each illustration. Many of these vital issues raised in contemporary scholarly discussion will be clarified by linguistic analysis and comparative study of religious ideas. The study of these parables in light of their Jewish background should answer these questions decisively. Faith in God is the basis of prayer. Faith can be viewed as determined persistence. True faith focuses on an awareness of what God is like.

---

[4] Jeremias, *Parables of Jesus,* 160.

[5] It would appear that the conclusion of the parable of the Corrupt Judge has been somewhat revised. Because the word "faith" is a strong parallel to the term "persistence" (RSV: "importunity") in Luke 11:8, it must be an original part of the saying. The reference to the coming of the Son of man, however, well may be the work of the evangelist, who sees the practical application to his setting in life. It is not out of the question that the humor of Jesus could have included a reference to the coming of the Son of man as a concept to undergird the importance of faithful persistence. One might compare the logion in Matthew "for truly, I say to you, you will not have gone through all the towns of Israel, before the Son of man comes" (Matt 10:23). Can one see an element of humor or irony in these sayings? Jesus' keen wit must be kept in full view.

[6] In the context of the parable, the translation "persistence" is preferable, as has been noted by BAGD, s.v. ἀναίδεια. The word "tenacity" in English would convey the original idea well.

"THE CONTEMPTIBLE FRIEND"

The opening question of the parable of the Contemptible Friend—"Which of you . . . ?"—is an effective rhetorical device that links the illustration with the following series of sayings about a father who gives good things to his children. The rhetorical question invites one response: no one among us would behave in such a way. The action of the man in the house is unthinkable.[7] What true friend could refuse in such a contemptible way to help his neighbor? In a similar fashion, it is impossible to imagine a father who would give his son a snake when he has asked for some fish to eat.[8] The parable assumes a knowledge of village life in the cultural setting of the first century. The word-picture describes a family dwelling and the interaction between neighbors. The beginning of the scene appears to be a quite plausible situation in the town. The opening question—"Who among you?"—captures the audience's attention because it leads them to listen for an unexpected turn in the story. In the metaphorical world of parable lore the typical everyday circumstances of the mini-drama are deceptively familiar. Everyone listens for the surprise. They are expected to participate in the thought processes of the story's plot and the action of the drama.

At midnight, a neighbor comes to the door of a friend and calls out for assistance. The listeners anticipate the turn of events. The neighbors are friends. The neighbor does not knock on the door at this time of night; that might cause unnecessary alarm. He calls out. His friend on the inside will recognize his voice, immediately open the door of his house, and come to his aid. The fact that the story occurs in the middle of the night emphasizes the urgency of the moment. One may consider the references to midnight in the Passover story (Exod 11:4; 12:29). The surprise in the mini-drama comes from the answer of the friend inside the house and the anticipated response of the neighbor outside.

Hospitality in the culture of first-century Israel was of inestimable value. The man inside the house had obligations to his neighbor, who in turn was obliged to provide a meal for his unexpected guest. The visitor traveling through the district would expect traditional hospitality. His friend, moreover, could rely on the other people in the village to assist him in fulfilling

---

[7] See Jeremias, *Parables of Jesus,* 158, correctly observing that the response to this question is "the emphatic answer 'No one! Impossible!' or 'Everyone, of course!' "

[8] The sayings reflect the realities of the setting of fishermen around the Sea of Galilee. In that lake the kind of fish without scales *(Clarias macracanthus)* resembles a catfish. It can crawl on land or in the mud. In many ways it has the appearance of a snake. Fishermen have noted that the nets at times bring up small stones and snakes from the bottom of the lake (cf. Matt 13:47, "fish of every kind"). Would a father give these to his children? Certainly the local color of these logia was not lost on the original audience. See Jeremias, *Parables of Jesus,* 226; Bailey, *Poet and Peasant,* 137; and Mendel Nun, *The Sea of Galilee and Its Fishermen in the New Testament* (Kibbutz Ein Gev: Israel, 1989) 10.

his obligation as a host. In many ways, the visitor is considered a guest of the entire village. On all sides, the culture of hospitality in Jewish village life is assumed in this colorful story. The links in this chain of cultural responsibility are clear to the listeners: visitor, friend, and neighbor. But the neighbor behaves very badly and shocks the audience. A small town in Galilee would be deathly quiet at this time of night, and others in the village would hear clearly each word of the conversation. The following day would bring news of the unexpected guest and the rich hospitality he received from his friends in the village filled with kind people. The event would be brought to the attention of everyone in the town. News travels quickly in such an environment. In the small village atmosphere, moreover, borrowing from a neighbor was not uncommon. In a later rabbinic text one finds the humorous anecdote concerning the proper way to borrow a needed item from one's neighbor.

The Clever Borrower

R. Acha said: One woman is clever at borrowing, and another woman is not clever at borrowing. The woman who is clever at borrowing goes to her neighbor, and though the door is open, she knocks at it, and says, "Peace be to you. How are you? How is your husband? How are your children? Is it convenient for me to come in?" The neighbor says: "Come in, what do you require?" The visitor says, "Have you such and such a utensil that you can give me?" The neighbor answers: "Yes." The woman not clever at borrowing goes to a neighbor, and though the door is closed, she opens it, and says to her, "Have you such and such a utensil?" The neighbor answers, "No."[9]

Rabbi Acha's illustration emphasizes the need to use acceptable custom and proper manners when approaching a neighbor for help. The story appears in *Leviticus Rabbah* in the context of several similar illustrations. It was not unusual to approach a neighbor to make a request. The humor of the story line, which contrasts two different women, teaches the desired lesson.

The humorous stories of lively rabbinic preachers are not infrequent in Jewish literature. Sometimes an attention-attracting illustration that betrays subtle dry wit may be used to emphasize a vital message. Such is the case with the story parable of R. Chanina from *Midrash Psalms:*

The Arrogant Traveler

R. Chanina told a parable about a traveler journeying on the highway. As it grew dark, he came to a lodge where the inn keeper said to him: "Come into the lodge away from the wild beasts and robbers!" But the traveler replied: "It is not my custom to enter into a lodge [at this time]." As he went on his way, midnight and thick darkness overtook him, and he returned to the lodge. He

[9] *Lev. Rab.* 5:8 (*Midrash Vayikra Rabbah*, ed. Mordecai Margulies [5 vols.; Jerusalem: Wahrmann Books, 1970] 1:123; see the English translation in H. Freedman, *Midrash Rabbah*, 74); noted by Jakob Jónsson, *Humour and Irony in the New Testament: Illuminated by Parallels in Talmud and Midrash* (Leiden: Brill, 1985) 128.

> cried and pled with the inn keeper that he would open up for him. The inn keeper answered: "It is not customary for the lodge to open up at night, and it is not the custom of the inn keeper to receive [a guest] at such an hour. When I asked you to come in, you were not willing and now I cannot open up for you." Thus also the Holy One, blessed be He, said to the children of Israel: "Return, O Backsliding children" (Jer. 3:14, 22) and "Seek ye the Lord while he may be found" (Isa. 55:6).[10]

The dry wit of the parable emerges from the dialogue between the arrogant traveler and the innkeeper. The innkeeper invited the traveler to enter as a guest out of concern for the traveler's well-being. But the time was wrong for the man on his journey, who probably thought that he would have another opportunity. He is too interested in continuing his journey. It is not his custom to lodge at this time. When the traveler realized his mistake, however, it was already too late. The innkeeper responds to his urgent pleas with the same words the traveler used, "It is not the custom of the innkeeper to receive guests at this hour."

The humor and dramatic action in the parable communicate an urgent message from the prophet Isaiah, "Seek the LORD while he may be found" (Isa 55:6). The colorful illustration of R. Chanina in *Midrash Psalms* illustrates the urgency of making matters right with the Lord immediately, because the future is uncertain. The text of Isaiah comes to life in the metaphorical world of parabolic illustration.

The parallel images in this rabbinic parable are quite similar to the Gospel illustration. The friend at midnight makes his urgent request in the Gospel text. Likewise in the rabbinic parallel, the Lord must be sought while he may be found. In the word-picture of the illustration, time is limited because the traveler must enter the inn while it is open. In the Gospel story, the door is shut and the friend inside the house will not open it. The rich repository of Jewish parabolic images may be used to illustrate different messages. The genre of parabolic teachings is similar even if the main theme and single point of the stories are quite different.

In the Gospel parable, the genius of the storyteller can be seen in the way he anticipates the reaction of his listeners. Jesus is closely attuned to the anticipated action of the two men who have this dialogue at midnight. The scene is familiar to the listeners. The humble home described in the parable would resemble many similar dwellings in a Jewish village in Galilee. The family sleeps together in the small house, which would be constructed close to other homes in the village. When the neighbor refuses to give the traditional hospitality, the audience is expected to complete the story in their minds.[11] While the Latin Vulgate completes the story, "Yet if he continues

---

[10] *Midr. Pss.* 10:2 (*Midrash Tehilim*, ed. S. Buber [Wilna: Wittwa & Gebrüder Romm, 1891] 46b–47a). See Str-B 2:186; Jónsson, *Humour*, 117–18.

[11] See A. Resch, *Die Logia Jesu* (Leipzig: J. C. Hinrichs, 1898) 75. Resch completes the story after this verse on the basis of the Latin text, "Yet if he shall continue knocking"

knocking" (v. 8), the parable itself is more colorful without the addition. This is perhaps the mark of the finest storyteller. The dramatic presentation of his story tells itself because of the vivid everyday life examples that require a minimum of narration. The plot of the story moves so quickly that the addition of unnecessary detail detracts from the way the action of one scene leads into the next. What happens when one's friend refuses a simple request because of a lame excuse? The man outside the door will be so indignant at the unacceptable behavior of his friend that he will take the house apart to obtain what he wants.

In a similar way, the parable of the Prodigal Son (Luke 15:11–32) does not give a conclusion to the story. The listener is expected to participate in the drama and decide how it will end. Will the elder brother respect his father's wishes? Will he be reconciled to the younger brother? In the parable of the Contemptible Friend the audience is invited to complete the action of the story as it is told. Originally parables were passed on orally. The performance of a story suffers when it is studied only as a written text. When hearers listen to the storyteller tell his tale in a parable about a neighbor who stands at the door of his friend at midnight with a simple request, they understand what will happen. The friend inside the house is expected to open his door and invite his neighbor to come inside and receive anything he needs. In modern Arab culture it is not unusual to hear the polite proverb "My house is your house." He must give his neighbor anything he requires.

Instead of the expected response, however, the friend in the house does not even open the door. He recognized his friend's voice, but he does not wish to help him with his emergency. The only acceptable excuse would be that he does not have the three loaves that his friend needs. The story, however, indicates that he does have them but refuses to give them. It is not difficult to open the door. In the home of a peasant villager, all the children sleep on the floor. They are probably already awake because they would certainly hear the friend's voice. In fact, it is probable that other neighbors would hear the dialogue as well. At this point the major transition occurs. The familiar territory suddenly changes. The man inside the house breaks every rule of accepted etiquette. The outrage of the listeners to the story will be directed toward this man. What will the neighbor standing outside the house do? He will pound the door and shout until this contemptible friend opens up. In the end, he will receive anything and everything he needs. The reason the homeowner opens the door, however, is not friendship but persistence. One cannot miss the humor of the parable.

The Greek term *anaideia* (ἀναίδεια) in Luke 11:8 is usually translated into English by "persistence," as in the NASV, or "importunity" (e.g., RSV).

(from cod. Colb. "At ille si perseveraverit pulsans"). He suggests that the story continued with the persistence of the man knocking at the door and reconstructs the Hebrew text: אמן ואם יתחזק הלז לדפק. One could note here the parallel saying, "knock, and it will be opened to you," from Luke 11:9, which has influenced Resch.

These translations do not miss the mark by very much. The term could be translated "tenacity" or "bold persistence." Literally the word means "shamelessness" (ἀ and αἰδώς).[12] Hence Bailey (following Fridrichsen) has argued for a meaning of "avoidance of shame" as a positive virtue in the Middle East. They claim wrongly that it is the man inside the house who has *anaideia*. Though he will not get out of bed to help his neighbor on account of friendship, he will give him whatever he wants because he desires to avoid shame. He will be criticized if he does not help his neighbor. Bailey and Fridrichsen's suggestion is entangled with difficulties, as Fitzmyer has pointed out.[13] On the contrary, the basic meaning of shamelessness does not mean "avoidance of shame." One without shame will do anything to achieve his or her purpose. The one who tries to avoid shame always behaves properly in order to maintain his or her personal honor. If this meaning were intended, the Greek word for honor, *aidōs,* would be more appropriate than *anaideia.* It is better to understand the word in the sense of bold persistence. It means unrelenting effort and is closely related to the English word "tenacity." A person with brazen tenacity demands what he or she requires without shame. The more important philological question refines the entire discussion: what term in Hebrew or Aramaic can be translated by Greek *anaideia*? Bailey and those who follow his approach are incorrect both linguistically and also culturally because they have not understood the context of the term *anaideia* in Jewish thought. The basic idea of shamelessness or without shame is quite different from avoidance of shame.[14] Linguistically it is essential to discover the meaning of key terms of the Gospel parables in the Hebrew language. Culturally one must understand the meaning of the terms within the proper Jewish context.

Greek *anaideia,* "shamelessness," in the Gospels is not easy to deal with. To understand the term in the parable, one must ask what it means in Hebrew, the original language of the *Vorlage* of the Gospels. Hebrew provides

[12] See LSJ, s.v. ἀναίδεια, citing Pausanias, *Periegeta* 1.28.5 "In the Areopagus, λίθος ἀναιδείας was the stone of *unforgivingness*, on which stood an accuser who demanded the full penalty of the law against one accused of homicide." The accuser would stand shameless and with determined persistence demand that justice be meted out to the one responsible for murder. This is shamelessness, not avoidance of shame.

[13] See J. A. Fitzmyer, *The Gospel according to Luke* (AB 28; 2 vols.; Garden City, N.Y.: Doubleday, 1981–1985) 2:912: "In this interpretation the *anaideia* is a quality of the petitioner. Some commentators have attempted to make it rather a quality of the neighbor roused from sleep: 'he will fulfill the request because of *his* own shamelessness, namely, that which will be brought to light through his refusal' (A. Fridrichsen, 'Exegetisches,' 40–43). But that interpretation fails because the *autou*, 'his,' that modifies *anaideia* has to be understood with the preceding *philon*, 'his friend,' a reference to the begging neighbor." Fitzmyer is certainly correct. For the other view see Bailey, *Poet and Peasant,* 119–33; as well as the earlier study of A. Fridrichsen, "Exegetisches zum Neuen Testament," *Symbolae Osloenses* 13 (1934): 38–46, esp. 40–43.

[14] See Fitzmyer, *Luke*, 2:912.

rich insight into the meaning of the parable. Certainly one must consider the original language of the parables and how a Greek translation would render a difficult Hebrew term. Is the Hebrew parable closer to the language of the Bible or the Mishnah? Does the conclusion of the text represent the redaction stage of the Gospels in Greek? When the text is carefully examined linguistically, the evidence leads strongly in one direction.

Probably the Hebrew word that best translates the Greek term *anaideia* is a form of the word chutzpah, which has become idiomatic in English as "chutzpah" as well as in modern Hebrew for "determined persistence." In current English, perhaps "raw nerve" would be a better definition. "Chutzpah" means "brazen tenacity" or "bold perseverance." "Relentless diligence" or even "impudence" is very near the meaning. Indeed, it may well be that the first recorded use of a form of the term appears here in the parable of Jesus that we have called the Contemptible Friend.[15] The conclusion is almost inescapable. Moreover, when the parable is studied in light of its partner, the Corrupt Judge, a fascinating question emerges: Does Jesus define faith as determined nerve?

In biblical Hebrew one does not find an exact equivalent to Greek *anaideia.* The verb *ezaz* (עזז) in the hiphil form is probably the closest word in biblical Hebrew. It means showing an impudent or defiant face, as in the idiom *heezah panim* (העזה פנים, e.g., Prov 7:13).[16] Probably in the language of the Bible one would need to translate Greek *anaideia* by the noun *ezut* (עזות) or the phrase *ezut panim* (עזות פנים), which means "impudence," though this exact idiom does do not appear in the OT. The language of the Mishnah, in all events seems to be nearer to the words of Jesus in this text. The term chutzpah, or the Aramaized form chutzpa, which means "tenacity," "impudence," "insolence," or "brazen persistence," is much nearer the word of the Gospel parable, *anaideia.* The colorful Hebrew word *chatzuf* (חצוף), from the same root in the paaul form of the passive participle, appears in the earlier literature and would be more appropriate to the language of the Gospel than the biblical idiom *ezut panim,* "impudence." The pail form (חציף) is also used.[17] The Hebrew phrase *ezut panim* and the Mishnaic Hebrew term *chatzuf* have similar basic meanings, but the connotation of the term in

---

[15] Of course the "Contemptible Friend" refers to the man inside the house who refuses to help his neighbor. In the partner parable, the "Corrupt Judge" tries to ignore the widow. The titles Contemptible Friend and Corrupt Judge emphasize by contrast the nature of God. One could entitle the parables the Impudent Friend and the Persistent Widow, which would stress the person who approaches God in prayer, but it appears that the primary theme of these colorful illustrations is the divine nature. They encourage persistent faith because of God's character.

[16] See KBL, 694–95.

[17] See Michael Sokoloff, *A Dictionary of Jewish Palestinian Aramaic* (Ramat Gan, Israel: Bar Ilan University Press, 1990) 213; cf. also 192. He translates the verb *chatzaf* (חצף) as "boldly insist upon."

Mishnaic Hebrew is quite different from the biblical Hebrew. In Mishnaic Hebrew a positive characteristic can be described by the term. It depends on the context. In usage, the Mishnaic term is much closer to the Gospel parable. In the Hebrew Scriptures, the expression *ezut panim,* "impudence," would almost always be a negative characteristic. A study of the term chutzpa in Mishnaic Hebrew demonstrates that when the expression means "brazen persistence" or "bold tenacity," it describes a positive virtue. One early Tannaitic teacher is even named R. Chuzpit, that is, Rabbi Impudence, or perhaps, in the more positive sense, Mr. Brazen Tenacity. In difficult circumstances hard-minded persistence is esteemed as a virtue. Chuzpit is considered an important scholar.[18] Determined persistence or brazen nerve can be a highly valued characteristic in one's religious faith.

A parable attributed to Rabbi Akiva in the Jerusalem Talmud uses the term *chatzuf* in a positive manner. It deals with the theme of faith-filled persistence in prayer for rain. Rabbi Akiva likens himself to one who had bold impudence or brazen tenacity. When his fasting and prayer for rain received a reply from heaven and those of R. Eleazar did not, R. Akiva told a parable.[19] He wanted the people to honor R. Eleazar even though his fast and prayer for rain were not answered. Rabbi Akiva's imaginative parable about a king who had two daughters teaches a message about prayer and the boldness with which a person may approach God. Perhaps it was to alleviate tension between Akiva and his senior, Eleazar. Faith is not easy to define. Nonetheless, in the context of the Jerusalem Talmud, the tenacity of a child toward her father is prized as a valid approach to one's heavenly Father, who will give a ready and sure reply.

The Tenacious Daughter

> R. Leazar[20] [Eleazer] observed a fast but no rain fell. R. Akiva observed a fast, and rain fell. He [R. Akiva] went in and said to them, "I will tell you a

---

[18] He flourished during the time of R. Akiva before the revolt. On his life and teachings, see Hyman, *Toldot*, 2:419.

[19] L. Finkelstein describes the circumstances of the story from both Talmuds:

> Akiba officiated [the fast], and hardly had he begun the services with the improvised prayer, 'Our Father, Our King, we have no King besides Thee. Our Father, our King, pity us for Thine own sake,' when the rain came! The general astonishment at this miracle—for it was interpreted as nothing less—is indescribable. God had indicated his preference for Akiba. Of course, it could not be that the pupil was either more learned or more pious than the Master. But, it was widely held, the incident did prove that Akiba's kindliness and his readiness to condone the faults of others made him superior to Eliezer. Akiba himself paid no attention to the congratulations which were heaped upon him. He only hastened to mollify Eliezer.

The stage is set for Akiva's parable of the two daughters (L. Finkelstein, *Akiba, Scholar, Saint, and Martyr* [New York: Atheneum, 1975] 105).

[20] The Jerusalem Talmud uses the spelling Leazar for Eleazer, which is probably closer to the original pronunciation in Israel during the time of Jesus. Consider the

parable. To what may the matter be compared? To a king who had two daughters. One was tenacious [*chatzufah*, חצופה] and the other was gracious [*kashirah*, כשירה]. When the tenacious one wanted something and came before him, he said: Give her what she wants so she will get out of here. But when the gracious one wanted something and came in before him, he lengthened his dealings with her because he enjoyed listening to her conversation."[21]

In the application of the parable, R. Akiva concludes that R. Eleazer by no means should be considered lacking in spirituality or religious piety because his fast did not receive a response from heaven. His prayer was proper. Akiva showed his appreciation and reverence for his senior, who was his respected teacher. Rabbi Eleazer is like the gracious daughter with whom the king loved to prolong his conversations. Rabbi Akiva describes himself as impudent by comparing himself in the parable to the tenacious daughter who always received what she wanted from her father because of her bold disposition. The entertaining anecdote captured the people's attention. Everyone would want to know what happens to a king who has two daughters so very different from one another. The parable deals with an apparent contradiction. Why did one fast receive a response from heaven when another did not? The paradox is compounded when one considers that R. Eleazer would be more esteemed in the eyes of the community. Akiva's parable does not alleviate the tension within the contradiction. Instead, he tells a story that logically explains that sometimes a child with bold tenacity receives a positive reply from a parent before the voice of a well-behaved child is heard. The parable itself is somewhat of a paradox. While honoring graciousness, the positive value of chutzpah is clearly seen. Bold tenacity is sometimes appropriate in prayers of strong faith. Akiva's prayer was answered even though Eleazer is more respected.

In another parable, the sages of Israel could compare the relationship between God and humanity to that between parent and child. Within the relationship of love in the family structure, a child may exhibit strong-willed

---

spelling of Lazarus in the Gospel of John and in Luke 16:19–31, which is the Greek form for Leazar. On the relationship between R. Eleazer and R. Akiva, see Finkelstein and Safrai in the next note.

[21] y. *Taan.* 66d; ch. 3, Hal. 4; see also b. *Taan.* 26b, where the occasion of the parable is described. The parable is cited by Str-B 2:187. See also the discussion of McArthur and Johnston, *Parables,* 25, 192. McArthur and Johnston translate *chatzufah* as "brazen." The parable is discussed by Finkelstein, *Akiba,* 105ff. Finkelstein translated the term *chatzufah* as "repulsive." The contrast between daughters is that one is repulsive and the other is lovable. See also the study on Akiva's life and teachings by S. Safrai, *Rabbi Akiva Ben Yosef Chayav Umishnato* (Jerusalem: Bialik Institute, 1970) 37–38. The language of the parable is of interest. It begins in Hebrew but changes to Aramaic in the middle of the parable. The change may indicate the redaction of the Jerusalem Talmud. Language change is not unusual in the talmudic literature. The language of rabbinic parables is Hebrew, although Aramaic portions may be contained within them (see Young, *Jewish Parables*, 40–42).

tenacity and receive his or her request, even though such behavior would not be acceptable in other situations of polite society. In a parabolic illustration, R. Simon observes that in the same way that a prince pesters his father for a single pearl of great price, so also Israel pestered God for the gift of Torah. The Hebrew word for "pester" (הטריח) is probably the same term used in the text of the parable of the Contemptible Friend (Luke 11:7) when the man inside the house tells his neighbor, "Do not bother me" (μή μοι κόπους πάρεχε) and in the words of the unjust judge (Luke 18:5) who decides to help the widow simply "because this widow bothers me" (διά γε τὸ παρέχειν μοι κόπον τὴν χήραν ταύτην). The word-picture that compares the people of Israel to the son of a king makes the relationship between God and his people one that must be described in terms of familial endearments. Persistence is a genuine expression of true faith.

The Prince Who Pestered His Father

> "The LORD is my strength and my shield; in him my heart trusts; so I am helped [Ps 28:7]." R. Simon told a parable: To a king who had a single pearl. His son came and asked him: "Give it to me!" The king answered: "It does not belong to you." But the son pestered him [הטריח עליו][22] until the king gave [the pearl] to his son. Thus Israel sang a song at the Red Sea to the Holy One, blessed be He, "The LORD is my strength and my song [Exod 15:2]." They entreated Him to give them the Torah. Thereupon, God answered them: "It does not belong to you but to those above." But because they pestered him, He gave them Torah, as it is said, "The LORD gives strength to his people [Ps 29:11]."[23]

Two other rabbinic parables appear in the context of prayers that were offered by the Jewish community for much-needed rain. The second parable resembles the story about a king and his two very different daughters. It is told by Samuel the Short[24] and is quite pertinent to the illustrations of Jesus because the terminology refers to waiting before God in prayer with perseverance.

---

[22] W. Braude translated הטריח עליו with the English phrase "wearied him with begging." The translation is good. The idea conveyed by the Hebrew expression is "pester" or "bother." Here the more literal sense has been maintained. See Braude, *Midrash on Psalms*, 1:378–79.

[23] *Midr. Pss.* 28:6. See *Midrash Tehilim*, ed. Buber, 116b; see also the *Yalkut Shimeoni* 2, Remez 708, on Ps 28:6 for some differences, where instead of a single pearl and a prince it is a portion of food and a friend. Buber (n. 22) feels that the present version is probably better because of its wide attestation. The parables circulated independently with some modifications.

[24] The name of Samuel the Short, Hebrew *Shmuel Hakatan* (שמואל הקטן) has been rendered in different ways. Many translators prefer Samuel the Little or Samuel the Lesser, but the name may well refer to his small stature, and therefore the translation "Samuel the Short" could accurately convey the idea of the name.

The Servant and His Perseverance

> Samuel the Short called a fast and rain fell before sunrise. The people thought that it was because of the merit of the community. But he said to them, "I will tell you a [parable]. To what may the matter be compared? To the servant who asked for a reward from his master. The master said to them, 'Give him [his reward] and do not let me hear his voice.' "
>
> Another time Samuel the Short called a fast and rain fell after sunset. The people thought that it was because of the merit of the community. But Samuel said to them, "It is not because of the merit of the community [that rain fell]. I will tell you a parable. To what may the matter be compared? To a servant who asked his master for a reward. The master said to them, 'Keep him waiting until he has languished and grieved himself [for a time]. Then give him [his reward].' "[25]

Samuel the Short uses two contradictory illustrations. Both parables teach the listeners that they should not assume that they have earned God's grace by their own merit or goodness. The stories focus upon God and his divine favor. That favor cannot be earned. Depending on the occasion, God may be moved by a fast or may answer prayer without fasting. Everything depends on God. Nevertheless, the people pray and seek his favor by fasting during a time of need. Because the Jewish community was so dependent on agriculture for its life during this period, one often finds references to prayers for rain. When the rains came even before the people began the designated fast, Samuel the Short said that it was not because of their merit. When the rain fell after the fast, again he warned that this is not because of the special merit of the community. A striking parallel to the parables of Jesus emerges from Samuel the Short's struggle to understand the divine nature and describe it to the community. Sometimes a master allows his servant to pine and be in grief before he grants his request. The words of the master, "Keep him waiting," describe the predicament of the faithful. They persevere and wait until God answers. They may experience hardship. They may even languish and grieve themselves until God breaks through to meet the need.

The second parable of Samuel the Short defines faith as waiting before God with perseverance. Fasting accomplished the purpose. The close similarity between Samuel the Short and the Gospel parables of the Contemptible Friend and the Corrupt Judge reveals the common Jewish heritage of waiting before God. The focus of the Gospel parable emphasizes the divine nature. The Hebrew term chutzpah accurately expresses the idea conveyed

---

[25] b. *Taan.* 25b. I am grateful to David Flusser, who called my attention to this parable and noted its pertinence to the study of the Gospel parallel. Consider also the persistence of the man who comes to Hillel and badgers him with questions (*Abot R. Nat.*, version A, ch. 15, and parallels).

by these parabolic illustrations. The friend at midnight, the widow, the tenacious daughter of the king, the prince who pesters his father, and the servant who waits and languishes until his master rewards him all have one thing in common: they all have the chutzpah, or hard-minded tenacity, to remain faithful until their petition is answered.

The concept conveyed by the term chutzpah is employed in its positive meaning in other contexts within the broader background of Jewish thought. Judah, the son of Jacob, who prevented Joseph from being murdered by his other brothers, is described in rabbinic literature as having chutzpah. Hence Jacob says to Judah, " 'Judah is a lion's cub' (Gen. 49:9). Thus we learn that he was given the strength of a lion and the tenacity (chutzpah) of a lion's cubs."[26] He possessed both strength and the raw nerve to use it. In difficult times he showed his bold persistence. The use of the term chutzpah here demonstrates its great value as a characteristic to be esteemed and employed for the benefit of others. The parallel Gospel parable, the Corrupt Judge, supplements and completes the powerful themes that appear in the parable of the Contemptible Friend. The Hebrew equivalent to the Greek term *anaideia* is chutzpah (or *chatzuf*). As one studies the two parables of Jesus together, the chutzpah of the impudent friend at midnight is described in greater detail as the characteristics of the persistent widow are portrayed in the humorous mini-drama of the Corrupt Judge.

THE CORRUPT JUDGE

The parable of the Corrupt Judge uses the term "faith" when it refers to the actions of the widow.[27] She deals with a magistrate who fears neither God nor man. Justice is not his concern. In the parable, he is primarily consumed with his interests for his own well-being. When the widow annoys him and he fears further attack, he is willing to hear her case. In Jewish thought, the judge is highly esteemed and must be fair-minded. The description of the divine judge and the widow in Sir 35:14–18 quite probably was common knowledge in the time of Jesus. One discovers a number of important parallels in word and thought from the text, which is dated in the second century B.C.E.

[26] *Gen. Rab.* 99:7 (cf. *Midrash Bereshit Rabbah,* ed. C. Albeck and J. Theodor [3 vols.; Jerusalem: Wahrmann, 1980] 3:1258).

[27] It is possible that "faith" in Luke 18:8 is redactional, like the words "when the Son of man comes." One can, however, note the close relationship between the difficult term "shamelessness" as meaning bold persistence in Luke 11:8 and the word "faith" here in Luke 18:8. Is faith an original part of the conclusion of the parable? When Jesus praises people for faith, often they have demonstrated extreme persistence in trying to reach him for help. This unwavering perseverance combined with a bold belief in God is often related to the essence of the word "faith" in the Gospels.

> He will not ignore the supplication of the fatherless, nor the widow when she pours out her story. Do not the tears of the widow run down her cheek as she cries out against him who has caused them to fall? He whose service is pleasing to the Lord will be accepted, and his prayer will reach to the clouds. The prayer of the humble pierces the clouds, and he will not be consoled until it reaches the Lord; he will not desist until the Most High visits him, and does justice for the righteous, and executes judgment. And the Lord will not delay, neither will he be patient with them till he crushes the loins of the unmerciful and repays vengeance on the nations; till he takes away the multitude of the insolent, and breaks the scepters of the unrighteous.[28]

Ben Sira describes the Lord as the righteous magistrate who vindicates the widow and the orphan. The references to prayer in the text are not without significance. God hears the prayers of people in need. The widow is helpless in the structure of society. She needs an advocate who will take up her case. Ben Sira presents God himself as the judge figure who will represent her with her special needs. The parable of Jesus portrays a corrupt judge, so different from the high ideal of the just magistrate in Jewish thought, who will not listen to a widow because he fears neither God nor man.[29]

Although the evangelist places the parable in the context of some eschatological discourses,[30] he introduces the story by the comment, "And he told them a parable to the effect that they ought always to pray and not lose heart" (Luke 18:1). For Luke the theme of persistent prayer may have emerged from the theme of the parable itself or may actually have been a part of his source. In any case it is fair to observe that the evangelist correctly viewed the emphasis of the parable on perseverance in prayer as the primary theme of the parable.[31]

Character descriptions are extremely important in parables. The storyteller must introduce the cast. The details of his portrayal of the characters are of inestimable value when one studies each scene of the mini-drama. The words in Luke 18:2, "In a certain city there was a judge who neither feared God nor regarded man" (Κριτής τις ἦν ἔν τινι πόλει τὸν θεὸν μὴ

---

[28] For the Hebrew text and a commentary see the fine edition of M. Segal, *Sefer Ben Sira Hashalem* (Jerusalem: Bialik Institute, 1972) 220.

[29] The close similarity between the Gospel parable and Ben Sira is more than coincidence. It is probable that the text from Ben Sira was known to the parable teller, who recognized how the listeners would respond to an extreme characterization that compared God with an unjust judge.

[30] See Luke 17:22–37. Chapter 18 of Luke contains other unique Lukan material that may have come from different contexts. He has collected the material here, but each unit must be studied individually. The Corrupt Judge is closely associated with the Contemptible Friend, even though these two parables are located in different contexts in Luke.

[31] The introduction to the parable is written in Greek and is probably the work of the evangelist. It does not show the evidence of a Semitic *Vorlage*, unlike the body of the parable itself.

φοβούμενος καὶ ἄνθρωπον μὴ ἐντρεπόμενος), introduce the judge as the major problem of the widow. In v. 6 he is referred to as unrighteous, which is the same term used for the dishonest steward in Luke 16:8. The conflict of the story focuses on the character of the judge. According to the Hebrew Scriptures, during the wise reign of Jehosaphat judges were given jurisdiction over the legal affairs of the people. The policy of jurisprudence for the land was established by instructing these judges, "Consider what you do, for you judge not for man but for the LORD. . . . let the fear of the LORD be upon you" (2 Chron 19:6). The judges must fear the LORD. They must not judge on the basis of partiality or bribes but, according to the description of the Chronicler, must represent the righteous judgment of God himself. This high view of justice makes the behavior of the corrupt judge in the parable that much more despicable.[32]

Perhaps the original description in Hebrew would be simply, "a judge who neither feared God nor human beings" *(shofet shelo yare et elohim vet haadam)* because the words "nor regarded" (μὴ ἐντρεπόμενος) were probably added in the Greek stage of the Gospels. That a judge does not fear God is the most serious charge against a court where justice is perverted in the interests of a corrupt magistrate.[33] The widow cannot plead her case on the basis of justice. She does not have an advocate who can represent her problem to a fair judge. As a widow she needs an influential intermediary who can approach the unjust judge and convince him to act in her behalf. Clearly her adversary occupies a position of power and superiority. Apparently her

---

[32]Fitzmyer, *Luke,* 2:1178, has pointed out that the description of the judge has parallels in extrabiblical texts. He notes, "Cf. Josephus' description of King Jehoiakim, 'neither reverent toward God nor fair toward human beings' (*Ant.* 10.5,2 § 283); Dionysius of Halicarnassus, *Rom. Ant.* 10.10,7; Livy 22,3,4." Cf. the parallel in Dionysius, where the phrase "without fearing the wrath of the gods or heeding the indignation of human beings" appears.

[33]A traveler's description from the ancient city of Nisibis in Mesopotamia has often been cited to illustrate this parable. "The *Kadi* (judge), who sits amidst cushions upon an elevated dais, is described as accepting bribes through intermediaries in the courtroom. It seemed to be ordinarily taken for granted that judgment would go for the litigant who had bribed highest. But meantime a poor woman on the skirts of the crowd perpetually interrupted the proceedings with loud cries for justice. She was sternly bidden to be silent, and reproachfully told that she came there every day. 'And so I will,' she cried out, 'till the *Kadi* hears me.' At length, at the end of a suit, the judge impatiently demanded, 'What does that woman want?' Her story was soon told. Her only son had been taken for a soldier, and she was alone, and could not till her piece of ground; yet the tax-gatherer had forced her to pay the impost, from which as a lone widow she could be exempt. The judge asked a few questions, and said, 'Let her be exempt.' Thus her perseverance was rewarded. Had she had money to fee a clerk, she might have been excused long before." (Quoted from H. B. Tristram, *Eastern Customs in Bible Lands* (London: Hodder & Stoughton, 1894) 228–29, by K. E. Bailey, *Through Peasant Eyes* (Grand Rapids: Eerdmans, 1980) 134.)

adversary dominates a corrupt court through his influence on an unscrupulous judge. The depiction of the widow in the OT often refers to her vulnerability in a society insensitive to her needs.[34] She is a forgotten member of the community. Her adversary controls the court to the extreme disadvantage of the widow. But the widow has faithful perseverance, which proves to be more effective. She would not give up. Against all odds, her headstrong tenacity wins the court's favorable decision.

The high value Jesus places on an outcast who makes good and a villain who becomes a hero can be detected in his parable of the Corrupt Judge. The story has a surprise ending. The widow plays the role of the outcast, and the wicked judge turns into the protagonist in the final act of the mini-drama. The common people loved stories filled with such unexpected outcomes. The central message of the parable is never far from the minds of the listeners. If an unscrupulous magistrate will be moved to act justly because of the unrelenting tenacity of a helpless widow, how much more will the one good God answer persistent prayer? If a corrupt judge can be influenced for good by someone of little importance and no worldly clout, how much more can the person created in the divine image pray expectantly to the compassionate God? Luke 18:3 emphasizes the point that the widow kept coming to him. She was tireless. As Fitzmyer notes, "Persistence was her only weapon."[35] The widow continued to demand, "Vindicate me against my adversary."

The judge refused for some time but was worn out by her perseverance (v. 4). The use of soliloquy is characteristic of parables. The judge reasons to himself. He does not fear God or human beings, but this widow is pestering him. His character has not changed. He is watching out for himself. His concern for himself is seen in his conclusion, which shows the unexpected turn in the drama: the unjust judge acts justly, "I will vindicate her, or she will wear me out by her continual coming'" (v. 5). The Greek word translated "she will wear me out" is *hypōpiazō* (ὑπωπιάζω), a word used for boxing. It can mean "strike [one] under the eye" or "give [a person] a black eye."[36] Diogenes Laertius uses the term to describe an exchange between Crates and Nicodromus in the gymnasium that resulted in a blow to the face because of an insult (*Crates* 6.89). Paul uses the term when he says that he "buffets" (i.e., strikes or beats) his body in order to subdue his nature and live a holy life (1 Cor 9:27). In the parable of Jesus, the word suggests that the judge will be

---

[34] See Fitzmyer, *Luke,* 2:1178: "Was she one of those whose 'houses' were being devoured (see 20:47)? She fits the OT picture of the widow to whom justice is often denied. See Exod 22:22–24; Deut 10:18; 24:17; Mal 3:5; Ruth 1:20–21; Lam 1:1; Isa 54:4; Ps 68:5; recall the OT implication of disgrace which was often associated with widowhood."

[35] Fitzmyer, *Luke,* 2:1179.

[36] See LSJ, s.v. ὑπωπιάζω, which also notes the metaphorical meanings of "bruise" or even "annoy greatly," and "wear out."

injured in either a metaphorical or a physical sense.[37] The Hebrew word *paga* (פגע) is very near in meaning because it can refer both to a physical blow and to an injury of a person's honor, though the latter meaning is much less frequent.[38] Scholarly consensus would probably support taking the verb in a figurative sense.[39] "She will keep wearing me down by her persistent coming."[40] But it is more to the point to take the term literally.[41]

The judge is really worried. He reasons that this widow is so persistent and determined that her next move might be to take a swing at him and strike him in the face. A physical blow from a widow in the public arena of his courtroom would be the ultimate disgrace. The judge is aware that he could not respond to such a physical attack. He must give her what she wants before she becomes uncontrollable and actually punches him in the eye. Culturally, the judge recognizes the fact that the widow's action would be justified under the circumstances, and that if he does not grant her request, the end result may be far worse. The best translation of the judge's soliloquy might be, "I will grant her justice lest in the end she comes and gives me a blow in the face!" The metaphorical sense is also possible: "I will grant her justice lest she keeps coming and beats me down [or wears me out completely]!" So concludes the heart of the parable and the most Semitic portion of the text. The widow's persistence beats the judge into submission.

The application of the parable is introduced when the Lord, that is, Jesus says, "Hear what the unjust judge says." The title "Lord" for Jesus is early and deeply embedded in the best sources of the Gospels,[42] but here it may be a Lukan insertion. The importance of the title "Lord," *adon* (אדון), must

---

[37] Fitzmyer, *Luke,* 2:1179, observes, "The vb. was, however, also used in a figurative sense, 'to blacken the face' (i.e. besmirch my character) or 'wear out completely.' See further Aristotle, *Ars rhet.* 3.11,15 § 1413a.20; Plutarch, *Mor.* 921F; Diogenes Laertius, *Vitae* 6.89. Cf. Derrett, 'Law,' 189–91; BDF § 207.3; E. Klostermann, *Lukasevangelium,* 178. Any of the figurative meanings would be possible, not to mention the physical sense itself, 'lest she come and give me a black eye.' "

[38] According to Sokoloff, *Aramaic*, 424, the term can mean "meet, disqualify, attack." The word is used in legal settings for the one who may be disqualified or attacked because of his ruling.

[39] See Moffatt's translation, "I will see justice done to her—not to have her for ever coming and pestering me." James Moffatt, *A New Translation of the Bible* (London: Hodder & Stoughton, Limited, 1948).

[40] See BDF 112, § 207, "in order that she may not gradually (pres. ὑπωπιάζῃ!) wear me out completely by her continued coming (pres.!)."

[41] At least if the Greek translator rendered the Hebrew term *paga* with the Greek word *hypōpiazō*, he probably understood the literal sense of the word: in the next phase of her persistent protest, she will strike him and give the corrupt magistrate a black eye.

[42] See Brad H. Young and David Flusser, "Messianic Blessings in Jewish and Christian Texts," in Flusser, *Origins,* 290, esp. n. 24. On the blessings in Luke 11:27 see also M. McNamara, *The New Testament and the Palestinian Targum to the Pentateuch* (Rome: Pontifical Biblical Institute, 1966) 131–33.

not be overlooked. It is possible that it appeared in the *Vorlage* of the parable in the Gospels. If the corrupt judge behaves in such a way that he can be influenced to grant justice to the widow, how much more will the just Judge hear those who persistently cry out to him day and night. The idiom "day and night" is excellent Hebrew. The term "elect" in v. 7 is unusual in Luke.[43] The Greek term for elect, *eklektos,* is parallel to the Hebrew word *bachir* (בחיר), which has a rich background in the Hebrew Scriptures and appears in the Dead Sea Scrolls. In Luke's parable it refers to the disciples who pray with determined perseverance.[44] The strong affirmation that God will work justice quickly for his people reinforces the word-picture in the parable. The conclusion of the parable, which refers to the coming of the Son of man, links it with the preceding context. The reference to faith in the saying, though often questioned by commentators, may well preserve a strong parallel to the term for raw nerve (chutzpah) in the parable of the Contemptible Friend.[45] Can true faith be viewed as determined persistence that borders on determined tenacity?

FAITH AND PERSISTENCE IN JEWISH THOUGHT

The problem of the Jewish context of these parables, from the richly diverse Judaism of the Second Temple period, must be studied carefully. Not only is one arrested by the startling references to bold tenacity as a form of true religious piety and devout faith in the parables of Jesus; an examination of Jesus' Jewish heritage reveals a strong current in ancient Judaism that extolled perseverance to the edge of blasphemy in the struggle contained within the relationship between God and humanity. Does the high view of divine transcendence in Jewish thought exclude the possibility of tenacious

[43] See esp. Lindsey and dos Santos, *Concordance,* 1:315–16. This is a favorite term for Mark, who has influenced Matthew. It would be remarkable if Luke had purposely deleted it. See the very fine study by Flusser in *Yahadut,* 253–74. Jesus did not ordinarily use the term "elect." The language of the parable may have influenced Mark's usage of the term.

[44] See, e.g., 2 Sam 21:6; Isa 42:1; 43:20; 45:4; 65:9, 15, 22; Pss 89:3; 105:43; 106:5, 23; 1 Chron 16:13; and in the Dead Sea Scrolls 1QpHab 5:4; 9:12; 10:13; 1QS 8:6; 9:14; 11:16; 1QH 2:13; 4QpPs 37 1:5; etc. The term is often used in the Dead Sea Scrolls for the chosen members of the community.

[45] The term "faith" in the parable will continue to be questioned by many fine exegetes. When one carefully studies the use of the term in the Gospels, however, it becomes clear that it may not be dismissed lightly as a redactional addition of Luke. R. L. Lindsey (private communication) has often spoken of faith as persistence, as in the case of the woman with the issue of blood who pursued Jesus through the crowds. Her faith saved her. The blind man in Jericho shouted for attention until Jesus healed him. Again, faith is said to have been exercised. Faith can be persistence. It can be shamelessness in the sense of *anaideia* in Greek, which seems to represent the word *chatzaf* in one of its various forms, probably *chatzuf.*

persistence on the part of people in the frustration of the human predicament? The profile of one outstanding figure of Jewish history from this period suggests close links with Jesus and his Jewish theology. Choni the Circle drawer in talmudic legend displayed outrageous daring toward God when he prayed for rain. When rain did not come as a result of his prayer, he drew a circle in the dirt and stood inside it. He had the audacity to tell God that he would not move until rain fell. In fact the action so outraged the conservative leader of the Pharisees, Simeon ben Shetach, that he had to resist the strong desire to excommunicate Choni. What could he do? Rain fell and, technically speaking, Choni had not violated the Torah.[46] In the end Simeon ben Shetach warned Choni and described his presumptuous actions in the strongest possible terms by using the word for sin in the reflexive sense (*mitchatae*, מתחטא). Choni "sinned himself" by exercising blasphemous tenacity toward God. In the same way that a child may act contemptuously toward his or her parents and receive what is requested, Choni's prayer was rewarded with the answer of much-needed rain.

Choni Prays for Rain

> Once they asked Choni the Circle drawer, "Pray that rain may fall." He answered them, "Go out and take inside the Passover ovens so that they may not be softened." He prayed, but the rain did not fall. What did he do? He drew a circle and stood within it. He spoke before him, "O Lord of the universe, your children have turned their faces to me, because I am like a son of the house before you. I swear by your great name that I will not move from here until you have shown mercy upon your children." Rain started to sprinkle. He said, "Not for such rain have I prayed, but for rain that will fill the cisterns, pits, and caverns." It began to rain with violence. He continued, "Not for such rain have I prayed, but for rain of goodwill, blessing, and graciousness." Then it rained in moderation [and continued] until the Israelites went up from Jerusalem to the Temple Mount because of the rain. They went and asked him, "In the same way you prayed for rain to come, so pray that it may go away!"[47]

Choni is also mentioned in Josephus.[48] His strong personality has left an enduring legacy in Jewish history. When the people asked him to pray that the rain would stop, he answered with clever wit in legendary fashion, "Go and see if the Stone of the Strayers has disappeared!" The stone was a high mark in Jerusalem that served as a kind of lost-and-found department in a city that was often inundated with numerous pilgrims from all over the

[46] See David Flusser, foreword to *A Hebrew Translation of the Gospel of Mark*, by R. L. Lindsey (Jerusalem: Baptist House, 1973) 5.

[47] See m. *Taan.* 3:8 (Danby, *Mishnah*, 198; Albeck, *Seder Moed*, Tel Aviv: Dvir, 1977, 339) and parallels. These texts have been discussed by G. Vermes, *Jesus the Jew* (London: Collins, 1973) 58–82.

[48] Josephus, *Ant.* 14.22–24.

world. Lost articles would be announced so that they could be claimed.[49] Choni, in his characteristic spirit, quips that he will not pray for the rain to stop until the stone is covered with the flood of rainwater. No one should miss the very significant terms used in this story about Choni. The first key term is the "son of the house," which describes his relationship to God. He says that God's children have turned to him because he is like the son of the house. The special sense of God's presence and Choni's keen awareness of his humble relationship to God as a household servant is expressed in the designation. The saying links Choni with other wonder-workers within this stream of Jewish life such as Chanan Hanechba, Aba Chilkiah, and Chanina ben Dosa.[50] Jesus is close to them. The reaction of Simeon ben Shetach is both predictable and also parallel to the way some religious leaders reacted to the ministry of Jesus. The inevitable tension between a radical approach to God in prayer and the more conservative or conventional way for offering a petition to heaven is not surprising. Simeon ben Shetach represents the more accepted concept of prayer when he warns Choni. The Circle drawer's devout piety, it seems, gives him a special relationship, like the son of the house. Choni resembles a misbehaving child according to Simeon ben Shetach.

Simeon ben Shetach's Reaction to Choni

> Simeon ben Shetach sent to him [saying], "If you had not been Choni I would have excommunicated you! But what can I do to you? You act with bold tenacity against [*mitchatae*, מתחטא, literally "sin"] the Omnipresent and He performs your will, like a son that acts with bold tenacity against his father and he performs his will! Concerning you the Scripture says, "Let your father and mother be glad, and let her who bore you rejoice" (Prov. 23:25).

Choni is like a son. His heavenly father responds to his unrestricted impertinent behavior by granting his request. His radical approach to God is accepted because he lives a holy life of obedience. God hears the prayers of this righteous man. In many ways, it is his life that is answered rather than a prayer.[51] The son can receive an answer from his father. Although Choni refers to himself as the son of the house, that is, a much-loved household servant, Simeon compares him to a son who goes to his father with bold tenacity to make a request. Such a petition is tolerated by parents who will indulge their children's improper behavior. Simeon warns Choni, but he does

---

[49] See b. *B. Metzia* 28b. See *Mishnah*, ed. Albeck, 4:340, on the text m. *Taan.* 3:8 and b. *Taan.* 19a. Albeck observes the humorous exaggeration of Choni.

[50] See the important treatment of these and similar figures in Jewish history in the fine study by A. Büchler, *Types of Jewish-Palestinian Piety* (London: Jews' College Press, 1922). See also S. Safrai, "Teaching of Pietists in Mishnaic Literature," *JJS* 16 (1965): 15–33; "Chasidim Veanshe Maaseh," *Tzion* (1985): 134–54.

[51] At least Simeon ben Shetach says that if he had not been Choni, he would ask for excommunication.

not deny the validity of his approach to God. After all, in a dramatic fashion, the determined prayer was answered.

The radical approach that extols strong faith in prayer for divine help in human need also finds acceptance in the mainstream of Jewish thought. In the period of the Amoraim, R. Nachman makes a strong statement in favor of headstrong perseverance in one's approach to God. Rabbi Sheshet builds upon the idea, because such boldness can achieve the desired result.

Bold Tenacity Against Heaven

> R. Nachman said: Tenacity [chutzpa, חוצפא], even against Heaven, is efficacious: first it is written, "You shall not go with them" [Num. 22:12] but subsequently it is written, "Rise up and go with them [Num. 22:20]." R. Sheset said, tenacity [chutzpa, חוצפא] is a kingdom without a crown, for it is written, "I am this day weak, though anointed king, and these men the sons of Zeruiah be too hard for me [2 Sam. 3:39]."[52]

In fact R. Abahu describes Moses as imploring God in the same way that a person grabs another's garments and demands action. Did Moses take God by the throat, so to speak, when he demanded that God forgive the people of Israel? It seems that a bold prayer characterized by brazen tenacity is acceptable under some circumstances.

The rabbis struggled with the implications of the biblical text when Moses challenged God. They realized that Moses was justified in his love for the people, which constrained him to implore God on their behalf. On certain occasions, prayer must issue forth with brazen tenacity and determined persistence. When the people sinned by making the golden calf, God was ready to destroy Israel. Moses pleaded with God to forgive them. In Exod 32:10 the Lord says to Moses, "now therefore let me alone, that my wrath may burn hot against them and I may consume them." Moses cries out to the Lord to spare the people. Rabbi Abahu describes Moses by explaining the biblical passage:

Moses Acts with Brazen Tenacity

> If it was not explicitly written, it would be impossible to say such a thing; this teaches that Moses took hold of the Holy One, blessed be He, like a man who seizes his fellow by his garment and said before him: "Sovereign of the Universe, I will not let You go until You forgive and pardon them."[53]

The mental image of Moses being compared to a person who takes another by his clothes to demand mercy is extraordinary. Should one use such boldness in prayer to God? Choni the Circle drawer would reply in the affirmative.

---

[52] b. *Sanh.* 105a; and see Str-B 2:186–87.

[53] b. *Ber.* 32a; see the fine discussion by Heschel, *Torah Men Hashamayim*, 1:196. R. Abahu seeks to emphasize the strong-willed tenacity of Moses when he spoke to God with such boldness.

Jesus of Nazareth would also agree. On a number of occasions in the healing stories of the Gospel texts, Jesus responds to someone who demonstrates strong-willed determination by saying, "Your faith has saved you."[54] This description of faith is firmly embedded in the Gospel tradition. When friends tear a hole in the roof of a house to help a sick person approach Jesus, he sees their faith, which could be defined as a brazen tenacity.[55] The woman with a hemorrhage displayed unrelenting resolve when she worked her way through a crowd and grabbed the hem of Jesus' garment, which no doubt was his prayer fringe.[56] In Luke's Gospel, the woman who broke into the home of Simeon with a bottle of ointment to pour on Jesus' feet gave evidence of her raw nerve. He says to her, "Your faith has saved you." Her actions were viewed as bold, to say the least.[57] In the story of the Canaanite woman who begs Jesus to heal her child, Jesus refers to her great faith in the account of Matthew's Gospel.[58] In the Lukan story of the ten lepers, they cry out for Jesus to help them. Their rude behavior is described along with the one who returned to thank Jesus. Jesus explains to him that his faith saved him.[59] Certainly their actions showed headstrong persistence. The example of the blind man in Jericho is more to the point. He is rebuked by the crowds. He refuses to shut up and shouts out with even more determination. Jesus heals him and describes his actions as showing faith.[60] Clearly, in the Gospels, sometimes faith is described as bold tenacity. The parables of the Contemptible Friend and the Corrupt Judge describe faith as unrelenting determination, but the illustrations press beyond an idea of persistence. They challenge the people to redefine their concept of the divine nature. What is God like? This is the problem of prayer. God is one's trustworthy friend. He is like a fair magistrate who will hear and answer the perseverance of an individual who approaches him with a personal need.

FAITH AS TENACIOUS PERSISTENCE

When these two parables of Jesus are studied together in light of their Jewish background, faith is defined as tenacious persistence. The person commits all of his or her needs to God in true faith. As fascinating as it may

[54] This fact and its importance for understanding faith have been pointed out by Lindsey. See his *Concordance*, 3:115. I am grateful to Lindsey for his rich insights into the Gospels on the subject of faith.

[55] Luke 5:20; Mark 2:5; Matt 9:2.

[56] Luke 8:48; Mark 5:34; Matt 9:22.

[57] Luke 7:50.

[58] Matt 15:28. The text is not in the Markan parallel.

[59] Luke 17:19. The reference to faith may be an addition to the story. It is missing in Codex Vaticanus.

[60] Luke 18:42; Mark 10:52. The example is vivid. The blind man is impudent, and Jesus praises his behavior as true faith.

be, Jesus' use of chutzpa in this parable is probably the first recorded instance of a use of a form of the word in this positive way.[61] Perhaps others in the company of Choni the Circle drawer spoke in a similar fashion before him. Certainly the rich Jewish heritage of Jesus from the days of the Second Temple, as well as from the period in which Israel's sages flourished in their centers of Jewish learning and community life, preserve clear parallels to the teachings of Jesus concerning chutzpah as a genuine expression of faith in God. The rabbis such as Simeon ben Shetach offer valuable warnings about taking the concept too far. Perhaps even Choni would recognize the limitations of such an approach when it is divorced from the proper lifestyle of Jewish piety. Certainly in the Gospels, Jesus teaches a life of discipleship that would preclude some of the inherent dangers of the excesses associated with unrestricted acts of impertinence in the presence of the holy and infinite God. True faith, however, in its proper context can be linked to chutzpa. Prayer with expectant faith in the nature of God may be expressed with bold persistence or brazen tenacity. Knowing who God is and recognizing one's place in the divine scheme of creation will build a solid life of prayer with perseverance even in the greatest of hardships. This radical concept of faith preserved in the Gospel texts is deeply rooted in early Jewish thought.

[61] One hesitates to make such a claim. It is important to consider all the evidence. Clearly our knowledge of the Hebrew language from this period is limited. The Gospels preserve significant materials for study. Nonetheless, the word *chatzuf* is the best Hebrew word for *anadeia* in the context of the parable. It defines the meaning of faith.

Part 3

Parables of Grace in the Gospels and their Theological Foundations in Ancient Judaism

3 The Fair Employer: Jewish Grace in Jesus' Parables

FOCUS

The parable of the Fair Employer (Matt 20:1–16) illustrates the divine character in concrete images of money, labor, management, and most especially the wealthy landowner. It deals in the realities of everyday life. God is like the gracious landowner who hires workers for his vineyard. People hearing the story see themselves in the day laborers—both those who were glad to receive full-time pay for part-time work and those who play the role of the grumblers. The crucial issues raised in the dramatic presentation surround these questions: What is just and fair? What is God like? In what ways do God's servants resemble him and reflect the divine character in their relationships with other people? First and foremost, the story attempts to imagine God in his immeasurable goodness and in his unmerited generosity. Second, it focuses attention on the welcome of the outcast into the community of faith.[1]

In the eyes of many interpreters, the grumblers in the colorful story have just cause in their grievous complaints. They were set up for the disappointment when the steward began to pay the wages from the last to the first. The

[1] I have discussed this parable in my book, *Jesus the Jewish Theologian,* 129–41 and see also my earlier treatment in *Jesus and His Jewish Parables* 259–66. Here I must give another perspective based upon further analysis of primary sources. My approach to the parable is much different from the accepted theory. Compare the discussion of Jeremias, *Parables of Jesus* 136–38, who wrongly claims that Jesus' illustration opens up "... the difference between two worlds: the world of merit, and the world of grace; the law contrasted with the gospel." Jeremias has misunderstood the world of ancient Jewish thought and the force of Jesus' message in the parable. See also Scott, *Hear Then the Parable,* 281–98.

eleventh-hour laborers joined the work team during the cooler part of the day, not long before evening, when everyone else would be thinking about quitting the job and receiving compensation for a day's work. The eleventh-hour laborers had worked one hour only, and yet they were paid the same amount of money as the workers who had toiled all day long in the scorching heat. All were made equals. Is this just and fair? The parable teaches that it is fair, the first are last and the last are first. They all receive the same wage in the mercy and justness of the magnanimous landowner.

SETTING IN LIFE

The setting in life for the parable reflects the depressed economic conditions in which able laborers wait in the marketplace daily, hoping to be hired for temporary work. A denarius was sufficient to provide food for the laborer and his family, but it was not a great amount of money. It was considered fair compensation for a day's work. The day laborer is on the bottom of the economic ladder.[2] When harvest season arrives, more positions are available to handle the pressing needs associated with gathering the crop. The parable does not mention the harvest, but the actions of the landowner who hires workers all day long would suggest the urgency of harvesting the produce. Harvesttime work in a vineyard is toilsome manual labor, which taxed even the strongest worker's physical stamina and concentrated energy.

The scorching heat of the day probably refers to the wind from the south. During certain climatic conditions of the summer, such desert winds bring a dusty and dry heat, which makes the weather unbearable especially during the afternoon. The Arabs refer to this time as a *chamsin*, i.e., fifty days, because one must withstand this terrible hot weather for approximately fifty days out of the year. In Hebrew these climatic conditions are referred to as a *sharav*, literally "dryness," because of the scorching nature of the dry heat. These uncomfortable conditions may last from a few days to three weeks at a time. Agricultural workers are particularly sensitive to this weather.

The urgency of the harvest, moreover, made each hour crucial. For maximun profit the grapes must be harvested at an ideal time. One day too late and the crop may be lost. One day too early may cost dearly in the marketplace. The wealthy landowner monitors the process very closely and hires laborers accordingly. The owner or his manager must calculate the amount of time required to gather produce from each section of his vineyard.

---

[2] Jeremias rightly pointed out this fact, *Parables of Jesus* 35–38, "There is no question here of a limitless generosity, since all receive only an amount sufficient to sustain life, a bare subsistence wage. No one receives more . . . they touch the owner's heart. He sees that they will have practically nothing to take home; the pay for an hour's work will not keep a family; their children will go hungry if the father comes home empty-handed." The life of the worker has been treated by M. Ayali, *Poalim Veomanim* (Jerusalem: Yad Letalmud, 1987), in Hebrew.

Some laborers are more proficient and gather the grapes in less time. All variables relating to the harvest must be carefully considered during the entire process, and above all the right number of laborers must be employed for a successful harvest. While the parable does not explain the actions of the landowner, bringing in new workers when others are tired may increase productivity by creating fresh morale among the weary laborers. Those who hear the parable follow the drama and pick out the major transitions in each turn of events. It is a story about the workplace. The land is the factory of agricultural society, and the labor dispute between the landowner and the day workers vividly portrays the blaming of God for what seems to be an injustice.

A similar agricultural setting is portrayed in a Greek fable in the collection of Babrius.[3] The center of the story is the crested lark who made his nest in the middle of a grain field. As is often the case in fables, the animals are wiser than the people. The plot of the story involves nature and a desire to learn from the higher level of life that is found in animal lore. Fables often seek wisdom through observation of animals and the natural life of the great outdoors. The crested lark has young who are growing older but are not yet able to leave the nest. The owner of the grainfield recognizes that harvest time has arrived. The young of the crested lark overheard his remark concerning the harvest, "Now is the time for me to call in all my friends that I may reap." The young birds are worried about their home. They tell their father that they must leave because the friends of the owner of the field are coming to reap. The wisdom of the crested lark is revealed when he tells his young, "It is not time for us to flee, a man who relies on his friends for help is in no great hurry." Time passes and the rays of the sun begin to make the ears of grain wither. When the owner of the field observed the crop being consumed by the sun, "he made arrangements right away to hire the reapers for tomorrow, and hire the binders too." After the landowner hired workers for the harvest, the crested lark told his little ones, "Now indeed the time has come, my children, for us to leave this place now that the man himself is reaping and no longer trusts his friends." The anecdote is designed to illustrate how hired help are more reliable than friends. The wise old lark understood human nature better than the landowner. The fable teller paints a vivid picture of the grainfield, the landowner, reapers, binders, and the natural fauna of the area. Love of nature and a keen interest in animal lore is found in the story. Many of the same images are used in Gospel and rabbinic parables.

In modern parable interpretation, the story of the Fair Employer is usually viewed as an illustration of the message of grace in Christianity, which must be contrasted to a theology of works in Judaism: the Gospel parable portrays salvation by grace, whereas its Jewish counterparts refer to

[3] Babrius, Fable 88 (*Babrius and Phaedrus*, ed. Perry, 108–11).

merit through works. The grumblers are identified with the Jewish leaders, and the latecomers with the rejected outcasts. Such undesirable outcasts in Gospel teachings may be linked to "tax collectors and sinners" or even to the followers of Jesus themselves. On the other hand, the message of Judaism did not reject the "tax collectors and sinners" but called upon all people to reform their lives.[4]

While strong evidence has been cited to support these allegorical elements in the parable, this anachronistic approach pulls the parable out of the social, economic, and religious context of the first century. It views Jesus as an outsider attacking Judaism. The religious beliefs of Jesus however, motivate him to call for social action that will alleviate human suffering. Jesus is a religious leader within first-century Jewish society who is calling the people to spiritual revitalization, which will result in social and economic reform. But he is preaching traditional Jewish values.[5] Because of the compelling parallels to Jesus' teachings in Judaism, it is far more convincing to place him within the mainstream of Jewish religious faith as an activist who sought renewal of the people by shaking the foundations of complacent belief without corresponding action. The belief is based on a firm foundation, but it must be demonstrated in practice. In fact, the conflict in the context of the Gospel seems to be more economic than theological. The story of the rich man that precedes the parable contrasts disciples who have abandoned all to follow the call of Jesus with a wealthy man who turns down his invitation. Jesus asks him to sell all, give to the poor, and follow him. This seems to be an invitation to join the inner circle of disciples. To be sure, the rich man was religious, but his reasons for rejecting the call of Jesus are related to his pocketbook, not his faith. Grounds for accepting Jesus' call would be religious, based on the finest teachings of Jewish wisdom during the period, teachings that address the social problems of the poor and encourage active study of Torah. His reasons for turning down the invitation of Jesus were financial. The other disciples within the inner circle ask Jesus about their reward for selling all and following him in discipleship. The Matthean context of the parable highlights the social issues related to Jesus' radical approach to discipleship. In short, the literary context of the Gospel parable does not support the Christian interpretation, which contrasts the grace offered by the church with the so-called legalism of the synagogue.

Many sources from Second Temple period Judaism as well as from nascent Christianity portray a compassionate God who is willing to receive the outcast. The Jewish sources seem to refute soundly the misrepresentation that the teachings of the religious leaders during the time of Jesus excluded undesirables from the fellowship of the community. On the contrary, they taught love and acceptance. The problem of preaching and practicing, how-

---

[4] Jeremias, *Parables of Jesus,* 136–37.

[5] See Flusser, 97f. and *Yahudut Umekorot Hanatzrut* (Tel Aviv: Sifriyat Hapoalim, 1979), 175–77. See also note 1 above.

ever, where some teach sound doctrine but fail to live up to the standard, seems to be present during Jesus' day in the same way that most religious communities tend to set higher standards than are actually practiced. But Jesus is a part of that standard, he is not rejecting another religious system. He should be viewed within the context of ancient Judaism rather than as a maverick or outsider trying to start a new religion. Like other Jewish teachers of the period, Jesus called the people to live up to the high spiritual values and ethical requirements of the Torah. The rich man in the preceding context was reminded of the requirements of the Ten Commandments pertaining to his responsibilities to others. Financially, he was able to help the poor. He was unwilling, however, to give up his riches and follow Jesus. The economic factors were more decisive than the theological motives. But the theology of the divine character as revealed in the parable of the Fair Employer will motivate Jesus' disciples to act.

The money in the parable captures the listeners' attention. Jesus uses humor to heighten the awareness of the financial circumstances of the laborers. "Why do you stand here idle all day?" the wealthy landowner asks the eleventh-hour laborers. Those listening to the story would catch the dry wit of Jesus. They had surely seen scores of day laborers waiting to be hired. It is all too obvious why they stand there. They want work. Without work for the day, most likely their families will not have food to eat. The landowner promises to give them what is fair. They rush to the vineyard as the sunset approaches. In an agrarian society, these economic conditions are familiar. The shock of the parable comes at its surprise ending.

What is fair and just according to the magnanimous landowner is shockingly contrary to accepted practice. His unconventional generosity toward the unfortunate laborers who were hired late in the day surprised the audience. But Jesus was comparing the generous landowner to God, who gives a just reward. The anticipation of reward and just compensation was customary. The saying of Antigonus of Socho in Abot 1:3 emphasized the fear of God and total devotion to him and at the same time minimized the concern for reward: "Be not like servants who serve the master for the sake of receiving a reward, but be like servants who serve the master not on condition of receiving a reward. And let the fear of heaven be upon you." The Hebrew term translated "reward" is פרס, which probably refers to some type of bonus compensation. The basic meaning of "just reward" is certainly conveyed by this term. The eminent commentator on the Mishnah, C. Albeck, understands the saying as emphasizing love. The person of piety serves God because of love rather than the hope of receiving a reward.[6] In the Synoptic Gospels, the value of reward (μισθός = שכר) pervades the ethical and practical teachings of Jesus, e.g., "for your reward is great in heaven" (Matt

[6] *Mishnah*, ed. Albeck, 4:35 on Abot 1:3; cf. also J. Levy, *Wörterbuch über die Talmudim und Midraschim* (4 vols.; Berlin: Benjamin Harz, 1924) 4:124. See b. *B. Bat.* 25a.

5:12) or "For if you love those who love you, what reward have you?" (Matt 5:46). The compensation is a reality but not a goal. The motive of love, which emerges from a deep awe and reverence for God, should be the guiding principle of moral action and spiritual life.

The fulfillment of a commandment, doing good to help someone or simply obeying God, is the quintessence of Jewish faith and practice. Faith begins with knowing who God is and having no other god (Deut 6:4). But true faith is accompanied by action because it involves so much more than belief. Doing a good deed to help another person in need is faith with corresponding action. It is love that will have its reward. The concept of a reward for obedience rests in part upon biblical promises, which speak about the blessing of long life for those who honor their parents or who let the mother bird go before collecting her young (Deut 5:16; 22:7). But the motivation for obedience is not based on the hope for a reward. Doing a mitzvah is for its own sake, and this in itself is reward enough. True faith is evidenced by a life devoted to the spiritual values of the biblical belief in God. These truths are expressed in the form of a later rabbinic parable that serves to illustrate these concepts as they developed within Jewish culture.

The Laborers in the Orchard

> R. Hiyya taught: To a king who had an orchard into which he brought laborers without revealing to them the reward for planting each of several kinds of trees in the orchard. Had he revealed to them the reward for planting each kind of tree in the orchard, the laborers would have picked out the kind of tree for whose planting there was the greatest reward and planted it; thus the work of the orchard would have been neglected in one section and not neglected in another section. Even so, concluded R. Abba bar Kahana, the Holy One, blessed be He, did not reveal to Israel the reward for heeding the different precepts of Torah. Had He revealed it to them, Israel might have picked out the most rewarding precept and heeded only that one. Then the Torah would be neglected at one Section and maintained only at another Section.[7]

While the reward is a reality, obedience to the teachings of Torah is the essence of a genuine faith in God. In the orchard, each tree must be planted and tended properly. One section cannot be maintained to the neglect of another. The motivation for service therefore is based more on total obedience than work to earn a reward. The workers in the orchard receive a reward, but they must serve out of an earnest desire to care for the needs of every planting. The rabbinic parable emphasizes total obedience to God without concern for the final compensation. It is similar in some respects to the saying of Antigonus of Socho. His people do not serve him on the condition of receiving a reward but rather out of love, which is grounded on awe and reverence.

---

[7] *Pesik. Rab.* 23/24; cf. the English translation of W. Braude, *Pesikta Rabbati* (2 vols.; New Haven: Yale University Press, 1968) 1:494–95; Hebrew edition, *Pesikta Rabbati*, ed. M. Friedmann (Vienna: Josef Kaiser, 1880) 121b–122a.

JESUS' JEWISH THEOLOGY

The Gospel text is best understood in the context of first-century Jewish thought. By raising the issue of divine justice in giving fair compensation, Jesus forces the listeners to evaluate their own relationship to others. The humor in the story, as seen in the lively conversations between the key actors, is a dynamic teaching tool that conveys the truth of the message. It is the reality behind the word-picture that challenges the people. After all, Jesus is a theologian, but his theology is rooted in the manifold diversities of Second Temple period Judaism. The parable describes the nature of God as it explores the meaning of justness and mercy in the biblical understanding of God.

Flusser has demonstrated the close identity between Jesus and early Judaism. In most ways, the Gospel parable falls in line with rabbinic teachings concerning divine grace and just reward for obedience. The rabbis also told a parable about two laborers who receive the same pay that is not based on the amount of work each accomplished. Performance alone is not the criterion for reward. In this story we find two laborers who are made equal in the same way that the daylong workers in Jesus' parable are made equal to the latecomers. The standard of payment for services rendered, a denarius for a day's work, is another point of identity between the rabbinic and Gospel texts.

Grace or Works

> How do the righteous come [into the world]? Through love, because they uphold the world through their good deeds. How do they depart—also through love. R. Simeon ben Eleazar told a parable. To what may the matter be compared? To a king who hired two workers. The first worked all day and received one denarius. The second worked only one hour and yet he also received a denarius. Which one was more beloved? Not the one who worked one hour and received a denarius! Thus Moses our teacher served Israel one hundred and twenty years and Samuel [served them] only fifty two. Nevertheless both are equal before the Omnipresent! As it is said, "Then the LORD said to me, 'Though Moses and Samuel stood before me' " (Jer 15:1); and thus He said, "Moses and Aaron were among his priests, Samuel also was among those who called on his name" (Psalm 99:6); concerning them and others like them He says, "Sweet is the sleep of the laborer whether he eats little or much" (Eccl 5:12).[8]

The element of time plays a prominent role in both parables, with latecomers working only one hour yet being paid the same wage as the others, one denarius. Is this fair? In the context of Jewish theology, all are rewarded

[8] Semachot de-Rabbi Chiyah 3:2; *Masekhet Semachot,* ed. M. Higger (Jerusalem: Makor Foundation, 1970), 220–21. See also Flusser's works in note 5 above.

justly according to their obedience rather than job performance alone. Moses served the people for 120 years, but Samuel for only 52 years, yet both receive equal reward from God. Is this justice? Both the Gospel and rabbinic parables imply identical replies to this question.

Frequently since the work of J. Jeremias, scholars have claimed that Jesus broke away from traditional Judaism by teaching grace instead of reward in this parable. The law of Judaism is superseded by the grace of Christianity. Jeremias based his interpretation of Judaism on the rabbinic parable of "The Industrious Laborer." The motifs in this classic rabbinic parable are very similar to Matthew's parable of the Fair Employer.

The agricultural setting of the story from rabbinic teachings is vividly clear, and its rich imagery reminds scholars of the Gospel parable. In the drama of the rabbinic parable a troupe of actors appears playing significant roles as the king, a proficient worker, and the other day laborers. The conflict of the story involves a wage dispute and a heated argument between the king and the day laborers. Every element of the story, however, is overshadowed by the close relationship between the king and the proficient worker. The king longs to have fellowship with him. While everyone else works, they walk together the lengths and breadths of the field enjoying each other's company. Unlike the parable of the Fair Employer, however, the proficient laborer is on the job all day long, whereas some of the latecomers in Jesus' parable work only one hour. The proficient worker distinguishes himself from the others by his outstanding performance in the first two hours of the day. The rest of the day he spends walking about with the king in full view of the other laborers, who are toiling away in the field. The proficient worker still receives a full day's wage like everyone else even though he did not work with the others throughout the day. What is the meaning of justice in this parable?

The Industrious Laborer

> To what may R. Bun bar Chaya be compared? To a king who hired many laborers. One of them was extremely proficient in his work. What did the king do? He took him and walked with him the lengths and breadths [of the field]. In the evening the laborers came to take their wages. But [to the one with whom he had walked—the king] gave a full day's wage. The laborers murmured and complained, "We worked all day long, but [the king] has given this one who only worked two hours a full wage like us." The king answered them, "He has done more in two hours than what you did for the entire day!" Thus though R. Bun labored only twenty eight years, he did more than a learned scholar could have studied in a hundred.[9]

[9] See R. Zeira, j. Ber. 5c, ch. 2, halakah 8. I am grateful to Rabbi Menachem Rubin who suggested to me the translation "lengths and breadths [of the field]" which aided me in translating the parable.

Who is R. Bun bar Chaya? Since mention of him introduces this colorful rabbinic parable, it is essential to understand who he is for a proper interpretation. Jeremias neglected the context of the story. The occasion of this parable was a funeral. Rabbi Bun bar Chaya had died at the young age of twenty-eight. In an effort to comfort the bereaved family, the parable was told as a part of a eulogy in honor of the young but distinguished scholar. When the solemn nature of the context of the parable is kept in view, the image of the king takes on much greater significance. The king is seldom a stock character in the rabbinic parables. Here he is drawn to the proficient worker and yearns to be with him. The reality behind the word-picture conveys a message of comfort for a bereaved family: God so loved the proficient R. Bun bar Chaya that he gave him a break from the toilsome labor of this life to be with him.

In my opinion, Jeremias was incorrect to suggest that the rabbinic parable teaches merit, in the sense that the proficient worker earned his reward by his industrious performance in comparison with the other laborers.[10] The focus of the rabbinic parable is God and his grace. His justice is beyond knowing. While it is true, as Jeremias points out, that the king comments on the productivity of the proficient worker, it should be observed that the laborer served the king all day long. He certainly earned a day's pay, but he was praised for his tremendous accomplishment in the first two hours. When the payment for services was given at the end of the workday, the other laborers grumbled about the fact that the proficient worker spent most of the time walking around with the king. The king countered their argument by saying, "He has done more in two hours than what you did for the entire day!" This element of apparent hyperbole and exaggeration is designed to defend the king's sovereignty and justice. The force of the message must be located in the reality behind the parable. Thus, though R. Bun bar Chaya labored only twenty-eight years, he faithfully served the King. As the King's beloved laborer, in the highest sense of divine justice he will be rewarded fairly along with the other workers. Although R. Bun bar Chaya died young, God's purpose is beyond human comprehension. His accomplishments are no less than those of others who are given more time, and his reward is just and fair. In many ways the parable of "The Industrious Laborer" is a story of theodicy that seeks to answer the perplexing questions, Why does tragedy strike the righteous? Why do bad things happen to good people?

The parable is not intended to give a completely satisfactory answer. Nevertheless, it portrays the grace and mercy of God in the image of a king who seeks companionship with the proficient worker. The phrase "He took him and walked with him" is a central theme of the story, which concludes with fair compensation for all.

[10] Jeremias, *Parables of Jesus,* 136–37.

THE CONFLICT

The conflict in the parable of Jesus centers on the fair wages paid to all workers in accordance with their agreement. Justness is the foundation of the landowner's action because he pays the same wage to all in spite of the unequal amount of time devoted to work by the various groups of workers. The first workers received exactly what they bargained for. The conflict is seen when the landowner pays the latecomers the same wage. After they saw the generosity of the landowner, the laborers who worked all day naturally thought that they would receive a bonus. Instead the first are last and the last are first. The grumblers complain to the owner of the vineyard that they deserved more because they withstood the heat of the day. They are angry about money and the generosity of the landowner.

In a religious perspective, the laborers should have been happy about the good fortune of their coworkers who, because of the generosity of the landowner, would now have enough provision for their families. In my opinion, often the poor are genuinely happy for an unexpected blessing that someone else in their station in life receives. But this is not the case in the parable. These laborers express their disgust by irately accusing the landowner of injustice. They grumble about their wages and are envious of the others.

THE FAIR EMPLOYER RESOLVES THE CONFLICT

According to Jesus, the landowner is a fair employer. He gave the first group of laborers what they agreed to at the beginning of the day; moreover, he compensated the latecomers with what was just. It is the noble and generous character of the landowner that will resolve the wage dispute.

The parable portrays a major farming operation with a large estate, management staff, and numerous groups of day laborers who are working in the vineyard. This picture emphasizes the power and authority of the owner of the vineyard. As the most prominent actor in the drama, he is not a stock character. On the contrary, he is the leading man, and the whole story revolves around him and his actions. He is not detached from the scene. In fact, as the magnanimous and wealthy nobleman of the estate, he is involved very much with the intricate affairs of the sizable operation. He hires the workers and gives orders to his steward concerning the amount of payment for each person as well as the process in which the last are paid before the others. The manager who holds the position of steward is of course quite privileged in the sense that he has steady work and the trust of the landowner. His role in the parable reveals another realistic feature of the story from its setting in life. Such a manager often handled these affairs for the wealthy landowner. In some respects, it may be somewhat uncommon for the landowner of such a large estate to be so involved in the day-to-day affairs of the vineyard. He is very concerned about the needs of his laborers as he oversees the work of his vineyard in a hands-on style of management. It is his view of fair pay that creates the conflict, and such a wage dispute must be solved from the top.

First, the landowner teases the disgruntled employees by deriding their self-serving attitude toward their coworkers. He describes their attitude by the strong pejorative idiom "evil eye." That term in Hebrew, עין רעה, referred to parsimonious illiberality. This accusation of stinginess was an insult that carried with it a certain measure of shame. Generosity was a virtue that was highly esteemed in Jewish culture. The landowner contrasts his good eye, i.e., generous and magnanimous spirit, with the stingy attitude of the day laborers who refused to rejoice in the good fortune of their fellow human beings. Second, it seems that the words of the landowner make a strong contrast between what belongs to him and what belongs to the disgruntled workers. It forms a play on words that is paralleled in similar Hebrew sayings. Such wordplays between what is mine and what is thine probably existed in other linguistic forms and diverse cultures as well. The Greek text of Matt 20:14–15 captures the force of the colorful Semitic background of the saying. If we examine the Greek text and make a theoretical Hebrew reconstruction, the words "evil eye" and the similar-sounding possessive pronouns for "mine" (שלי) and "thine" (שלך) give greater force to the words of the owner of the vineyard in this Gospel parable.

> ἆρον τὸ σὸν καὶ ὕπαγε· θέλω δὲ τούτῳ τῷ ἐσχάτῳ δοῦναι ὡς καὶ σοί. ἢ οὐκ ἔξεστίν μοι ὃ θέλω ποιῆσαι ἐν τοῖς ἐμοῖς; ἢ ὁ ὀφθαλμός σου πονηρός ἐστιν ὅτι ἐγὼ ἀγαθός εἰμι;

> קח [טול] את שלך ולך: ברצוני לתת לזה האחרון כמו גם לך: הלא מותר לי לעשות בשלי כרצוני אלא עינך רעה אף [אני טוב] שלי טובה היא

> "Take thine and go! I desire to give to this last one as I also gave to you. Am I not permitted to do with mine as I want? Even if your eye is evil, mine is [I am] good?"

What is the owner of the vineyard like? He is generous and liberally gives to the last workers what belongs to him. The wordplay is similar to a saying in Jewish wisdom that describes four different types of human beings. It is a classic parallelism that humorously compares the four different ways of combining the possessive pronouns "thine" (שלך) and "mine" (שלי).

Four Kinds of People

> Four characters of people:
>
> He who says, what is mine is mine and what is thine is thine. This is the average type. Some say it is the character of Sodom.

> He who says, What is mine is thine and what is thine is mine. He is ignorant.
>
> He who says, What is mine is thine and what is thine is thine. He is a saint.
>
> He who says, What is thine is mine and what is mine is mine. He is wicked. (*Abot* 5:13)

The quadripartite structure of the rabbinic text made it easier to remember and served to heighten the humorous element of the saying from oral teachings. The listener would follow all the four possible combinations of the two words "mine" (a) with "thine" (b). The first is obvious, (a) (a) and (b) (b). "What is mine is mine and what is yours belongs to you" represents the average person who respects his property and recognizes your ownership of your belongings. The funny character of the next combination, (a) (b) and (b) (a), is mixed up completely. This type has everything reversed. "You own my property and I own yours" is his or her approach to life. He or she is ignorant. The next person is very much like the landowner in the parable of the Fair Employer. Such a person is very generous, viewing his or her possessions as belonging to others. The combination, (a) (b) and (b) (b), describes true piety. The saint says, "What belongs to me is yours and what belongs to you is yours." This describes the nature of the landowner! The final combination produces the thief, (b) (a) and (a) (a). In many ways, this would also describe the grumblers in the parable. They both want what is theirs and also what belongs to the landowner. They refuse to accept the latecomers or share in their joy at receiving a full day's wage.

Jesus' parable is designed to describe the divine character in the teasing words of the fair employer. In his justness, he makes all the laborers equal. The action of the magnanimous nobleman challenges the listeners to follow his example. After all, such a generous spirit is a quality to be admired. The parable does not, however, break the image of God in Judaism. The story actually upholds many descriptions of the divine nature in the writings of Israel's wise teachers. Do Jesus' parables teach Jewish grace? The theological significance of the Gospel parable is embodied in a later rabbinic parallel about divine mercy, "The King and the Lazy Workers." The king in the anecdote merits praise because he is determined to pay unproductive employees their full wage in spite of their poor job performance.

The King and the Lazy Workers

> Solomon said to the Holy One blessed be He: Master of the Universe! When a king hires good laborers who perform their work well and he pays them their wage—what praise does he merit? When does he merit praise? When he hires lazy laborers but still pays them their full wage!"[11]

[11] *Midr. Pss.* 26:3; *Midrash Tehilim*, ed. S. Buber (Wilna: Wittwa and Begrüder Romm, 1891), 109a and cf. The English translation, Braude, *Midrash on Psalms*, 1:359.

Unlike this rabbinic parallel, all the workers in the parable of the Fair Employer seem to have performed their jobs well, even though some worked much longer than others. In fact, all the laborers in the vineyard fulfilled the requirements of their assigned tasks. The issue was time and not job performance. In the rabbinic story, however, lazy workers who have not fulfilled their obligations still receive wages. The rich king, who pays them even though they do not deserve it, is worthy of esteem because of his generous and magnanimous spirit.

The Jewish theological concept of grace, God's unmerited favor, can be seen in Jesus' parable of the Fair Employer. His story was not an iconoclastic attack against a Jewish theology of salvation through works. Grace, merit, and reward are crucial elements in the teachings of Jesus as well as the rabbis. Their approaches to these theological issues are quite similar. The sophisticated didactic method of Jesus' parable invites the listeners to participate in the story. They see themselves in the grumblers and realize that each person must seek those godlike qualities which were embodied in the actions of the generous landowner. He was fair and just when he showed grace to the latecomers. His generous nature challenged the others to follow his example. First and foremost the story tells us about God and his unlimited grace for each person.

4 God's Gracious Gifts

FOCUS

The underlying theme of the parable of the Talents and its parallels in the Synoptic Gospels is stewardship.[1] What will the steward do with his master's goods? Everything that a person has, whether it be goods or abilities, is given from above. In Jewish thought, God's creation of the world makes every person a caretaker of what really belongs to God. Each individual who is created in the divine image is endowed by God. One's concept of God, moreover, is viewed as the primary determining factor in faithful stewardship. In contrast to the fear of the one-talent servant, the good servants trust in the goodness of their master and as a result of their faith are willing to take risks in order to achieve a maximum return for their master's money.

All of these similar versions of the story introduce a dramatic conflict. What will the servants do while their master is far away? The popular English expression "When the cat is away, the mice will play!" probably captures a major element of the basic plot underpinning the entire story. Although the cat is away at present, he will be coming back. The master is out of town, and the servants are in charge of the affairs of his estate. The question the parable asks could be put another way: "How do people behave in the absence of God?"

While the master is gone now, he will return. He has entrusted his possessions to his servants, who act as caretakers. What reward will they receive when the master returns to settle his accounts? Will they be punished for mismanagement?

In Matthew, the servants use what is graciously bestowed as a sacred trust—each according to his ability (Matt 25:15). Sizable sums of money are

---

[1] The Talents, Matt 25:14–30; The Pounds, Luke 19:11–27; Watchfulness, Mark 13:34.

used to illustrate faith in God and responsible stewardship.[2] In Luke's version, the master carefully instructs his servants, "Trade with these till I come" (Πραγματεύσασθε ἐν ᾧ ἔρχομαι, 19:13). In Matthew, the most capable servants take risks and double their master's money.[3] The surprise element in the story is that all the servants had the proper attitude. The five-, two-, and one-talent servants have one common characteristic: to please the master. The one-talent servant, however, desired to save the master's money, so hid it. Though his action was based upon the best of intentions, he forfeited the potential benefits that could have been gained from low-risk investment. By burying the money, he lost all possible profit. Fear, in fact, guided the actions of this one-talent servant, who failed to grasp the essence of his master's character. His good intention, misled by a wrong understanding of his master, produced the opposite result. In the end, he was severely punished. According to the message of the parable, good intentions are not enough. With a clearer understanding of the attributes of his master, he would have had sufficient vision to use his talent wisely.

THE PARABLE'S CHRISTIAN INTERPRETATIONS

Christian interpretations of the parable can already be seen in the placement of the text in the Synoptic Gospels. In Matthew's Gospel it is positioned in the midst of eschatological teachings, with the parable of the Wise and Foolish Maidens preceding it and the Judgment of the Nations following it. The parable of the Pounds in the Third Gospel is used by Luke to conclude the special section of his text known as the Travel Narrative (Luke 9:51–19:28). The reader is reminded of the trip to Jerusalem and different views concerning the kingdom of heaven (v. 11). The third evangelist positions the parable between the story of Zacchaeus and the triumphal entry into Jerusalem. Mark gives a slight allusion to these parabolic teachings when he speaks about the unknown day and hour that urge constant preparation. The drama begins, "It is like a man going on a journey, when he . . . puts his servants in charge" (Mark 13:34). But the man will return. In Luke, the nobleman comes back to receive his kingdom, and in Matthew, after a long

[2] The talent was equal to about fifteen years' wages for a day laborer. The English use of the word "talent" to mean ability is derived from this parable. In the Gospels, the talent only means money and in the case of the parable may include the idea of some goods or possessions, i.e., "his property," τὰ ὑπαρχόντα αὐτοῦ (Matt 25:14). As the story unfolds, it becomes clear that the cash value is the major import of the story. Harrington has commented on the difficulty of ascertaining the precise amount of money and goods spoken of here. As he notes, "At any rate, the point is not the precise amount but rather that it was a large sum (like a 'million dollars' or a 'huge amount' in modern speech)." See D. J. Harrington, *The Gospel of Matthew* (Collegeville, Minn.: Liturgical Press, 1991) 352.

[3] In Luke, the best servant increased the initial deposit tenfold.

delay, the wealthy man returns to seek an accounting of the deposits he entrusted to his servants.

In modern scholarship, the delay of the master followed by his sudden return has been interpreted as illustrating the coming of the Son of Man.[4] This eschatological interpretation has been understood as preserving the original context of Jesus' story. The warning of the end-time crisis has been emphasized by all of the evangelists in the way they collected the parables and arranged them thematically in their Gospels. On the one hand, the stress on the last judgment is deeply rooted in the message of Jesus, but on the other hand, the real focus of Jesus' teachings is the cultivation of personal piety and active involvement in helping people. The preparation theme should be stressed more than the final judgment. In fact, originally the parable was likely concerned more with the daily lives of the disciples than with the imminent end-time crisis. The eschatological meaning was overemphasized after the parable had been incorporated into the Gospel tradition or at the time the evangelists made collections of parables according to perceived themes. The problem surrounding the delay of the Parousia in church teachings tended to turn the original force of the parables into an apologetic explanation rather than a strong call for urgent life-changing action.

As a Jewish teacher in the first century, Jesus combined apocalyptic thinking with practical living. The practical message of the parables should never be eclipsed by an overemphasis on the coming of the Son of man. In fact, many eschatological sayings of Jesus also speak about ethical living and social action that must characterize the lives of the disciples. It is Jesus' theology of dedicated service to others, divine justice, and holy living that forms the foundation of his teachings concerning the end times. Even in the lofty description of the eschatological judgment of the nations, the greater emphasis is placed on social action and moral responsibility. The king who becomes the final judge rewards or punishes the nations on the basis of their activities in behalf of the less fortunate ones, who do not have food to eat, clothes to wear, or a friend to visit them when they are sick or in prison. Jesus calls his listeners to effective service that will meet the needs of hurting people. The apocalyptic coming of the Son of man was an accepted fact that called for ethical action in the present time as the provision for the future reality soon to be revealed.

Even if the context in the Gospel of Matthew highlights the theme of preparedness for the end times, the parable's deeper message teaches the disciple to recognize God's gifts, to be a responsible caretaker of his gracious endowment, and to serve God faithfully. In Matthew, the story warns against apathetic inactivity in the face of the coming of the Son of man, who is gloriously described in the dramatic scene of judgment. The Son of man comes with the glory of his Father and appears as the royal judge of the

[4] See, e.g., Harrington, *Matthew*, 351–55.

nations. The parable is placed here after the parable of the Wise and Foolish Maidens. Though it may have been natural for Matthew to see some parallel between the delay in the coming of the bridegroom in the story about the wise and foolish maidens and the long time that passed between the wealthy man giving talents to his servants and his sudden return, the truth is that the parable may well have had a different context in the oral teachings of Jesus. In rabbinic thought, either death or the end of the present world may cause the final accounting to determine a person's reward or punishment. In any case, moral action and righteous living are the only way to be prepared for the unknown time of the Last Judgment. Clearly the idea of a final accounting is firmly established in the parable. In truth, it could take place either when the Son of man comes or when a person dies. In either case, the parable stresses the urgency of acting before it is too late. The master will return from the far country. Hence the ultimate concern of the story is the faithful stewardship of God's gracious gifts.

A major issue of the parable is the just reward. In Christian interpretations, the seeming injustice of the master's harsh treatment of the one-talent servant becomes a serious problem. In Luke's version, the others charge the nobleman with wrong. When he takes the one pound from the last servant and gives it to the servant with ten pounds, the others murmur, "Lord, he has ten pounds!" (Luke 19:25). The verse is missing in a number of manuscript readings. Though it is well attested in other manuscripts, it is probably a scribal gloss that was added later to deal with the seemingly unfair action.[5] But the most faithful steward receives more, and the one who did not act wisely loses everything. The stakes are high in the parable.

The living of life is a serious business in the parables of Jesus. The nobleman's actions are defended, because "to every one who has will more be given; but from him who has not, even what he has will be taken away" (Luke 19:26; cf. Matt 25:29). This saying is closely related to a Jewish tradition that speaks about the giving of the law. The Torah was freely given by God. In like manner, it is taught freely. The one who learns the most from Torah receives more, while the one who neglects the study of the ways of the Lord will lose what he or she has acquired. The more learning, the more life. The more one has, the more one will receive. In Matthew's version, the gloss does not appear, but the explanation of the man's action is given: "For to every one who has will more be given." This is the way God acts. When it comes to reward and punishment, the divine view of justice is not consistent with human understanding of equitable recompense. The point is that he or she who has used wisely what God has given will receive so much more. Learn as much as possible and faithfully follow the teachings of the sages in daily practice.

---

[5] Cf. B. Metzger, *A Textual Commentary on the Greek New Testament* (New York: United Bible Societies, 1975) 169.

On the one hand, Matthew's version of the parable is a masterpiece of creative folklore, which builds on the artistry of language, storytelling technique, culture, and tradition to communicate an urgent message. On the other hand, Luke's version seems to be a fusion of two different stories with competing themes. The similarities in wording between Luke and Matthew are striking. Equally remarkable are the distinctive characteristics of the parable of the Talents and its secondary parallel in Luke's parable of the Pounds. Are the differences the result of Jesus telling two similar but distinctive stories on different occasions? A storyteller may use a similar form, structure, stock characters, etc., in two different contexts, which would account for the striking differences between the two parables. The strong verbal identity between them, however, makes another approach more plausible.[6] Matthew and Luke seem to be related through common literary sources. In the present case, Luke's version was revised for its literary context according to its subsequent Christian interpretation.

Luke's version of the parable makes subtle allusions to the historical events surrounding Archelaus' rise to power. Herod the Great's will stipulated that Archelaus succeed him in power. Hence Archelaus received the most significant portion of Herod's vast kingdom. The people had had their fill of Herod and the political intrigues of his household, which often resulted in cruel oppression. They especially despised Archelaus, who was so much like his father in brutality and the political aspirations that motivated him to seek the favor of Rome. The people yearned for a change. An embassy composed of Jews and Samaritans traveled to Rome in an effort to persuade the political powers to find a more suitable leader. In the words of the parable: "But his citizens hated him and sent an embassy after him, saying, 'We do not want this man to reign over us'" (Luke 19:14: οἱ δὲ πολῖται αὐτοῦ ἐμίσουν αὐτόν, καὶ ἀπέστειλαν πρεσβείαν ὀπίσω αὐτοῦ λέγοντες· οὐ θέλομεν τοῦτον βασιλεῦσαι ἐφ' ἡμᾶς). In Luke's parable, the idea of a king coming from a far country to receive his kingdom introduces a new concept, which showed that the royal judge would come at the end of time rather than when Jesus arrived in Jerusalem.[7]

The parable's basic message concerning stewardship is linked with the theme of a nobleman who is given a kingdom. It is very much like the events surrounding Archelaus's rise to power. Furthermore, the word-pictures of servants being rewarded with cities for each pound they had earned conjures up the image of king and kingdom. The revised introduction explains why the kingdom will not soon appear in Jerusalem. When the time comes, the

[6] For the strengths and weaknesses of these two different approaches to the Synoptic parallels see Fitzmyer, *Luke*, 2:1230.

[7] Lindsey has argued convincingly in a private communication that the kingdom was a secondary theme introduced by the pre-Lukan redactor rather than Luke himself. Therefore the wording probably reflects the editing of the third evangelist's source rather than his own revisions.

king rewards his subjects with cities. No doubt such an oriental monarch is searching for able administrators who will be able to pull the maximum tax benefit from the economy of these cities. At first, the introduction of the kingdom idea seems to result in an intrusive aside that distracts from the core message of faithful stewardship, which is so much clearer in the Matthean parallel. Here ten servants receive one pound each. This was the equivalent of about three months' wages for a day laborer. The storyteller does not mention each of the ten servants on the day of reckoning, which would go too far. The mention of ten servants, however, may lend support to the dramatic background of the parable, which portrays the concentrated blocks of opposition that tried to stop Archelaus. In the parable, each of the ten servants received a pound.

In the final accounting, only two groups of servants are discerned in the drama of the story. In the first group of good servants, the most productive was able to gain a ten-pound increase on the initial investment, a huge profit of ten times the original deposit. The second member of this group produced five pounds, which also demonstrated remarkable productivity. In the second group, only one servant is represented. He hid the nobleman's money in a napkin.[8] Because of fear, he did not invest the money and was unable to show a yield on his master's trust. In saving the money he lost it and was punished for mismanagement even though his efforts to preserve the nobleman's deposit were based on good intentions. In the final analysis, the competing theme of the nobleman who travels to a far country to receive a kingdom (Luke 19:12) seems to work contrary to the major focus of the picture, which describes the master who rewards his servants for taking care of his deposit. The message of stewardship is essential for the parable, while the opposition to the coming king remains secondary. In the Christian interpretation, however, the parable brought comfort and understanding to a persecuted community of faith waiting for the return of their master. The shocking result, which compares the loving Jesus of Christian kerygma to the cruel Archelaus of Second Temple period communicated the message of divine sovereignty during hard times. The final judgment will bring recompense in line with divine standards, which are difficult to comprehend in the present time.

Eusebius refers to a version of this parable in the *Gospel of the Nazarenes*.[9] He explains that this Gospel text was written in Hebrew letters,

---

[8]Cf. Jeremias, *Parables of Jesus,* 61 n. 51: "Burying (Matt. 25:18), according to rabbinical law, was regarded as the best security against theft. Anyone who buried a pledge or a deposit immediately upon receipt of it, was free from liability (b. *B.M.* 42a). On the other hand, if anyone tied up entrusted money in a cloth, he was responsible to make good any loss incurred through inadequate care of the entrusted deposit (*B.M.* 3.10 f.). It should be observed that both Matthew and Luke presuppose Palestinian conditions. The napkin is a woven head-covering, about a yard square."

[9]Eusebius, *Theoph.* 4.22 on Matt 25:14–15. It has been discussed by T. W. Manson, *The Sayings of Jesus* (London: SCM, 1977) 248; cf. R. W. Funk, B. Scott, and J. R. Butts,

which probably refers to its early origins among Hebrew-speaking Jewish Christians. For Eusebius, this important source for the life and teachings of Jesus seems to explain difficult-to-understand passages from the Gospel tradition. In the Christian understanding of the parable of the Talents and the parable of the Pounds, the question of just reward for good intentions was difficult to deal with. Why should the man who stored the master's deposit for safekeeping be punished? Eusebius quoted the *Gospel of the Nazarenes* in his discussion of the parabolic teaching of Jesus. He may have seen this ancient source in the famous library at Caesarea.[10] In any case, the version of the parable from the *Gospel of the Nazarenes* describes the reward and punishment given to three servants who had received talents on loan from their master. One servant wasted his master's money on harlots and flute girls. He was punished by being sent to prison. The servant who multiplied his master's deposit was rewarded, while the third servant, who hid his talent, was only rebuked. Was this approach attempting to justify the apparently unfair treatment of the well-meaning servant who hid his talent?

> But since the Gospel [*written*] in Hebrew characters which has come into our hands enters the threat not against the man who had hid [*the talent*], but against him who had lived dissolutely—for he [*the master*] had three servants: one who squandered his master's substance with harlots and flute-girls, one who multiplied the gain, and one who hid the talent; and accordingly one was accepted (with joy), another merely rebuked, but the other cast into prison—I wonder whether in Matthew the threat which is uttered after the word against the man who did nothing may refer not to him, but by epanalepsis to the first who had feasted and drunk with the drunken.[11]

In reality, it is very difficult to treat the textual questions relating to the *Gospel of the Nazarenes* without more evidence. We know this source only from secondary quotations in patristic literature. The reference to riotous living with the harlots and flute girls may hint at the parable of the Prodigal Son, in which the elder brother accuses the younger with the charge "devoured your living with harlots" (Luke 15:30). Such a crime, in the *Gospel of the Nazarenes*, is worthy of prison, but the one who preserves the master's deposit by hiding it should receive only a rebuke. The servant who hid his talent is given a reprieve. Certainly the irony of the canonical Gospels better preserves the reality of the parable, which would be more characteristic of Jesus' original teachings.

The Parables of Jesus (Sonoma, Calif.: Polebridge Press, 1988) 55. See also P. Vielhauer and G. Strecker in *NTApoc*, 1:137–39.

[10] Cf. Ray Pritz, *Nazarene Jewish Christianity* (Jerusalem: Magnes, 1988) 84 n. 6.

[11] *Gos. Naz.* 18 as translated in *NTApoc* 1:161–62. Cf. also M. R. James, *The Apocryphal New Testament* (Oxford: Clarendon, 1924) 3; and William D. Stroker, *Extracanonical Sayings of Jesus* (Atlanta: Scholars, 1989) 45.

THE SETTING IN LIFE

The actual setting for the parable is found in dramatic scenes from the everyday life of the people during the time of Jesus. Big money and the high risk of investing capture the interest of the audience. Entrusting a deposit to servants was not unusual. In fact, the book of Tobit in the Apocrypha provides an outstanding parallel for the setting in life. The situation of the parable is seen in the instructions that the elderly Tobit gives to his son Tobias. Young Tobias is to go on a long journey to Media in order to recover a deposit that his father had left in the safekeeping of Gabael the son of Gabrias. On this journey he is accompanied by his faithful dog and assisted by the angel Gabriel. The deposit is the crucial element in a long and interesting travelogue, which teaches divine reward in the difficulties of life. Tobit gives these instructions to Tobias: "And now let me explain to you about the ten talents of silver which I left in trust with Gabael the son of Gabrias at Rages in Media. Do not be afraid, my son, because we have become poor. You have great wealth if you fear God and refrain from every sin and do what is pleasing in his sight."[12]

The theme of reward for faithful stewardship as well as the dramatic motifs of the master's departure into a faraway place and his return after a delay also appear in rabbinic parables. In Jewish theology, the issues pertaining to the love and fear of God fascinated and perplexed the rabbis. A parable is told in a search for insight, that about a king and two servants. As has been seen, although the Gospel parables have more servants, in fact there are only two types. The faithful servants are of one type, while the slothful, unimaginative servant is of the second type. The rabbinic parable emphasizes the special characteristics of the two servants. The first one loved and feared the king, while the other merely feared his royal master. The rabbis were keenly aware of each person's need to stand in awe and reverence before God. But as this parable illustrates, the emotion of love is of primary importance. The parable is used in a sermonic portion that explains Deut 6:5, "you shall love the LORD your God."

Love and Fear of the King's Servant

What is the difference between love and fear? [The distinction] may be illustrated through means of a parable. To what may the matter be compared? To a king who had two servants. One loved the king and feared him. The other feared the king but did not love him. The king went into a far country. The servant who loved the king and feared him, rose up to plant gardens, orchards and all varieties of fruit. The servant who feared the king remained inactive and did nothing at all. Upon returning from the far country, the king saw the gardens, orchards and many varieties of fruits arranged before him according to the design of the servant who loved him. When the one who loved the king

[12] Tob 4:20–21.

> came before him, he saw the many varieties of fruits arrayed before him. He was greatly contented in correspondence to the joy of the king. But when the king entered the domain of the servant who feared him but did not love him, he saw all the desolate grounds which lay before him according to the failure of the servant who feared him. When the one who feared the king came before him, he saw all the desolate grounds which lay before him. He was greatly distressed in accordance with the anger of the king. As it was said, "He provides food for those who fear him" (Ps. 111:5). This refers to [the quality of justice].[13] Hence you learn that the reward of the one who loved [the king] was a double portion while the reward of the one who feared the king was only a single portion.[14] Thus the ones who worship foreign gods only receive their portion in this world but Israel merits [favor] by enjoying her portion in both worlds.[15]

The plot of the rabbinic parable is developed around the departure of the king and the activities of his two servants during his absence. The attributes of the servants, their relationships to the king, determine the success or failure of their stewardship. The servant who has the proper faith in God, based upon reverence and love, works diligently to win divine approval through dedicated service. Fear without love is not enough. Those who love the king will obey his commandments and seek to please him in their daily lives.

In another rabbinic parable dealing with the theme of stewardship, the relationship between the written and oral Torahs is debated. In the eyes of some, the written word should be sufficient for Jewish faith and practice without consulting the oral teachings of Mishnah. The purpose of Mishnah however, is to refine the deeper meaning of the written Torah as it explores the mysteries of everyday living. The concept of stewardship is portrayed in the simple pictures from home life. The process of using wheat to bake bread from flour and using flax to make a tablecloth illustrates the way that Mishnah is used for a proper interpretation of the Bible. The Bible is given as a trust from God. Employing Mishnah to understand the written word properly is good stewardship of the sacred trust.

---

[13] Other authorities read, "this world." See *Seder Elijah* (25) 26 (*Seder Eliyahu Rabbah*, ed. M. Friedmann [Jerusalem: Wahrmann, 1969] 141). The food given to those who fear the LORD is understood as the reward they receive in this world.

[14] It should be remembered that according to Deut 21:17 the eldest son inherited the double portion.

[15] *Yalkut Shimeoni*, vol. 1, Remez 837; and *Seder Elijah* (25) 26 (*Seder Eliyahu Rabbah*, ed. Friedmann, 140–41). The original source of the parable is difficult to determine. Friedmann notes that the wording of the text is preserved better in the *Yalkut*. The style of the text is similar to *Seder Elijah*. The wording of the parable in its present form betrays some linguistic problems, which may have been caused by unattentive scribes. See C. G. Montefiore, *Rabbinic Literature and Gospel Teachings* (New York: KTAV, 1970) 331; and S. T. Lachs, *A Rabbinic Commentary on the New Testament*, (Hoboken, N.J.: KTAV, 1987) 340–42.

The King's Wise and Foolish Servants

> My son, were not both Bible and mishnah spoken by the mouth of the Almighty? If so, what is the relationship between them? The distinction between them may be illustrated by a parable. To what may the matter be compared? To a mortal king who had two servants whom he loved with utter love. To one he gave a measure of wheat and to the other he gave a measure of wheat, to one a bundle of flax and to the other a bundle of flax. What did the wise one of the two do? He took the flax and wove it into a tablecloth. He took the wheat and made it into fine flour by sifting the grain first and grinding it. Then he kneaded the dough and baked it, set the loaf upon the table, spread the tablecloth over it and kept it to await the coming of the king. But the foolish one of the two did not do anything to it. After many days the king came into the house and said to the two servants: My sons, bring me what I gave you. One brought out the table with the loaf baked of fine flour on it, and the tablecloth spread over it. The other brought out his wheat in a basket with the bundle of flax over the wheat grains. What a shame! What a disgrace! Need it be said which of the two servants was the more beloved? He of course who laid out the table with the loaf baked of fine flour upon it.[16]

The parable uses the sharp contrast between two servants, one wise and the other foolish, to illustrate the relationship between Bible and Mishnah. The oral teachings of the sages are fundamental for the proper stewardship of biblical revelation. Both are the words of God. The written word requires refinement through careful study and proper interpretation. This parable uses the common motif of the king who leaves his servants in charge of a trust while he is away. The images in the story are taken from the daily lives of the people, who were familiar with the hard work required to make bread from the raw ingredient of wheat or to make a tablecloth from flax. After hearing the parable, the routine of baking bread or making cloth would remind the audience of the way the Mishnah refines the deeper meaning of the Bible.[17]

These Jewish parallels illustrate the setting in life of Jesus' parable of the Talents. The Gospels use stock characters, from wealthy aristocrats to common servants, as well as money and banking practices, to communicate effectively the message of faithful stewardship. In the plot of the story,

---

[16] *Seder Elijah* (*Seder Eliyahu Rabbah*, ed. Friedmann, 171–72). Cf. the English translation in W. Braude, *Tanna Debe Eliyyahu* (Philadelphia: Jewish Publication Society, 1981) 408–9. See also David Flusser, "Aesop's Fable and the Parable of the Talents," in Thoma and Wyschogrod, *Parable and Story*, 9–25; and A. Jülicher, *Die Gleichnisreden Jesu* (1888; 2 vols. repr., Darmstadt: Wissenschaftliche, 1963) 2:485.

[17] Some scholars have discerned in the parable a polemic against the Karaites or the Christians, who did not use Mishnah. On the contrary, I tend to see the argument as pertinent in all periods of Jewish life, in which general discussions of the relationship between Bible and Mishnah have always been relevant. In this matter I have been impressed with S. Safrai's discussion of *Seder Elijah* (private communication).

moreover, the fearful precaution of the one-talent servant leads to disaster and gives a solemn warning to the audience not to make the same mistake.

THE DISASTER OF FEARFUL PRECAUTION

In the rabbinic parables studied above, the servants are basically good or bad. Two groupings or types emerge from the drama of the stories. The servant who loved and feared his master is contrasted with the one who only feared him. A similar distinction is made between the wise and the foolish servants: the servant who only feared the king was inactive and did nothing. The parable of Jesus uses yet another element in story lore, an element of dynamic reversal that surprises the listeners when an unnecessary precaution produces the opposite of the intended result, an element that in present-day terminology has been called a *motifeme.*[18] Precaution is usually esteemed as a virtue, but it often becomes excessive, preventing creativity and stifling productivity. The precaution of the one-talent servant caused a financial reversal and resulted in his punishment.

Flusser has pointed out the strong similarities between the parable of the Talents and Aesop's fable of "The Miser," in which excessive precaution resulted in a serious loss. The fable is a dramatic presentation of a *motifeme*.

The Miser

> A miser sold all his property and bought a mass of gold, which he buried in a secret place to which he made frequent visits of inspection. Someone who had noticed his coming and going found the treasure and carried it off, and when the miser returned and discovered his loss he wailed and tore his hair in a frenzy of grief. Someone who saw him agonizing, after learning the cause, said to him, "Don't grieve, my friend, just take a stone and bury it in the same place and think of it as gold in a vault. Even when the gold was there you made no use of it."[19]

Flusser explains, "In both stories an untimely precaution seduces a man to bury his own property in a hiding place in the ground, and in both cases the action results in disaster."[20] The irony of the parable is seen in the good intention of the servant. He feared his master and determined to guard the money by burying it in the ground. Rabbinic sources indicate that burying money was considered the most effective way of guarding it against theft. But money is an investment that should be used in producing income.

In an interesting variation of the fable in the writings of Antiphon, a man asks the miser for a loan of money for a business venture in which the miser

---

[18] See Flusser, "Aesop's Fable," 15.

[19] Noted by ibid., 16–21. Translation of Fable 225 (*Babrius and Phaedrus*, ed. Perry, 465); see also C. Hahn, *Corpus fabularum Aesopicarum* (Leipzig: B. G. Teubner, 1875) 198–99, no. 412.

[20] Flusser, "Aesop's Fable," 19.

will be paid interest. Instead of taking advantage of an opportunity that would guarantee him capital gains, the miser hides his money in the ground. When it is stolen, it is the man who sought the loan from the miser who gives the words of wisdom: a stone of no financial value will serve the same purpose as unused capital.[21] Antiphon's version, which includes the idea of an interest-bearing investment, is even closer to the parable of Jesus because the wicked and slothful servant is criticized for not giving his money to the bankers, who would at least have paid a dividend for the investment.

The miser in the fable lost everything. The unwise servant in the parable of Jesus lost the deposit, which is taken away from him and given to the servant with the ten talents. He is rebuked by the words "For to every one who has will more be given, and he will have abundance; but from him who has not, even what he has will be taken away." Finally the "worthless servant" is thrown into outer darkness, where tormented people weep and gnash their teeth. The severe punishment urges right thinking and decision making. Stewardship in the teachings of Jesus is very serious business.

THE THEOLOGICAL FOUNDATION OF JESUS' PARABLE

The theological foundation of Jesus' parable embraces the Jewish worldview of God and his creation. The world belongs to God. This concept is reflected in daily prayer. Since the earth and the fullness thereof is the work of God and belongs to God, each person must recognize God's sovereignty by giving thanks to him whenever one benefits from God's world in any way. This pervasive Jewish understanding of the world is found in the practice of giving thanks. "Rab Judah said in the name of Samuel: To enjoy anything of this world without saying a blessing is like making personal use of things consecrated to heaven, as it is written, 'The earth is the LORD's and the fullness thereof' (Psalm 24:1)."[22] While this text comes from a later period, the idea that the world belongs to God is rooted in the Bible in passages like Psalm 24. To enjoy God's world without giving thanks with the appropriate blessing was like robbing God.[23]

In the story of the death of R. Johanan ben Zachai's son (see above, ch. 1, pp. 35–37), the concept of stewardship gave comfort to the bereaved father. The major element of comfort in the illustration appears in R. Eleazer's affirmation of God's gift. The son is given to his father as a sacred trust. Such a trust, as every parent knows, is accompanied with the hard struggles associated with taking good care of the child. In the case of R. Johanan ben Zachai's son, the object of value had been returned to the "king" with a

---

[21] See ibid., 18; K. Freeman, *Ancilla to the Pre-Socratic Philosophers* (Oxford: Basil Blackwell, 1948) 151–52; cf. H. Diels and W. Kranz, *Die Fragmente der Vorsokratiker* (3 vols.; Berlin: Weidmann, 1971) 2:361–63.

[22] b. *Ber.* 35a and parallels.

[23] See R. Hanina b. Papa, b. *Ber.* 35b and parallels.

record of faithful stewardship. The parable makes sense only because of the Jewish idea that all of life is a gift from God.

Rabbi Akiva made this clear when he taught that everything in life is given on pledge from God and that each person is held accountable before him. The famous teacher compared the loan from God to a storekeeper who gives credit to his customers. It is his practice to keep an accurate record of every account. He will demand payment when the time arrives.

The Pledge

> Everything is given on pledge, and the net is spread for all the living: the shop is open; and the dealer gives credit; and the ledger lies open; and the hand writes; and whosoever wishes to borrow may come and borrow; but the collectors regularly make their daily round; and exact payment from man, whether he be content or not; and they have that whereon they can rely in their demand; and the judgment is a judgment of truth; and everything is prepared for the feast.[24]

For Akiva, colorful images taken from the practices of commerce, such as the dealer, the ledger, the collectors, and the customer's responsibility to make payment on his account, were pictures of a person's obligations to God. The world is a trust given to God's servants.

The sense of obligation to God is overshadowed by a recognition of his merciful nature. He is a compassionate God, who cares for his servants. In the rabbinic conception of God, it was natural to compare a lease agreement involving tenant farmers and their landlord to the way God has entrusted his world to humanity. An earthly landowner will expect due payment of the obligations of his tenants. God, in contrast, is viewed as being far more noble and gracious than any human landlord.

The Landlord's Portion

> R. Nehemiah said: Even when we regard our actions, we are filled with shame. Why is this so? Ordinarily, one gives over his field to a tenant, and the latter supplies the seed and the labour, yet he [the owner] receives an equal share [of the crops]; but the Holy One, blessed be He—His name be exalted and his mention extolled—is not so, for though the world and all that is therein is His, as it says, *The earth is the Lord's and fulness thereof,* etc. (Ps. xxiv, i), and though the earth and the fruit thereof are His, and He also causes the rains to descend and the dews to spring forth in order to make the fruits to grow, as well as preserving them and doing everything else for them, yet God said to them: "I have only commanded thee to give Me one-tenth as tithe, and one-fiftieth as *terumah.*" This is why it says, "*Unto Thee, O Lord, belongeth righteousness, but unto us shamefacedness.*"[25]

---

[24] *Abot* 3:20 (J. H. Hertz, *The Authorized Daily Prayer Book* [New York: Bloch, 1959] 661–63).

[25] *Exod. Rab.* 41:1, trans. ed., H. Freedman, *Midrash Rabbah,* 467–68; *Midrash Tanchuma,* Ki Tisa, 14.

Ordinarily a landlord expects 50 percent of the income from the produce on his estate even though the tenant farmers provide all of the seed, raw materials, and labor required to bring in the harvest. In contrast, God is much more beneficent because he asks only the tithe and the terumah offering even though everything associated with his estate comes directly from him. Every person stands in his presence with a shamed face because of his great goodness. The world is given in *arisût* (אריסות), a land-lease type of agreement to God's tenant farmers. They enjoy the benefits of the land according to the gracious attributes of their noble landlord, but they must fulfill their part of the bargain.

In fact, the image of a strong figure of a landowner is used by the one-talent servant to defend his actions that produced no profit on the deposit. The justification for his actions was based on his view of the master. This fact is very important for the parable. The failure was based upon a misunderstanding of the divine nature. The servant defends his actions: "I knew that you were a hard man, harvesting where you did not sow and gathering where you did not scatter" (Matt 25:24).[26] With such a master, the steward should have realized that he could not lose. After all, if he harvested where he had not sown and gathered where he did not scatter seed, a steward should have been willing to accept some risk when investing for growth and profit. Because of fear, the steward sought to avoid failure by burying the talent. His attempt to preserve capital brought about his ruin. Instead of faith, he had fear of his master.

DECISIVE ACTION

The message of the parable, then, focuses on decisive action. The steward must take steps to increase what has been graciously given. Simply put, he or she must use what is in hand. No matter how great or small, it is given by God and must be used for his service. In recognizing the rabbinic concept of native ability as God's gift, Flusser has pointed to a fascinating parallel that reveals a play on words from the Hebrew text of Prov 3:9, "Honor the LORD with your substance." The Hebrew word for substance, הון, which probably refers to goods, assets, or money, was interpreted to mean חן, grace that is given by God. His divine favor is graciously given (חנן) to a person to be used for his glory. The son of Bar Kapar's sister, Rabbi Chaya bar Adda, was gifted in his strong and beautiful voice. It could be used to bless others and glorify God during the worship service when he led the people in reciting the Shema.

---

[26] My translation. The words of the servant could be reconstructed into good idiomatic Hebrew by translating the Greek text with אדון אני יודע שאתה איש קשה [קשיח] קוצר במקום שלא זרעת וכונס במקום שלא פזרת. The Greek διασκορπίζω should be translated "scatter" and is parallel to the Hebrew פזר, which refers to scattering seed. This is preferable to the RSV, which renders the term by "winnow."

God's Gracious Gifts

Rabbi Chaya bar Adda the son of Bar Kapara's sister had a good voice. Before he would recite the prayer, *Shema Yisrael,* that is "Hear O Israel the LORD our God is one" (Deut. 6:4), Bar Kapara used to say to him, "My son, when you take your stand before the reader's desk, recite the *Shema* in a strong voice, as to comply with the teaching: 'Honor the LORD from your substance (מהונך, *mehonchah*)' (Prov. 3:9). From your substance, that is from what He has graciously granted to you (ממה שחננך, *memah shechananchah*)!"[27]

The story about R. Chaya bar Adda reveals the Jewish understanding of exceptional abilities. These qualities are given by God and must be used faithfully. Decisive action is required to make the most of God's gracious gifts. The parable of the Talents drives home this point. The servants must use what they have received, each according to his ability. These exceptional qualities are bestowed from above.

FAITHFUL STEWARDSHIP

In the world of parable lore, faithful stewardship of these divinely given talents determines the servant's success and the final reward in the serious business of life. Perseverance in the task of stewardship is the foundation of success. The master praises the productive stewards with words that describe their successful efforts as well as their just reward, "Well done, good and faithful servant; you have been faithful over a little, I will set you over much; enter into the joy of your master" (Matt 25:21, 23). They were faithful with the little that they had received, and they will be rewarded with abundance. For the original audience, the amount of money represented in the talents was immense. For the wealthy landowner, however, the sum is little, but the reward is granted on the basis of his view of wealth. The servants faithfully served in overseeing his loan; now they will be rewarded with his immeasurable favor and enter into his joy. The reference to joy brings the divine into the picture. The reality behind the story overtakes the simple images of the master, servant, deposit, and reward. First and foremost, the parable is about God and his character.

In Jewish theology, the concept of faithfulness and its reward was accepted as a given. The rabbis derived their view from examples in the Bible. One such prominent teaching concerning faithfulness came from the models of Moses and David, both of whom began their careers in the biblical narrative as humble shepherds. Because of their faithful service in the small task of keeping the flocks, they are elevated to fulfill the high position of

[27] *Pesiq. Rab. Kah.* 10:3 (*Pesikta Derav Kahana*, ed. B. Mandelbaum [2 vols.; New York: Jewish Theological Seminary, 1962] 1:164–65); see also the English translation in W. Braude, *Pesikta de Rab Kahana* (Philadelphia: Jewish Publication Society, 1975) 189.

caring for God's sheep, the people of Israel. Their faithfulness in minor roles as shepherds was the necessary training to lead the people. First they were tested. After they proved themselves faithful, they were elevated to the highest role.

Faithfulness in the Least

> "Now Moses was keeping the flock" (Exod 3:1): It says, "Every word of God is tried" (Prov 30:5). Before God confers greatness on a person, first He tests him by a little thing and then promotes him to greatness. Here you have two leaders whom God proved first by a little thing, found faithful, and then promoted them to greatness. He tested David with sheep. . . . God said to him, "You have been faithful with the sheep; come therefore, and tend My sheep," as it is said, "From the ewes that give suck He brought him" (Psalm 88:71). Similarly also in the case of Moses it says: "And he led the flock to the farthest end of the wilderness". . . God took him to tend Israel, as it is said, "You did lead your people like a flock, by the hand of Moses and of Aaron" (Psalm 87:21).[28]

Moses and David were faithful in their work as shepherds. After being tested in a small matter of the stewardship of sheep they were elevated to positions of greatness. The message drawn from the biblical stories of Moses and David is based upon the Jewish understanding of faithful service. He who is faithful in the least matter will also be faithful in a more significant position. The teachings of Jesus are firmly rooted in ancient Jewish thought and Bible interpretation.

When the Gospel parable of the Talents is studied in light of its Jewish tradition and Christian interpretations, its deeper message is understood. Although the eschatological force of the master's return to give reward or punishment to his servants on the basis of their performance pervades the rich imagery of the plot of the parable, its primary message is on stewardship of God's graciously bestowed resources in the present. God is good, and the stewards of his divinely given abilities and assets must use them creatively and faithfully to achieve a maximum return on their master's investment. In the business of life, the parable gives a sound financial forecast for the productive use of God's resources.

---

[28] *Exod. Rab.* 2:3 (A. Shinan, *Midrash Shemot Rabbah,* Jerusalem: Dvir, 1984, 106). Cf. the English translation in H. Freedman, ed., *Midrash Rabbah,* 49–50.

Part 4

Teaching in Parables: The Theology of Reconciliation between God and Humanity in Both Judaism and Christianity

5 The Samaritan: Love Your Enemies

FOCUS

The message of the parables reaches the audience on different levels (Luke 10:25–37).[1] The parable of the Good Samaritan teaches a clear message on the level of a child. But does it challenge the minds of the learned? Because Christian scholars often misunderstand the Jewish background to the teachings of Jesus, they frequently miss the deeper level of meaning in the story of the Good Samaritan. The simple meaning of the parable is understood universally, but the far-reaching implications of the story in its Jewish context would be appreciated only by the specialist in haggadah and halakah. Here the Jewish roots of the parable will be explored for an enriched understanding of the story in its historical setting.

The parable of the Good Samaritan has been viewed from many perspectives. It is the classic form of the story parable. As a mini-play with a colorful cast of characters, the parable is an action-packed drama. One scene moves quickly to the next. The plot captures the attention of the listeners. The story is not, however, designed to entertain but rather to communicate. The parable introduces the members of the cast and then takes the listeners on a journey in which they come into contact with the internal conflict of the drama. The resolution of the conflict communicates the deeper meaning of the story. The genre of story parables in their classic form functions in this way. The drama communicates the deeper message of the storyteller.

The literary form is Jewish. At least the clear parallels to the parables of Jesus are found only in rabbinic literature. When one explores the Jewish

[1] See my brief discusion of the parable in *Jewish Parables*, 239–41, 269–70, treating some of the beautiful stories in rabbinic literature that tell how a stranger in trouble is given help. The Jewish literature emphasizes the need to show compassion (e.g., *Eccl. Rab.* 11:1,1). See also Flusser, *Gleichnisse*, 70ff.

world in which Jesus lived and taught his message, fresh insights emerge from comparative study. The parable of the Good Samaritan's deeper level of meaning is best understood in light of its rich Jewish background.

THE CONTEXT IN LUKE

In Luke, the parable is given as an answer to the question of the Torah scholar (Gk. *nomikos*),[2] who asked, "And who is my neighbor?" The question is genuine because the term for neighbor in Hebrew (*rea*, רע) has a range of meanings. One could legitimately claim that the term referred only to a friend. In Hebrew, the root meaning of the word could be understood as meaning "friend" or "a person who is close." The name Ruth, for example (Hebrew *rut*, רות, a shortened form of *reut*, רעות), is derived from the root *rea*. The meaning of the name is understood as "close companion."

Probably in biblical Hebrew the term was originally more general and had the broader meaning "anyone." The earlier general meaning is seen in the Siloam Inscription from the days of Hezekiah, when the tunnel was constructed in Jerusalem. A worker who began at one end of the tunnel call out to his *rea* in the group working from the other end. When the call was heard, the workers knew that they were nearing the end of the project. This use of *rea* means "coworker" or "colleague" and would not necessarily denote a close friend.

In the time of Jesus the Hebrew language was in transition. The meanings of words change and develop with use. How would the people at the end of the Second Temple period understand the term *rea* in the holiness code of the book of Leviticus? The code commands the people of Israel, "love your neighbor as yourself." Does the commandment refer merely to a close friend or to every person? Could it even be pushed to further limits and be defined to include a known enemy?

In the Lukan context of the parable of the Good Samaritan, the Torah scholar approached Jesus and asked him a question, "Teacher, what shall I do to inherit eternal life?" Jesus answered him by asking another question, "What is written in the Torah? How do you read?" In Luke's version of the episode, the Torah scholar answered his own question by giving a reply to Jesus' question.[3] At least Jesus responded to the Torah scholar's inquiry with

[2] The Hebrew meaning of the term is difficult. Ezra Fleischer has recently translated it as *chakam* (חכם), "sage." See Ezra Fleischer, "On the Beginnings of Obligatory Jewish Prayer," *Tarbiz* 59 (1990): 418. Possibly the term *ben Torah* (בן תורה), "son of [or disciple of] the teachings of Torah," was used in the *Vorlage* of the Gospels. The translation "lawyer" in the AV is unfortunate. In modern usage, as Howard Ervin once suggested to me, "theologian" or "student of Scripture" might be more appropriate.

[3] This is the most probable reading of the text. The assumed subject of the sentence in Luke 10:27 would be the Torah scholar, who gave the answer ἀγαπήσεις κύριον τὸν θεόν σου. Mark refers to the reading of the Shema directly. See Flusser, *Yahadut*, 35–37.

another question, "What is written in the law? How do you read?"[4] Because of the way Jesus presented his questions, the Torah scholar could arrive at the proper approach, "love the Lord your God" and "your neighbor as yourself." The entire episode is imbued with the fresh air of the land of Israel in the first century C.E. Questions concerning the law and the proper approach to others were not uncommon. The emphasis of early Jewish thought during this period is expressed in the well-known biblical passage "Hear O Israel, the LORD our God, is one LORD," which precedes the commandment "you shall love the LORD your God" in the Torah passage (Deut 6:4–5).

The dialectic discussion between Jesus and the scholar was not characterized by hostility or confrontation, as many NT scholars have assumed.[5] The question is a genuine inquiry. Jewish learning involved asking questions and answering questions with more questions. The Torah scholar is viewed much more positively in Luke's version, for he answers the question correctly. Not only is this the case in regard to the two commandments that speak of love for God and love for people; it is also true in regard to the conclusion of the parable of the Good Samaritan. When Jesus asked him who was the neighbor to the man in need, the Torah scholar answered correctly, "The one who showed mercy."[6]

This answer at the conclusion of the parable has often raised questions in the minds of interpreters. To many scholars the answer is incorrect. The neighbor is the person in need. Correctly defined, the neighbor would be a friend in need, not an enemy who showed compassion. The Torah scholar,

---

[4] Flusser has emphasized the dramatic aspects of this lively discussion. In the Hebrew of that period Jesus' questions would have been precise and decisive: מה כתוב בתורה איך אתה קורא.

[5] The translation in the GNB emphasizes the idea of hostility by suggesting that the scholar of Scriptures was trying to trap Jesus. The suggestion is proleptic. It anticipates the questioning of Jesus by the priests on the Temple Mount during the events of the last week before his passion in Jerusalem. In contrast, instead of Sadducean priests, here one sees a learned man of Scriptures asking Jesus a legitimate question. See b. *Ber.* 28b and *Abot R. Nat.*, version B, ch. 31, where R. Eleazer is asked a similar question by his disciples.

[6] I have learned so much from Fitzmyer that I hesitate to disagree with his fine scholarship, but I feel that he may have missed the exact point of the parable. In his commentary (*Luke,* 2:884) Fitzmyer writes, "The point of the story is summed up in the lawyer's reaction, that a 'neighbor' is anyone in need with whom one comes into contact and to whom one can show pity and kindness, even beyond the bounds of one's own ethnic or religious group." The one who showed mercy is the Samaritan. He was not beaten, robbed, and left dying in the middle of the road. The Torah scholar, perhaps from the artful way in which Jesus phrased the question, understood that his *rea* could be defined as a Samaritan. On the other hand, the Samaritan would be defined by the culture and the historical period as an enemy. But in the parable an enemy could behave like a neighbor. He showed compassion. Even one's enemy is a *rea.* While it is certainly true that the injured man would be included in the definition of neighbor in the story, this is not the main point of the parable.

however, understood the message of the parable. He concludes that even one's enemy, i.e., every person, is one's *rea.* Logically, however, for many hearers of the parable, the man who was abandoned to die would be the neighbor in question. By no means would they think of the good Samaritan. Why is the Samaritan considered the "neighbor" of the story? Clearly, the parable invites serious reflection and careful study of its cultural milieu.[7]

Many interpreters have suggested that this is an artificial context created by Luke. Here it is important to observe that the Torah scholar is viewed in a much more positive manner in Luke than in the synoptic parallels. Moreover, only Luke preserves the parable. It would seem that Mark transferred the answer to the question about the commandments to Jesus, and Matthew followed Mark's lead. Certainly it is difficult to imagine that Luke would have taken words attributed to Jesus in his source and then placed them into the mouth of an inquiring Torah scholar![8] If Luke respected the meaning of a red-letter edition of the Gospels, he would not take away from the words of Jesus. In any case, the tension between Jesus and the Jewish theologian is on a much different level from that frequently assumed by NT exegetes of Luke's Gospel. The conclusion of the parable connects the story to the question of the Torah scholar in a way that does not appear to be the work of a clumsy redactor. The opening comment of the story, however, "but he, desiring to justify himself," seems to be a connecting sentence that was not in Luke's source but was added as an editorial suture.

Flusser has emphasized to me that the parable of the Good Samaritan is closely linked to the saying of Jesus in the Sermon on the Mount "You have heard that it was said, 'You shall love your neighbor and hate your enemy.' But I say to you, Love your enemies" (Matt 5:43–44).[9] The relationship between the logion and the parable of the Good Samaritan was independently affirmed by Max Lüthi, the specialist in the study of fairy tales.[10]

---

[7] Indeed, Jesus asked a leading question, "Which of the three . . . ?" He wanted to focus attention on the reciprocity of being a neighbor in action and understanding the meaning of neighbor in the broader sense of the term. The meaning of neighbor encompassed the totality of human need for every person, because each individual is created in the divine image.

[8] See the penetrating discussion of this Gospel text in Flusser, *Yahadut,* 35–37, treating the interrelationships among the Synoptic Gospels.

[9] I highly value a private discussion I had with Flusser concerning this parable in Lucerne, Switzerland, on June 3, 1987. On a visit to Jerusalem in June 1991, I was able to clarify these questions with Flusser. He views the parable as a part of Jesus' teachings concerning the need to love one's enemy. See especially Flusser, *Gleichnisse*, 70–71.

[10] It is quite possible that this portion of the Sermon on the Mount was originally a part of the story of the Torah scholar and the parable of the Good Samaritan. Flusser and Lüthi believe that it should be inserted between the pericope concerning the lawyer's question and the parable (private communication). Matthew preserved the saying from his source, which he had in common with Luke. Matthew added it to his collection of sayings for the Sermon on the Mount. The meaning of the parable of the Good Samaritan,

More is involved than just the mention of the term "neighbor." One must recognize that the Samaritans were considered enemies of the Jewish people. At least many would have viewed the sudden appearance of a despised Samaritan as the hero of a Jewish parable somewhat perplexing. Perhaps the people would have anticipated the appearance of a Pharisee or one of Jesus' own disciples. The element of shock in the parable emerges from the unexpected turn of events. A Samaritan saves the dying man. An enemy becomes a friend. The astonishing conclusion of the parable demonstrates that the Torah scholar was sincere, because he arrives at the proper answer after hearing the parable.

The entire episode in the Gospels captures the original setting of the life situation. A story parable in its classic form often finds its place in active dialogue and live communication. The Gospel story portrays a question-and-answer session between Jesus and a Torah scholar. A parable settles a bewildering issue that pertains to love of God and love of humanity. Who is one's neighbor? How far does love extend? How should Lev 19:18 be translated? Does it read, "Love your friends"? Perhaps it should be translated, "Love even your enemies."

LEADING CHARACTERS

The colorful cast members of the mini-drama provide insight into the plot of the story. A man is stripped and left half dead. Without identifying clothes, one cannot recognize to which cultural community he belongs. Is he a Pharisee? Is he a priest? Is he a Roman? Jesus does not tell the listeners. They know, however, that those who pass by the scene of the crime cannot identify the victim's family or tribe with certainty.[11] He is simply a dying man in urgent need. Is he dead? Is he alive? What is the proper religious duty for every person who encounters such a situation? How will the diverse characters in the cast of the parable treat the dying man?

The inner structure of the parable is seen in the other three characters.[12] The Lukan context of the parable would indicate that the Torah scholar asking Jesus questions was one who accepted the oral law, perhaps a Pharisee. In contrast, the first two characters who pass by the injured man do not embrace the oral tradition. The priest and the Levite were probably Sadducees, who would not have accepted the validity of the oral Torah. They would, however, follow the written law with literal exactitude. Here

properly understood, is love of enemies. The suggestion of Flusser, with some independent confirmation by Lüthi, is ingenious and has much to commend itself. Also see S. Lachs, *Commentary*, 282. Lachs noted the importance of Matt 5:43 and that the meaning of the term "neighbor" must be interpreted in the broad sense for the parable.

[11] Only circumcision could provide some identification of the dying man, but it is doubtful that the listeners would have considered this aspect of the story.

[12] See the discussion in McArthur and Johnston, *Parables*, 132ff.

one begins to appreciate the artistry in the parable. The three key actors, the priest, the Levite, and the Samaritan, have both similarities and distinctions within the diverse religious cultures of the first century C.E. The original audience of the parable would have been keenly aware of these distinctions.

Whether Luke would have created the context intentionally is questionable. It appears that the Hebrew *Vorlage* of the Gospel would have preserved these points in the story. The three characters are typical of sound storytelling techniques, from a well-known nursery rhyme, "The butcher, the baker, and the candlestick maker," to more sophisticated narrative fiction.[13] The rule of threes is often followed.[14] The priest and the Levite serve religious functions in the temple. Historical sources from the period indicate that large numbers of priests lived in Jericho.[15] The road to Jerusalem from Jericho was known as a dangerous route because of the robbers and brigands who would lie in wait for travelers.[16] Within this realistic setting for the story, one discovers the wealthy class of priests and Levites, who no doubt made the road lucrative for robbers. These religious functionaries, furthermore, did not follow the oral interpretation of the Torah that flourished within the broader movements of Jewish theological reflection and that characterized the discussions of the Pharisees.

The artistry of the story's plot is seen in how the Samaritan saves the life of the injured man. The priest and the Levite pass him by on the road.[17]

[13] See Fitzmyer, *Luke*, 2:883: "The storytelling devices are to be noted in the episode: the threesome in the dramatis personae (the priest, the levite, and the Samaritan [like the Englishman, the Irishman, the Scotsman]); the Palestinian details (olive oil, wine, animal, and inn) . . . "

[14] See McArthur and Johnston, *Parables*, 132–34.

[15] See S. Safrai, "The Temple," in Safrai et al., *Jewish People*, 2:870: "Most of the priests, particularly the ordinary priests, did not live in Jerusalem. During this period we find families and larger groups of priests living in Sepphoris, Jericho, in a town in the Judaean Hills, and elsewhere." See j. *Yoma* 1:4; j. *Taan.* 68a; b. *Taan.* 27a; Luke 1:39; also Jacob Mann, "Jesus and the Sadducean Priests: Luke 10:25–37," *JQR* 6 (1914): 415–22, esp. 421; and A. Büchler, *Die Priester und der Cultus im letzten Jahrzehnt des jerusalemischen Tempels* (Vienna: Hölder, 1895) 161–81. On the priests and the Levites see M. Stern, "Aspects of Jewish Society: The Priesthood and other Classes," in Safrai, et al., *Jewish People*, 2:561–630, esp. 596–612; also J. Jeremias, *Jerusalem in the Time of Jesus* (London: SCM, 1969) 147–221.

[16] Lachs observes, "This road was infamous in antiquity for its rocky and desert terrain and for the presence of brigands. Jerome records that in his day bands of marauding Arabs traveled this road" (*Commentary*, 282). See ibid., n. 3: "Jerome, *De Locis Heb.*, s.v. 'Adummim.' Cf. 2 Chron. 28:5–15; Strabo, *Geog.* XVI.2, 41 states that Pompey destroyed strongholds of brigands near Jericho." The Gospel parable portrays a realistic setting for the story, one in which the people could visualize the robbery from known experience.

[17] See the valuable insights of Bailey, *Peasant Eyes*, 53–54. In discussing the final payment promised by the Samaritan, Bailey has pointed out the storyteller's method of

In the parable, Jesus describes the action-filled scene of a traveler who (1) "fell among robbers, who" (2) "stripped him and beat him," and (3) "departed, leaving him half dead." The religious men make no effort to help him because of their understanding of biblical law. Like the robbers, they abandon him. But the Samaritan reverses the actions of the robbers in dramatic movements that retrace their steps. The substructure of the parable emerges in the way the injured man is saved by the emergency care of the Samaritan, who (1) "went to him," (2) "bound up his wounds, pouring on oil and wine," and (3) "set him on his own beast and brought him to an inn, and took care of him." In contrast to the robbers who took the victim's money, the Samaritan paid for the inn and gave the innkeeper two denarii in advance payment. The Samaritan makes a promise that when he returns, he will cover all expenses related to the convalescent care of the man in need. Thus he provided additional protection for the injured man by explaining his intention to return. The injury renders him vulnerable. But the Samaritan will check back with the innkeeper to make certain that adequate care has been provided for the man in need. The Samaritan will reward the innkeeper for his best care. The leading characters of the story play significant roles in the structure of the parable's plot. The priest and the Levite continue the action of the robbers; the robbers abandoned him to die and they pass by in like manner. The Samaritan, however, reverses the actions of the thieves and makes every effort to restore the man whose life was at risk. Though the Samaritan had no obligation to fulfill the oral law, in essence he did what was required.

The tremendous importance given to the oral interpretation of the Torah in Pharisaic teachings can hardly be overemphasized. The Torah was delivered to Moses with its oral commentary and practical application in every aspect of human experience.[18] The written law will not be understood without its clear explication in everyday life from the oral teachings of the sages. In the Mishnah, it may well be that the sages had the Sadducees in mind when they taught, "And these are they that have no share in the world to come: he that says that there is no resurrection of the dead prescribed in the Law, and [he that says] that the Law is not from Heaven, and an Epicurean."[19] The Sadducees rejected the teachings of the oral law. They were literalists in the sense that they followed only the written law. The priest and the Levite in the parable of the Good Samaritan were Sadducees, who typically would not only reject the oral law but might even have a certain amount of contempt for those who obey

developing a carefully arranged parabolic structure in the action of "the play within a play."

[18] See E. E. Urbach, *The Halakhah: Its Sources and Development* (Jerusalem: Yad la-Talmud, 1986), esp. 43–58.

[19] m. *Sanh.* 10:1 (Danby, *Mishnah*, 397; *Mishnah*, ed. Albeck, 4:202). The Mishnah text here emphasizes the authority of the sages' teaching.

both Torahs.[20] The concept of the two laws, a written Torah and an oral Torah with all its diverse applications, is embodied in the teaching of *Sifra*, the Tannaitic commentary on the book of Leviticus. The significance of this point and the origin of the oral teachings of Torah at Sinai with Moses can be seen in this instructive text, which gives a commentary on the plural form of the Hebrew word Torah in Lev 26:46: " 'and laws [plural of Torah, תורות]' (Lev. 26:46). This teaches that two laws [Torahs] were given to Israel, one written and the other oral." The midrash continues with the end of the verse, " 'which the LORD made between him and the people of Israel on Mount Sinai by Moses.' Moses was granted the merit of being made the mediator between Israel and their Father in heaven. This teaches that the Torah was given, encompassing all its laws, all its details and all its interpretations by the hand of Moses on Mount Sinai."[21] The written law will not be understood without its traditional interpretations and practical application in the oral commentary from the second law given to Moses on Mount Sinai. The difference between the Torah scholar asking Jesus a question such as "Who is my neighbor?" and the leading characters in the parable is decisive. The oral interpretations of the written law, which were so very important to Jesus and the Torah scholar, have little meaning for the priest and the Levite.

While it is clear that the Samaritans were not viewed favorably by the Jewish people during that period, it is not often recognized that they did have at least one common characteristic with the Sadducees: rejection of the oral law. They lived by the letter of the law in the five books of Moses. Hence the priest, the Levite, and the Samaritan are indeed a threesome in that they have one common characteristic: all three would not have accepted the halakah of the Pharisees, and groups closely associated with the Pharisees, who devoted great energy to the proper interpretation of the written Torah. The Samaritans therefore had more in common with the Sadducees than might be expected at a first reading of the parable.

The Samaritans as a group were viewed quite negatively in Jewish sources from the period. In Sir 50:25–26, the point is emphasized, "With two nations my soul is vexed, . . . and the foolish people that dwell at Shechem."[22]

---

[20] It is true that some priests from the period were Pharisees (see Jeremias, *Jerusalem*, 256ff.). Nonetheless, the priestly clans and Levites were predominantly Sadducees, as can be seen from clear references such as Acts 5:17, "But the high priest rose up and all who were with him, that is, the party of the Sadducees."

[21] *Sifra* on Lev 26:46 (*Sifra*, ed. J. H. Weiss [Vienna: J. Salsberg, 1862] 112c). I have not cited the saying of R. Akiva, which shows the meaning of Torah as instruction concerning specific issues in Jewish life. See the helpful discussion of Heschel, *Torah Men Hashamayim*, 3:1–22. Clearly the sages had diverse views concerning the written Torah and its various applications in oral tradition.

[22] See Segal, *Sefer Ben Sira Hashalem*, 348–49, who notes the hostility between Jews and Samaritans from Josephus, *Ant.* 12.154–156. Josephus comments that after Antiochus

Fitzmyer has correctly referred to the “attitude shared by Palestinian Jews concerning the Samaritans, summed up so well in the Johannine comment, ‘Jews, remember, use nothing in common with Samaritans’ (John 4:9 . . .).”[23] When Jesus and his disciples seek a night’s lodging in a Samaritan village, they are not accepted with traditional oriental hospitality. In Luke 9:52–54 a clear picture of hostile relations between the Samaritans and Jews is vividly described. The Samaritans reject Jesus and his disciples because they are Jewish pilgrims making their way to Jerusalem to observe the feast. The Samaritans will not allow Jews to spend the night in their village. James and John are ready to call fire down from heaven to burn the Samaritans alive. Tensions between the communities sometimes erupted into war.[24] When the word “Samaritan” was said among the Jewish people in the first century, no one thought of the descriptive term “good.” The Samaritans were considered enemies of the people. History gives good reasons for the ancient hatred between the Samaritans and the Jewish people. Jesus and the Torah scholar arrived at a much different understanding when they examined the message of “Love thy neighbor as thyself.” The story parable shocked the listeners with an unexpected hero.

THE PRIESTHOOD, RITUAL PURITY, AND THE ORAL LAW

The people listening to the parable are keenly aware that the Sadducees in the priestly service are extremely concerned about their ritual purity.[25] In the eyes of a Sadducean literalist, the prohibition in the written Torah (Lev 21:1) “And the LORD said to Moses, ‘Speak to the priests, the sons of Aaron, and say to them that none of them shall defile himself for the dead among his people’ ” superseded all humanitarian concerns. The Pharisees would never have agreed. The underlying current of thought in the parable emerges in the figures of the priest and the Levite, who were more interested in ritual purity than saving the life of another human being. As will be seen, the priests were sharply criticized in the rabbinic teachings because they were overly concerned with ritual cleanness, to the neglect of other ethical and moral

---

(203–180 B.C.E.) made a treaty with Ptolemy, “the Samaritans, who were flourishing, did much mischief to the Jews by laying waste their land and carrying off slaves; and this happened in the high-priesthood of Onias.”

[23] Fitzmyer, *Luke*, 2:883.

[24] Josephus, *War* 2.232–240; *Ant.*, 20.118–136. See H. Graetz, *Popular History of the Jews* (6 vols.; New York: Hebrew Publishing Co., 1949) 2:168–71; and esp. E. Schürer, *The History of the Jewish People in the Time of Jesus Christ* (rev. and ed. G. Vermes, F. Millar, and M. Black; 3 vols.; Edinburgh: T. & T. Clark, 1974–1987) 1:459.

[25] See S. Safrai, “Religion in Everyday Life,” in Safrai, et al., *Jewish People*, 2:828–32. As he points out (p. 828), “The question of ritual purity and impurity (טהרה and טומאה) was a major issue in the temple era and in tannaitic times. But most of the laws in question affected only the priests.”

questions. How far does religious cleanness go for the priest? How does the oral law treat the question of ritual purity?

In 1914, Jacob Mann, in a penetrating study, noted the importance of the tension between Jesus and the Sadducean priests.[26] The strong tension, according to Mann's carefully argued position, arose because Jesus accepted the oral Torah and the priests did not. Mann believed that the priest and the Levite thought that the man in the parable who was abandoned on the road was already dead. The oral law treats the question of the urgent need to bury an abandoned corpse. If the man was dead, the oral law required the priest and the Levite to bury him even though they would contract uncleanness. The *met mitzvah*, מת מצוה, is a law concerning a dead person who has no one to bury him. The oral law requires even a high priest to pollute himself with ritual impurity in order to bury a *met mitzvah*. The written law states clearly, "The priest . . . shall not go in to any dead body, nor defile himself, even for his father or for his mother" (Lev 21:11). The priest and the Levite acted properly according to the literal meaning of the Torah. In the oral law, however, as preserved in the later codification of the Mishnah, the early tradition presents a different approach for the *met mitzvah*. The oral Torah says, "A High Priest or a Nazirite may not contract uncleanness because of their [dead] kindred, but they may contract uncleanness because of a neglected corpse" (m. *Naz.* 7:1).[27] The only response of the priest and the Levite, according to the oral law, was to bury the person and disregard the question of ritual impurity raised by a literal reading of the written Torah.[28]

---

[26] Mann, "Sadducean Priests."

[27] The Mishnah has a discussion of different views concerning who will bury the corpse if both the high priest and a Nazir, who is temporarily set apart for ritual sanctity, find the *met mitzvah* (see esp. *Mishnah,* ed. Albeck, on m. *Naz.* 7:1 and Albeck's comments, 3:215; also *Mishnayoth,* ed. and trans. Philip Blackman [7 vols.; New York: Judaica, 1990] 3:313, on m. *Naz.* 7:1). R. Eliezer says that the high priest should bury him, but the sages were of the opinion that the Nazirite should accept the responsibility. In any case, the oral law makes the duty of burying a corpse mandatory. The antiquity of the tradition cannot be questioned. Josephus (*Ag. Ap.* 211) is keen to mention it: "The duty of sharing with others was inculcated by our legislator in other matters. We must furnish fire, water, food to all who ask for them, point out the road, not leave a corpse unburied, show consideration even to declared enemies . . ."

[28] Mann, "Sadducean Priests," 418, notes, "The rabbis tried hard to deduce מת מצוה from the Bible . . . (cp. Siphra to Lev. 21.1, Nazir 47a, 48a–b, Zebahim 100a and parallels.)." See also Jeremias, *Jerusalem,* 152, concerning the controversy between the Pharisees and the Sadducees regarding the *met mitzah:* "The Pharisees upheld it, placing compassion above the strict maintenance of ceremonial purity for the high priest. The Sadducees, however, those staunch upholders of the letter of the law, rejected even this one exception (M. Nazir vii. 1)." The Sadducee would never accept the interpretation of Lev 21:1, 11 from the Pharisees who taught that the priest had a duty to bury an abandoned corpse. The Sadducean priests would have no qualms about leaving a dead body or someone in the agony of death.

In fact, even in pagan thought it was an accepted ethic of civilized conduct to provide burial for an abandoned corpse. Travel in ancient times was dangerous. At times a traveler might encounter an unknown person who had been killed by an accident of nature or by robbers. One must bury the corpse, no matter what inconvenience it might cause.

With all the high regard that should be given to Mann, one cannot be certain that the parable raised the critical issue of a *met mitzvah* and the duty of burying the dead. The more important issue was saving a life. Whether the priest and the Levite realized that the man was still living or wrongly assumed that he was already dead, they failed to act. In either case, the oral law is certainly at issue. E. P. Sanders wisely notes, "In the parable, Jesus criticizes a priest and a Levite for not being willing to risk coming into contact with a corpse. The point seems to be that they did not know whether or not the man by the side of the road was dead, and they were unwilling to risk incurring corpse-impurity simply on the chance that they might have been able to help."[29] What should be emphasized here is that well-known oral Torah teachings treated the issues that confronted the priest, the Levite, and the Samaritan, who all encountered the scene of a cruel and brutal robbery. The oral law teaches proper ethical conduct whether the man was dead or still alive. The priest and Levite could ignore the teachings of the oral law in good conscience because of their literal approach to the Pentateuch.

According to the story, the robbers abandoned the man, leaving him "half dead" (ἡμιθανῆ, Luke 10:30), indicating that the man was still alive. The language of the parable betrays considerable stylization in Greek, but the Hebrew background of the text is still apparent. The term "half dead" is probably an attempt to capture in Greek the force of the Hebrew word *goses* (גוסס).[30] The oral law treats the situation of the dying man who is in agony. The Hebrew word *goses* would best render the concept of the Greek "half dead." He is between life and death, beaten so badly that one cannot be certain whether he will survive. It is highly doubtful that he will live.

[29] E. P. Sanders, *Jewish Law from Jesus to the Mishnah* (Philadelphia: Trinity, 1990) 41–42.

[30] I am grateful to David Flusser, who strongly argued this point to me (private communication). The term ἡμιθανής, "half dead," is Greek and not Hebrew. It appears in *Jos. and Asen.* 27:3 (see J. H. Charlesworth, ed., *The Old Testament Pseudepigrapha* [2 vols.; New York: Doubleday, 1983–1985] 2:244 n. 27f) as well as in Diodorus Sicilus and Dionysius of Halicarnassus (cf. BAGD, s.v. ἡμιθανής). The phrase חצי המות does appear in Hebrew literature in discussion of payment of damages for a goring ox, but with a different meaning from that in Luke 10:30 (cf. *Mekilta Derabbi Shimeon Bar Yochai,* ed. Y. N. Epstein and E. Z. Melamed [Jerusalem: Hillel, 1980] 188, on Exod 21:35). It is doubtful that ἡμιθανής could have been a Greek mistranslation of מת מצוה. Probably *goses,* with its meaning in Jewish thought and halakic tradition, is the best Hebrew term for ἡμιθανής.

In Jewish oral tradition, the principle of saving life at all costs gained unsurpassed and uncompromised priority. The rabbis treated the question of preservation of life *pikuach nefesh* (פקוח נפש) or *safek nefashot* (ספק נפשות) with great severity. All written laws of the Torah must be violated to preserve life.[31] Clearly a dying man's life is more important than ritual purity. The oral law teaches that the *goses*, a person who is in agony, must be treated as a living person in every respect. He may marry, divorce, contract property, or sell his possessions. In the early Tannaitic tractate on death and dying, *Semachot,* the religious law clearly states, "A dying man is to be considered the same as a living man in every respect."[32] The talmudic literature preserves the wide understanding that most of the persons in the condition of the *goses* will indeed die (*rov gosesim lamitah,* רוב גוססים למיתה).[33] The priest and the Levite treated the dying man as if he were already dead. They did not accept the oral tradition concerning the preservation of life at all costs, and they feared that their ritual impurity was at risk. If he were dead, they should have buried the *met mitzvah.* If he were still living, they should have done all to preserve his life. But they passed by the dying man.

Flusser has called attention to a similar incident, which occurred in the temple itself. The talmudic literature preserves this dramatic episode from the history of the Second Temple period. One senses the extreme tension between the priestly class of Sadducees and the broader religious movement closer to the Pharisees, which is represented by the saying of Rabbi Zadok. He sharply criticized the attitude of the priests.[34] Is religious purity more

---

[31] The basic law regarding preservation of life in rabbinic literature is found in b. *Yoma* 85a; see also *Mekhilta Derabbi Ishmael,* ed. H. S. Horovitz and Ch. Rabin (Jerusalem: Wahrmann, 1970) 340–41, on Exod 31:12; also the article in *EncJud* 13:509–10.

[32] *Sem.* 1:1 (see the fine edition by Z. Zlotnick, *The Tractate Mourning* [New Haven: Yale University Press, 1966] with the Hebrew text, vocalized by E. Kutscher], 31,1; also the critical edition of the Hebrew text, *Masekhet Semachot,* ed. M. Higger [Jerusalem: Makor, 1970] 97). On the definition of a *goses* in halakah, see Zlotnick, p. 9, who observes, "Although the Sages accept the rule that 'most gosesim die,' i.e. succumb to their illness, yet up to the moment of death the goses is legally alive, the rule itself conceding that some may live." The *goses* in the parable of Jesus does survive.

[33] See b. *Arak.* 18a, where the third-century Palestinian sage R. Abahu recites the halakah "Most of the people in a dying condition really die." See also b. *Git.* 28a (where the saying appears in the name of Raba, the fourth-generation Amoraic sage, who says that most people who become ill will live but most of the *gosesin* will die); *Kidd.* 71b (R. Papa); b. *Shebu.* 33a, 37b; cf. also Str-B 2:182. In b. *Sanh.* 78a the question of the *goses* as a dying man and the *terefah,* one who is mortally wounded, is discussed. The rabbis took care to study the question in the oral law that developed from issues in the Torah. Though the references to the halakah are later than the Second Temple period, one should not exclude the possibility that the teaching in regard to the dying person *goses* was early. The Amoraic sages probably based their discussions on earlier traditions concerning inheritance and temple sacrifices, which had a place in the time of the temple.

[34] Though R. Zadok was himself a priest, he was not a Sadducee but was closely

important than saving a life? According to the story of talmudic literature, some priests were more concerned about ritual purity than about the shedding of blood.

The Priests and Ritual Purity

> Our Rabbis taught: It once happened that two priests were side by side [שוין] as they ran to mount the ramp. When one of them came first within four cubits of the altar, the other took a knife and thrust it into his heart. R. Zadok stood on the steps of the Hall and proclaimed: "Our brethren of the house of Israel, listen carefully! Behold it says: 'If one be found slain in the land . . . then thy elders and judges shall come forth . . .' (Deut 21:1). On whose behalf shall we offer the heifer whose neck is to be broken, on behalf of the city or on behalf of the Temple?" All the people burst out weeping. The father of the young man came and found him still in convulsions. He said: "May he be an atonement for you. My son is still in convulsions and the knife has not become unclean." [His remark] comes to teach you that the cleanness of their vessels was of greater concern to them even than the shedding of blood. Thus it was also said: "Moreover Manasseh shed innocent blood very much, till he had filled Jerusalem from one end to the other (2 Kings 21:16)."[35]

The shocking episode does not betray evidence of being a legend. The story assumes a knowledge of the temple's sanctuary. The two priests seem to be running up the ramp where only one of them would make the sacrifice. Josephus has reported that the priests did have serious disagreements among themselves, which, according to his account, resulted in priests dying of starvation.[36] The priests argued over their various forms of income, such as the profits for the many skins of the sacrificial animals offered in the temple.[37] Apparently these two priests were competing with one another to

---

associated with the Pharisees.

[35] See b. *Yoma* 23a (Epstein, *Babylonian Talmud,* 105); t. *Yoma* 1:12 (*Tosefta,* ed. with commentary S. Liebermann [15 vols.; New York: Jewish Theological Seminary, 1955–77], 224); t. Kifusta, 735; Sifre Numbers, end of Masae (*Sifre Al Bemidbar Vesifre Zuta*, ed. H. S. Horovitz [Jerusalem: Wahrmann, 1966] 222); j. *Yoma,* ch. 2; *Hal.* 2, 39d, where at the end of the story the word for their condemnation (לגנאי) is added to criticize the priests even more strongly; t. *Shebu.* 1:4 (*Tosefta,* ed. Zuckermandel, 446); m. *Yoma* 2:2. (The editors of the Mishnah were so scandalized by the story that they changed the incident from a story of murder to one of how a priest's leg was broken and how lots were cast to determine each priest's place in temple service to prevent tragedy; see especially *Mishnayoth,* ed. Blackman, 278, on *Yoma* 2:2.) I have appreciated the opportunity of discussing the text with both Flusser and Safrai. See also the discussion of Flusser's discovery in G. Cornfeld, ed., *The Historical Jesus: A Scholarly View of the Man and His World* (New York: Macmillan, 1982) 58.

[36] See Josephus, *Ant.* 20.179–181, where he describes disputes between the high priests and the ordinary priests during the reign of King Agrippa.

[37] See b. *Pesach.* 57a and parallels, where "men of violence" among the priests break into the storage house for the skins. Cf. also Jeremias, *Jerusalem*, 105–7.

offer the sacrifice. Perhaps it was an especially good portion or very profitable in some other way. They may have been younger priests, though this cannot be certain simply from the details in the story that they ran up the ramp and that one of their fathers was still living and apparently serving in the temple.[38] From his position on the steps of the hall, R. Zadok could witness the entire event clearly.[39] His words of rebuke indicate that the entire temple worship and its corrupt priesthood probably should be separated from the people of Jerusalem. The temple should be viewed as another entity outside the holy city. R. Zadok's question concerning the heifer betrays an extreme tension between the priesthood of which he was a part and the growing movement of the sages, where R. Zadok was also accepted.[40] It would be more natural to view the temple worship as a source of national pride and a symbol for the religious piety of the entire city of Jerusalem. Instead, R. Zadok is suggesting that the priests should bear the blame and responsibility for the tragic slaying on the ramp of the altar.

The shock of the slaying is probably not as great as that of the father's reaction to the death of his son. Rabbi Zadok was deeply grieved when he witnessed the killing of one priest by another. The father of the dying man, in contrast, is more concerned about ritual purity of the knife. His son is still alive, although in the throes of death. Perhaps he could still be saved. But the father shows little concern for his son's life. He is more concerned with the ritual cleanness of the sacrificial knife than with the violent death of his son.

One may question whether all of the details in the talmudic legend are accurate. The episode may well, however, as Flusser has suggested, provide the historical event that inspired the parable of the Good Samaritan. The Sadducean priests who denied the oral law had too little concern for the sanctity of life. When their sacred task of the religious service and their ritual purity were concerned, preservation of life *(pikuach nefesh)* was of secondary

[38] The priests could serve in the temple when they reached twenty years of age, according to R. Eliezar ben R. Jose (see *Sifra* on Lev 21:16; *Sifra,* ed. Weiss, 95b; and b. *Chul.* 24b; also the article by David Flusser, "... To Bury Caiaphas, Not to Praise Him," *Jerusalem Perspective* 33/34 (1991), 23–28.

[39] On R. Zadok see W. Bacher, *Die Agada der Tannaiten* (5 vols.; Strassburg: Karl Tübner, 1890) 1:43–46; Hebrew translation of Bacher by A. Rabinovitz, *Agadot Hatannaim* (5 vols.; Jerusalem: Davir, 1919); Bacher 1:34–36; A. Hyman, *Toldot Tanaim Veamoraim* (3 vols.; Jerusalem: Boys Town, 1963) 1:201–2. See also *EncJud* 16:914–15.

[40] See the preceding note. Being of priestly descent, R. Zadok served in the temple, but he was known for his piety and was close to Gamaliel (see j. *Sanh.* 19c, ch. 1, halakah 7). Though some priests were Pharisees, this seems to be the exception, as can be seen from Acts 5:17, where the priests are said to be of the party of the Sadducees. As Jeremias (*Jerusalem,* 230) notes, "The chief priests, too, were generally Sadducees," though he recognizes that some Pharisees belonged to the priesthood (p. 256). The strong influence of the Pharisees among the people is seen by the fact that some priests joined their movement. The images of the priest and Levite in the parable naturally portrayed members of the Sadducees in the minds of the listeners.

importance. The Pharisees would never accept the Sadducean approach to the written Torah. The strong rabbinic criticism in the story of the two priests running up the ramp of the altar could have been stated in the parable of the Good Samaritan: "the cleanness of their vessels was of greater concern to them even than the shedding of blood."

THE SAMARITANS AND RITUAL PURITY

The Samaritan who passed along the same road, like the priest and the Levite, also had no part in the oral tradition of the Pharisees. The Samaritans accept the Pentateuch with some variant readings and live their religious faith in a closely knit community.[41] Emil Schürer observed, "Basically, therefore, their [the Samaritans'] observance of the Torah could be compared to that of the Sadducees."[42] On matters of religious purity, the Samaritans were not meticulous enough for the Pharisees.[43] But by no means did they disregard the biblical injunctions concerning purity and impurity.

Schlatter, and Jeremias after him, suggested that the relationship between Jews and Samaritans may have improved during the days of Herod the Great, when he married a Samaritan woman.[44] These improved relations did not endure a serious violation of the ritual purity of the temple during Passover. The Samaritans spread human bones in the temple to disrupt and scandalize the people during celebration of the Passover. Jeremias reports:

> But they [the Samaritans] must already have lost this right [access to the inner court of the Temple] some twelve years after Herod's death when one Passover at the time of the Procurator Coponius (6–9 C.E.), some Samaritans strewed human bones in the Temple porches and all over the sanctuary in the middle

[41] See the critical edition by A. Tal, *The Samaritan Targum of the Pentateuch* (3 vols.; Tel Aviv: Tel Aviv University Press, 1980), with a valuable introduction.

[42] Schürer, *History*, rev., 2:20. Though Jeremias has raised doubts about the early date of the documentation that served as a basis for Schürer's view, he has not presented strong evidence to the contrary; see Jeremias, *Jerusalem*, 358 n. 25. Because the foundation of Samaritan faith is the first five books of Moses and the Sadducees also lived their lives according to the written Torah, some parallels would naturally emerge. See m. *Nid.* 4:2 (Danby, *Mishnah*, 748; *Mishnah*, ed. Albeck, 386): "The daughters of the Sadducees, if they follow after the ways of their fathers, are deemed like to the women of the Samaritans." For further support of his view, Schürer quoted Epiphanius, *Pan.* 14, who made the point that the Sadducees τὰ πάντα δὲ ἴσα Σαμαρείταις φυλάττουσιν.

[43] See Schürer, *History*, rev., 2:19: "Inasmuch as their observance of the Torah in regard to tithes and the laws of purity falls short of Pharisaic requirements, they are judged by the rabbis to be in many respects on a par with Gentiles."

[44] See Jeremias, *Jerusalem*, 353; and A. Schlatter, *Die Theologie des Judentums nach dem Bericht des Josefus* (Gütersloh: C. Bertelsmann, 1932) 75.

> of the night (*Ant.* 18.29f.). This was obviously an act of revenge for something about which Josephus is characteristically silent. This appalling defilement of the Temple, which probably interrupted the Passover feast, added fresh fuel to the old fires of hatred.[45]

Clearly, when Jesus referred to the Samaritan in a positive manner, it was an ingenious shock element in the parable. Even a Samaritan cared more for human life than the priest or the Levite! The guardians of the temple neglect basic human values.

The story is so shocking that some commentators have suggested that Luke himself added the reference to the Samaritan because Jesus could not have spoken about an enemy of the Jewish people in such an affirming way. According to this approach, originally the hero in the parable would have been a common Israelite or even one of the *am haaretz,* who did not observe Torah as carefully as the priests and Levites.[46] These suggestions appear improbable when the question of the Torah scholar and his final answer at the conclusion of the parable are carefully studied. Luke also preserves another story about a Samaritan in a positive light. Out of ten lepers who were healed of their disease only the Samaritan thanked Jesus. The miracle story also contains a similar shock element. Are these fictional creations of Luke?[47] Clearly, in the parable only the Samaritan can fulfill the function. He is considered an enemy. While the listeners probably would have expected a hero who followed the oral law, such as a Pharisee, they were surprised by an enemy who showed compassion. Therefore the teaching of Jesus from the Sermon on the Mount collection of sayings is clearly illustrated. The meaning of "neighbor" must include not only those who are near but even an enemy. The parable affirms the words of Jesus, "You have heard that it was said, 'You shall love your neighbor and hate your enemy.' But I say to you, Love your enemies" (Matt 5:43–44). Jesus wanted the Torah scholar to understand the point. He chose three characters to play leading roles in the parable. He asked the scholar, "Which of these three, do you think, proved neighbor to the man who fell among the robbers?" When the Torah scholar answered, "He who showed mercy on him," he was saying, "An enemy is my neighbor," or, to be more exact in the context of the first century, "Even my enemy is my neighbor."

It is important to note that, because the Samaritan himself took the written Torah according to his version seriously, he accepted the risk of ritual defilement by helping the man in need. In the modern period, Ayala Loewenstamm has noted the Samaritan custom: "After the death, they read the Pentateuch all night long. On the next morning they wash the corpse. Anyone touching it becomes unclean and is obliged to bathe. They place the

[45] Jeremias, *Jerusalem*, 353.
[46] See the discussion by Manson, *Sayings*, 262.
[47] See the comments of Jeremias, *Jerusalem*, 358.

body in the coffin and carry it to the cemetery. The high priest eulogizes the person but does not make himself ritually unclean by touching the body (Lev. 21:10–15)."[48] Further study is needed by specialists in Samaritan religious law and custom in antiquity, but it may well be that the Samaritan understood the risk of ritual defilement that he accepted when he helped the injured man.

But the Samaritan risked much more than ritual defilement. He could have been implicated in the crime. At least, if a despised Samaritan had been found with a man who had been brutally murdered by brigands, it is not unlikely that he would have been charged with the crime.[49] The good Samaritan was willing to risk any danger in order to preserve life.

WHO IS MY NEIGHBOR?

The answer to the question "Who is my neighbor?" is not as simple as one thinks at the first reading of the parable. Many would answer, "Any human being in need." But the Torah scholar, because of his great learning, understood the deeper level of the parable. He did not respond by saying, "The injured man," "any person in need," or even the identity of the character in the parable, "the Samaritan." Instead he answered with profound wisdom, "The one who showed mercy." Of course Jesus gave him the three options, and this emphasized the point of reciprocity. Each person must understand the needs of his neighbor in order to become a neighbor. He no longer defined the Samaritan only as a member of another religious and cultural community. He did not call him "the Samaritan" but defined him by his actions. He is the one who showed compassion. In order to understand or define the meaning of neighbor *(rea)*, one must first become a neighbor. One discovers a strong reciprocity in the sense that to define "neighbor," one must first become a neighbor. The Torah scholar did not categorize the Samaritan according to his cultural and religious community. He saw him for what he did. He realized from the story of Jesus that

[48] See Ayala Loewenstamm, "Samaritans," *EncJud* 14:747. He notes, "These laws [on ritual impurity and purity] are completely binding within the Samaritan community."

[49] Bailey, *Peasant Eyes,* 52, has made this point quite well:

Much of what we are arguing for requires no special Middle Eastern cultural attitude but is rather a common human response. An American cultural equivalent would be a Plains Indian in 1875 walking into Dodge City with a scalped cowboy on his horse, checking into a room over the local saloon, and staying the night to take care of him. Any Indian so brave would be fortunate to get out of the city alive *even* if he had saved the cowboy's life. So with the Samaritan in the parable, his act of kindness will make *no* difference. Caution would lead him to leave the wounded man at the door of the inn and disappear.

While the point Bailey makes is well taken, he moves toward the allegorical approach so cherished by the church fathers when he says that Jesus is the good Samaritan in the parable. Bailey often misses the content of first-century Jewish thought.

every human being, whether friend or enemy, is of inestimable value and must be esteemed[50] according to the biblical commandment "you shall love your neighbor as yourself." Jesus made his point clear enough for the Torah scholar; one should interpret the verse in the broadest sense: "you shall love *even* your enemy as yourself."[51]

[50] See also Lapide, *Sermon,* 78–84.

[51] The parable is a quite striking example of what Flusser referred to as the "new sensitivity," which had its origin in the Jewish wisdom from the Second Temple period. See his fine study, "A New Sensitivity in Judaism and the Christian Message" in his *Origins,* 469–93, revised from the earlier publication in *HTR* 61 (1968): 107–27.

6 The Merciful Lord and His Unforgiving Servant

FOCUS

The parable of the Unforgiving Servant (Matt 18:23–35) focuses on the meaning of divine forgiveness within the context of human relationships. God's mercy is not given to those who do not forgive others. The drama centers on relationships among people. True religion builds relationships not only with God but also with other people, who are created in the divine image. The foundation of this powerful teaching is emphasized also in rabbinic thought. Rabbi Gamaliel Beribbi once said, "He who is merciful to others, will have mercy shown to him by Heaven. He who is not merciful to others will not have mercy shown to him by Heaven."[1]

In the business of life, people injure one another. Human relationships are not perfect, but even in their imperfection, Judaism and Christianity teach people to show mercy and compassion to one another. To illustrate this, Jesus portrays the relationship between God and humanity through a colorful word-picture about a lord and his servants. The business accounts must be settled. The outrageous sum of money used in the parable to portray the debt of the unforgiving servant captures the attention of the audience while it enhances the keen humor of the story.[2] Ten thousand talents, somewhat like the numbers associated with the national debt, were simply an incomprehensible sum for the average worker. Even the very wealthy could not conceive of so great an amount of money. The exaggerated figure provides a clear setup for the punch line, "as he could not pay," as well as the bold, yet ridiculous, answer of the servant, "Lord, have patience with me, and I will

[1] b. *Shabb.* 151b.

[2] See also Jónsson, *Humour,* 134–36.

pay you everything." No matter how such a debt is incurred, whether by accumulated interest on a defaulted loan or a case of embezzlement, no single individual could ever hope to repay it.

Although humor is difficult to define and understand because of cultural barriers, Jesus' dry wit comes through in this story of one very fortunate servant. Additional time will not enable the servant to pay. Nothing short of a miracle will turn around his circumstance. The first phase of the story is filled with surprise. As the servant begs for mercy, his lord does not give him more time to prolong the agony of his inability to pay. Instead he is moved with compassion and forgives the entire debt. Only an extremely noble and generous king or landowner was able to demonstrate such an unexpected display of compassion.

The servant and his family are spared lifelong slavery. The significant turn in the plot of the story occurs when this same servant is given the opportunity to do likewise. Unlike his merciful lord, he sends his fellow servant to debtors' prison for a trifling sum. In the end, the wicked servant is severely punished. Though he had received mercy, he was unwilling to extend it to others.

The fiction of the story is made real as members of the audience consider their relationship with God. Each must soberly evaluate his or her relationship with other people as a prerequisite for approaching God. Human forgiveness is crucial for divine mercy.

THE PARABLE IN CHRISTIAN TRADITION

Christian tradition has upheld the high ethical teachings of Jesus concerning forgiveness. While the parable of the Unforgiving Servant is found only in Matthew's Gospel, its message is stressed in the Lord's Prayer, which became a vital expression of Christian faith. The prayer for Jesus' disciples with its dynamic petition, "Forgive us our debts as we also have forgiven our debtors," finds a prominent position in the *Didache,* which demonstrates that the early Christians emphasized the theme of forgiveness in the life of the church. In fact, the prayer in the *Didache* uses the singular form of ὀφειλή, in contrast to the plural of the Synoptic version but very much in line with the singular in the wording of the parable in v. 32.[3] The lord refers to "all that debt" (πᾶσαν τὴν ὀφειλὴν ἐκείνην, כל החוב הזה) that he had forgiven. Could the Lord's prayer as it is recorded in the *Didache* have been influenced by the wording of this parable?[4] I am inclined to believe that this is the case,

[3] The Greek form ὀφειλή for "debt" was once thought to appear only in the NT. Deissmann discovered it used with the same meaning as in our parable in papyri from the Fayyûm. See Adolf Deissmann, *Bible Studies* (1901; repr., Peabody, Mass.: Hendrickson, 1988) 221.

[4] See A. H. McNeile, *The Gospel according to St. Matthew* (London: Macmillan, 1949) 270. He notes, "For ὀφειλή, a late word (not in the LXX), cf. Rom. xiii. 7, I Cor. vii. 3.

although it is possible that later Greek usage influenced the prayer's wording in the *Didache*. The parable dramatically illustrates the necessity of human forgiveness as a condition for divine mercy, which is also taught in the prayer. Whatever the case, the lack of forgiveness by the wicked servant is considered a grave wrong in Christian tradition.

The parable itself appears as the climax of the fourth of five sections in Matthew's Gospel. This fourth division begins with the rejection at Nazareth and ends with this story concerning forgiveness. Matthew's placement of the parable may show his understanding of how crucial forgiveness is for the life of the Christian community. This is especially true when the parable is juxtaposed with 18:15–17, where instructions are given for restoring fellowship with a brother or a sister who has sinned. The church discipline is described in terms of forgiveness and reconciliation.[5] If one person does not succeed in dealing with the fault, the entire congregation may need to become involved. On the one hand, these Matthean teachings represent the later practices of church discipline, but on the other hand, the parable goes beyond the limits of a community of faith. In Jesus' teachings, forgiveness must be extended to everyone, even an enemy.

The parable is introduced by the standard Matthean phrase "Therefore the kingdom of heaven may be compared to a king who wished to settle accounts with his servants," Διὰ τοῦτο ὡμοιώθη ἡ βασιλεία τῶν οὐρανῶν ἀνθρώπῳ βασιλεῖ ὃς ἠθέλησεν συνᾶραι λόγον μετὰ τῶν δούλων αὐτοῦ (Matt 18:23). The mention of a king in this introduction seems somewhat odd, because in the body of the parable the creditor is always referred to as the lord, ὁ κύριος. Although this title is appropriate for a king, it might be more suitable for a wealthy landowner.[6] The mention of a king in the introduction probably represents an interpretation by the evangelist, and may well call attention to the concept of the eschatological king who is coming to settle accounts with every person on the great day of reckoning.[7] The enormous sum of money involved in the parable is fitting for a dispute involving either a king or a wealthy landowner.[8] For Matthew, the urgency

It occurs in the Lord's Prayer in the *Didache*. . . and in the papyri of the 1st and 2nd cent." Cf. Klaus Wengst, *Schriften des Urchristentums* (Munich: Kösel, 1984) 79, on *Did.* 8:2.

[5] See especially the discussion by Manson on the nature of Christian fellowship in *Sayings*, 206–14.

[6] In its oral form, the parable might have started with "It may be compared *to a man*" (לאדם) or "It may be compared *to a landowner*" (לבעל הבית). The term "king" might have been used by Matthew for greater clarity in a story about high finance. The reviser (Matthew) who added the "kingdom of heaven" introduction probably also introduced the "king" into the first part of the parable. For a kingdom parable, he would have reasoned, one needs the actor who plays the role of king.

[7] Cf. McNeile, *Matthew*, 268. In Matt 25:31–46 the Son of man, who is the eschatological judge, is referred to as "the King" (v. 34).

[8] See also W. F. Albright and C. S. Mann, *The Gospel according to Matthew* (AB 26; New York: Doubleday, 1981) 223.

of constant preparation is revealed in the dramatic presentation of the king who summons his servants for an audit of their accounts. The banking motif is a powerful image of financial accountability, which conjures up the concept of God's reckoning of each person's transactions in the course of a human life.

Matthew's interpretation of the parable seems to stress forgiveness in the life of the community of faith, as in 18:15–17. The core elements of the parable, however, are deeply rooted in the best sources for the life of Jesus and its cultural context. The wording of the parable reveals rich Semitic imagery that would have characterized the teachings of Jesus. The word "debt" in the parable is another way of saying "sin."[9] In Semitic thought "debtor" had a connotation that went beyond the world of finance and referred to other wrongs. Often a debt is metaphorically related to interpersonal relationships on a moral and ethical level. The verb ἀφῆκεν (v. 27) is also significant. It meant both release from a monetary debt and forgiveness for an injury or wrong. This was a familiar Hebrew expression. The colorful phrase "seizing him by the throat" also is found in many Hebrew texts (חנק). Such action is even discussed in the Mishnah. Under such physical pressure a person is not required to make good on his or her pledge. "If a person seized a debtor by the throat in the street and his fellow found him and said to him, 'Leave him alone and I will pay you,' he is not liable."[10] Most significantly, the Jewish worldview, with its concept of God and the absolute necessity for each person to forgive his or her neighbor, has impacted the early Christian interpretations of this parable.

The weight of sin against God is felt in the Christian treatment of the parable. Augustine believed that the number ten associated with the thousands of talents referred to the Ten Commandments.[11] The Decalogue summarized the law of God and human responsibility to the divine initiative. Breaking these commandments was considered a terrible violation of God's will. The enormous debt owed to God cannot be emphasized enough. The famous biblical exegete Alfred Plummer wrote, "Why is the debt to God represented as so enormous? Partly as a true contrast to offences between man and man, and partly because every sin is an act of rebellion, and thus small acts, which attract little or no attention, may be great sins."[12] The grace of God is dramatized when the lord forgives his servant of a debt that could never be honored.

---

[9] This was properly understood by Luke in his interpretation of the Lord's Prayer. McNeile notes, "The thought of sins (Lk. τὰς ἁμαρτίας) as debts was thoroughly Jewish" (*Matthew*, 80).

[10] See m. *B. Bat.* 10:8 and parallels.

[11] Cf., e.g., W. Kissinger, *The Parables of Jesus: A History of Interpretation and Bibliography* (Metuchen, N.J.: Scarecrow, 1979) 22.

[12] Alfred Plummer, *An Exegetical Commentary on the Gospel according to St. Matthew* (5th ed.; 1920; repr., Grand Rapids: Eerdmans, 1953) 256.

The Venerable Bede (ca. 673–735) is best known as the "Father of English History," but he was deeply involved in biblical scholarship as well. Unfortunately, in spite of his contributions to biblical scholarship and distinguished accomplishments as a church leader, Bede wrongly viewed this parable as describing the relationship between the church and the synagogue. He interpreted the unforgiving servant as the Jews who would not forgive the Gentile church.[13] Without a foundation in the larger context of Jesus' teachings, he allegorized the meaning of the parable. This type of religious polemic undermined the rich Jewish heritage of the parable and its application to daily life. For that matter, such an allegory could just as easily be turned in the opposite direction. A negative approach to Jews and Judaism always proves detrimental in the exegetical study of the parables of Jesus.

Jesus and his teachings must be placed in the midst of his own people rather than in conflict with them. In fact, without a proper understanding of the Jewish background of the parable, we will forever miss the true force of its message, which is based on its cultural and religious setting. The parable is a hallmark of traditional Jewish teachings from this historical period. It should not be viewed as a polemical commentary that criticizes the ethical values of early Judaism. The story line of this parable is not concerned with the church and the synagogue. On the contrary, it focuses attention on the relationships among individuals on a personal level. The parable deals more with individual bitterness than it does with the community of faith as a whole. The warning is jolting. Unforgiveness in the realm of personal relationships will cast a person out of God's presence forever.

THE PARABLE IN THE LIGHT OF JEWISH TRADITION

In the cultural context, the sacred calendar of the Jewish people may provide the setting in life for this parable. The ten-day period between the Jewish New Year and the day of Atonement was designated for seeking forgiveness between individuals. A person was not prepared to seek divine mercy during the great fast on the day of Atonement if he or she had not first sought reconciliation with his or her neighbor. The day of Atonement was the experience of the community as every person participated in the fast. The preparation for this collective experience, however, focused on the necessity

---

[13] See the fine discussion by Kissinger, *Parables,* 39–40, who mentions Bede's view: "The unmerciful servant represents the Jews, who though they were the subject to the Decalogue, nevertheless, were guilty of many transgressions. They were ungrateful to the Savior who could have freed them from the law. Moreover, they submitted to a new sin, that of despising their fellow-servants, the Gentiles." For a more positive view than these very unfortunate remarks, see some of Bede's other homilies in *Bede the Venerable: Homilies on the Gospels,* trans. L. Martin and D. Hurst (2 vols.; Kalamazoo, Mich.: Cisterican, 1991).

to forgive one another on a personal level so as to approach God without a bitter heart. Mercy from above depended upon showing mercy to those below.[14]

The Mishnah has provided striking evidence for these oral traditions regarding preparation for the day of Atonement. Forgiving one another was stressed by the sages:

> For transgressions that are between a person and God, the Day of Atonement effects atonement, but for the transgressions that are between a person and his or her neighbor, the Day of Atonement effects atonement only if one first has appeased one's neighbor.[15]

While the Gospel of Matthew does not mention the time of the year in which Jesus taught this parable, it does mention the question of Peter, "Lord, how often shall my brother sin against me, and I forgive him? As many as seven times?" This particular question is fitting for the issues concerning reconciliation during the ten days of Awe. Quite likely, Jesus told the parable during this time, when Judaism focused on the task of interpersonal reconciliation.

The theme of forgiveness between individuals as a prerequisite for divine mercy was a pervasive teaching in ancient Judaism. One of the finest examples is found in the words of Ben Sira. The issue of forgiveness is treated in a discussion about prayer and healing. One should not dare approach God in prayer with enmity in one's heart.

> Forgive your neighbor the wrong he has done, and then your sins will be forgiven when you pray. Does a person harbor anger against another and yet seek for healing from the Lord? Does he have not mercy toward a man like himself and yet pray for his own sins? If he himself, being flesh, maintains wrath, who will make expiation for his sins? Remember the end of your life, and cease from enmity.[16]

In early Jewish thought, the concept of *imitatio Dei* demanded that genuine mercy be granted by one person to another in the same way that God himself gives grace to the sinner. The close similarity between the two mini-dramas of the parable portrays how each person must strive to be like God. The first dramatizes God's love, when the lord forgives his servant. The second exactly re-creates the first mini-drama except for the change in roles between the merciful lord and his unforgiving servant, which shows how much every

---

[14] Compare also Matt 5:23–24, where the call for reconciliation goes beyond giving forgiveness. Jesus teaches that one must seek forgiveness from a person who has been offended before offering a gift at the altar of the temple.

[15] See m. *Yoma* 9:9 (*Mishnah*, ed. Albeck, 247) and the parallels: j. *Yoma* 42a, ch. 8, halakah 7; b. *Yoma* 85a; and *Sifra* on Lev 16:30 (*Acharei Mot* 8; *Sifra*, ed. Weiss, 83a). The teaching is attributed to R. Eleazar ben Azariah. See also *Torah Shelemah*, ed. M. Kasher (43 vols.; New York: Talmud Institute, 1951–1983) 31:102.

[16] Sir 28:2–6a. See the important discussion by Patrick Skehan and Alexander Di Lella, *Wisdom of Ben Sira* (AB 39; Garden City, N.Y.: Doubleday, 1987) 363–64. For the Hebrew text, see Segal, *Sefer Ben Sira Hashalem*, 168.

human being is like God. Every individual is created in God's image and must seek to understand and imitate his ways. Being made in his likeness, people must love and forgive in the same way, which God shows mercy, those who have done wrong.

In another passage from the teachings of Jesus, the temple sacrifice is portrayed. What happens when a person enters the temple to offer a gift and remembers that someone feels ill will against him or her? Jesus stresses total reconciliation. Even if the other person is the one at odds with the giver of the gift, Jesus teaches his followers to leave the sacrifice and go make matters right: "first be reconciled to your brother, and then come and offer your gift" (Matt 5:23–24). Forgiveness and reconciliation should precede prayer and worship.

MERCY AND JUDGMENT

The drama of the parable of Jesus leads the listener through trial and triumph all the way to tribulation. The character of the lord dominates the story. His strong presence is felt in every scene. First his awesome power summons the listener to do some self-inventory, when the lord calls his servants before him to audit the records. This is the trial. The strength of his character is revealed in the noble act of canceling the debt as well as in his response when he discovers that the one who had received mercy failed to show compassion to his coworker. The debtor triumphs in receiving total remittance of his huge debt, but he enters travail when his lord punishes him for not forgiving. The lord is sovereign in the story, which first and foremost reinforces the Jewish understanding of God as a compassionate and just judge, who will show limitless mercy as well as pronounce severe judgment.

In the first scene of the parable, the trial begins when the lord summons his servants for an accounting of the records. Such an accounting, somewhat like an intensive IRS audit, would discomfit even the honest business executive who keeps the most scrupulous records. This sense of tension is heightened when the books reveal that one servant owes the master ten thousand talents.[17] This is a grave situation. The talent was the equivalent of 6,000 denarii. Judea, Idumaea, and Samaria together paid in one year only 600 talents, while Galilee and Peraea paid 200.[18] The Dead Sea Scrolls help us to understand the magnitude of the debt. The *Copper Scroll*'s fabulous treasure would be described in terms of 6,000 talents.[19] J. T. Milik observes,

---

[17] On the translation of the amount μυρίων ταλάντων (v. 24), compare the way that the LXX rendered Esth 3:9. MS א* (as well as Coptic sa and bo) substitutes the Greek word "many" (πολλῶν), and c reads *centum.* Cf. *Novum Testamentum Graece,* ed. S. C. E. Legg (2 vols.; Oxford: Clarendon, 1935–1940).

[18] Josephus, *Ant.* 17.318–320.

[19] See J. Allegro, *The Treasure of the Copper Scroll* (London: Routledge & Kegan Paul, 1960) and B. Luria, *Megilat Hanachoshet* (Jerusalem: Kiryat Sefer, 1963).

"The total of gold and silver said to be buried exceeds 6,000 talents, or 200 tons—a figure that obviously exceeds the resources of private persons or of small communities."[20] If a day worker who received a denarius a day could work every day of the week and save all of his wages, it would have taken him over 150 years to obtain this kind of money.

The second scene illustrates the quality of mercy. Because the servant could not pay his debt, his wife, children, and he himself would be sent to prison. They would spend the rest of their lives subjected to a terrible penal system that showed little concern for human dignity. The practice of sending someone to prison for failing to honor financial obligations is confirmed from the Greek papyri as well as from the rabbinic literature.[21]

The lord orders the man to be sold along with his immediate family until payment is made. His friends and relatives will not be able to find the necessary financial resources to secure his release. His debt is so great that all he can do is seek the mercy of his lord. The threat of imprisonment is very real. The practice of selling a person in order to exact payment is used in the Gospels in another illustration of Jesus, "Make friends quickly with your accuser, while you are going with him to court, lest your accuser hand you over to the judge, and the judge to the guard, and you be put in prison; truly, I say to you, you will never get out till you pay the last penny" (Matt 5:25–26; Luke 12:58). The fear that a person would be imprisoned until he paid the last penny was not groundless. The selling of a person for financial debt was strongly criticized already by the prophet Amos: "because they sell the righteous for silver, and the needy for a pair of shoes" (Amos 2:6; cf. 8:6). In 2 Kgs 4:1 the widow expresses her concern to Elisha that the creditor will sell her children into slavery to pay off her debt: " 'Your servant my husband is dead; and you know that your servant feared the LORD, but the creditor has come to take my two children to be his slaves.' "[22]

In a rabbinic parable, a king makes a loan to a man with the condition that he would pay him back 1000 kors of wheat a year. This is an enormous amount, which would exceed his ability to fulfill his loan obligations. The parallel in thought and structure to the Gospel drama is striking. Like the unmerciful servant, the man is punished severely in the conclusion of the rabbinic parable. The man is compared to King David, who was recompensed for his misconduct but who ultimately received grace in the biblical account describing his life.

---

[20] J. T. Milik, *Ten Years of Discovery in the Wilderness of Judaea* (London: SCM Press, 1963), 42.

[21] The debtor could be taken to prison by his creditor: see Plautus, *Poen.* 3.5.45.

[22] See also Lev 25:39: "And if your brother becomes poor beside you, and sells himself to you, you shall not make him serve as a slave." Cf. Neh 5:5; Isa 50:1.

The Auction Block

> A parable: A man borrowed from the king a thousand *kor* of wheat per year. Everyone said, "Can it be possible for this man to manage a loan of one thousand *kor* of wheat in one year? It must be that the king has made him a gift of it and has written him a receipt!" One time the man had nothing left over and could not repay anything to the king, so the king entered the man's house, seized his sons and daughters, and placed them on the auction block, whereupon everyone knew that the man had received no pardon from the king.[23]

A family sold to pay the debt is portrayed in the rabbinic parable. The Greco-Roman background of these practices has been observed in the studies by Adolf Deissmann in the Greek papyri. Deissmann called attention to the close parallels in wording between the parable of Jesus and the language of the papyri. The judicial proceedings that attest to the practice of imprisoning debtors is revealed in these fascinating texts. For example, a man named Phibion committed a crime when he had a worthy man imprisoned along with women without sufficient grounds. The king or a nobleman is not the only one with such authority. Like the unmerciful servant in the parable, who takes legal action against the colleague who owes him a mere 100 denarii, the papyri demonstrate that a common person also had this prerogative when he or she was unable to collect payment on a bill.

> Phibion's offence was that he had "of his own authority imprisoned a worthy man [his alleged debtor] and also women." The Florentine papyrus is thus a beautiful illustration of the parable of the wicked servant (Matt. xviii. 30; cf. also Matt. v. 25f. Luke xii. 58f.) and the system, which it presupposes, of personal execution by imprisonment for debt. Numerous other papyri and inscriptions show that this was Graeco-Roman Egypt, and elsewhere, a widespread legal custom. Probably the most interesting example for us is an inscription in the Great Oasis containing an edict of the governor of Egypt, Tib. Julius Alexander, 68 A.D. The technical expression here has the same ring as in the gospel. "They delivered them into other prisons," says the Roman governor; "he cast him into prison," says Jesus.[24]

---

[23] *Sifre Deut.* 26 (*Sifre Devarim,* ed. Finkelstein, 38); Reuven Hammer, *Sifre: A Tannaitic Commentary on the Book of Deuteronomy* (New Haven: Yale University Press, 1986) 47; see also *Midrash Tannaim* (*Midrash Tannaim,* ed. D. Hoffmann [1908; repr.; Jerusalem: Books Export, n.d.] 13–14. Cf. also the discussion by Ignaz Ziegler, *Die Königsgleichnisse des Midrasch beleuchtet durch die römische Kaiserzeit* (Breslau: Schlesische Verlags-Anstalt v. S. Schottlaender, 1903) 251.

[24] Adolf Deissmann, *Light from the Ancient East* (1927; repr.; Peabody: Hendrickson, 1995) 270. Deissmann comments on the Greek text, παρέδοσαν καὶ εἰς ἄλλας φυλακάς, in a note, observing its similarity in wording to Matt 18:30, ἔλαβεν αὐτὸν εἰς φυλακήν. One should observe also that the same verb is used in Matt 18:34, παρέδωκεν αὐτὸν τοῖς βασανισταῖς ἕως οὗ ἀποδῷ πᾶν τὸ ὀφειλόμενον.

The Gospel parable describes a situation very similar to that portrayed in the papyri. The trial of the servant who owed a colossal sum that he could never pay is colorfully depicted in the Gospel account. His family will be sold as slaves. The hopeless circumstance can be changed only by the grace of the master.

The debtor's trial is turned to triumph because his lord unexpectedly responds to his dramatic plea for mercy. Here one catches a clear view of a foundational tenet in Jewish theology: God is quick to show mercy to one seeking forgiveness. In the great theophany given to Moses on Mt. Sinai revealing the true character of the God [YHWH] of Israel, God is described as "merciful and gracious, slow to anger, and abounding in steadfast love and faithfulness, keeping steadfast love for thousands, forgiving iniquity and transgression and sin" (Exod 34:6–7). This and similar passages were very important during the observance of the day of Atonement at the time of Jesus.

The conclusion of Jesus' parable, however, is filled with tribulation and despair. The servant who had seen his family snatched away from the grim sentence of lifelong slavery is quick to send his colleague to prison for a much smaller debt. The one hundred denarii is one six hundred thousandth the debt he had been forgiven. It was about three months wages for a day worker, which shows that it was enough for imprisonment but quite minute in comparison with the grand amount forgiven by the king. The scene is déjà vu. The servant seeks payment of a debt. The difference in the scene is found in the quality of mercy. The unmerciful servant does not forgive like his master. The lord of the servants, however, is not only merciful but also just. The one who would not forgive will not receive a reprieve. His fellow servants recognize the injustice and report the actions of their unmerciful coworker to the lord. He is enraged. The continuation of Exod 34:6–7 is seen here. On the one hand, God forgives iniquity and transgression; on the other hand, he "will by no means clear the guilty." The anger of the master is vented on the servant who would not learn from the example of compassion modeled for him in the act of acquittal that he had just experienced. Now he will be delivered into the hands of the tormentors: "And in anger his lord delivered him to jailers [torturers]" (καὶ ὀργισθεὶς ὁ κύριος αὐτοῦ παρέδωκεν αὐτὸν τοῖς βασανισταῖς [Matt 18:34]). The term *basanistais* most certainly refers to torture and extreme physical pain.[25]

In early Jewish thought, such punishment for the unmerciful servant may appear harsh, but his misconduct was considered unpardonable. He had received bountiful mercy but was unwilling to forgive a minor debt. Such teachings were especially emphasized during the time leading up to the day

[25] BAGD 134. Delitzsch (in *Haberit Hechadashah* [trans. F. Delitzsch; Tel Aviv: Bible Society, 1976]) translates it as מיסרים, and Salkinson (in *Haberit Hechadashah* [trans. J. Salkinson; London: Trinitarian Bible Society, 1957]) rendered the phrase ויתנהו ביד נגשים.

of Atonement.[26] God will not forgive someone who has not made matters right with one's neighbor. Even though the message of the parable is abundantly clear, Jesus reaches beyond the word-picture into the realm of reality. He makes direct application for the mashal by drawing the focus of attention on the *nimshal* behind the story. He warns, "So also my heavenly Father will do to every one of you, if you do not forgive your brother from your heart" (Matt 18:35).

CONCLUSION

The parable shows the deep roots of Jesus' teachings in ancient Judaism. Jesus' Jewish theology of God saturates the drama of the story as the action moves from scene to scene. The listener is caught up into the plot of the mini-play and participates in the trial, triumph, and tribulation of the servant. What happens when it is impossible to pay one's creditor? Will debtors' prison become the final solution for a father and his family? The economic setting creates a realistic circumstance for the action of the story. The conflict of the drama involves money and a harsh prison sentence. The cultural and religious background is based on the teachings concerning the great day of fasting in Israel's sacred calendar, when each person seeks forgiveness from God. The creation of humanity, in the very image of God, demands full accountability, which means that one must be merciful in the same way that God shows mercy. The images created by the parable lead the listener to join the actors on the stage. Each individual must ask God for forgiveness of a colossal debt. To what extent, however, do I extend mercy to others who have wronged me?

[26]The fast of the day of Atonement is probably behind Matt 6:16–18. The mention of almsgiving, prayer, and fasting (i.e., repentance) was related to the preparation for seeking God's forgiveness on the fast during the days of awe. Cf., e.g., Tobit 12:8 and this remarkable passage from j. *Taan.* 65a, ch. 2 hal. 1: "R. Eleazar said: Three things annul a difficult decree. They are prayer, almsgiving and repentance. These three are found in one verse, 'If my people which are called by my name will humble themselves and pray' (2 Chron. 7:14) this is prayer, 'and seek my face'—this is almsgiving, as it is written, 'I will see your face by righteousness [almsgiving]' (Ps. 17:15). 'And turn from their wicked ways,'—this is repentance. If they do thus, it is written, 'then I will forgive their sin and heal their land' (2 Chron. 7:14)." See Matt 6:1–18.

7 The Father of Two Lost Sons

FOCUS

By dramatizing a family tragedy, the parable of the Prodigal Son (Luke 15:11–32) focuses on the crisis of broken relationships between a human being and God. A person living without God is like the younger son running away to a far country. But the elder brother living at home with his father is no better off. He is much like a religious person who misunderstands the divine nature and lacks a meaningful relationship with God. The elder son does not show love for his father and struggles, perhaps unsuccessfully, to forgive his brother. He cannot share the joy of his father over the return of the runaway.

The plot of the parable revolves around a father and his two sons. The parable, moreover, begins and ends with both of them. Although traditional interpretations have tended to stress the wrongs of the runaway younger son, both elder and younger brothers are equal players in the dramatic scenes of this compelling story of broken family relationships. They both have needs and are lost, but they are lost in different ways. As Leslie Weatherhead explained in his insightful popular book on the parables, "The story, then, is the story of a loving father who had two boys, one of whom walled himself off from his father's love by doing evil, while the other walled himself off from that same love by doing good. . . . In both cases the sons were prodigals, for they were estranged from their father, and the love relationship between them and him was broken."[1] They did not love their father and they were not capable of loving one another.

The value of family relationships sets the stage for a parable that reaches out to the most irreligious sinner as well as to the one who is outwardly pious while deficient in true religion. The relationship the brothers have with each

---

[1] Leslie D. Weatherhead, *In Quest of a Kingdom* (New York: Abingdon, 1944) 87.

other influences their relationship with their father. Genuine faith begins by developing a solid relationship with God. It involves a fellowship between the religious person and his or her Creator. The one who loves God must also love other people. In every scene of the story, the father plays the major role as the compassionate parent. He loves his sons enough to allow them the freedom of decision. But when they make a wrong choice that is harmful for them, the loving father is always there waiting to help them in the time of crisis. He seeks restoration and healing of relationships. Neither of the sons understands him as a loving parent. They view him from a financial side; he is like a banker who has the money to supply their needs and pay their wages. The parable challenges the audience to respond and accept the compassion of the committed parent.

THE PRODIGAL SON IN CHRISTIAN INTERPRETATIONS

Christian interpretations of the parable of the Compassionate Father and His Two Lost Sons have tended to emphasize the return of the prodigal rather than the entire family situation. The dramatic images of the father restoring the wasteful son are allegorized for Christian meaning.[2] Not surprisingly, the unforgettable scene of the father forgiving his wayward son overshadows all other concerns. The high Christology of Christian interpretations has invited an identification of Jesus and his actions with some facet of the parable.

In fact, Karl Barth discerned christological meaning in the action of the drama. The prodigal is like Jesus in the sense that, in his coming, Jesus assumed the shame of every human being but then seeks and brings restoration to the father. Barth recognizes "a most illuminating parallel to the way trodden by Jesus Christ in the work of atonement, to His humiliation and exaltation."[3] It is hard for Barth to avoid seeing the Christian doctrine of the atonement in the parable: "Or better, the going out and coming in of the lost son, and therefore the fall and blessing of man, takes place on the horizon of the humiliation and exaltation of Jesus Christ and therefore of the atonement made in Him."[4] Little from the context of the Gospel or the words of Jesus,

---

[2] Cf., e.g., Clement of Alexandria, "Greek Fragments in the Oxford Edition, Marcius Chrysocephalus: Parable of the Prodigal Son" (ANF, 2:581–84), where the robe given to the prodigal is baptism, the ring symbolizes the mystery of the trinity, and the shoes are those who ascend to heaven.

[3] Karl Barth, *Church Dogmatics* (trans. G. W. Bromiley; 4 vols.; Edinburgh: T. & T. Clark, 1936–1962) 4/2:23. Barth claims (p. 24), "Primarily, originally and properly, the scribe and Pharisee does not reject merely a distasteful doctrine of sin and forgiveness, but the God who is the God of this man, the man who is the man of this God, the actuality of the Son of God and His humiliation, and of the Son of Man and His exaltation, the atonement which takes place in this One."

[4] Ibid., 23.

however, support this imaginative interpretation. Why must the humiliation of Christ and his atoning death be forced upon the role of the prodigal son in the parable? Barth's great contribution to Christian theology can hardly be underestimated, but he seems to view the parables through the eyes of the church's beliefs about Jesus rather than first-century Jewish beliefs about God. If the parable has a historical setting in the time of Jesus, the interpreter must seek the significance of the images in the illustration from the setting of the Second Temple period.

The story originally involved three family members, but seldom has the significance of the elder brother been carefully considered. The prodigal, his elder brother, and the father must be kept in full view. One of the main issues for Christian interpretation, moreover, concerns the father figure. This major point of controversy is crucial for proper interpretation. Does one discover a major correspondence between Christ and the father? Is God himself compared to the compassionate parent figure of the story? What is the the reality behind the image of the compassionate father?

In his treatise on repentance, the Latin church father Tertullian gives an unequivocal answer: "Who is that father to be understood by us? God, surely; no one *is* so truly a Father; no one so rich in paternal love."[5] Edward Schweizer, the eminent professor of New Testament theology and exegesis at the University of Zurich, as well as Bailey, however, have argued that in some way Jesus should be identified with the father in the parable. While Schweizer claims, "In the parable of the prodigal son, Jesus does not appear,"[6] Schweizer does try to show a correspondence between Jesus and the father in the parable. Bailey also argues for a christological interpretation. He makes it clear: "In conclusion, then, the atonement is at least 'overheard' in the parable."[7] He hears echoes of the incarnation and the atonement in the parable. Bailey claims, "When the father leaves the house to come out to his son in love and humility, he demonstrates at least in a part of the meaning of the incarnation and the atonement."[8] Unlike Barth, who sees a parallel between Jesus and the prodigal, Bailey finds a correspondence between the

[5] Tertullian, *On Repentance* 8 (ANF, 3:663).

[6] E. Schweizer, *Jesus* (London: SCM, 1971) 28. He suggests that "it is wrong even to speak in terms of whether he 'appears' in the parable or not. A parable cannot be treated like an allegory, with each of the characters representing something specific; the father cannot be equated with God, or the younger son with the sinner. A parable has a single goal: to lead the listener along a certain path." At the same time, Schweizer claims a "correspondence" between the conduct of the father and Jesus.

[7] Bailey, *Poet and Peasant*, 190. Cf. p. 188 n. 204, where Bailey confronts a problem he faced as a Christian living in the Middle East: "For centuries Islam has used the parable of the Prodigal Son in anti-Christian polemic attempting to prove that Christian theology is at odds with the message of Jesus." In trying to refute Muslim teachings that say that the atonement is not in the parable, Bailey has labored to give a Christian response. See also Kenneth E. Bailey, *Finding the Lost* (St. Louis: Concordia, 1992) 9–11.

[8] Bailey, *Poet and Peasant*, 190.

father who humbles himself in the parable and Jesus who comes to humanity in the incarnation and offers himself on the cross for the atonement.

While Schweizer claims that Jesus "does not appear" in the parable, his interpretation stresses the correspondence between the actions of Jesus and the conduct of the father. These actions that are paralleled by the conduct of the father would, in Schweizer's view, be considered blasphemous by the Jewish audience. On the one hand, Schweizer rejects allegory, but on the other hand, he claims, "Of course there must be certain correspondences. . . . he [Jesus] equates God's own merciful conduct with his own conduct toward the tax collectors."[9] Perhaps for Schweizer Jesus does appear in the parable after all. At least the actions of Jesus find correspondence with those of the father. In fact, it is in the parable of the prodigal that Schweizer finds cause for the crucifixion of Jesus. He recognizes the blasphemy that caused his opponents to nail Jesus to the cross. Schweizer argues,

> Who but Jesus would have the authority to assume the role of God in his parable and proclaim a celebration on behalf of the sinner who has been restored to fellowship with God? Those who nailed him to the cross because they found blasphemy in his parables—which proclaimed such scandalous conduct on the part of God—understood his parables better than those who saw in them nothing but the obvious message, which should be self-evident to all, of the fatherhood and kindness of God, meant to replace a superstitious belief in a God of wrath.[10]

When the theological significance of the parable is understood in light of Jewish tradition, Schweizer's accusation of blasphemy is unfounded. The act of forgiveness, when one human being is reconciled to another, does not constitute blasphemy. Each individual should be like God in showing compassion to others. Moreover, it is highly doubtful that the parable was designed to combat the "superstitious belief in a God of wrath." The concept of God's mercy is not a new notion that would cause hostility. As Petuchowski has convincingly argued, the theological message of Jesus demonstrates remarkable solidarity with the religious teachings of rabbinic-Pharisaic Judaism.[11]

No one crucified rabbis for telling parables.[12] Even if the parable focused attention on the compassion of God to receive sinners, this message in and

---

[9] Schweizer, *Jesus*, 28.

[10] Ibid., 29.

[11] Petuchowski, "Significance," 76–86; see also "A Panel Discussion of the Parable," *Christian News from Israel* 23 (1972–1973) 144ff.

[12] Cf. the needed critique by E. P. Sanders, *Jesus and Judaism* (London: SCM, 1985) 39–40. The mistake has been made by Scott, *Hear*, 423–24. See also the chapter "The Parables and the Crucifixion" in Charles Smith, *The Jesus of the Parables* (Philadelphia: Westminster, 1948) 17–35. Petuchowski's "Significance" has not had the influence that it deserves. Some of the issues raised in the study of the parables of Jesus and their rabbinic counterparts relate directly to the Jewish origins of Christianity and the original

of itself would not have been considered blasphemy. The community would rejoice when a wayward one was restored by repentance. In fact, as will be seen in the study of rabbinic parallel parables, the concept of God's mercy to receive a repentant sinner was a major doctrine in Jewish theology. God loves the wrongdoer and receives each one who repents. The necessity of forgiving one another, as a prerequisite for seeking forgiveness from God, is also a major tenet in Jewish thought, one that appears already in Sirach.[13] Jesus makes this a major theme in the prayer he taught his disciples: "Forgive us our debts, as we also have forgiven our debtors."[14] On the day of Atonement, the Mishnah instructs the people to make things right one with the other before seeking forgiveness from God.[15] Thus the idea of human forgiveness is strong in Jewish theology. The elder brother in the parable should forgive the younger. The theme of forgiveness and reconciliation are very much consistent with Jewish traditional values.

It is difficult to see a clear allusion to the cross in the story, and one must ask whether such an allegorical approach does a terrible injustice to the original context of the story and the powerful message of Jesus in the parable. Of course, in the context of the Gospels, Jesus is on the way to Jerusalem. The cross figures prominently in the message of the Gospel texts. Nonetheless, the primary point of contact between the metaphoric world of the parable and the reality behind the story should not be abandoned. The father figure more naturally is related to God and his great compassion both for those who pretend to serve him (the elder son) and for those who flagrantly abandon him (the younger son).

Does Jesus appear in the parable? I believe that Tertullian's answer, that the compassionate father must certainly be identified with God himself, is the only proper response. Tertullian seems closer to the setting of the Gospels than Barth, Bailey, or Schweizer. First-century Judaism viewed God as full

context of Jesus' teaching. It is of great benefit to consider the work of Clemens Thoma, *A Christian Theology of Judaism* (Mahwah, N.J.: Paulist, 1980). The foreword by David Flusser, "Reflections of a Jew on a Christian Theology of Judaism," is of great import in the present discussion. Flusser observes, "Many modern theologians increasingly attempt to define the message of Jesus over against Judaism. Jesus is said to have taught something different, something original, unacceptable to the other Jews. . . . Even though he gave his own personal bent to Jewish ideas, selected from among them, purged and reinterpreted them, I cannot honestly find a single word of Jesus that could seriously exasperate a well-intentioned Jew" (p. 16). When one considers the vast amount of parabolic teaching in talmudic literature and the identity of theological constructs between Jesus and the Jewish sages, it is difficult to maintain a theology of hostility. The parables are a point of solidarity between Jesus and the Jewish people of his time.

[13] Sir 28:2–4.

[14] Matt 6:12; Luke 11:4. Surely the Matthean version with the aorist tense is better. See my book *The Jewish Background to the Lord's Prayer* (Austin, Tex.: Center for Judaic-Christian Studies, 1984) 28–30, 45.

[15] m. *Yoma* 8:9.

of compassion for those who sought forgiveness and reconciliation. Surely the whole story of Jesus' life is a parable in and of itself, and his mercy for sinners is parallel to the love of God. But such mercy in ancient Judaism is required from everyone who seeks to love and serve God. It does not in any way constitute blasphemy, as Schweizer has implied. In fact, the reading of the later Christian theological reflection into the dramatic story may indeed undermine the force of Jesus' parable. Jesus' clear message in the parable must be heard. The need to seek forgiveness from God and to forgive one another should not be distorted by the high theological issues relating to the doctrines of the incarnation and the atonement.[16]

Some parables reveal a veiled christological attestation of Jesus and his mission. But all Gospel parables begin with an understanding of the compassionate God. The interpreter must see God in the parables. For Bailey, "the visible demonstration of love in humiliation is seen to have clear overtones of the atoning work of Christ."[17] Although the father runs to meet the prodigal and leaves the celebration to seek out his angry elder son, it is difficult to impose the doctrine of the atonement or the meaning of the incarnation on the parable. While Christians may see these teachings from the position of later faith, one is hard pressed to attribute such theological implications to Jesus himself. Jesus is teaching about God's loving nature and challenging a response.

Surely this is first and foremost a parable about God, who is revealed in the actions of a compassionate parent. Tertullian seems to have grasped the essence of the story. Each listener may find himself or herself in one of the two sons. The younger runs away from his father. In hunger and desperation he realizes that he is in need. The older has exactly the same need, but has fooled himself by thinking that his relationship with his father is in fine order.

Have Christian interpretations stressed the christological implications of the parable to the point that they have distorted the original message? How would the story be understood in a first-century Jewish setting? Instead of viewing the parable through the eyes of later Christian theologians, the

---

[16] No doubt the Christian response to the issues raised by the parable would have been different after the cross. See Manson, *Sayings,* 286: "This lies in the fact that there does not seem to be any place in it for the doctrine that God's forgiveness of sinners is made possible by the sacrificial death of Jesus. On this point it may be said first that the Christian doctrine of the Atonement is not based on this parable alone, but on the whole set of facts presented in the life and teaching of Jesus in the experience of Christians." Fitzmyer agrees: "There seems to be no place in it for the teaching that God's forgiveness of sinners actually comes through the 'sacrificial death of Jesus.' Manson rightly rejects such criticism of the Lucan parable because it misses its point, which is not to be a summary of 'the Christian doctrine of the Atonement' or a compendium of all of Christian theology" (*Luke,* 2:1086).

[17] Bailey, *Poet and Peasant*, 206.

interpreter must seek to see the illustration through the eyes of first-century Jews. The best answers for these difficult questions can be found by exploring the parable in light of Jewish tradition.

THE PARABLE IN THE LIGHT OF JEWISH TRADITION

When viewed through the lens of Jewish tradition, the parable cannot be interpreted as a polemic against the Pharisees. The story deals with two types of people. It should be interpreted universally, for these types are found everywhere, appearing in every group. In many ways, Pharisees would identify with the message of the parable because it reinforces their teachings.

The theme of the parable does not appear in a strong personal attack against the Pharisees, but emerges in the clear message of God's love for both the prodigal and the elder brother, who had lost his godlike feeling of compassion for his younger brother, who needed forgiveness and acceptance. The sectarian polemic against the Pharisees emphasized by many commentators does not appear in the body of the parable itself.[18] Jesus may have criticized the hypocritical practices of some Pharisees, but he did not attack Pharisaism as a religious movement.[19] The profound message of this story is intimately related to the Jewish theological understanding of God and people. This worldview was the legacy of Pharisaic thought.[20]

Clearly the method of parabolic teaching found its place both in the teachings of Jesus and in the instruction of Israel's sages, but more than this fact must be recognized. The theological messages of the parables share much common ground. The theological distinctives that unite the message of Jesus' parables with ancient Jewish thought have not always been fully appreciated. Here we will consider one of the outstanding achievements of the parables of Jesus and parallel rabbinic parables that have common theological concepts. By studying the rabbinic parables in light of Jesus' parabolic instruction, both texts become clearer, and our understanding of the Jewish thought of the Second Temple period and postbiblical Judaism is enriched.[21]

---

[18] The placing of this parable in Luke may have contributed to some of the misunderstanding. The Semitic background of the Gospels and the redactive stage of their final compilation contributed to the church's miscomprehension of Judaism. See the valuable article by David Flusser, "The Crucified One and the Jews," *Immanuel* 7 (1977): 25–37, reprinted in *Origins*, 575–87 (German original, "Der Gekreuzigte und die Juden," *Jahresbericht* 6 [1975] for the Lucerne Theological Faculty and Catechetical Institute).

[19] Cf. John Bowker, *Jesus and the Pharisees* (Cambridge: Cambridge University Press, 1973); and my *Jesus the Jewish Theologian*, 143–54.

[20] See David Flusser, "Sensitivity," in *Origins*, 469–93.

[21] A number of modern NT scholars have achieved a greater appreciation of the Jewish sources of nascent Christianity, as can be seen in the title of James Charlesworth's popular book, *Jesus within Judaism* (Garden City, N.Y.: Doubleday, 1988). Charlesworth acknowledges, "Jesus' teaching was characterized by parables, and by the proclamation

THE FAMILY CRISIS DRAMATIZED

In the Gospel parable, the crisis of the family is dramatized. Personal relationships are shattered as the younger brother asks for his inheritance, sells everything, and leaves home. The elder brother's silence speaks louder than anything he says. His actions at the end of the parable are not surprising because he did nothing to prevent the breakup of the family. The crisis is revealed in what the younger son says as well as in what the elder son does not say. The younger wants his father to die, and the elder quietly receives his double portion of the inheritance, doing nothing to bring reconciliation. Neither of them tries to build a relationship with the other or their father. In the first-century context, such a major family crisis riveted the listener with the shock effect of unusual events.

In fact, the parable is of the classic type that contrasts the actions of two sons. The story could contrast two servants, two sons, two workers, etc.—any such contrast that attracts attention. A fine example is the parable of the Two Sons in Matt 21:28–32. Both sons were asked by their father to work in the vineyard. The first son was impolite to his father and refused to work in the vineyard. In the end, however, he obeyed his father. The second son gave honor to his father and said that he would work in the vineyard. He, however, did not obey. Neither of these two sons was completely righteous in his actions. The surprise ending of the episode evokes the recognition that it is the first son who obeyed, though at first he insulted the dignity of his father. The parable emphasizes that it is never too late to make a decision and to act upon it.[22] The main theme of the parable has strong parallels in early Jewish thought. The ethical and theological point of view expressed in these parables certainly has a place in the context of Judaism in all its diversity during the time of the Second Temple period.[23] The evil prodigal son of the parable turns out to be all right after he comes to himself. It is never too late to make the right decision. The parable contrasts two seemingly different sons who are the same beneath the surface. Both need a meaningful relationship with their father.

---

of the present dawning of God's rule (or the Kingdom of God). These two phenomena, and the Lord's Prayer itself, are deeply Jewish and paralleled abundantly in literature roughly contemporaneous with Jesus" (p. 167). See also the preceding note. On the kingdom of heaven theme and how it relates to the parables and to the teaching of Jesus, see especially my *Jewish Parables*, 189–235.

[22] See Flusser, *Gleichnisse*, 39. In many respects the parable of the Laborers in the Vineyard has a parallel motif, because God's grace is shown to the workers who did not do a full day's work. The other laborers, who had started working early in the day, should have been thankful for the generosity of the landowner. See also my *Jewish Parables*, 259–66.

[23] Flusser has discussed Jewish parallels to this classic type of parable in his *Gleichnisse*, 39, 48 n. 19.

YOUR MONEY OR YOUR LIFE

Life experience teaches that even closely knit families sometimes fall apart when the will of a deceased parent is read. The shock of this story, however, strikes the listener at the beginning, when the son asks for his inheritance before his father's death. These words echo a death wish. The son wants the money more than he desires the life of his father. The request was tantamount to seeking his father's death.

The division of the property is evident at the very beginning of the story. Sadly it has not always been recognized that both sons received their inheritance. This fact is crucial for following the plot of the story and the role of each character. The elder brother received a double portion, two-thirds of the family's accumulated wealth while the younger brother received only one-third. The elder brother's silence shouts at the first-century audience. He quietly receives his share of the money without involving himself with the broken relationships in his family.

Both Joachim Jeremias and David Daube have discussed the Jewish laws of inheritance that can clarify a number of points concerning the parable's setting in life.[24] According to mishnaic law, a father could execute a will even before his death. This is what takes place in the parable of the Prodigal Son. The Jewish law of inheritance describes what happens in the parable. Even so, it would have been presumptuous for the younger son to initiate the execution of the will by the division of the estate while his father was still living. His request would have shocked the original audience of the parable. The provisions of the oral law, however, allowed a father to implement his will before his death. Hence, in accordance with the stipulations of the law, the father in the parable divided his estate between the heirs because of his younger son's request. In this parable, the dramatic shock effect of the story results from a son who takes the initiative and asks his father for the inheritance before his father dies.[25] In essence the younger son was telling his father that he wanted him to die.

According to the provisions of the mishnaic law, the father would retain usufruct rights even if for some reason he divided his estate between his heirs before his death, so he could make use of the estate. He had a legal right to

[24] See the possible interpretations of the Jewish laws regarding inheritance discussed by David Daube, "Inheritance in Two Lukan Pericopes," *ZSRG.R* 72 (1955): 326–34; and the conclusions of Jeremias, *Parables of Jesus*, 128–32. A great deal has been written concerning the legal background of the parable. See also the work of J. Duncan M. Derrett, "Law in the New Testament: the Parable of the Prodigal Son," *NTS* 14 (1967): 56–74. For a working bibliography, by no means complete, see Kissinger, *Parables*, 351–70; and the treatment by Fitzmyer, *Luke*, 2:1092–94.

[25] The son's actions were not at all acceptable, and may have brought to mind Deut 21:18–21 (cf. A. Wünsche, *Erläuterung der Evangelien aus Talmud und Midrasch* [Göttingen: Vandenhoeck & Ruprecht, 1878] 460).

retain a certain amount of control over the sons' property and assets after the will had been executed. The Jewish oral tradition sought to protect an aging parent from possible lack of responsibility by the heirs. This would explain why the father was able to give orders to the servants of the estate (vv. 22–24) after he assigned his living between his two sons (v. 12). In the mishnaic tractate *Baba Bathra* the law states:

> If a man assigned his goods (הכותב נכסיו) to his sons he must write, "From today and after my death." So R. Judah. Rabbi Jose says: He need not do so. If a man assigned his goods to his son to be his after his death, the father cannot sell them since they are assigned (כתובין) to his son, and the son cannot sell them because they are in the father's control (ברשות). If his father sold them, they are sold [only] until he dies; if the son sold them, the buyer has no claim on them until the father dies. The father may pluck up [the crop of a field which he has so assigned] and give to eat to whom he will (שרצה האב תולש ומאכיל לכל מי), and if he left anything already plucked up, it belongs to all his heirs. If he left elder sons and the younger sons, the elder sons may not care for themselves out of the common inheritance at the cost of the younger sons, nor may the younger sons claim maintenance at the cost of the elder sons, but they all share alike.[26]

Jeremias summarizes the implications of the Jewish law in this passage from the Mishnah: "(a) the son obtains the right of possession (the land in question, for example, cannot be sold by the father), (b) but he does not acquire the right of disposal (if the son sells the property, the purchaser can take possession only upon the death of the father), and (c) he does not acquire the usufruct, which remains in the father's unrestricted possession until his death."[27] The law of the Mishnah, or more probably an earlier version of the tradition, apparently was known during the time of Jesus. At least, the father in the story divides his living between his two sons. After he divides his estate, the younger son sells his portion and travels into a land far way. In mishnaic law, the buyer of the inheritance could not take possession of the land until the death of the father. Also, we find that when the son returns, the father can give orders to the servants of the estate. Therefore it is clear that he has been able to retain a limited control over the estate. Again this

---

[26] m. *B. Bat.* 8:7 (*Mishnah,* ed. Albeck, 146; trans. Danby, *Mishnah,* 376); cf. b. *B. Bat.* 136a. See also Sir 33:19–23; b. *B. Metzia* 75b.

[27] Jeremias, *Parables of Jesus,* 128–29. While final conclusions differ from Jeremias, Daube ("Inheritance," 330) observes this facet of Jewish law as described in the talmudic literature: "The father at the same time as he paid off his younger son, made a gift of the rest to the elder, keeping back for himself the usufruct and the running of it for life. This transaction, fully recognized in the Talmud, may be alluded to by the phrase 'he divided unto them the goods,' which, on this premise, would not be inexact at all. The younger son obtained absolute control and enjoyment of his share at once. The elder was also given his share—so that on the father's death there would be nothing for the younger to inherit."

situation is perfectly described in the oral law, because "the father may pluck up the crop of a field which he has so assigned."[28] It is impossible to know with absolute certainty that the mishnaic law as stated in m. *B. Bat.* 8:7 was in existence at the time of Jesus, but the parable portrays this legal setting with remarkable precision.

While the Mishnah passage may represent a later formulation of the oral tradition, there is little reason to doubt that the mishnaic law was in effect at that time. Moreover, it seems that this law was assumed to be common knowledge by Jesus the storyteller, because he makes a parable that illustrates the family laws of inheritance with exactitude. One should not doubt that the laws of inheritance would have been well known, because the disposition of family possessions was a major concern that affected the everyday life of the people. Nonetheless, it would seem that the son displayed considerable audacity when he asked his father for his portion of the inheritance before his father died. It was as if a child said to his parent, "Drop dead! I want your money."

THE THREE ACTORS

The parable has three actors. Each of them plays a very significant role in the drama. Each one of them surprises the audience. The audience expects the actor to play a different role. Jesus loves to use role reversal in his parabolic teachings to break normal expectations. He shocks the listener by turning the world upside down. The audience probably expects the elder son to fill the role of a family mediator. Instead, he acts out the part of a greedy hypocrite. It expects the younger son to die of starvation rather than accept the shame of returning to his father. It would have understood severe punishment from a father who suffered such abuse from his sons. Instead, the audience is overwhelmed by his compassion. The plot of the story and the unexpected role reversals make a lively drama that captures the attention of the listeners and leads them to embrace the type of love that comes from God alone. Here we will begin with the elder son, consider the family crisis created by the younger, and learn from the compassion of a committed parent.

THE FAMILY MEDIATOR OR THE GREEDY HYPOCRITE

The obedient son of the parable is just as lost as his younger brother, but in different ways. He separated himself from his father's love by doing good and being a model of obedience. In that regard, his conduct is fine—but his

[28] The financial implications of this aspect of the law should not be forgotten. The elder brother would have realized that, because of the father's usufruct rights, the return of his younger brother could place some of the remaining family assets at risk.

heart relationship with his father and brother is fragmented from the very beginning of the parable. According to Middle Eastern culture and Jewish traditional values, such an elder son would hold the position of mediator in a family crisis. When the younger son asked for the inheritance, the responsibility and obligation of the elder son was clear to the first-century listener. The father should have been told to leave the matter in the hands of the elder son, because the younger boy did not really mean what he said or realize how much such a request would hurt his father. The elder son should have demanded that his younger brother apologize to their father. As mediator, the elder brother could have sought reconciliation between his brother and their father.

Instead he silently waited for his share of the property and family assets. By not doing anything, he was just as wrong as his younger brother. As can be seen in his speech at the conclusion of the parable, he viewed his father strictly from a commercial perspective. The older son based his relationship to his father on finances. He boasts about his faithful service to his father and reveals his true feelings when he speaks about his father as a boss to be obeyed or a banker to be respected. He is interested only in the money that he deserves and the reward that, in his view, he has earned by his hard work. He does not love his father as a parent or see the needs of his younger brother. Instead of the family mediator the elder boy became a greedy opportunist.

The older son is often thought to have been in the right until his brother returned home. After the younger son had hurt his father and wasted his family's life savings, the elder brother may have felt justified in being angry at the joyous celebration over the return of the prodigal. But at the beginning of the crisis he had been silent. Because of his inaction he shared the guilt for what had happened. He had not seized the opportunity to act. One cannot assume that such conduct would be accepted without criticism. The original audience would have understood his obligation to mediate between his father and younger brother.[29] But if the inheritance was divided early, before the father's death, the elder brother would receive his portion of the estate along with the younger brother.[30] Thus the listeners learn (v. 12) that the father "divided his living between them" (διεῖλεν αὐτοῖς τὸν βίον).

The interpreter must listen to the silence of the elder brother. Since he was to receive twice as much of the estate, his lack of initiative may well have been influenced by the financial benefit of not doing anything. In all events, he does nothing to bring about reconciliation between the family members.[31] While he is a model of obedience, he does only what is required. While he

---

[29] Bailey's insight (*Poet and Peasant; Peasant Eyes*) into Middle Eastern culture and thought has further elucidated this point.

[30] Fitzmyer has observed (*Luke*, 2:1087), "In any case, the firstborn son was to inherit or receive a 'double portion,' i.e. twice the amount that would be given to each of the other sons. See Deut. 21:17. In this case, since there were only two sons, the elder would receive two thirds and the younger one third of the property."

[31] See preceding note.

does not disobey his father, he fails to fulfill the role of mediator. The original audience would have seen through him. They understood his pretense at the very beginning of the story, long before he humiliates his father at the banquet given in honor of his brother.

Here the elder brother also had a broken relationship with his father, whom he viewed primarily as a source of money. Note the elder brother's reaction when he discovers that his brother has come back home and that his father is celebrating the prodigal's safe return: "Lo, these many years I have served you, and I never disobeyed your command" (v. 29). The younger brother had the same difficulty, though the problem manifested itself in a different way. The elder brother viewed his father as an employer who must be obeyed instead of a parent who must be loved. The younger son viewed his father in a similar fashion. When he finally decided to return to his father's house, he rehearsed his speech: "I am no longer worthy to be called your son; treat me as one of your hired servants."[32] The younger son also considered his father merely as a banker who controlled the finances and paid a wage. When he returned, the father interrupted his speech about becoming a hired servant. He was restored as beloved son into the father's care.

The broken relationships are clear in the older son's speech to his father in the outer courtyard. He does not address his father with a title of honor. He fails to acknowledge any family ties with his brother. The pronouns used in the speech communicate the situation effectively. He refers to the prodigal as "this son of yours," which stresses his determination to break all ties with his brother. He laments the fact that his father never made a celebration in his honor with his friends. He has no part with his father and those members of the community who have gathered to celebrate the restored fellowship between the father and his wayward son. The community is rejoicing with the father, but the older son insults his father and the guests by refusing to join in the festivities. His father implores him to accept his brother who was dead but now has come back to them alive and well.

The theological concept portrayed in the story has deep roots in postbiblical Judaism. The elevated religious idea that one cannot serve God merely for the sake of personal benefit or for the sake of receiving a reward and of avoiding punishment is already reflected in the saying of Antigonus of Socho (second century B.C.E.): "Be not like slaves that serve the master for the sake of receiving a reward, but be like slaves that serve the master not for the sake of receiving a reward and let the fear of Heaven be upon

[32]Though some manuscripts have added the phrase "treat me as one of your hired servants" to the conversation between the younger son and his father after he returns (v. 21), this phrase is certainly an addition from the rehearsed speech in v. 19 (see Metzger, *Textual Commentary*, 164). The difference may be significant. Apparently the father will not allow his wayward son to make his offer of repayment but, rather, accepts his return in compassion and restores him without further question. Hence the story further speaks of the unmerited love of a father for his son.

you" (*Abot* 1:3).[33] In Jewish thought, God was not considered an employer who paid a wage but was more accurately conceived of as a father who desired a proper relationship with his children. He is to be served not in order to receive compensation but out of love.[34]

THE REBELLIOUS BOY OR THE TRUE SON

The man's younger boy is a rebel to the core. It is unthinkable that a child would ask his father for the inheritance before his father dies. But after committing this terrible offense, to make matters even worse, he sells everything and runs away. At heart this boy is insubordinate and recalcitrant like the rebel child of Deut 21:20, whom his parents bring before the elders of the city with the complaint, "This our son is stubborn and rebellious." The younger boy is disobedient and seeks to flee as far away from his father as possible. As a blatant sinner, he defies his father's love. After implying that his father should drop dead, he takes the inheritance and turns all his assets into cash.[35] Then he runs away to a far country. One third of the accumulated wealth of the family is liquidated. The buyers of the property will not be able to take possession of their newly bought land until the father dies. Perhaps they could obtain such property at exceptional value because of these special terms relating to the sale. The younger son takes his money and travels as far away from his family as is possible.

In *Poet and Peasant* Bailey reports one occasion in the Middle East when a son asked his father for his inheritance before his father died. The father was a physician and in good health. "In great anguish" the father reported to his pastor, " 'My son wants me to die!' The concerned pastor discovered that the son had broached the question of the inheritance. Three months later the

[33] On the early tradition behind this saying in *Abot*, see L. Finkelstein, *Haperushim Veanshe Keneset Hagedolah* (New York: Jewish Theological Seminary, 1950) 40–45. Perhaps more than other scholars, Flusser has observed the pervading influence this approach had on early Jewish thought. On Antigonus's saying he notes, "Yet we have to bear in mind that this logion is but *one* expression of a new, profound sensitivity that developed within Judaism, which later on was so much taken for granted that it became a second nature, a sensitivity that, in turn, Christianity took over from contemporary Judaism." Flusser concludes, "If we now take into consideration the many references in rabbinic literature that compare the awe and the love of God as superior modes of worship, we find that in the majority of these passages love is rated superior to awe in the service of God. . . . This superior rating of love over awe prevailed and took hold upon all Jewish groups" ("Sensitivity," 110–11 [*Origins*, 472–73]).

[34] Ibid., especially Flusser.

[35] Here the aorist participle indicates the purpose of gathering all together, i.e., selling all. See J. Nolland, *Luke* (WBC; 3 vols.; Dallas: Word, 1989–93) 2:783: "συνάγειν, 'to gather together,' is used in Plutarch, *Cato Min.* 6.7 (672c) of converting an inheritance into cash, and may be so used here." Probably the original audience thought of all property and possessions being sold.

father . . . died. The mother said, 'He died that night!' meaning that the night the son dared ask his father for the inheritance the father 'died.' "[36] While modern examples from the Middle East must be used with great caution when exploring the cultural context of the first century, it is quite possible that this story provides some insight. At least, in light of the law of inheritance in the Mishnah, which constantly refers to the death of the father, such a request for the inheritance from the son would be like telling his father that he wished he were dead. The original audience hearing such a tale is in shock. What will the father do? Severe punishment or complete rejection would not be out of the question.

Instead the father divides the inheritance between his two sons. The elder quietly receives his share while the younger son converts his share into money. The dream of many rural boys is travel, and he is eager to leave his family far behind. He takes his money and travels to a faraway country, where he wastes his inheritance going his own way. Like many runaway children, the boy has lost his support base in the relationships of his family. Without skill or training he is vulnerable. The younger son lives the life of a playboy until his money is gone and a great famine sweeps through the land. A food shortage hurts the poor and the homeless first. The severity of the situation, however, seems to have affected everyone in the land. Food is the precious commodity that is lacking. When he becomes desperate, the rebel son realizes his mistake. His broken relationship with his father has placed him in exile. He is far from home and the traditional values with which he is familiar. The inheritance did not last long in his wasteful way of living.

The powerful famine sweeping through the far country has reduced him to absolute poverty. Out of his hunger, he joins himself with one of the citizens of that country, an obvious reference to a non-Jew. The wealth of the citizen is implied by the terminology used to describe him. Even during the time of famine, this citizen of the land has livestock, and the poor seek his benevolence. By making himself valuable to a wealthy person of the land, the boy hopes to receive food. He tries to ingratiate himself to this Gentile by doing him favors and begging for a gratuity. The situation is most desperate. Jesus is artistically drawing a picture of life with a broken relationship. In exile and at the mercy of a heartless Gentile, the poor Jewish boy tries to alleviate his hunger. By placing himself in the service of the Gentile, he hopes to receive some benevolence. The non-Jew obviously wants to get rid of the boy. Perhaps the anti-Semitism of the Greco-Roman world is portrayed in this illustration of the boy's deprivation. The Gentile sends him to feed the pigs, apparently knowing how offensive swine would be to a Jew. The parable teller builds upon the Jewish audience's repugnance for eating pork. The privileged son of a landowner

[36] Bailey, *Poet and Peasant,* 162 n. 73.

from the land of Israel is reduced to feeding pigs. In the end, the Jewish boy is completely rejected.

The text says that no one gave the young man anything. While the citizen of the land has fodder for the pigs, he does not give food to the young Jewish boy. It is more important to care for the pigs than to feed a son of Abraham. Not only is he reduced to feeding the swine; he would gladly have "filled his belly" with the pigs' fodder.[37] This fodder, κεράτιον, is usually identified as the pod of a carob tree.[38] The pods of the carob tree are sometimes described as the food of the poor. The parable seems to illustrate graphically the great poverty of the young man. In fact, as has often been noted, in later Jewish literature the rabbis made a play on words between the Hebrew terms for sword, *chareb* (חרב), in Isa. 1:21 and carob pod, *charob* (חרוב), the food of the poor. When times are prosperous, it is difficult for the people to remember God. But when they are in need and want food, they repent and seek him. When the people are desperate, they will seek to eat carob to survive.

The Carob and Repentance

> This may be deduced from the Bible text, "If ye be willing and obedient, ye shall eat of the good of the land; But if ye refuse and rebel, ye shall be devoured with the sword" [or eat carob]. R. Acha said Israel needs carob [*i.e.* poverty] to be forced to repentance [*i.e.* only when Israel are reduced to such a state of poverty that they must eat carob do they repent of their evil ways].[39]

When poverty causes the people to eat the carob pod, then they seek God in repentance. While it is doubtful that this interpretation was widely circulating during the time of Jesus, it does indicate that the carob pods were used as food for the poor. In the minds of the sages, poverty could lead the people into a recognition of their need for God. In the experience of the younger son, his desperate need leads him to seek restoration to his father. In his desire for restoration, he is even willing to pay back what has been lost.

When he comes to himself, out of desperation the boy realizes his responsibility for the wrong. He wants to make matters right. His repentance is based more on his own need than a theological revelation. Indeed, he seems to view his father more as a bank manager than as a loving parent, but this attitude is rooted in his sense of shame for the wrongs he has committed against God and his father. Crucial for proper understanding is the expression "he came to himself." The Greek words, εἰς ἑαυτὸν δὲ ἐλθών, form a dynamic equivalent to the Hebrew phrase חזר בו. In Hebrew and Aramaic

[37] The expression "fill the belly" is somewhat crude and atypical of Lukan style. It would, however, be more fitting in the Hebrew language, which is fond of using references to the body such as hand, foot, mouth, head, or belly.

[38] Cf. P. Lagrange, *The Gospel of Jesus Christ* (2 vols.; Westminster, Md.: Newman, 1951) 2:65: "he is reduced to the desire of filling his empty stomach with the carob pods or locust beans thrown to the swine—no great feast!"

[39] *Lev. Rab.* 35:6, quoted by Feldman, *Parables and Similes,* 124.

such terminology was often used to describe repentance. It refers to a coming home. The issue has been debated among scholars whether the phrase has a Greek background, such as in Epictetus, or the force of a Semitic idiom for repentance.[40] Epictetus describes the young man Polmeo, who sought the vanity of a wayward life's pleasures until he had a radical transformation by coming to himself and discovering the essence of life's meaning. While strong similarities between the young man who "comes to his senses" in Epictetus and the prodigal of the Gospel parable emerge from a comparative study, the story of Jesus is much nearer to the Jewish world of repentance. In the Gospel parable, the wayward son returns home. In fact, numerous rabbinic parables use the same imagery and language in describing repentance. In the same way that a loving father will receive a rebellious child who returns home, God in his mercy will receive the one who has done wrong. The Hebrew phrase חזר בו is the exact equivalent of the parable's Greek εἰς ἑαυτὸν ἐλθών. It means that the young man repents of his wrong. He is ready to come home. He desires to pay back what he has wasted.

While the phrase "come to oneself" is known in both Greek and Hebrew (and Aramaic), it is far better to see a Semitic background for its use in the parable. Though Luke reveals a rich knowledge of Greek but only a little understanding of Semitic languages outside of the linguistic influence of his sources, the parable of the Prodigal Son is imbued with the flavor of Hebrew. For instance, though Luke almost always changes the wording of his source from the word "heaven" to "God" to clarify the meaning for his readers, in the parable the younger boy declares that he sinned against "heaven," i.e., God himself. The Jewish background of the boy is brought out because he uses a circumlocution for God, like many pious Jews during this period. His repentance is deep and sincere. He is anxious to pay back all that he has wasted. He is ashamed of his wrongs. His sense of shame makes him feel unworthy to be treated as a son. His sin is against heaven, i.e., God himself, as much as against his earthly father. The fact that he is owning his wrong before God as well as before his father makes it clear that he is repenting for the terrible wrongs that he had committed. The use of the term "heaven" as a circumlocution for God is widely recognized in Jewish literature. Luke studiously avoids it, often replacing the more Semitic phrase "kingdom of heaven" with "kingdom of God." Here he fails to make the change, probably indicating the early source of the parable. At the least, this type of language came before the editing of Luke's Gospel.

When the son returns, the father does not even allow him to complete his eloquent speech about becoming a hired servant. Instead he puts a ring on his finger, which again reflects the Semitic language of Luke's source. The young man is restored as a son rather than as a hired servant. It is probably

---

[40] Cf. BAGD 311: "εἰς ἑαυτὸν [ἔρχομαι] *come to oneself* (= to one's senses) (Diod. S. 13, 95, 2; Epict. 3, 1, 15; Test. Jos. 3: 9; Sb 5763, 35) Lk 15:17."

a signet ring that is placed on the boy's finger, which gave him some access to the father's financial resources. In all events, the wording has often been recognized as a Semitism. T. W. Manson observed, " 'Put a ring,' literally 'give a ring.' The Greek reflects the Semitic idiom whereby the verb 'to give' is used in the sense of 'to place.' "[41]

The Semitic atmosphere created by the story is directly linked with language. The boy runs away to a "far country." This is fine Hebrew imagery.[42] The boy experiences a strong famine and feeds pigs. He would "fill his belly" with the pods. Such a phrase is unseemly for Luke's Greek, but Semitic languages love idioms using the terms for the body: one holds an object "in the hand," words are not merely spoken but proceed forth from "the mouth," and here the boy longs to fill "his belly." The hired servants of his father have "bread" enough and to spare. In Hebrew, "bread," by way of extension, refers to all the physical needs of the person. The boy was lost but is found, he was dead but is made alive. This strong condemnation of his wrong employs Semitic parallelism by using sharp contrasts between lost and found as well as between death and life. Again, the imagery of the parable recalls the rich terminology of Hebrew. Without a doubt, the expression "he came to himself" is best understood as the Hebrew or Aramaic terminology for repentance. The essence of repentance in Jewish thought means to come home. The core meaning is clearly portrayed in the story of a wayward boy who returns to his father. In a Hebrew setting of first-century Israel, the boy's action in the parable defines repentance by a dramatic portrayal of a family crisis.

Even with the joyful celebration begun by the father at the prodigal's return, the reference to dead and lost is a clear description of the wayward son. He had done serious wrong. While he broke the commandments, his greatest sin is his broken relationship with his father, the cause of all wrong-doing in his life. He must go back home and make matters right with his father.

THE COMPASSIONATE FATHER OR THE BANKER

The major role in the parable is played by the compassionate father. He loves his sons enough to allow them the freedom to make their own decisions. Even when they make the wrong choices, he is waiting and willing to help them. The comparison between God and the compassionate father of the parable would be obvious to a first-century audience.[43] Jesus could compare the all-powerful God in Jewish traditional thought to a helpless parent. After

---

[41] Manson, *Sayings*, 289.

[42] In rabbinic literature this is a מדינת הים, "province of the sea," which appears in the parable as a faraway land with no Jewish citizens. In Hebrew it is literally ארץ רחוקה. The same idea pervades several rabbinic parables.

[43] Such would be clear at least from the later rabbinic parables.

all, no parent can control the will of a child. The correspondence to God is striking, for, like the helpless father of the parable, the Creator of heaven and earth allows people to choose even when they make the wrong choice.[44] Some make decisions like the younger son, and others are more like the elder. The caring parent is always waiting and willing to help the children with their individual needs. The father of the parable is willing to give all for the well-being of his boys.

God is like the compassionate father of the parable. He is eager to receive each one who comes to him. He allows his children the freedom to choose. Even if they make the wrong choices and bring disaster, he is always ready to accept them back into the family when they return home. The interpreter must find this type of father in rabbinic parables to appreciate his actions in the Gospel story. A father will receive his son even if he has done serious wrong and broken all the rules. A son must never be ashamed of returning to his father.

No one should miss the strong links the parable has to the Jewish theology of the period and how it reminds the listeners of the nature of God and the need of each individual to respond not only to the divine expression of compassion but also to forgive and to accept the outcast. The theme is not entirely new or revolutionary in its message, but it is powerful and innovative in the way that it is expressed.

The Gospel text's high view of a compassionate God and his concern for every person can be clearly seen in the message of rabbinic parables. One example is especially near to the illustration of the prodigal son in Luke. The parable deals with the theme of repentance and God's parentlike desire to forgive and to receive the one who repents with joy and acceptance. It is attributed to R. Meir in the text of *Deuteronomy Rabbah:*

The Compassionate Father and His Lost Son

Another explanation: "You will return [ושבת] to the LORD thy God (Deut. 4:30)." R. Samuel Pragrita said in the name of R. Meir: To what may this matter be compared? To the son of a king who took to evil ways. The king sent a tutor to him who appealed to him saying, "Repent, my son [חזור בך בני]." The son, however, sent him back to his father [with the message], "How can I have the effrontery to return? I am ashamed to come before you [באלו פנים אני חוזר בי ואני מתבייש לפניך]." Thereupon his father sent back word, "My son, is a son ever ashamed to return to his father? And is it not to your father that you will be returning?" Thus the Holy One blessed be He, sent Jeremiah to Israel when they sinned, and said to him: "Go, say to My children, Return." Where do we learn this? It is said, "Go and proclaim these words . . ." (Jer. 3:12). Israel asked Jeremiah, "How can we have the effrontery to return to God?" How do we know this? It is said, "Let us lie down in our shame, and let our confusion

[44] The Dead Sea sect, teaching predetermination, could not accept the message of the parable.

cover us . . ." (Jer. 3:25). But God sent them word, "My children, if you return, will you not be returning to your Father?" How do we know this? "For I am a father to Israel . . ." (Jer. 31:9).[45]

The theological worldviews of the parable of the Prodigal Son and the rabbinic parallel are identical. The concept of God, the need of every human being, and the desire for reconciliation are clear. The concept of God as a compassionate father who desires a relationship with his children is the same in both. The rebellious son who goes into a far country and needs reconciliation with his father in the parable of the Prodigal Son is also seen in the rabbinic text. Here R. Meir's parable is closely related to the biblical text of Jeremiah, which calls the tribes of the north to return to their father in heaven, whom they have abandoned. Hence they have suffered exile to a far country. Their rebellion against the God of compassion is complete because they have taken to evil ways and have involved themselves in idolatrous worship. They have committed the ultimate sin. In *Deuteronomy Rabbah* the text is closely related to the verse in Deut 4:30, "you will return [i.e., repent] to the LORD your God."

Jeremiah is given the task of calling the wayward people back to a compassionate God, who will forgive the most serious of all transgressions. In the minds of the rabbis, idolatry denied the very essence of God and was the greatest evil. The people had broken the first of the Ten Commandments and violated the sacred affirmation of Deut 6:4, "Hear O Israel: the LORD our God is one LORD." The rabbinic parable views the transgression in light of individual action as well as corporate responsibility. Each individual person can see himself or herself in the son of the parable. When every person returns to the worship of the one God, the nation will receive restoration. The rich imagery of a father who reaches out to his wayward son is a development of the theme of Jeremiah, where God is referred to as the Father of Israel.

The parable in *Deuteronomy Rabbah* is preserved in the name of R. Meir, one of the five disciples of R. Akiva.[46] It should be remembered that Meir

---

[45] *Deut. Rab.* 2:24. See *Midrash Rabbah* (2 vols.; Wilna: Wittwa & Gebrüder Romm, 1887); and the new edition with commentary by the Institute of Midrash Hamevuar, ed. A. Steinberger (Jerusalem: Hanachal, 1983) 81. Israel Abrahams observed the theme of the two sons as parallel to the Prodigal story in *Studies,* 1.92. Paul Fiebig had already noted the importance of this parable from the regular edition of *Deuteronomy Rabbah* for the study of the parable of the Prodigal Son. Cf. P. Fiebig, *Rabbinische Gleichnisse* (Leipzig: J. C. Hinrichs, 1929) 35; *Die Gleichnisreden Jesu* (Tübingen: J. C. B. Mohr, 1912) 197ff. This had already been discussed by A. Wünsche, *Erläuterung,* 460–61. Concerning the difficulties with the methodology of Fiebig, see Young, *Jewish Parables,* 22–26.

[46] See Bacher, *Tannaiten*, 2:59, discussing this parable and the life of R. Meir. E. P. Sanders also has related this parable of R. Meir to the Prodigal Son in *Paul and Palestinian Judaism* (London: SCM, 1977) 178; see also note 159, where Sanders observed the same theme in the similar parable in *Midrash Acher,* which is printed in *Bet Hamidrash,* ed. A. Jellinek (6 vols.; Jerusalem: Wahrmann, 1967), 1:21ff.

was made a disciple by the learned master Elisha ben Avuya, who later departed from the faith and was referred to as *acher*, literally, "the other." *Acher* came to be viewed as a heretic who not only rejected the true belief in God but also failed in the practice of Judaism, where ritual observance is highly esteemed. After *acher* abandoned his belief in the God of Israel and become involved in some form of theosophic speculation, R. Meir longed to see his beloved master return to the faith of his people.[47] In a legendary account, the talmudic literature explains how R. Meir tried to convince his former teacher to repent. Some evidence may be found for Elisha ben Avuyah's repentance, and it is possible, though not entirely certain, that he returned to his faith immediately before his death.[48] Hence R. Meir is known for his teachings concerning repentance. He is also celebrated for his teaching in parables. Several parables have also been preserved in the name of Elisha ben Avuyah. Rabbi Meir learned the art of telling parables from his contemporaries. Though the memory of the wit and humor of his illustrations left a lasting impression on R. Meir's numerous disciples, many of his parables have not been preserved in the literature, and it may be that some of the stories attributed to him are derived from a later period. Probably many more parables circulated within the world of Jewish learning in late antiquity that have not been preserved. Enough parables have come down to the modern scholar, however, to indicate the wealth of thought and depth of expression these powerful illustrations portrayed. Rabbi Meir's parable of "The Compassionate Father and His Lost Son" in *Deuteronomy Rabbah* is a fine example of the significance of repentance in Jewish thought. A father, according to the parable, will always be anxious to welcome his rebellious boy who comes home. Although *Deuteronomy Rabbah* was compiled later, it is quite possible that the illustration is derived from an authentic memory of Rabbi Meir's teaching in the oral tradition. In any case, the theme of repentance and God's compassion toward a wayward child is characteristic of Meir's teaching.

Moreover, the theme of repentance, and God's willingness to accept the person who truly repented, became an integral part of Jewish faith and practice. The day of Atonement and the days of awe preceding the New Year emphasized the urgent need for individuals to restore faith with each other and with God. The homiletical midrash *Pesiqta Rabbati* also preserves a rabbinic parable that deals with the theme of repentance. If a person will make the first step toward God, God will help to complete the return. The

---

[47] See j. *Chag.* 77b, ch. 2, halakah 1; b. *Chag.* 16b. R. Meir calls Elisha b. Avuyah to repent [חזור בך], but *acher* refuses to listen to his disciple.

[48] Ibid. See also Hyman, *Toldot*, 1:155–57. At least, R. Meir felt that his master had repented at the point of death. In addition, see the important study of these texts in David Halpern, *The Merkabah in Rabbinic Literature* (New Haven: American Oriental Society, 1980) 167–70.

parable has many similarities with the text from *Deuteronomy Rabbah* but seems to be derived from another source. A son has run away to a far country. He needs his father's help to return home. The parable dramatizes the experience of repentance for the listener. The divine love and compassion for the person who has gone astray is evident.

The Compassionate Father and His Runaway Son

> "Return, O Israel, to the LORD your God" (Hos. 14:2). The matter may be compared to the son of a king who was far away from his father—a hundred days' journey. His friends said to him, "Return to your father!" He replied, "I am not able." His father sent him a message, "Come as far as you are able according to your own strength and I will come to you the rest of the way!" Thus the Holy One Blessed be He said, "Return to me and I will return to you" (Mal. 3:7).[49]

According to the concept of repentance as taught by Israel's sages, if a person will do what he or she can in his or her own strength to start the journey home, God will respond and provide all the help that is needed. He will give more strength to help the person complete his or her return home. Like the parable of Rabbi Meir from *Deuteronomy Rabbah,* the illustration from *Pesiqta Rabbati* is closely related to the parable of the Prodigal Son. The rabbinic counterpart reflects the same theological themes. God yearns for the return of his people. They may have run away to a far country. Even if it is a hundred days' journey away, they must only go as far as they can in initiating their return. God will go the rest of the way to meet them.

Another very important parallel to these rabbinic illustrations appears in the text of *Deuteronomy Rabbah* published by Saul Lieberman. The parable stresses the friction between father and son. The clear disobedience is emphasized in the intense family argument. The compassionate father of the story calls upon his son always to remember that, no matter what happens to him because of his direct disobedience, a sinful son will be welcomed home by his father. Even though the son's misfortune is a direct result of his rebellion, the father will always be ready to receive him.

---

[49] *Pesiq. Rab.* 44 (*Pesikta Rabbati,* ed. Friedmann, 184b–185a). See the translation by W. Braude, *Pesikta Rabbati* (2 vols.; New Haven: Yale University Press, 1968) 2:779. The context of this parable is important. Braude notes in his summary, "Israel's repentance moves God to annul his own edicts. . . . Repentance soars straight up to God. Even if the heap of a man's iniquity reaches all the way up to God, return to God is possible" (pp. 769–70). Consider the significance of this text and its place in rabbinic thought in light of M. Kadushin's discussion of God's love and compassion in his work, *The Theology of Seder Eliahu: A Study in Organic Thinking* (New York: Bloch, 1932) 108–62. W. O. E. Oesterley's popular study, *The Gospel Parables in the Light of Their Jewish Background* (New York: Macmillan, 1936) 186–87, saw the strong reference to confession and repentance in the parable of the Prodigal Son.

The Compassionate Father and His Obstinate Son

> R. Abbahu in the name of R. Yose ben Chalafta, it is written, "When you beget children . . ." (Deut. 4:25) and it is written, "I call heaven and earth to witness against you this day . . ." (Deut. 4:26). To what may Israel be compared? To the son of a man who said to his father, "I intend to depart into a far country by way of the sea." The father warned, "But the time for sailors to ship out for sea has already passed!" He was vehement about the matter and argued, "You must understand that if you go to sea now, you face certain destruction! In the end your ship will be wrecked and all that you own will be lost. Listen I am telling you that if you disobey my word and insist on going to sea, all these things will happen to you which I have warned you about. However even if the ship is wrecked, you lose everything in it and all of your personal belongings are swept away and only you yourself are delivered, remember one thing. Do not be ashamed to return to me. Do not say, 'How can I have the effrontery to return to father [Abba].' Now I am telling you, even if you disobey and all these terrible things happen to you—you must never be ashamed to return to me and I will surely receive you." Thus the Holy One said to Israel, "I call heaven and earth to testify against you . . ." (Deut. 4:26). Thus he called them, "But from there you will seek the LORD your God, and you will find him, if you search after him with all your heart and with all your soul. When you are in tribulation, and all these things come upon you in the latter days, you will return to the LORD your God and obey his voice, for the LORD your God is a merciful God . . ." (Deut. 4:29–30). And also he affirmed, "And when you beget children . . ." (Deut. 4:25).[50]

The rabbinic parable attributed to R. Abbahu in the name of R. Yose ben Chalafta dramatizes the meaning of repentance by showing the correspondence between a human parent and God. The son in the story has decided on a journey to a far country, a plot also contained in the Gospel parable of the prodigal. The father pleads with his son not to leave home. The far country is emblematic of living a life of rebellion against God. The father of the story is called "Abba." He pleads with his son, "Do not be ashamed to return to me. Do not say, 'How can I have the effrontery to return to father [Abba].'" In rabbinic thought, it is never too late for the sinner to repent and receive divine compassion.

The rabbinic parables, like the illustration of the prodigal son, are filled with the great imagery of divine mercy, which is always bestowed on the person who truly repents. This example models God's grace in the drama of a son who disobeys his father. Like the prodigal in the Gospels, his sense of shame is immense. In desperation after losing everything at sea, he might be tempted to ask himself, "How can I have the effrontery to return to my father after such willful disobedience?" The message of the father echos the senti-

---

[50] *Midrash Devarim Rabbah,* ed. S. Liebermann (Jerusalem: Wahrmann Books, 1974), 55. This is my translation.

ment from the Gospel text. A child should never be ashamed to return home. The love of a compassionate parent is unlimited.

In the same way, God is compassionate and longs for the repentance of his people. The people themselves have a great need to return to their God. The sin is so immense that they are ashamed to seek repentance. At least in like manner, the son in the parable feels the weight of his wrong and does not wish to return to his father. How can he return when his sin is so great? The prophet Jeremiah refers to God as the father of the Jewish people.[51] They have rejected their father and have sinned by committing idolatry and false worship of foreign gods. How can they have the audacity to seek forgiveness? In the midrash, R. Meir refers to God as the father who sends the messenger to encourage his son to return home. The son sends word to his father that he cannot have the effrontery to return, i.e., to repent. The father is even more vehement. He does not give up but sends his son another message. No matter how great the transgression, a compassionate father is always eager to receive his son.

In "The Compassionate Father and His Runaway Son," the rebellious boy has gone a hundred days' journey and does not have the strength to return home. His compassionate father sends word that he will come to meet him. All he must do is to make the first step and go as far as he is able. The father will do the rest. In "The Compassionate Father and the Obstinate Son," Rabbi Abbahu in the name of Rabbi Yose ben Chalafta dramatizes the breakup of a relationship between father and son in a heated argument. The son wants to ship out. The father believes it is too dangerous. The willful boy is determined to break his father's word and disobey. The father vehemently pleads with his rebellious son that no matter what happens, he must always remember that he is welcome to come home. No distance is too great and no disobedience is too rebellious. Like a parent who loves his or her child, God has compassion for the sinner who returns home from a far country.

In the parable of the Prodigal Son, the father is not so intent on calling his wayward sons. The listener senses his helplessness, which is related to the silence of the elder brother. Unlike the rabbinic parallel, the father in the Gospel story does not argue and try to convince his two lost sons of their wrongs.[52] He is, however, ready to receive them when they repent. His compassion is strong, but he does not try to persuade his sons until the conclusion of the drama. At the end of the parable, the compassionate father pleads vehemently with the elder brother to receive his brother, who was lost but has been found. The father takes a more prominent role in dialogue and interaction with the older boy, who refuses to forgive the younger.

In the rabbinic parables, the wayward son is always called upon to return home to his compassionate father, who will not allow the serious transgression

---

[51] Jer 3:4, 19; 31:8–9.

[52] In Luke 15:31–32, the father does explain to his elder son the reason for gladness and hopes that the elder son will respond to his example of loving acceptance.

to break the relationship. All the parables view sin more as a broken line of fellowship that results from misunderstanding the divine character than as merely violating a religious precept. The Prodigal Son has a miniparable attached to it. The man had two sons, and the elder has conflict both with his father and his brother. The story illustrates the need for each person to forgive and to accept the outcast. The rabbinic parables do not contain this second motif, but it should be remembered that the concept of forgiveness for the outcast and for one's fellow who has given offense is deeply embedded in ancient Jewish thought. The idea itself is clearly articulated in the text of Sirach, and the theme is greatly emphasized during the day of Atonement in the Mishnah.[53] No one can approach the Almighty and request forgiveness for his transgressions unless first he has forgiven his neighbor for every wrong. The parable of the Unmerciful Servant in Matthew clearly expresses this high ethical code.[54] The rabbinic parable focuses upon the theme of God's great compassion for his children and his active concern that they will accept him.

The similarities between the Gospel parable of the Prodigal Son and its rabbinic counterparts are striking indeed. The theological significance of the details of each of these powerful stories emerges in the compelling image of a concerned father reaching out to disobedient children who need his love. The identity of theological content of the two parables marks the close relationship between their original settings. Both stories betray their deep roots in the Jewish thought and religious piety of the time of Jesus.

THE STORY THAT DOES NOT END

The precision of storytelling technique emerges in the courtyard scene. The father has left the joyous festivities to rush outside. His older son is angry and refuses to go inside. On such an occasion he would be expected to serve as a gracious host and at least pretend that he is pleased to see his long

---

[53] See Sir 28:2; m. *Yoma* 8:9 (Albeck, 247). The teaching that divine forgiveness is dependent upon reconciliation between individuals, as stated in m. *Yoma* 8:9, is attributed to Eleazar ben Azaryah in *Sifra* on Lev 16:30 (*Sifra*, ed. Weiss, 83 a–b). On the prayers of the synagogue, cf. S. Goldschmidt, *Seder Haselihot* (Jerusalem: Mosad Derav Kook, 1975). The high idea of forgiveness between individuals as a step toward divine forgiveness is well documented in ancient Jewish thought. See, e.g., *T. Zeb.* 5:3; 8:1–3; *T. Gad* 6:3–7; *T. Iss.* 5:2; 7:6; *T. Dan* 5:3. Note also that the concept pervades rabbinic thought; see, e.g., the talmudic sources, *Mekilta Derabbi Simeon Bar Yochai* on Ex. 12:32 (ed. Epstein and Melamed, 231); *Mekilta Derabbi Yishmael* on Exod 15:21 (*Mekhilta Derabbi Ishmael*, ed. Horovitz and Rabin, 127); *Sifre Zuta* on Num 6:26 (*Sifre Al Bemidbar Vesifre Zuta*, ed. Horovitz, 248); *Eliyahu Rabbah* (*Seder Eliyahu Rabbah*, ed. Friedmann, 86–87, 109, 157); t. *B. Kam.* 9:27; b. *Shabb.* 151b; and *Tg. Ps.-J.* on Lev 22:28.

[54] Matt 18:23–35; cf. Matt 5:8, 6:12, 14–15; Mark 11:25; Luke 11:4, 6:37 (cf. Col 3:13). See the preceding note.

lost brother, who had made it back home. Instead, he is fuming with anger out in the courtyard. The father and son engage in a heated argument. But the conclusion of the exchange remains uncertain. The listener does not know what happened. The story does not end.

Parables often lead the listener on a collision course with destiny. Each one who follows the path of the drama must make a decision. The listener is invited to step up onto the stage of the play and act out the final scene. In reality, the conflict could be resolved in two different ways. Everything depends on the final decision of the elder brother, i.e., the listener.

JESUS AND THE PHARISEES

With regard to the parable of the Compassionate Father and the Two Lost Sons, Jesus and the Pharisees had much in common. Like Jesus, the Pharisees stressed God's willingness to receive the wayward sinner who repents. At least when studying the religious and ethical teachings of the rabbis who are the spiritual descendants of the Pharisees, one encounters a strong outreach to sinners. No matter how wrong one has been or what evil conduct has been practiced, the compassionate God is willing to receive each person who repents. In fact, the rabbis stressed the love of God in parables portraying the family relationship. A wayward son will be restored to the care of his father when he returns home. The rabbinic parables call upon the wayward children to come home for the welcome of a caring father.

The impact this high ideology had upon subsequent Jewish thought is considerable. S. Safrai's study of R. Akiva has demonstrated the results of this concept. In *Abot* 3:16, according to the superior reading of the text, Akiva teaches, "All is foreseen, but freedom of will is given, the world is judged by grace and everything is not according to the excess of works [either good or evil]."[55] It is not according to the wages earned but according to divine grace (i.e., טובה, goodness) that people will be judged. The compassionate father of Jesus' parable had two wayward sons, each of whom had gone his own way. Both of these sons had a distorted view of their father's love and parental concern. When the sayings of Antigonus and Akiva are studied in the context of the Second Temple period, it becomes clear that the Gospel parable is closely associated with the thought

[55] S. Safrai discusses the manuscript evidence and presents compelling arguments to accept this reading of *Abot* 3:16, "and all is not according to the excess of works," instead of the reading in many translations, "and all is according to the excess of works." See his "Vehakol Lefi Rov Hameaseh," *Tarbiz* 54 (1984): 33–40; and cf. his work on R. Akiva's life and teachings, *Rabbi Akiva*. Cf. also C. Taylor, *Sayings of the Fathers* (2 vols.; Cambridge: Cambridge University Press, 1877), where some of the manuscript evidence can be seen, although the translation is less than reliable. Safrai's discussion enables us to gain insight into the teaching of Akiva and his emphasis on divine mercy.

that was part and parcel of early Judaism.[56] The emphasis of the parable is on the younger son's recognition of his need and his decision to return to his father. The terminology of the parable, εἰς ἑαυτὸν δὲ ἐλθών, "when he came to himself" (v. 17), and ἀναστὰς πορεύσομαι πρὸς τὸν πατέρα μου, "I will arise and go to my father" (v. 18), reflect the high Jewish concept of repentance. He recognizes his need and desires to return to his father.[57] The theme of repentance was an important part of Israel's worship and the liturgy of the synagogue. The artistry of the story is seen in the fact that the elder brother is left in the courtyard with his father pleading with him.

TWO SONS AND TWO TYPES OF SINNERS

Both of the man's sons were sinners. They represent two types of sinners, but their sins are remarkably similar. Both view their father more as a banker than as a parent. He is the master who controls the finances, and they are laborers who desire more money. They speak about their relationship with their father strictly from their financial ties and work obligations. They view themselves as hired servants in their master's house. As heirs, the younger wants an unlimited overdraft and the elder desires a fat savings account with the prestige of wealth and position. While they seem so different in the way they go about obtaining what they want, they are really quite similar. The message of the story stresses that love is a relationship. The commandment is important. They violated the commandment. But of even greater significance than the commandments is the relationship. Fellowship

[56] See the saying of Antigonus in Abot 1:3 and compare the discussion of Flusser, "A New Sensitivity in Judaism and the Christian Message," *Judaism and Origins of Christianity*, 471–72.

[57] While others have questioned the concept of repentance in the parable, a careful linguistic analysis of the Semitic background and context makes the idea apparent. Cf. Jeremias, *Parables of Jesus*, 130; and Str-B 2:215. See also the earlier study of Jeremias, "Zum Gleichnis vom verlorenen Sohn, Luk. 15, 11–32," *TZ* 5 (1949) 228–331. Of course it is interesting to note that Greek εἰς ἑαυτὸν ἐλθών, "he came to himself," has a Hebrew equivalent in the rabbinic parallel parable considered in the present study, חזר בו. Also the sentence of v. 18, ἀναστὰς πορεύσομαι πρὸς τὸν πατέρα μου, betrays a strong Semitic background in wording and imagery. The Greek verb πορευέσθαι could reflect either Hebrew הלך or שוב. In the LXX the verb שוב is much more frequently translated by the Greek ἀποστρέφειν or ἀναστρέφειν, whereas πορεύεσθαι is usually the translation for הלך. The context of the parable clearly carries the meaning of return. But in reality it is not a major point for proper interpretation because whether one translates הלך or שוב, the import of the story emphasizes the return of the younger son. Compare also, e.g., the wording in 2 Sam 3:21, where the LXX has ἀναστήσομαι δὴ καὶ πορεύσομαι for אקומה ואלכה in the Hebrew text. For the wider range of meanings of the Hebrew phrase, see also E. Ben Yehuda, *Milon Halashon Haevrit* (17 vols.; Jerusalem: General Federation of Jewish Labor in Eretz-Israel, 1959) 3:1496.

with the father is of far greater importance than strict obedience. In fact, true obedience is based firmly upon a strong relationship.

CALL TO ACTION

The parable gives a strong call to action. Each person must understand God as a compassionate father who yearns for a strong and meaningful relationship with his children. There are indeed two types of sinners. The outwardly righteous sinner is just as wrong as the blatantly wicked evildoer. The cause of wrongdoing is rooted in a broken relationship. The elder brother is poisoned with hatred and resentment. Though outwardly righteous, inwardly he is in great need. He must not only be restored to a right relationship with his father but forgive his brother. Forgiveness and reconciliation between individuals greatly influence their relationship with God. These two concepts permeate the thought of the parable. God is a compassionate father. Sin is a broken relationship. The parable first and foremost portrays God as a compassionate parent who longs for a strong and healthy relationship with his two boys. The drama of this family crisis leads the listener on a path of urgent decision.

How does the parable end? Commentators have sometimes divided the parable into two parts.[58] The illustration speaks both about one who recognizes personal need, the younger boy, and one who does not, i.e., his older brother. The end of the parable is determined by the listeners' response. Everyone must decide how he or she will respond to the love of the father in the parable. The decision one makes determines the conclusion of the parable.

In this quintessential parable of Jesus from the Gospels, the Jewish view of God and two types of wrongdoer are portrayed in a manner remarkably similar to the world of rabbinic thought. In fact, parables from the talmudic literature also the tell the story of a family crisis where a son is instructed never to be ashamed to return home. The call to action is urgent. Men and women must seek God's face in the same way as a wayward child comes back home. No matter what wrong has been done, each must recognize his or her need and seek God's help.

---

[58] See, e.g., George Buttrick, *The Parables of Jesus* (New York: R. R. Smith, 1928) 188ff.

8 The Two Debtors

FOCUS

No other parable is so embedded in its context as Jesus' story of the Two Debtors (Luke 7:41–43). A banquet with an unexpected intruder is the background for the parable. The attention of the listener is riveted on Jesus' illustration, which gives an answer to an offended host. Jesus' charismatic personality dominates the scene. The occasion of the illustration is crucial for Luke, who stresses the sharp contrast between the two debtors, one who owed much and one who owed little. All those reclining around the table recognize the comparison of Simon the host to the one who owed little, as well as of the woman to the one who owed much. Forgiveness of great wrong will produce much gratitude, whereas the one who is forgiven little will not have the same feelings of thankfulness. Jesus is the teacher of parables who builds a bridge of understanding between the woman, who is likely a harlot, and Simon the Pharisee. Both are seekers needing divine approval. Jesus' teaching of Torah gives the affirmation that provides the acceptance necessary for both seekers.

The sharp contrast between the pious Simon and the unrighteous woman emerges from the parable. Jesus' parables make use of opposites, sometimes with extreme exaggerations: the publican is the antithesis of a Pharisee; the wise maidens are the opposite of the foolish; the obedient son is the one who does not pay lip service to his father, while the polite son is disobedient; the wise man builds his house upon the rock, but the fool upon the sand. Here also two extremes appear. In the context they refer to Simon and the woman. They are like two debtors who are forgiven their debts. One is forgiven a whole year's salary, the other a month's pay. How will each respond when his debt is eliminated?

The narrative about Jesus' association with Simon the Pharisee and his encounter with this sinful woman sets the stage for the parable about two debtors. The context emphasizes the feeling of gratitude expressed by one who has been forgiven of many wrongs. At the conclusion of the story, a christological controversy is introduced into the episode, taking up the question, To whom has God given the right to forgive sins? The earlier comment of Simon concerning the prophetic call of Jesus already had directed attention toward the true character of Jesus' ministry. Who is Jesus? Why was he invited to eat with Simon the Pharisee? Why would an uninvited guest intrude? The woman brings an alabaster flask of ointment and anoints Jesus' feet. She does not plan on becoming overwhelmed with emotion, but her gratitude for God's grace overpowers her. She breaks down in tears and weeps over the feet of Jesus. She wipes them dry with her hair while kissing his feet. Her actions are extraordinary under any circumstances. One should not be surprised that her behavior elicited a reaction from the host. Jesus responds to Simon's inquiring thoughts by telling a parable. The parable addresses issues specifically pertaining to Simon and the woman. In fact, the message of the parable itself is akin to the spirit of the Pharisees and many of their teachings.

CHRISTIAN INTERPRETATION

Christian interpretations have tended to view Simon as an antagonistic Pharisee. No doubt, rich diversity characterized the various circles of Pharisees and their followers in the first century. But contrary to the simplistic descriptions in our Christian tradition, the Pharisees believed that each person was created in the image of God. Even one who had committed a terrible sin could be forgiven and restored to the fellowship of the community of faith. Were this woman a prostitute or an adulteress, the grace of God would be sufficient. The Pharisee did not reject a sinner who repented. On the contrary, the Pharisees longed for the spiritual renewal of the people.

On the one hand, our Christian tradition has vilified the Pharisee without understanding the basic teachings of Pharisaism. On the other hand, Christian tradition has rightly stressed the central significance of grace and forgiveness in the story. But the first-century context demands a careful analysis of Pharisaic beliefs and practices for a proper understanding of the parable and its powerful message. The woman who is described as a sinner was filled with strong emotion because of her gratitude to God. Jesus defended her actions by explaining her extraordinary behavior in the context of first-century culture. He told a simple but compelling story that made the point clearly. Her actions were accepted customs of welcome, and the parable stresses the nature of true gratitude.

Too often commentators assume that the Pharisee invited Jesus to dinner in order to trap him or insult him.[1] The Gospel text simply reads, "One of

---

[1]Cf., e.g., I. H. Marshall, *The Gospel of Luke* (NIGTC; Grand Rapids: Eerdmans, 1978) 308, claiming that the word order of Luke's text "stresses the unusual nature of the

the Pharisees asked him to eat with him, and he went into the Pharisee's house" (v. 36). There is no reason to assume that Simon had ill intentions. On the contrary, there is ample reason to believe that the Pharisee wanted to honor Jesus and find out more about him. The personal interest of Simon is especially apparent in v. 39, where he entertains the thought that Jesus may be a prophet or, according to some manuscripts, "the prophet."[2] Simon must have invited Jesus to his home in order to learn more about him and his teachings. While it is true that consideration of the external evidence alone would support the position that the definite article was added later, making Simon's statement more specific, I do not endorse this conclusion. In the twenty-fifth edition of the Nestle-Aland text, the definite article appears bracketed in the text,[3] indicating that the editors thought it might have been in the original text. A Greek scribe would be inclined to delete the article for stylistic reasons.[4] Moreover, such a scribe would not have recognized that the definite article was a messianic reference stemming from Deut 18:15. Athough the evidence is not conclusive, when the internal evidence is carefully weighed, there is a solid basis for accepting the definite article and translating "the prophet."

That Simon had invited Jesus over to his home with a sincere heart was argued by Jeremias. Jeremias did not claim that the definite article must be accepted as the better reading, but he did recognize that Simon's reference to Jesus as a prophet is a clear indication of his good intention: "The meal to which the Pharisee invited Jesus is clearly a banquet (κατακλίθη, v. 36); it is in honour of Jesus, since Simon is allowing for the possibility that Jesus may be a prophet, and that with him the departed Spirit of God has returned, bringing the New Age."[5] Simon the Pharisee was a seeker. He invited Jesus to his home because of his curiosity. He thought that Jesus might indeed be the prophet like Moses who would come. In the original reading of the Gospel episode, the audience would have viewed Simon in a positive light. One of the pious members of the community from among the Pharisees is inviting Jesus over for a dinner. Simon may be interested in following Jesus. At least in the earlier version of Luke's Gospel, and most likely in his source, the messianic allusion was originally a part of the story. Simon's statement

---

invitation." On the other hand, he observes that similar situations appear in Luke 11:37 and 14:1.

[2] See, e.g., A. Plummer, *The Gospel according to St. Luke* (ICC; New York: Scribner, 1900) 211: "The reading ὁ προφήτης (B Ξ) would mean 'the great Prophet' of Deut. xviii. 15 (comp. Jn. i. 25, vii. 40), or possibly 'the Prophet that He professes to be.' The art. is accepted by Weiss, bracketed by WH., put in the margin by Treg., and rejected by Tisch."

[3] Now, sadly, in the twenty-sixth and twenty-seventh editions it has been relegated to the critical apparatus.

[4] While there are many exceptions, "predicate nouns as a rule are anarthrous" (BDF, §273).

[5] Jeremias, *Parables of Jesus*, 126.

hinted at the idea of one who was coming. Could it be that Jesus is a prophet, even the prophet like Moses? But the eschatological prophet would recognize what sort of woman is touching him.

In addition, the fact that Simon himself did not wash Jesus' feet should not be a surprise. Such customary foot washing would have been done by a household servant and certainly not by the host. Perhaps the woman began to anoint the feet of Jesus before the servants began their tasks associated with welcoming the guests during the dinner, like washing their feet. She may have slipped in with the other guests and started as soon as the guests had taken their places. In John's Gospel, the foot washing occurred during the meal after the disciples were reclining.[6] In any event, there is not sufficient reason to assume that Simon invited Jesus to dinner and then insulted him by refusing to wash his feet in the traditional manner. Simon's servants may have already washed the feet of the guests, or the woman could have begun to anoint Jesus' feet before the household servants tended to this duty. She could have come forward to attend to the task like one of the servants.

Jeremias even suggested that the dinner invitation was given to Jesus following a Sabbath sermon that he preached. In traditional Jewish custom, inviting a traveler to a Sabbath meal is a meritorious deed. If Jesus taught in the synagogue, as he did on many occasions during his ministry, Simon may have seized an opportunity to extend a dinner invitation in order to honor the guest preacher, to fulfill the meritorious task of hospitality, and above all to learn more about Jesus and his teachings. In such a case, the woman may have been moved by the message and trailed behind the others as they went to Simon's home to honor their guest speaker. Would Jesus have preached a message on God's reign and forgiveness for the outcasts? Such a Sabbath message might explain the unusual actions of this woman, who is described as a sinner. At least, Jeremias suggests that "Jesus had preached a sermon which had impressed them all, the host, the guests, and an uninvited guest, the woman."[7]

In all events, the words of Jesus, "I entered your house, you gave me no water for my feet," most certainly emphasize the "you." Simon as the host would not have performed this task. The shock of the host doing this job is seen in the Gospel of John as well as in rabbinic literature. In John the disciples are appalled when Jesus their master washes their feet. In a well-known story of the distinguished R. Gamaliel, his disciples are shocked when he rises to serve them at a banquet. Is Gamaliel a common household servant? Rabbi Gamaliel exploits the occasion to teach his followers. He serves them like a servant, but there is one greater than Gamaliel who serves. Consider Abraham, who served his visitors. But there is one greater than Abraham who serves. Consider the Holy One, Blessed be He, who provides food for

---

[6] See John 13:1–3; and the discussion by R. Schnackenburg, *The Gospel according to St. John* (3 vols.; New York: Crossroad, 1975) 3:6, 16–17.

[7] Jeremias, *Parables of Jesus,* 126.

all his creation.[8] These lessons would not be meaningful if the host was expected to greet his guests in such a way. The household servants made sure that the guests were welcomed properly. It was their duty to wash the feet.

Jesus was merely stating that the woman's actions were not provocative within the context of accepted cultural norms and customs. If a household servant performed such tasks, the woman's actions should not be offensive to anyone. After all, she was overcome with feelings of gratitude for a renewed awareness of God's mercy and forgiveness, which she seemed to attribute to Jesus' teachings. While the exact motive for her actions is not stated explicitly, quite probably Jesus' message had changed her life, since she sought him out to show her appreciation. Disciples often showed their devotion to a respected teacher who had impacted their lives. A kiss on the head or on the feet was not unusual in that cultural setting.[9]

In a number of passages in rabbinic literature, a teacher kisses his disciple on the head and recites a blessing of thanksgiving and praise when a wise answer to an important question is given. On one such occasion, Johanan ben Zachai and Eleazer ben Arach were contemplating the meaning of the divine chariot. The master teacher, Johanan ben Zachai, kissed his disciple Eleazer ben Arach on the head and blessed him, "Blessed is the LORD God of Israel who gave to a son of Abraham our father understanding and knowledge to interpret the glory of his Father in heaven."[10] The custom of greeting a respected teacher with a kiss is also attested. King Jehosaphat is anachronistically described by the rabbis as greeting the wise sages of his domain with a kiss. While the description is far removed from the historical setting of the Hebrew Bible, it probably does shed light on the cultural traditions of the rabbinic era.[11] Judas approached Jesus to give him a kiss when he came to betray his master into the hands of the soldiers.[12] The kissing of the feet was less common but showed greater honor and appreciation. Out of heartfelt gratitude, a man delivered from a death sentence in court kissed the feet of the one to whom he attributed his successful defense.[13] Great appreciation

[8] See *Sifre Deut.* 38 (*Sifre Devarim,* ed. Finkelstein, 74); *Mekilta* on Exod 18:12 (Horovitz, 195); b. *Kidd.* 32b; and cf. my book, *Lord's Prayer*, 38.

[9] See, e.g., Str-B 1:995–96.

[10] See t. *Chag.* 2:1 (*Tosefta,* ed. Lieberman, 380); and cf. the parallels.

[11] Cf. " 'He honors them that fear the LORD' (Ps. 15:4) that was Jehoshaphat king of Judah, who every time he beheld a scholar-disciple rose from his throne, and embraced and kissed him" (b. *Mak.* 24a and parallels). See Lee Levine, *The Rabbinic Class of Roman Palestine in Late Antiquity* (New York: Jewish Theological Seminary, 1989) 99–101.

[12] See Plummer, *Luke,* 211: "The word is used of the kiss of the traitor (Mt. xxvi. 49; Mk. xiv. 45), which was demonstrative, of the prodigal's father (Lk. xv. 20), and of the Ephesian elders in their last farewell (Acts xx. 37), and nowhere else in N.T. Comp. Xen. *Mem.* ii. 6. 33. Kissing the feet was a common mark of deep reverence, especially to leading Rabbis (Xen. *Cry.* vii. 5. 32; Polyb. xv. 1. 7; Aristoph. *Vesp.* 608)."

[13] See b. *Sanh.* 27b; and cf. Jeremias, *Parables of Jesus,* 126: "All that is disclosed is a boundless gratitude; since to kiss a person's knee or foot (v. 38) is a sign of the most

was demonstrated to R. Jonathan when an old man came up and kissed his feet as he was walking through the promenade.[14] Rabbi Jonathan had assisted him in obtaining financial support from his son. Such support may have been vital for his daily sustenance. The old man was filled with gratitude. In the Gospel story, the woman who kissed the feet of Jesus expressed her strong feelings of thankfulness and respect.

Jesus contrasts the actions of the woman with those of Simon. The symmetry of his words form a beautiful antithetic parallelism, a common poetic form in Hebrew literature. The first part refers to what Simon has not done, the second part to what the woman has done. Simon gave no water for his feet. The sinful woman wet the feet of Jesus with her tears and wiped them with her hair. Simon did not greet Jesus with a kiss on the face, but the woman had not ceased to kiss his feet. Simon did not anoint his head with oil, but she anointed his feet with aromatic ointment (μύρον). By kissing the feet of Jesus, she was demonstrating the highest esteem that could be bestowed.

Stressing the insult by a host who failed to wash Jesus' feet misses the point of the Gospel story. The woman who wanted to follow Jesus was overcome with gratitude for God's mercy and for the teacher who had helped her. Because of overwhelming emotion, she was willing to assume the role of a servant. In contrast, Simon, who also was probably interested in following Jesus, was willing to play the role of a gracious host, but he did not demonstrate the kind of devotion that can proceed only from someone who had experienced a life of sin and had felt the joy of forgiveness. The greatest one, in the teachings of Jesus, is the one who is a servant of all. Simon answered Jesus' question at the end of the parable with sincerity and understanding. There is no reason to assume that he did not embrace the message of the parable. He understood what Jesus was saying and accepted it.

Traces of Christian interpretation already appear in Mark, Matthew, and John.[15] All of these Gospel accounts contain descriptions of a woman who anoints Jesus with ointment. Some commentators have discerned more than one anointing, and others have viewed the various accounts as conflicting versions of the same event. In any case, the common vocabulary and similarities of style strongly suggest that, at the written stage, the sources have overlapped one another. Apart from prevailing synoptic theories, the account

heartfelt gratitude, such as a man might show to one who had saved his life." Compare also Levine, *Rabbinic Class*, 99–101.

[14] See j. *Kidd.* 61c, ch. 1, halakah 7; j. *Peah* 15c, ch. 1, halakah 1; and *Pesik. Rab.* 23/24 (*Pesikta Rabbati*, ed. Friedmann, 122b; English trans., Braude, *Pesikta Rabbati*, 1:497). Consider also the linguistic parallel in the late Hebrew midrash *Measeh Kahana* 1:3: "Immediately the owner of the beast kissed his foot and said to him, 'Blessed art thou and blessed is the one who gave birth to you and blessed is the one who taught you' " (ed. S. A. Wertheimer and enlarged by A. J. Wertheimer, *Batei Midrashot* [2 vols.; Jerusalem: Ketav Vesefer, 1980] 1:307).

[15] Mark 14:3–9; Matt 26:6–13; John 12:1–8.

of Luke shows certain independent features and historical elements that indicate highly reliable sources.[16] First Luke mentions that the people are reclining in traditional Middle Eastern style. The woman does not crawl under the table, but stands behind Jesus. In the liturgy of the Passover haggadah, the reclining position is noted for association with the ancient custom of a festive meal, "Why on this night are we reclining?" The "standing behind him" may well refer to a symposium with a triclinium table, which is so familiar from archaeological discovery and historical record.[17] The other Gospels do not preserve this crucial element of the scene's description. Christian theology is the most prominent feature of John's account because he stresses that the ointment was an anointing for the burial of Jesus. Mark and Matthew also mention the burial of Jesus. In Luke the focal point is the incident involving Simon, the woman, and Jesus. The moment of determination is reached in the parable that speaks about two debtors. Luke makes no mention of the death, burial, and resurrection of Jesus, which would be more relevant in later discussions of the early church.

Mark, Matthew, and John also raise the issue of the cost of the ointment.[18] The dispute about money and the poor does not appear in Luke. Mark and John actually place a price on the ointment (three hundred denarii), while Matthew (26:9) merely states that it could have been sold for a huge sum that could have been given to the poor (ἐδύνατο γὰρ τοῦτο πραθῆναι πολλοῦ καὶ δοθῆναι πτωχοῖς). Maybe the money was obtained through ungodly business, which might have intensified the issue for some of Jesus' disciples.[19] In Matthew it is the disciples who become indignant at such a

[16] See, e.g., Fred B. Craddock, *Luke* (Interpretation; Louisville: John Knox, 1990) 104: For example, Matthew and Mark agree with Luke that the name of the host was Simon, but they identify him as a leper. John agrees with Luke that the woman anointed Jesus' feet, not his head; but John also agrees with others that the anointing was in Bethany, while Luke's story is apparently set in Galilee. Matthew and Mark agree with Luke that the woman is unnamed; John says she was Mary sister of Lazarus in whose home the incident occurred. The three others place the event late in Jesus' ministry and relate it to his death; Luke's story is one of love and forgiveness. What can we say about all of this? It may be that the Gospels reflect sources oral or written that spoke of one, two, or even three anointings, but as we receive the traditions, Luke must be understood as sufficiently distant from the others in location, time, and purpose to be considered entirely on its own.

[17] See S. Stein, "The Influence of Symposia Literature on the Literary Form of the Pesah Haggadah," *JJS* 8 (1957): 13–44.

[18] See C. S. Mann, *The Gospel according to Mark* (AB 27; New York: Doubleday, 1986) 556.

[19] Cf. Philo's discussion of the wages earned by a prostitute: "There is a very excellent ordinance inscribed in the sacred tables of the law, that the hire of a harlot should not be brought into the temple [Deut 23:18]; the hire that is, of one who has sold her personal charms and chosen a scandalous life for the sake of the wages of shame" (*Spec.* 1.280 [F. H. Colson and G. H. Whitaker, LCL]).

waste, and Mark simply says that some of those present were upset and commented among themselves about the extravagance (ἦσαν δέ τινες ἀγανακτοῦντες πρὸς ἑαυτούς). John identifies the opposition to the woman's action as coming from Judas Iscariot, who would ultimately betray Jesus. These colorful asides are better understood as having entered the Gospel tradition after the story had circulated in a Semitic source among the Hebrew- and Aramaic-speaking followers of Jesus. In this later Greek stage of the story, moreover, Mark and Matthew forget the meaning of the moment, when they speak of the gospel being preached in the whole world. They seem to be thinking of their communities of faith, who cherished this memory of a woman disciple who showed her love and devotion for Jesus. None of these parallel literary accounts preserves the parable, which is so indicative of Jesus' style of teaching. Luke's account, however, is imbued with a Semitic style and Jewish cultural orientation. Only Luke describes the posture of the woman, who stood behind Jesus while his feet probably were beside a triclinium as he reclined at the banquet table. The parable begins with a classic Hebrew idiom, "And Jesus answering said to him" (καὶ ἀποκριθεὶς ὁ Ἰησοῦς εἶπεν πρὸς αὐτόν, Luke 7:40). In Hebrew the phrase is well known in narrative texts, ויען ויאמר אליו. The wordplay involving the terms for "sin" and "debt" is also a common characteristic of both Hebrew and Aramaic texts during the first century.

In Luke's version, the conclusion of the story (vv. 47b–50) is likely the result of the third evangelist's own emphasis on forgiveness and love. The issues regarding who can forgive sin recall the episode of the healing of the paralytic man (5:17–26 and parallels).[20] Originally the story probably ended with v. 47a after the powerful saying "Therefore I tell you, her sins . . . are forgiven." At least this may well have been the ending in Luke's source. Some manuscripts delete 47b, "for she loved much; but he who is forgiven little, loves little." Hebrew stories are concise and often conclude with a strong wisdom pronouncement. The declaration that her many sins are forgiven focused attention on the tremendous gratitude that she showed to God. Such gratitude provided convincing evidence that this sinful woman had repented and experienced the power of God's mercy and forgiveness, to which Jeremias has already called attention:

> How completely the woman was overcome by gratitude towards her saviour is shown by the fact that unselfconsciously she took off her head-covering and unbound her hair in order to wipe Jesus' feet, although it was the greatest disgrace for a woman to unbind her hair in the presence of men; evidently she was so shocked at having bedewed Jesus with her tears, that she entirely forgot her surroundings.[21]

---

[20] Cf. also the saying of the early pious ones, "Blessed is he who has not sinned but everyone who has sinned may be forgiven" (t. *Sukka* 4:2 [*Tosefta*, ed. Lieberman, 272; j. *Sukka* 55b, ch. 5 hal. 4).

[21] Jeremias, *Parables*, p. 126.

In Christian preaching emphasis has often been placed on the grace and mercy of God, who accepted a woman who was an outcast. This emphasis is crucial for understanding the central theme of Jesus' proclamation of the kingdom. The power of God is revealed when men and women obey his commandments and experience the divine presence in daily living. The woman is thankful for her spiritual awakening, which seems to be associated with Jesus' ministry. While a sharp contrast between the two debtors is made in Jesus' illustration, both of them are forgiven. The Pharisee would not object to this theme of divine mercy. On the contrary, many Pharisees wanted others to experience God's power in a dynamic spiritual renewal, and no doubt most of them applauded Jesus' efforts in corralling the lost sheep of the house of Israel. Without sufficient attention to the primary sources that inform us about the Pharisees' approach to other people, one is prone to misread Simon's initial intentions and his response to the parable.

THE PARABLE IN THE LIGHT OF JEWISH TRADITION

The theme of two debtors is not so foreign to rabbinic literature. The idea that debt is a sin against God pervades the use of the term in rabbinic literature. The well-known blessing recited on the occasion of being rescued from danger reminds the one praying that he or she is a debtor to God: "Blessed art thou O LORD our God King of the Universe who grants grace to debtors (sinners)."[22] A humorous rabbinic text compares God to a moneylender and the sinner to a debtor who owes a great sum.[23] The wealthy moneylender is willing to forgive the debt. These sources bring out the basic meaning of "debtor" as a sinner.[24] Not only is a debtor a sinner; it is also true that the one who repents of sin is sometimes given a place greater than the wholly righteous. Isaiah 57:19 mentions those who are far away and others who are near. Such a text invited further interpretation by Jewish preachers and teachers.

One rabbi in particular, R. Abbahu, may represent a line of earlier interpreters within the chain of teachers in Pharisaic-rabbinic Judaism when he links those who are far with the ones who repent from sin and those who are near with the completely righteous (צדיקים גמורים). In any case, his approach could have developed at any time in Jewish exposition of Scripture. He believes that the ones who repent from sin will be given a better place in the world to come than those who are completely righteous. His conception of the relationship between the wholly righteous and the repentant sinners is similar to Jesus' teachings concerning the two debtors. Who will be more

[22] See, e.g., j. *Ber.* 14a, ch. 9, halakah 2, and parallels.

[23] See Jónsson, *Humour*, 135; C. G. Montefiore and H. Lowe, *A Rabbinic Anthology* (New York: Schocken, 1974) 324, discussing the rabbinic text in *Exod. Rab.* 31:1; and *Pesik. Rab.* 44 (*Pesikta Rabbati*, ed. Friedmann, 184a).

[24] Cf. Levy, *Wörterbuch*, 2:19–20.

grateful to God? "For R. Abbahu said: In the place where the repentant sinners stand even the completely righteous cannot attain because it says: 'Peace, peace, to the far and to the near' (Isa. 57:19)."[25] Of course, Jesus is not dealing with reward and punishment in the world to come. He does, however, explain why the woman who had become overwhelmed with thankfulness was so very moved. She was forgiven of much. The saying of R. Abbahu distinguishes the wholly righteous and the repentant sinners in much the same way as the Gospel parable distinguishes the two debtors. In Judaism of late antiquity the rabbis stressed how ready God was to receive the person who repented without concern for the amount of sin. In a series of selected homilies on the theme of repentance, the midrash stresses the nature of divine grace. "The Holy One, blessed be He, replied: Dread not the heap of your iniquities. If they are heaped up unto the heavens, and you resolve to return in repentance, I shall forgive you—even if they are heaped up not merely to the first, or the second, or the third, but the seventh heaven, indeed to the throne of glory itself, if you resolve to repent, I shall at once receive you."[26] The certainty of divine mercy is unquestioned in these sources. A woman who is described as a sinner would be restored to the community if she truly repented. Her demonstrative actions at the banquet in the home of Simon the Pharisee are evidence of the intensity of her commitment. Jesus explains what has happened and defends her behavior by using the parable. He builds a bridge of understanding to resolve the conflict that her behavior has caused.

The imagery itself of the parable is paralleled in Jewish literature. Even though the context and the main point are different, the same theme of two debtors appears. From the folklore perspective, the analogies are very similar because they both deal with the issues of payment of the amount owed in the same cultural milieu. The debtor who is a friend to the lender will receive a credit extension.

The Creditor and His Two Debtors

> "I will explain it by a parable," he replied. "To what may it be compared? To a man who is the creditor of two persons, one of them a friend, the other an enemy; of his friend he will accept payment little by little, whereas of his enemy he will exact payment in one sum!"[27]

---

[25] b. *Ber.* 34b; b. *Sanh.* 99a, *Otzar Midrashim,* ed. J. D. Eisenstein (2 vols.; Jerusalem: Hillel, 1969), 408. Cf. *Pesik. Rab.* 44:44; and esp. *Sifre Num.* 42.

[26] *Pesik. Rab.* 44 (*Pesikta Rabbati,* ed. Friedmann, 185a; English trans. Braude, *Pesikta Rabbati,* 2:780).

[27] See *Abod. Zar.* 4a (Epstein, *Babylonian Talmud,* 14) and compare Str-B 2:163, discussing the context of *Abod. Zar.* 4a, in which R. Abbahu answers a question of heretics relating to Amos 3:2, "You only have I known from all the families of the earth; therefore I will punish you for all your iniquities."

The rabbinic parable is similar in motif only. However, it is remarkable that the same images of a creditor and his two debtors, one whom he loves and the other whom he despises, could be used in a way that reminds us of Jesus' parable about two debtors. The one who owes five hundred denarii will be much more grateful than the one who owes fifty. Like the Gospel parallel, the rabbis speak about a creditor and his two debtors. The overlap of the world of motifs in parable lore is a very significant area of research. The parable teller may use the same motifs for diverse purposes in different contexts.

THE PARABLE AND ITS MESSAGE

The main point of the parable is to teach each person to be grateful for God's grace, whether one has been forgiven of many sins or few. Are not both great debtors to God? Secondary to this practical application, but very much the underlying theme, one must be like God in forgiving the sinner and welcoming him or her into the community of the faithful. The context of this parable is crucial. Simon should feel gratitude to God. The woman should not be criticized or ostracized for her expression of thanks to God. Jesus pronounces her sins forgiven. The entire episode revolves around the parable teacher and his message of love and acceptance. Jesus is a Jewish theologian who is consumed with a passion for preaching divine grace.

God's grace is unconditional. The one who is forgiven will give thanks for his mercy. The one who has committed many sins must be accepted into the community of faith in the same way that God receives each individual who repents of the wrong he or she has done. Everyone must rejoice when he or she witnesses the return of the outcast who is seeking acceptance and restoration. The parable communicates the deeper theological message of the human response to divine grace. Spiritual renewal will involve the giving of thanks to God, who has shown mercy on human weakness. The grace of God is extended to all without measure.

Part 5

The Disciple's Call:
A Life of Learning and Doing

9 The Urgent Invitation

FOCUS

First and foremost the parable of the Great Banquet[1] focuses on the call to a banquet meal and the various possible responses that may be given to the invitation. Only one response is acceptable in the case of this banquet. The whole story stresses the open invitation to the outcasts. The reversal and surprise of the parable's plot emerges from the actions of the invited guests, who come up with less than adequate excuses to avoid attending the banquet. Jesus employs humor and irony to teach his message concerning the kingdom of heaven and the divine initiative that calls all the people to come to his banquet table. The urgency for the hour of invitation is revealed when the ones who are called do not recognize the significance of the time. The humor of the episode is seen in the invited guests' trumped-up excuses, and the irony in the poor and needy, who are outside the boundaries of high society, enjoying the great feast. Jeremias has identified the poor, maimed, blind, and lame of the parable with the beggars of the Orient, and those from the highways and hedges with the homeless.[2] The beggars and the homeless feast at the great banquet while the respected members of the community exclude themselves with their worthless excuses.

The parallel account in Matthew produces some innovative changes by introducing the theme of a marriage feast and emphasizing punishment. Instead of a man preparing a great banquet, Matthew speaks about a king who gave a marriage feast for the prince. When the invited guests refuse to attend the prince's wedding feast, and some even go so far as to kill the servants who deliver the invitations, the king is filled with anger. He creates a shock when

---

[1]The Great Banquet, Luke 14:15–24; The Marriage Feast, Matt 22:1–14; The Dinner, *Gos. Thom.* 64

[2]Jeremias, *Parables of Jesus,* 176.

he sends his soldiers to punish the invited guests and burns their city. Then he sends his servants into the thoroughfares to invite as many as possible. But even after these outcasts who accept the king's invitation are gathered together, there is still a mixture of good and bad. Admission into the marriage feast is no guarantee of acceptance. The good and bad among the guests at the banquet are further separated from one another. Hence, the "many are called, but few are chosen" theme is stressed in the story when a guest attending the marriage feast without a proper garment is punished. At least this one guest from among those who responded positively to the king's invitation is punished. Matthew builds upon a number of common theological concepts as he draws upon his textual resources. In spite of the conflicting themes that underlie Matthew's version, the crucial importance of accepting the invitation remains in focus.

The *Gospel of Thomas*, on the other hand, preserves the motif of a man who prepared a dinner, which is closer to the Lukan account. While *Thomas*'s dinner is not the great banquet of Luke, the outline of the story is similar. Four excuses appear in *Thomas*, which breaks the rule of threes in folklore and storytelling. This secondary element weakens the original force of the story. The first excuse highlights the shortcomings of an entrepreneur who puts a business meeting before the obligation of his dinner invitation. The basic social conflict of *Thomas*'s version is seen also in the final emphasis, "Tradesmen and merchants [shall] not [enter] the places of my Father."

Both Matthew and Luke emphasize the moment when all is prepared and the time has arrived. The call that the banquet is ready is the original, challenging focal point of the parable. The time has come. The invitations have been sent. The servants announce that the supper is ready and call the guests to their places. The surprise in the parable is the unrealistic answers of the ones who are called to the dinner. The central question revolves around their responses. Each individual is given the opportunity to make his or her decision.[3] The plot of the story invites the proper reply and stresses the urgency of proclaiming that the time of the banquet is now.

THE PARABLE IN THE LIGHT OF CHRISTIAN INTERPRETATION

Certain Christian interpretations of the parable of the Great Banquet are found already in the Synoptic Gospels. This is especially true if one accepts the hypothesis that Matthew and Luke take the parable from a common source and adapt it for their own purposes. While Jesus could have told parables about a great banquet and a marriage feast on two different occasions, most interpreters tend to view Matthew and Luke as preserving two

[3] See Young, *Jewish Parables*, 169–76.

versions of the same parable.[4] If the evangelists are quoting two different parables, the main theme and message are parallel, much in the same way that a teacher may use two illustrations to drive home the same point. In all events, early Christian interpretation of the parable is revealed in the way the evangelists incorporated it into their respective Gospels.

Matthew placed the parable in the final week before the passion of Jesus, following the parable of the Wicked Tenants and the parable of the Two Sons.[5] These three parables were told in Judea as a part of Jesus' confrontation with the "chief priests and the elders" on the Temple Mount (Matt 21:23). Most probably an eschatological emphasis is revealed in Matthew's treatment of the judgment scene (Matt 22:11–14). The man without a proper wedding garment is severely punished: "Bind him hand and foot, and cast him into the outer darkness; there men will weep and gnash their teeth" (v. 13).[6]

Luke's version, however, places the parable in the context of a meal that seems to have occurred during the last journey to Jerusalem, quite possibly in a village of Galilee. Jesus had been invited to dine in the home of a leader of the Pharisees (Luke 14:1). He was eating with his followers and those who came to hear his teachings when someone declared, "Blessed is he who shall eat bread in the kingdom of God!" The preceding teaching on humility also is cast in the setting of a dinner where the invited guests were scrambling to obtain the seats of honor (Luke 14:7). Here the parable is introduced by a blessing related to eating bread in the kingdom of God. The people are gathering together to enjoy a meal. The seating arrangements are very important in a society where shame is avoided and honor is prized. Many of the respected community leaders who always made an appearance at important affairs such as this great banquet will miss the opportunity. An excuse is liable to ruin everything.

Both synoptic versions of the parable stress the call, "Come; for all is now ready."[7] The parable would probably be better entitled the invitation or even by a name that evokes the theological ramifications of the word-picture, such as God's Gracious Call. The story circulated in its earlier Semitic form before it was translated into Greek and adapted for the setting in each Gospel text. The version of Luke is clearly closest to the core text and preserves the heart of its original message. Its setting is authentic. The force of the parable's challenge is heard distinctly. Matthew's text weaves several strands of Jesus'

---

[4] This argument was made forcefully by Oesterley, *Gospel Parables in the Light of their Jewish Background*, 124–25.

[5] I have come to call the parable of the Wicked Tenants the parable of the Only Son; see Young, *Jewish Parables*, 282–316.

[6] This punishment should be compared with *1 En.* 10:4: "And to Raphael he said, 'Go, Raphael, and bind Asael; fetter him hand and foot and cast him into darkness' " (M. Black, *The Book of Enoch* [Leiden: Brill, 1985] 30).

[7] Luke 14:17 and Matt 22:4 with different wording.

teachings into this one parable. Matthew seems to give a clear allusion to the destruction of Jerusalem: "The king was angry, and he sent his troops and destroyed those murderers and burned their city" (v. 7). The preceding verse stresses the evil that these invited guests worked against the king's servants. The murder of the servants probably recalled the persecution of the early church, which would be fresh in the minds of some of Matthew's readers. The old motif of the killing of the prophets, which is certainly pre-Christian, is carried over into this parable from the preceding story (Matt 21:35, 39). The context of Matthew's version represents a later Christian interpretation. This motif is completely lacking in Luke's version. The change of audience is decisive in such cases. The parable in Luke reminds us of Jesus' ministry, while the version of Matthew is aimed at a different audience. The transition from a man in Luke to a king in Matthew, as well as the aggrandizement from a large banquet to a marriage feast for the prince himself, are also familiar developments in folklore, where the tendency to dramatize a story with more sensational elements is well known.[8]

The Gospel of Matthew seems to direct its focus more on a later audience than on a setting during the life of Jesus. Certainly the emphasis on the situation in the temple complex, when the Sadducees and priests questioned Jesus, provided a background for the message. But Matthew is speaking to another audience, guiding his own listeners, as they overhear Jesus speaking to the priests in the temple. Daniel J. Harrington has explained the background of Matthew's version of the parable:

> The parable of the wedding feast is an outline of salvation history from a Christian perspective. It explains the fall of Jerusalem and the inclusion of marginal people in God's kingdom. But it also provides a warning that mere admission is not enough; an appropriate response is needed. Care must be taken lest Matt 22:7 be made an indictment of the whole Jewish people and part of the "wandering Jew" myth, that is, that Jews are condemned to wander the earth without a homeland because they killed Christ. The target of the parable was (some) "chief priests and Pharisees" (21:45).[9]

Of course, Matthew does not teach that the Jewish people as a whole are responsible for the crucifixion of Jesus. Some of the chief priests cooperated with the Romans in their efforts to suppress all popular messianically oriented movements. The Romans crucified Jesus.

Matthew speaks from a pastoral concern for his community when he emphasizes the problem of the wedding garment at the end of the illustration. The good and the bad are among those gathered in the community of faith, and there will most certainly be a division. The theme of the tares among the

[8] See, e.g., Harvey K. McArthur and Robert M. Johnston, *They Also Taught in Parables* (Grand Rapids: Zondervan, 1990) 132–34; Propp, *Folklore*, 25–26.

[9] Harrington, *Matthew*, 308. On the ramifications of this redaction of the Matthean parable see Flusser's important work, *Origins*, 552–74.

wheat as well as the bad fish among the good appears here, where anticipation rises concerning the judgment scene. Early in her work, Eta Linneman suggested that the parable of the Marriage Feast combined two parables, one concerning the banquet and another about the man who did not wear the proper garment.[10] Her suggestion makes good sense in light of the way Matthew has forged his version of the parable together from the various components of Jesus' teachings. He employs rich imagery from the culture and customs concerning accepted wedding etiquette as he seeks to communicate the need for all to be prepared for the great messianic banquet. Matthew places the parable in Jesus' ministry. Jesus spoke to the Jewish people. Many among them were his supporters (Matt 21:46). Reading this parable anachronistically does a terrible injustice to his life and ministry by imposing a later setting for the parable that envisions the sharp separation between the church and the synagogue. The allegorical interpretation that views the invited guests as the Jewish people and the others who accepted the invitation from the highways and thoroughfares as the Gentiles must be rejected.

For the historical Jesus there was only the synagogue. This is not a parable about Christianity and Judaism but an urgent message for all people to accept God's gracious invitation and to remain faithful to his call. Even after the wedding guests have been admitted into the celebration of the feast, a man is discovered who does not have the proper garment. Irenaeus identified the garment as the Holy Spirit, and Augustine explained its significance as charity in light of 1 Cor 13.[11] Since the context of the parable does not provide a clue for an allegorical interpretation, it is difficult to support the efforts of Irenaeus, Augustine, or a host of others who have tried to determine the meaning of the garment. One thing, however, is clear: according to Matthew, not all who are participating in the life of the community will be accepted in the final judgment ("Many are called, but few are chosen").

The Jesus of history did not speak about the end of one religion so that a new one could be started. The Matthean form of the parable stresses acceptance of the invitation and purity of purpose. The proper wedding garment must be worn if one is to participate in the festivities associated with this grand feast prepared by the king for his son. The Gospel of Thomas version contrasts four excuses which are supremely more important than the dinner invitation.

GOSPEL OF THOMAS 64: THE DINNER

Jesus said: A man had guest-friends, and when he had prepared the dinner (δεῖπνον), he sent his servant to (ἵνα) invite the guest-friends. He went to the

[10] See Eta Linnemann, *The Parables of Jesus* (London: SPCK, 1977) 96–97.

[11] See Irenaeus, *Against Heresies* 4.36.6 (ANF, 1:517); Augustine, *Sermons on the New Testament Lessons* 40.6; 45.7 (*NPNF* 6:394, 407). See the fine discussion in Kissinger, *Parables*, 2, 24.

> first, he said to him: "My master invites thee." He said: "I have some claims against some merchants (ἔμπορος); they will come to me in the evening; I will go and give them my orders. I pray to be excused (παραιτεῖσθαι) from the dinner (δεῖπνον)." He went to another, he said to him: "My master has invited thee." He said to him: "I have bought a house and they request (αἰτεῖν) me for a day (ἡμέρα). I will have no time." He came to another, he said to him: "My master invites thee." He said to him: "My friend is to be married and I am to arrange a dinner (δεῖπνον); I shall not be able to come. I pray to be excused (παραιτεῖσθαι) from the dinner (δεῖπνον)." He went to another, he said to him: "My master invites thee." He said to him: "I have bought a farm (κώμη), I go to collect the rent. I shall not be able to come. I pray to be excused (παραιτεῖσθαι)." The servant came, he said to his master: "Those whom thou hast invited to the dinner (δεῖπνον) have excused (παραιτεῖσθαι) themselves." The master said to his servant: "Go out to the roads, bring those whom thou shalt find, so that they may dine (δειπνεῖν). Tradesmen and merchants [shall] not [enter] the places (τόπος) of my Father." (*Gos. Thom.* 64)

While the *Gospel of Thomas* avoids much of the added wedding imagery of Matthew, the text does refer to the business interests that are prominent in Matthew's list of the three excuses (Matt 22:5).[12] *Thomas* presents four excuses. The first refers to a business meeting that takes precedence over the dinner.[13] *Thomas* seems to view the social position of the merchants with disdain. The next man bought a house and does not have time to attend the dinner. The third person was asked to prepare the wedding dinner for a friend. Here the wedding theme of Matthew's parable does appear, but preparation for the dinner is the excuse. In Luke's parable the man making the excuse is the bridegroom himself. The stress on excuses (παραιτεῖσθαι) in *Thomas*'s parable is very much like Luke. Matthew's text, on the other hand, highlights the wedding theme, mentioning the meal (ἄριστον instead of δεῖπνον) for the first time in v. 4. *Thomas*'s fourth excuse is given by a man who had bought a farm (κώμη) and must collect the rent. Luke's version probably represents the actual life setting of a farmer more precisely. For the most part, a farmer lived in the village but farmed a field adjacent to his community. Generally speaking, a person did not buy a farm in the same sense as today. In our Western culture, one might acquire a house, barn, fields, and possibly other equipment for cultivation when purchasing a farm. More frequently, the people of first-century Israel lived together, enjoying community life in a village and farming the fields around the village. In that regard, Luke's description is precise. Buying a farm as described in *Thomas* is less characteristic of the agricultural circumstances of the first century. The secondary nature of *Thomas* is also reflected in the difficulty of translating the Greek word κώμη into a good Hebrew dynamic equivalent. The Lukan term

[12] Cf. Funk, Scott, and Butts, *Parables*, 42–43.

[13] This excuse, as well as the conclusion, should probably be considered secondary to the parable (cf. ibid.).

for field (ἀργός) is much closer to the Hebrew background of the Gospels. In Hebrew a dynamic equivalent is the word שדה, which is more appropriate for the story line of the parable (Luke 14:18; Matt 22:5). The fields are adjacent to the villages. The *Gospel of Thomas* suggests that the man is a wealthy landowner who bought the farm and collects the rent from the tenant farmers. This picture is somewhat problematic, because a nobleman with tenant farmers would send his servants to collect the rent. Nonetheless, tenant farming was a significant part of the agricultural economy and *Thomas* is betraying a suspicion and dislike of the wealthy who make excuses. Although Jesus himself had a high view of the poor who sought God without the entanglement of riches, the wealthy landowners in the parables of Jesus are portrayed in a positive sense as noble and benevolent. In any case, *Thomas* has four excuses that accentuate the need to accept the invitation, as his parable portrays the temptations of tradesmen and merchants who will not have a place in the presence of the Father. *Thomas*'s version of the parable is likely a later Christian interpretation based upon Matthew and Luke. The origins and sources of the *Gospel of Thomas* will continue to be debated by scholars for many years to come. Its parable of the dinner is a homiletical performance of a familiar story that gives special emphasis to the precarious position of tradesmen and merchants.

THE PARABLE IN THE LIGHT OF ITS JEWISH BACKGROUND

The version of Luke gives the clearest parallels to the Jewish setting and historical background of the parable. The beginning of the drama is crucial in Luke: "A man once gave a great banquet, and invited many." So characteristic of Jesus' teaching, the emphasis is on a call to the many. The story describes the scene of a great banquet.[14] The man is preparing a large dinner because he must make room for many guests. There is little reason to assume that the invitations were given only to the wealthy. All of the invited guests make excuses (v. 18).[15] The introduction for the plot of the parable emphasizes the great size of the dinner and the numerous invitations that were sent out. The "many" (πολλούς) must refer more to the common people than to the select members of high society.[16] Much food

[14] While the word "great" (μέγα) was deleted in X and e, there is little doubt that it is an original part of the parable. The textual attestation for it is decisive. As internal evidence, moreover, a sizable dinner is required for the plot of the story.

[15] The parable gives three excuses. Two of the three would probably come from those with sufficient wealth to buy land or acquire five yoke of oxen. Nevertheless, there is no reason to assume that the "many" in Luke only refers to wealthy people.

[16] On this point I must strongly disagree with Jeremias, *Parables of Jesus*, 176: "The invited guests are well-to-do people, large landowners (see on v. 19)." This assumption is not justified from the introduction of the parable: The man invited "many," which is

was prepared for this large banquet. As the introduction itself teaches, the banquet was intended to be inclusive.

The setting in the culture of the Second Temple period is described with great authenticity in this colorful portrayal of village life. A banquet for so many required extensive preparation. Generous hospitality was prized highly. The best foods, finest wines, and carefully prepared meats would have been served. The home of the host would have been a bustle of activity. The servants would have already invited the guests, who would be waiting for the second call given when the dinner was ready.[17] In essence they would have already accepted the invitation with an obligation to attend. Under normal circumstances the invited guests would wait eagerly for the festivities to begin. In oriental society, drums may have been used to alert the people that a special festive dinner was being prepared. In any case, one would expect a troupe of musicians to be present at the feast. During the day, long before the time of the meal, the smells of the meats roasting and the aromatic food preparations would fill the fresh country air of the streets in the village. Anticipation would grow regarding the great banquet, a social occasion where many of the people could share their lives in one of the favorite communal activities of the culture. During the feast, the village people had the opportunity to interact with one another in a festive atmosphere.

When the meal has been prepared, the host sends his servant to call the guests to the feast. The words of the call became very familiar which can be seen from the fact that Rabbi Akiva also uses them when he teaches about being prepared for God's banquet in the future. Rabbi Akiva used the words of invitation from God to instill a sense of awe in his disciples. God's call to the banquet will come. But will the people be ready? The wonder of God's pledge to the people and the certainty of judgment are stressed in this saying attributed to Akiva. Everything in life is given to people on loan from God. There will come a time of reckoning: "a net is spread for all the living." This saying demonstrates that great responsibility accompanies the pledge given to people by God. In this early rabbinic source, the image of judgment is heard in Akiva's words "and everything is prepared for the feast." The theological foundation for the teaching of Akiva is paralleled in the familiar words of the parable of Jesus.

Akiva and the Feast

> He [Akiva] used to say, Everything is given on pledge, and a net is spread for all the living: the shop is open; and the dealer gives credit; and the ledger lies open; and the hand writes; and whosoever wishes to borrow may come and borrow; but the collectors regularly make their daily round and exact payment

---

an inclusive term. The invited guests were much better off than the street people, but the dinner list is not limited to the "well-to-do, . . . landowners."

[17] In the introduction of the parable, the phrase "and called many" (καὶ ἐκάλεσεν πολλούς) refers to the first invitation announcing the banquet.

> from man, whether he be content or not; and they have that whereon they can rely in their demand; and the judgment is a judgment of truth; and everything is prepared for the feast. (*Abot* 3:20)[18]

The words "everything is ready for the feast" are closely paralleled in the Gospel parable when the servant calls the people to the great banquet by saying, "Come; for all is now ready" (ἔρχεσθε, ὅτι ἤδη ἕτοιμά ἐστιν, Luke 14:17). The Hebrew text of Akiva's saying, והכל מתוקן לסעודה, may well represent the form of the invitation customary at that time. For Akiva, the banquet refers to life in the world to come.

The servant's call to the dinner is also found in traditional Middle Eastern culture. Jeremias noted the prevalence of the custom: "The repetition of the invitation at the time of the banquet is a special courtesy, practised by upper circles in Jerusalem."[19] While one should not make a practice of accepting modern customs to illustrate the life setting in the first century, the experiences of W. M. Thomson merit some attention in this particular instance. Thomson lived in the Middle East for twenty-five years before the impact of Western culture became felt so strongly. Modern oriental culture has undergone many changes, especially with the advent of Islam in the seventh century and the encroachment of Western influence since World War I.[20] Nonetheless, many of the customs and traditions have persisted, so it is helpful that Thomson shares his interesting experience from the year 1857.

The Invitation

> I noticed that the friend at whose house we dined last evening sent a servant to call us when dinner was ready. Is this custom generally observed? Not very strictly among the common people, nor in cities where Western manners have greatly modified the Oriental; but in Lebanon it still prevails. If a sheikh, beg, or emeer invites, he always sends a servant to call you at the proper time. This servant often repeats the very formula mentioned in Luke xiv.17: Tefuddulû, el 'asha hâder—Come, for the supper is ready. The fact that this custom is mainly confined to the wealthy and to the nobility is in strict agreement with the parable, where the certain man who made the great supper, and bade many, is supposed to be of this class. It is true now, as then, that to refuse is a high insult to the maker of the feast, nor would such excuses as those

[18] *Abot* 3:19 (J. H. Hertz, *The Authorised Daily Prayer Book* [New York: Bloch, 1959] 661–63).

[19] Jeremias, *Parables of Jesus,* 176.

[20] This is, of course, one of the major drawbacks to what Bailey has referred to as "Oriental exegesis" in his fascinating book *Poet and Peasant*, 29–37. Bailey's fresh approach has much to commend it. It is crucial, however, to find materials from Jewish sources such as the Apocrypha, Pseudepigrapha, Dead Sea Scrolls, Talmud, and midrash that support the other later witnesses to the culture represented in the parables. In the present case, the rabbinic parables concerning banquets reinforce the observations made by Jeremias and Thomson. These sources also speak of the invitation that is given when the servant comes to announce that all is ready.

> in the parable be more acceptable to a Druse emeer than they were to the lord of this "Great supper"; but, however angry, very few would manifest their displeasure by sending the servants into the highways and hedges after the poor, the maimed, the halt, and the blind. All these characters are found in abundance in our streets, and I have known rich men who filled out the costume of the parable even in these particulars; it was, however, as matter of ostentation, to show the extent of their benevolence, and the depth of their humility and condescension. Nevertheless, it is pleasant to find enough of the drapery of this parable still practiced to show that originally it was, in all its details, in close conformity to the customs of this country.[21]

In the Gospel parable, the host sends his servant to call the many to the feast. Up to this point of the story, everything is familiar to the audience. They understand these customs well. The invited guests recognize their obligation to come to the banquet when all is ready. The urgency of the invitation is emphasized by the Greek word "already" (ἤδη), which told them that the hour for the meal had come and that they should lose no time in attending. It is at this point that the shock element is introduced into the plot of the story. Instead of responding to the second call, all the invited guests refuse to honor the invitation. The words of the parable describe the bizarre situation: "But they all alike began to make excuses."[22]

The nobleman preparing the banquet is terribly insulted. His honor has been forever put to shame in the eyes of the village people. But the man is very generous, and he has prepared a great feast. Enough food is prepared for many people. In a single act of charity he can reclaim his honor and shame those who insulted him. He invites the needy people who are completely outside the parameters of respected social circles. The culture and religion of the people taught them to care for the poor and the disabled with generosity and kindness, but the actual practice of the community sometimes left segments of the people with serious social needs. The action of a nobleman who helped the needy was highly esteemed by everyone.

The Jewish background of the parable gives rich insight. In the Jerusalem Talmud, the story is told about the village tax collector Bar Maayan. He was an irreligious moneyman who prepared a dinner for the honorable councilors of the town. They insulted him by refusing to come. He then invited the poor and the needy to the banquet. In such a move he brought honor to himself and shamed the councilors who refused to attend his dinner. His deed of kindness is highly praised in the Talmud. This good deed for the

[21] W. M. Thomson, *The Land and the Book* (2 vols.; New York: Harper, 1859) 1:178–79.

[22] They had already been informed of the invitation and are referred to in Greek as the κεκλημένοι, "called ones" (v. 16), which in Hebrew would be קרואים or נקראים. The verb παραιτεῖσθαι, "make excuses," "excuse oneself," or "decline an invitation," is translated in Hebrew as להתנצל by Delitzsch in *Haberit Hechadashah* (trans. F. Delitzsch; Tel Aviv: Bible Society, 1976) and may have been לסרב in the Hebrew language as spoken and written in the first century.

poor overshadowed the evil things he had done as a tax collector. In fact, he received more recognition in his death for this one righteous act than a pious scholar who was buried about the same time. Thus, even though Bar Maayan was a tax collector who was much disliked and held in contempt for his self-centered lifestyle, he was eulogized for his one act of great charity.

The Tax Collector's Dinner for the Needy

> But when Bar Maayan, the village tax collector died, the whole town took time off to mourn him. . . .
>
> Now what was the meritorious deed which Bar Maayan the village tax collector had done?
>
> Heaven forfend! He never did a meritorious deed in his life. But one time he made a banquet for the councilors of his town but they did not come. He said, "Let the poor come and eat the food, so that it does not go to waste."[23]

The Jerusalem Talmud is probably recalling a historical event that is paralleled in the parable of Jesus. It is fascinating that Thomson also refers to similar occurrences in his experiences in the Holy Land during the Ottoman period. He writes about a feast that all the invited guests refuse to attend. The host of the banquet invites the beggars and the homeless people to enjoy the delicacies of his feast. In rabbinic literature, the motif of the banquet is used to illustrate a number of key themes in Judaism. As noted above, R. Akiva spoke of the invitation to a banquet as a way of reminding his followers that each person must be prepared for the unknown time of his or her entrance into the world to come.

In a rabbinic parable about a banquet, the size of the feast is stressed. Though the parable is taken from a late source, *Midrash Psalms*, it gives rich insight into the cultural and folkloric elements in the Gospel story. The theme of the parable is a great banquet and the types of guests who are invited. Here the plot and message as well as the word-picture are parallel to the Gospel parable. Like the Gospel parable, the list of invited guests is changed and expanded to include more and more people. Unlike Jesus' parable, no one insults the king by refusing his hospitality.

The Great Banquet for Many

> R. Eleazar told a parable of a king who prepared a great banquet and charged his steward: "Invite me merchants; do not invite me artisans." There-

[23] y. *Sanh.* 23c, ch. 6, halakah 8 (English trans. J. Neusner, *The Talmud of the Land of Israel Sanhedrin and Makkot* [Chicago: University of Chicago Press, 1984] 181). See also j. *Chag.* 77d, ch. 2, halakah 2. Jeremias (*Parables of Jesus,* 178) wrongly assumed without sufficient evidence that Jesus made reference to Bar Maayan in the parable of the Great Banquet and in the Rich Man and Lazarus. The story does, however, add much to the cultural realism of the parables.

> upon his steward said: "My lord king, so abundant is thy banquet that the merchants will not be able to eat it all, unless the artisans are part of the company." Even so, David said: *"According to Thy mercy remember Thou me, for Thy goodness' sake, O Lord,"* as is said *The Lord is good to all* (Ps. 145:9).[24]

The parable emphasizes God's mercy and goodness, which are given for all people. The inclusive nature of divine grace spoken of in Ps 25 is illustrated in the rabbinic parable attributed to R. Eleazer. The wealthy merchants are not the only ones who will enjoy this feast. There is too much food for the merchants by themselves; the artisans must also be included in the festivities of this great banquet.

This parable of R. Eleazar is followed by a second parable, which is attributed to R. Jose bar Chanina. The second illustration is also about a king's banquet and the many invited guests. The word-picture describes the delay in the gratification of those invited to the banquet. They do not come in the fourth hour. They do not appear in the fifth and sixth hour, but finally in the evening. They all receive the great bounty of the dinner when the king welcomes them and thanks them for attending his banquet.

The Banquet and the Guests

> R. Jose bar Chanina told a parable of a king who prepared a banquet and invited the guests. The fourth hour passed, and the guests did not come. The fifth and sixth hours passed, and still the guests did not come. By evening the guests began to arrive. The king said to them: "I am beholden to you. Had you not come, I would have had to throw the whole banquet to my dogs." Even so, the Holy One, blessed be He, says to the righteous: I consider this a great favor on your part, for I created My world because of you; and were it not for you, all the goodness which I have prepared for the future, of which it is said *Oh how abundant is Thy goodness, which Thou has laid up for them that fear Thee* (Ps. 31:20), to whom could I give it?[25]

The banquet in this rabbinic parable implies the great reward prepared by God for his people. The blessing of this reward is reserved for the future time. The goodness of the present world is only a shadow of the blessing yet to come. Those invited to the banquet will arrive at the proper time. God is pictured as a benevolent king who longs to bestow upon the righteous his abundant blessings, which are being stored for those who fear him. Like the Gospel parable, which is introduced by a man eating with Jesus who declares, "Blessed is the one who shall eat bread in the kingdom of God!" and which teaches a message concerning the blessing reserved for the many, the rabbinic parable illustrates the great reward reserved for the righteous.

---

[24] *Midr. Pss.* 25:9 (Braude, *Midrash on Psalms,* 1:352; *Midrash Tehilim,* ed. S. Buber, 107a).

[25] Ibid.

WORTHLESS EXCUSES

The parable of Jesus reports three of the excuses given to the servant. The rule of three is observed. These archetype excuses are used to illustrate the others that certainly would have been supplied by the many other invited guests who express their regrets to the nobleman's servant and thus insult the host. The first excuse deals with the buying of a field, the second with the purchase of five yoke of oxen, and the third with marriage. Only the last excuse has any credence. In fact, the third reason for not attending the banquet likely conveyed an element of humor to the listeners. Defining wit and humor in the context of diverse cultures is no easy task. But it is likely that the third excuse was very funny to the first-century listeners.

The first excuse betrays the irony of the situation. The man accepted the first call. In the meantime, he has purchased a field that he has never seen. Does anyone buy property without first examining it carefully? Surely he could honor the invitation and then tend to his other business concerns. The absurdity of the reason for not coming is designed to illustrate the urgency of such an invitation and the danger of allowing any worthless excuse to prevail against the only proper response. The second excuse would be very difficult for a farmer to understand. The man has bought five yoke of oxen and must test them. Again, the people listening to the excuses would ask themselves why he would buy livestock for ploughing without considering the needs of his field work and testing the beasts before the transaction had been completed. An effective pair of oxen would pull the plough together, one helping the other as they moved at the same pace. In all events, he would have ample opportunity to test them in the field during the months of agricultural work. This character would rather plough than eat! He can test his oxen any time. The man's first obligation would be to attend the banquet.

Only the third excuse, "I have married a wife, and therefore I cannot come," would have a measure of validity. Although this is true, the timing of the wedding is the problem. In the interim between the first call and the second, the man has gone through the engagement proceedings and is already preparing for the seven blessings of the wedding ceremony. This excuse also is absurd. Many have noted the similarity between the three excuses in the parable and the reasons given in Deut 20:5–7 for a young man who is released from his duty of military service.[26] If he has built a new house, planted a vineyard, or betrothed a wife, he may be exempt from battle lest he die in the war and someone else enjoy the blessings of these experiences. The most striking similarity is with the man who had married a wife. It is quite possible

[26]See Young, *Jewish Parables,* 185 n. 24. Derrett has suggested that the parable's banquet actually refers to the dinner before the holy war (J. Duncan M. Derrett, *Law in the New Testament* [London: Darton, Longman & Todd, 1970] 126–55), but his approach has been wisely rejected by Scott, *Hear*, 170.

that this verse and its Jewish interpretations may have come to mind as the colorful story of the great banquet was being told. But the whole complex of excuses and their similarity to the biblical text does not have any real significance for the interpretation. The Hebrew text of the Torah is the common cultural background of the people, who appreciate faint linguistic allusions to their religious heritage. The major point made from the three excuses, however, stresses the idea that no cause or reason would justify refusal. The invited guests must attend the banquet. Their worthless excuses break an important rule of etiquette and insult the host.

THE BEGGARS AND THE HOMELESS ARE FED

On the one hand, the behavior of the invited guests was inexcusable. On the other hand, the generous nobleman hosting the banquet knew just what to do with the great feast that had been prepared. The Middle Eastern culture highly values food and recognizes the needs of the less fortunate. Food is precious. The invited guests had shamed the nobleman. By inviting the beggars and the homeless to his banquet, he brought honor to himself and put the rest of the people to shame. He absorbed the shame that the invited guests heaped upon him and shared the pain of other suffering human beings. The parable intensifies this action. The servant is sent out a second time to invite more needy people. After all, this was a huge feast that had been prepared.

John A. T. Robinson believed that the first sending was directed toward the Jews and the second to the Gentiles.[27] This assumption is anachronistic, being based upon the unjustified presupposition that the parable is concerned with Judaism and Christianity. Allegorizing the parable in this way divorces the parable from its historical setting in Luke, which focuses on Jesus' own ministry. His healing missions and teaching sessions were taking place among his own people. Many received his teachings and many did not. A Gentile mission is not alluded to in the parable. Closer to the life setting of Jesus was the ministry of John the Baptist. One could argue in a similar vein that the first sending out symbolized the mission of John and the second pictured the work of Jesus. But this whole approach to the parable is wrong from its inception. If the major focus of the parable was on Jews and Gentiles or on John the Baptist and Jesus, the storyteller and the context would make the association clear. Allegory may lead in many different directions but often follows the path of the interpreter who is bent on forcing his or her favorite themes upon the parables of Jesus. The interpreter must listen carefully to the parable teacher. This parable deals with the invitation, the excuses, and the outcome.

[27] John A. T. Robinson, *Redating the New Testament* (London: SCM, 1978) 19–20; cf. also my earlier discussion, Young, *Jewish Parables*, 175.

The outcome of the unusual events brought food to the hungry. The generous nobleman commands his servant, "Go out quickly to the streets and lanes of the city, and bring in the poor and maimed and blind and lame" (Luke 14:21). These needy people are those who were neglected and sometimes excluded. In an interesting contrast to Luke's parable, the *Rule of the Congregation* among the Dead Sea Scrolls excludes the maimed, blind, and lame from the fellowship of the congregation. In Jewish faith and practice it was imperative to provide financial support through almsgiving for these persons with physical limitations. Among the Essenes there was an unusual zeal to maintain ritual purity. In their eyes, the lame, blind, and deaf were considered somehow impure. The Essene congregation should be set apart and holy in a way similar to the priesthood as described in the Pentateuch. "And no man smitten with any human uncleanness shall enter the assembly of God. . . . No man smitten in his flesh, or paralysed in his feet or hands, or lame, or blind, or deaf, or dumb, or smitten in his flesh with a visible blemish; no old and tottery man unable to stay still in the midst of the congregation."[28]

The excluded ones are included in the parable of Jesus. Long ago J. T. Milik observed the sharp contrast between Jesus' teaching in the parable and the exclusiveness of the sectarian writings of the Dead Sea Scrolls: "These lists of defects are expansions of the lists of priestly disqualifications found in the Pentateuch—another example of how the Essenes universalized regulations once proper to the priesthood alone. One immediately thinks of the Gospel parable of the invitation to the banquet as St. Luke records it."[29] In contrast, the nobleman summons the poor, maimed, blind, and lame to fill the places of the original guests in this great feast in the kingdom of God. Jesus' parable calls on these humble members of society, who are outside the privileged circles of the village, to enjoy the feasting of the specially prepared banquet.

The servant returns and tells his master that there is still more room available. The nobleman urges his servant again, "Go out to the highways and hedges, and compel people to come in, that my house may be filled." As noted above, Jeremias identified the people found in the highways and hedges with the homeless. While it is fair to say that the people listening to the story recognized the universal call of the invitation for all people regardless of economic status or physical conditions, Jeremias probably goes too far in saying that this second group was only the homeless. The stress of the command is found in the strong words "compel [them] to come in" (καὶ ἀνάγκασον εἰσελθεῖν). The supper is indeed great, and the man wants his

[28] 1QSa 2:3–7 (G. Vermes, *The Dead Sea Scrolls in English* [3d ed.; Baltimore: Penguin, 1988] 102); and see especially J. Licht, *Megilat Haserachim* (Jerusalem: Bialik Institute, 1965) 264–65. Compare Licht's notes on lines 5–6, where he observes similar lists in parallel Hebrew texts. See also Fitzmyer, *Luke*, 2:1057.

[29] J. T. Milik, *Ten Years of Discovery in the Wilderness of Judaea* (London: SCM, 1959) 114–15.

house to be full. The first call went to the economically disadvantaged and to the disabled members of the community, who most probably were reduced to begging for their physical needs. The second sending, however, is completely unlimited and universal. Go into the highways and hedges, wherever people are to be found, and urge them to enter into my home. The call is for all people. The entire focus of the parable makes it clear that the invitation to the feast of the kingdom is offered to the many.

The master's high aim is to fill his house. Certainly the Greek term οἶκος, "house," means more than the physical dwelling. It is probably best understood in light of the Semitic background of the Synoptic Gospels. The word "house" in Hebrew, בית, should be interpreted in its meaning of family relationships. The master wants everyone to feel welcomed into his home as a family member. The meal is not complete if a member of his family does not come. In the second sending, the servant must compel the people to come in. The word "compel" is very strong.[30] Hence, the repetition of the servant's command is filled with meaning. First he is sent to the poor, maimed, blind, and lame. These take precedence over the normal folks. Then he is sent to gather all the other people he can find in an intensive campaign to fill the house. No one should be left outside the banquet except one group.

Those who rejected the invitation will not taste of the banquet (v. 24). While many scholars have determined that the concluding verse is a redactional addition, it is a suitable end to the parable.[31] The parable needs this ending to drive home the point. The time of the invitation is crucial. The master affirms, "For I tell you, none of those men who were invited shall taste my banquet."[32] The solemn warning is clear. While the great invitation is open to all, the invited guests stand in mortal danger of missing a never-to-be repeated opportunity.

---

[30] See BAGD 52.

[31] In addition, v. 24 may be rendered into good Hebrew, which may indicate that it comes from the better sources of the Synoptic tradition.

[32] It is similar to the conclusion of the parable of Johanan ben Zachai, "But those who did not adorn themselves for the banquet, let them stand and watch [the others eat]" (b. *Shabb.* 153a).

10 *The Search: The Parables of the Lost Sheep and Lost Coin*

FOCUS

The twin parables of the Lost Sheep and the Lost Coin (Luke 15:1–10; Matt 18:12–14) stress the diligent search for what has strayed or been misplaced. When the lost is found in the Lukan version, both illustrations focus on the joy of restoration, which must be a shared experience with friends and neighbors. Matthew preserves only the parable of the Lost Sheep and describes the sheep as going astray rather than emphasizing the lost and found theme as in Luke. The first evangelist concludes the parable by raising the concern for the little ones. It is not the will of the Father for them to die.

"What was lost has been found" is the message in all these versions, but scholars have felt other competing themes in the telling of the story. Who was responsible for the loss? Are the shepherds of Israel to be held accountable? Does the story stress the joy of discovery or the strenuous efforts required for the search? The shepherd and the woman rejoice, and both seek to share their joy with friends and relatives. Does Jesus stress the joy of the community over the happiness of the shepherd and the woman? Yet another theme is found in the Lukan version when Jesus speaks about the one who needs to repent. All will agree that there are those in need of repentance. But the counterquestion should be asked: Are there people who need no repentance? Was the story designed to challenge Jesus' disciples or to attack the scribes and Pharisees?

These simple illustrations present serious and complex problems for the interpreter. The parable is designed to teach one message. But the original cultural and literary context is held captive by conflicting messages. The major focus of the illustrations is difficult to understand because of the various themes that have been secondarily introduced into the stories. Here we shall suggest that these twin parables draw upon scenes of daily life in order to propose a solution to one of the most pressing questions in first-century Jewish religious life.[1] The problem is related to study and action. What takes precedence, learning Torah or practicing it? When these beautiful illustrations are silhouetted against this issue, the primary meaning of the parable is clear: All must search diligently for the lost.

On the one hand, the search for the lost is the overriding theme of the stories, but on the other hand, theological significance must be seen in the underlying cluster of ideas used to underpin this central message. The joy of discovery that must be shared with friends and relatives makes the vigorous effort involved in the search and the taxing burden required for restoration pale when compared with the rejoicing of a community. The lost has been found, the sinner has been restored, and the people are filled with joy. But the thrust of the parable focuses on the diligent search. The intensive work required to find the lost is the main theme. Many are in urgent need, and they will be restored only by the active efforts of a loving and caring community.

THE CHRISTIAN INTERPRETATIONS

The finest approach among the Christian interpretations of the parables has stressed compassion and outreach to those who are in need of spiritual restoration. Other approaches have sometimes maligned Judaism as deficient in compassion when compared with the church's concern for the sinner.[2] The setting in Luke intensifies the entire issue of the historical context in the ministry of Jesus. In Luke the setting for the parable is introduced: "Now the tax collectors and sinners were all drawing near to hear him. And the scribes and the Pharisees murmured, saying, 'This man receives sinners and eats with them.' " The table fellowship that Jesus enjoyed with all strata of society, even those of ill repute, becomes a point of contention in the story of Levi the tax collector, too. The Pharisees and scribes offer a similar criticism on the occasion of the great feast that Levi sponsored after he left all to follow Jesus as a disciple. After all, many of Levi's acquaintances from his days as a tax collector had joined the festivities. A spiritual leader such as Jesus should not eat with these types of irreligious people. His association with them

[1] As has been stressed to me by Lindsey, Jesus often taught in partner parables. The Lost Sheep and the Lost Coin are excellent examples of twin illustrations that reinforce one another. Lindsey and Flusser have suggested (private communication) that in the *Vorlage* of the Gospels these parables originally followed the story of the call of Levi (Matt 9:9–13; Mark 2:13–17; Luke 5:27–32).

[2] Both of these trends can be seen in Tertullian. On the one hand, he stresses divine grace for the sinner who returns and the earnest search. On the other hand, he teaches that Jesus refutes the Jews and not the Christians. He attacked the Jews because they were indignant at the notion of God giving hope to the heathen. See *On Repentance* 8 (ANF, 3:663); and *On Modesty* 8 (ANF, 4:81).

might be viewed as his endorsement of their questionable lifestyle. When asked why he ate with tax collectors, Jesus responded, “Those who are well have no need of a physician, but those who are sick; I have not come to call the righteous, but sinners to repentance’“ (Luke 5:31–32).

In every religious community some members may be criticized for association with undesirable outsiders who are viewed as antagonistic to the life of piety. While some Pharisees and scribes would not have approved of Jesus’ free association with wrongdoers, one should not lose sight of the fact that the Pharisees themselves highly valued the return of the sinner. One story taken from the later rabbinic literature, which most probably reflects earlier Pharisaic views, is a case in point. The story concerns R. Meir and his wife, Beruria. Even though R. Meir is a very high-profile leader, credited for his pervasive influence in the compilation of the Mishnah, his wife often is portrayed as having greater wisdom. In one of the areas where they lived, wrongdoers and sinners were troubling them. Rabbi Meir prayed that the sinners would die. He justified his prayer by quoting Ps 104:35, which, according to his translation, called for the “sinners” being brought to an end. Beruria, however, corrected his misreading of the Hebrew text. In her eyes, the Hebrew vowels should be read to say that “sins” should be brought to an end.[3] In other words, when the sins cease, there will be no more wicked men. Being a man of wisdom, R. Meir recognized that his wife was correct and began praying that the sins, rather than the sinners, should be brought to an end. According to Beruria, “Since the sins will cease, there will be no more wicked men!” In the end, R. Meir “did pray for them, and they repented.”[4] In all events, Jesus’ response to criticism is not unlike the major trends toward spirituality in the teachings of the Pharisees. The piety, spirituality, and welcome for the sinner who truly repents is the same for both Jesus and the Pharisees. The success of Jesus’ energetic outreach to sinners such as Levi should be received with joy rather than skepticism. Skeptics, however, do emerge from every tradition. Joy over a person who repents is in perfect harmony with traditional Jewish values.

Contrasting Judaism and Christianity on this point is an exercise in the pot calling the kettle black. Extremes and failures may be seen in both religious traditions. But the activities of Jesus as a spiritual leader who associated with every type of individual in society must be kept in clear view. He was at home in the company of the disreputable tax collector Zacchaeus as well as the honorable Simon the Pharisee. The introduction to the parables of the Lost Sheep and the Lost Coin in Luke 15:1 seems to be a carryover from the story about Levi in Luke 5:30: “And the Pharisees and their scribes murmured against his disciples, saying, ‘Why do you eat and drink with tax

[3] Instead of חַטָּאִים (“sinners”) as in the Masoretic Text, Beruria read חֲטָאִים (“sins”) in Ps 104:35, “Let [sins] sinners be consumed from the earth, and let the wicked be no more!” The wicked will be no more because their sins have been consumed.

[4] b. *Ber.* 10a (Epstein, *Babylonian Talmud,* 51) and parallels.

collectors and sinners?' " The issue was Jesus' willingness to search diligently for the lost. He sought spiritual renewal for others through personal involvement with them. He did not wait for the undesirables of society to approach him as a religious leader for spiritual guidance. Rather, he sought them out and demonstrated love and compassion through his personal association with them. Jesus' teachings were filled with popular images and animated characters from everyday life that commanded the attention of the common folk. All of this was part of Jesus' reaching out to the lost coins and straying sheep. Eating with the tax collector friends of Levi was near to the heart of Jesus. Levi was an influential man who had turned his back on his former questionable life in order to follow Jesus. In fact, Flusser and Lindsey have suggested that the original position of these two parables in Luke was after the story of Levi in the Hebrew undertext of the gospels.

This fascinating suggestion becomes quite plausible when the language and composition of the Gospels are studied to learn as much about their sources as possible. The present placement of the parables in the Gospel narratives is literary and artificial, as the synoptic comparison illustrates. The same parable may be placed in different literary contexts by each evangelist. His arrangement may be due to his sources or own creative instincts. The parables, however, may have had a different literary context in the earlier sources used by the evangelists. In any case, such an intuitive suggestion, that the parables of the Lost Sheep and the Lost Coin originally formed the continuation of the discourse about Jesus coming to help the sick who need a physician, is compelling. He told these stories at the dinner table of Levi. At the very least, both the story of Levi and the parables contain nearly identical themes. The mission of Jesus to help those in need, in an intensive search for the lost, emerges from both the Gospel account of Levi the tax collector and the twin parables of the sheep and the coin.

Matthew's approach to the parable, however, places the story in his discourses concerning "these little ones" (Matt 18:6, 10, 14). He seems to understand Jesus' parable as dealing with those inside the Christian community who have strayed. Unlike Luke, who says that the sheep is completely lost (ἀπολέσας), Matthew uses the verb that means strayed (πλανηθῇ) from the flock. Matthew, somewhat qualifying the search, leaves the actual recovery of such a stray sheep an open question, "And if he finds it" (καὶ ἐὰν ψένηται εὑρεῖν αὐτό), whereas Luke stresses the intensive effort of the shepherd who will search until he finds it.[5] Pheme Perkins observes, "Notice that Matthew even leaves the actual finding of such a lost sheep an open question."[6] Matthew seems to see a warning in the parable for the spiritual leadership of the church. More love and concern should be given to the straying sheep who need help from the leaders. They must seek them out. They are responsible for their restoration.

[5] See Harrington, *Matthew*, 266.

[6] See Pheme Perkins, *Hearing the Parables of Jesus* (New York: Paulist, 1981) 31.

GOSPEL OF THOMAS 107: THE LOST SHEEP

> Jesus said: The Kingdom is like a shepherd who had a hundred sheep. One of them went astray, which was the largest. He left behind ninety-nine, he sought for the one until he found it. Having tired himself out, He said to the sheep: I love thee more than (παρά) ninety-nine. (*Gos.Thom.* 107)

The parable of the Lost Sheep in the *Gospel of Thomas* differs from the canonical texts of Matthew and Luke. *Thomas*'s version illustrates the shepherd's concern for the one. Why would the shepherd leave the ninety-nine sheep to find one that had strayed? Because the sheep is the largest and most valuable. Jeremias describes *Thomas*'s approach: "The motive for the shepherd's laborious search is represented as being the loss of the largest and most valuable beast, which he loved more than all the rest." Jeremias is certainly correct when he argues, "A comparison with Matthew and Luke, as well as with the general trend of Jesus' message, shows that this is a complete misunderstanding of the parable."[7] *Thomas* represents an early interpretation that missed the major thrust of the parabolic teaching of Jesus. The security of the ninety-nine sheep is derived from the fact that the shepherd will indeed search out even one that is lost, regardless of its size or value. The contrast between the great value of the ninety-nine sheep in comparison with the relatively little value attached to one straying sheep, which was integral for the original parable, is obliterated by *Thomas.* On the other hand, *Thomas* does grasp the strong efforts involved in restoring the lost sheep. In its coloring of the story, the shepherd tired himself out in the process of searching for and restoring the fat sheep to the rest of the flock.

Perhaps Manson best captured the essence of these two parables. He focused attention on their primary message. Manson perceptively observed, "But the characteristic feature of these two parables is not so much the joy over the repentant sinner as the Divine love that goes out to seek the sinner before he repents."[8] This message is most lucidly preserved in Luke's version. God's love reaches out to the lost person, and Jesus is consumed with a passion to find those outcasts who need divine compassion.

THE JEWISH BACKGROUND

The original force of the parables is best appreciated when viewed within the context of early Jewish thought and culture. The shepherd seeking the lost sheep was reminiscent of God in the Hebrew Bible. Ezekiel 34:11–12 dramatizes God in the role of a shepherd who seeks the lost sheep: "For thus says the Lord GOD: Behold, I, I myself will search for my sheep, and will seek them out. As a shepherd seeks out his flock when some of his sheep have

---

[7] Jeremias, *Parables of Jesus,* 134.
[8] Manson, *Sayings,* 284.

been scattered abroad, so will I seek out my sheep." This strong prophetic word is greatly needed because the sheep have not received adequate care. The prophet sharply castigates the spiritual leaders by saying, "The weak you have not strengthened, the sick you have not healed, the crippled you have not bound up, the strayed you have not brought back, the lost you have not sought" (34:4). Jesus may well be alluding to this OT passage by stressing that God's shepherding work must be carried out by people. God seeks the lost through the social involvement of other concerned human beings. Jesus' ministry as characterized in the Gospels served the lost sheep. He is the type of shepherd who goes after the ones who stray in the wilderness. The challenge is for the disciples to become shepherds who are fully dedicated to the task of helping the lost experience restoration. They must perform the vigorous labor involved in recovery.

A similar image of God appears in a Jewish exposition of Ps 119:3, where R. Haggai bar Eleazer teaches that it is the shepherd who seeks the stray sheep and not vice versa. Who is the shepherd? It is God who goes after the lost.

The Shepherd Looks for the Lost

> Another comment: Why did David say at the end of the Psalm *I have gone astray like a lost sheep; seek Thy servant?* R. Judah the Levite bar Shallum answered in the name of R. Haggai bar Eleazar: As things go in the world, when a sheep strays from the flock, or an ox strays from the pasture, who seeks whom? The sheep, the shepherd? Or the shepherd, the sheep? Obviously the shepherd, the sheep. So David said to the Holy One, blessed be He: Master of the universe, seek me as the sheep is sought. . . . I have gone astray like a lost sheep; seek Thy servant, for, like a sheep, I am innocent—*a ewe lamb . . . without blemish* (Lev. 13:10).[9]

Not much is known about Rabbi Haggai bar Eleazer, and the date of this passage is uncertain. The metaphoric language, however, demonstrates the prevalence of the theme. Like a shepherd seeking the lost sheep, God himself seeks the one who has strayed.[10] Already in Ezekiel, the Hebrew prophet was using this metaphor, which was well known from everyday experience. When he compared God to a shepherd, the prophet criticized the religious leaders of his day for irresponsibly caring for their flocks.

Luke's version of the parable accentuates the shepherd imagery to a greater degree than Matthew's. In Luke the shepherd picks up the lost sheep and places it on his shoulders. This dramatic element is very significant. The shepherds listening to the story would realize that such a sheep is quite heavy, probably weighing seventy to ninety pounds. When the sheep is lost, it is often overcome with fright and will bleat loudly until help arrives. Being caught up with its paralyzing fear, the poor animal is motionless. The

---

[9] *Midr. Ps.* 119:3 (Braude, *Midrash on Psalms,* 2:249).
[10] See Hyman, *Toldot,* 1:411.

shepherd must take the sheep by its legs and saddle it around his neck, where he will carry it back to the flock.

The shepherd in the land of Israel customarily counts his flock before leading them into the fold for the night. With a flock of one hundred, the shepherd needs a number of undershepherds to assist. No doubt, he would leave some of the undershepherds in charge of the ninety-nine when he departs to find the lost sheep.[11] The listeners may assume that the search begins in the evening after the discovery of the lost sheep has been made. The other sheep will be led into a makeshift sheepfold or driven into a cave for protection. The Arab shepherd boy Muhammad ed-Deeb, credited with the discovery of the Dead Sea Scrolls in Qumran Cave I, is said to have counted his sheep at the unusual hour of 11:00 A.M.[12] He is sometimes viewed as an incompetent shepherd because he had neglected to count them on the two previous evenings. As the story goes, after he discovered that a sheep was missing, he entrusted his flock of fifty-five head to two undershepherds who tended to the needs of the herd while he searched for the lost animal—and then, by chance, discovered the Dead Sea Scrolls. While the entire story has been subject to what may well be justified skepticism, it is a fine illustration of the work of shepherds in the land today, which probably has not changed significantly over the centuries.[13] The listeners were familiar with the labor associated with shepherding the flock. Some no doubt had experienced the joy of finding a lost lamb after an intensive search through the dangerous wilderness.

These twin parables in Luke make use of sharp contrasts that would include all members of the original audience. Those who did not know the joy of finding the lost sheep might be more familiar with losing a coin in a dimly lighted home. The first parable speaks about a man and the second about a woman. Probably the shepherd with one hundred sheep would be considered well off, while the woman who lost one of her ten silver drachma coins would be viewed as poor.[14] Nevertheless, they share a common feeling

[11] H. Daniel-Rops, *Daily Life in Palestine at the Time of Christ* (ET; London: Weidenfeld & Nicholson, 1961) 230–31, observed: "Sometimes a number of shepherds would agree among themselves and bring their different flocks to the same place in the evening, so that each shepherd might watch in turn, which would allow the others to get some sleep in the tent. To make the watching easier, it was usual to make huge sheep-folds with dry-stone walls, high enough to be difficult to get over. Some pasture-grounds even had towers. . . . The watchers could keep a look-out for the approach of robbers, whether they had four legs or two."

[12] See W. H. Brownlee, "Muhammad ed-Deeb's Own Story of His Scroll Discovery," *Journal of Near Eastern Studies* 16 (1957): 236; and the discussion by Jeremias, *Parables of Jesus,* 134.

[13] Jeremias, *Parables of Jesus,* 133. He carefully describes these parallels to the work of the shepherd in the parable.

[14] See ibid.: "Among the Bedouin the size of a flock varies from 20 to 200 head of small cattle; in Jewish law 300 head is reckoned as an unusually large flock. Hence, with 100 sheep the man possesses a medium-sized flock; he looks after it himself."

of loss when something valuable to them is missing. Both of them recognize the effort involved in finding what is missing. The woman lights a lamp and sweeps the house.[15] The houses were usually constructed without windows and with a low doorway that would admit minimal light. She needs a lamp and a broom. The fuel of the wick lamp will be olive oil, and the broom will be of a primitive variety made from twigs tied together. She searches by sweeping, hoping that the silver coin will shine in the light of the flame. The drachma was a Greek coin equal to a denarius, the amount paid to part-time rural laborers for a day's work. Many of these houses were insular structures where most activities occurred in the courtyard. Such houses required little inside lighting.[16]

A very similar parable is told in rabbinic literature. The illustration focuses attention on the study of Torah. The dedication required for a life of Torah scholarship is compared to the search for a lost coin.

The Search for Torah Treasure

> R. Phinehas b. Jair opened his exposition with the text, *If thou seek her as silver,* etc. (Prov. II, 4). If you seek after the words of Torah as after hidden treasures, the Holy One blessed be He, will not withhold your reward. If a man loses a *sela'* or an *obol* in his house, he lights lamp after lamp, wick after wick, till he finds it. Now does it not stand to reason: if for these things which are only ephemeral and of this world a man will light so many lamps and lights till he finds where they are hidden, for the words of Torah which are the life both of this world and of the next world, ought you not to search as for hidden treasures? Hence "*if thou seek her as silver,* etc."[17]

The imagery of this fascinating illustration is very similar to the parable of the Lost Coin. The activity associated with lighting the lamp and searching in the dark is intensified in both illustrations. The distinctive feature of Jesus' parable, however, is the *nimshal,* or reality, behind the word-picture. Jesus speaks about the vigorous efforts required to restore a lost person to the community of faith, while R. Phinehas b. Jair illustrates the search for the hidden treasures of the Torah.

Both of the Lukan parables stress the boundless joy of recovering what was lost. The joy is so immense that it must be shared with friends and family. This aspect of the cultural background continues to appear in the

---

[15] Jeremias (*Parables of Jesus,* 134–35) assumes that the woman was searching for a coin from her headdress, which was bedecked with coins as a part of her dowry, but this assumption is not justified without further evidence closer to the time period or the Jewish cultural heritage. No hint of a dowry is given in the parable.

[16] See the fine work of John McRay, *Archaeology and the New Testament* (Grand Rapids: Baker, 1991) 81. For a description of modern examples, see S. Amiry and V. Tamari, *The Palestinian Village Home* (London: British Museum, 1989) 17–33.

[17] *Song. Rab.* 1.1.9 (Freedman, *Midrash Rabbah,* 10–11). *Song of Solomon Rabbah* contains early material, as here in citing R. Phinehas ben Jair.

village life of the Middle East.[18] Few secrets are kept private in a small Galilean village. The joy of discovery will be shared by the shepherd and the woman with their friends and acquaintances. Today many parable interpreters tend to view the joy as the main message.[19] While this point is well taken, the theme of joy is only a powerful undercurrent in the mainstream of Jesus' primary message concerning the intensity of a search for people in need, which may cause close association with undesirable characters such as tax collectors and sinners.

Luke seems to preserve some of the original dry wit of Jesus in his conclusion of the parable of the Lost Sheep: "Just so, I tell you, there will be more joy in heaven over one sinner who repents than over ninety-nine righteous persons who need no repentance."[20] The question is, How many people need no repentance? Rabbi Eleazer taught his disciples to repent every day.[21] The later rabbinic teachings regarding the ten days of awe and the day of Atonement mention three categories of people, the completely righteous, the completely wicked, and the "in-betweens."[22] The rabbis obviously believed that most people fall into the "in-between" category and need to repent. The house of Shammai taught, "There will be three groups at the Day of Judgment—one thoroughly righteous, and one thoroughly wicked and one of the intermediate."[23] Therefore Bailey may be correct when he notes, "Christ's subtle humor shows through in this verse. The 'righteous' who 'need no repentance' do not exist."[24] Most people need to repent and maintain a living relationship with God in their cultivation of personal spirituality. But the theme of repentance is emphasized more by Luke (or the source he is using for the story) than by the other evangelists. Matthew does not mention repentance in his version of the parable of the Lost Sheep. Nonetheless, the saying of Jesus "there will be joy in heaven over one sinner who repents" seems to be an original part of the parable. The lost has been found, and the people rejoice with God and his heavenly entourage.

In the story of the tax collector Levi, which likely served as the springboard for Jesus' pair of illustrations, Matthew and Mark do not mention repentance.[25] In Luke 5:32 Jesus declares, "I have not come to call the

[18] See, e.g., Eric F. F. Bishop, *Jesus of Palestine* (London: Lutterworth, 1955) 166.

[19] See, e.g., John Dominic Crossan, *In Parables: The Challenge of the Historical Jesus* (Sonoma, Calif.: Polebridge, 1992) 38.

[20] Luke 15:7. Cf. the parallel ending to the Lost Coin: "Just so, I tell you, there is joy before the angels of God over one sinner who repents" (v. 10).

[21] See b. *Shabb.* 153a and parallels.

[22] See b. *Rosh Hash.* 16b and parallels.

[23] See b. ibid., 16b–17a, and parallels. The school of Hillel stresses the grace of God at the day of judgment.

[24] Kenneth E. Bailey, *The Cross and the Prodigal* (St. Louis: Concordia, 1973) 24. Bailey's rich insight into Middle Eastern culture is greatly beneficial, but sometimes his allegorical interpretation and misunderstanding of Judaism are alarming.

[25] Cf. Matt 9:9–13; Mark 2:13–19; Luke 5:27–32.

righteous, but sinners to repentance." Jesus was calling for active discipleship, which involved learning his teaching and putting it into practice. Luke uses the perfect tense for "I have not come" (οὐκ ἐλήλυθα) together with the aorist infinitive for "to call" (καλέσαι), which stresses the idea of purpose. The perfect tense captures the force of the Semitic idiom לא באתי, which conveys the past action with present and continuing results. His purpose is to call the sinners to be his disciples, pursuing this objective by eating and fellowshiping with them. Moreover, the term "to repentance" (εἰς μετάνοιαν) does not appear in Mark or Matthew and is most likely a Lukan emphasis. One must fellowship with sinners and tax gatherers in order to make disciples.[26] The "righteous" ones, on the other hand, are beyond this type of table fellowship. Perhaps they have become too engrossed in academic study and personal piety to reach out to others who have strayed from Torah learning. Jesus was certainly maintaining the traditions of the Pharisees and Jewish wisdom teachers, who stressed that each meal was an opportunity to exchange the words of Torah and that each home must be a meeting place for the disciples of the wise to drink in their teachings.[27] When one eats a meal without discussing Torah, it is as if he or she had partaken of a pagan sacrifice.[28] The majority of Pharisees would have seen truth in the answer of Jesus. His emphasis on finding the lost was a concern that most Pharisees would have shared.

Two attitudes toward sinners can be discerned in early Jewish thought. One regarded association with wrongdoers as a temptation to sin. The other recognized the value of personal involvement with the irreligious in the effort to restore them to Torah observance. For instance, Nittai the Arbelite is remembered for his fear of sin. He did not wish to become associated with wrongdoers because of the ever present danger that such fellowship would lead to disobedience to God. He warns, "Keep far away from an evil neighbor, do not associate with the wicked, and do not lose hope of the final reckoning."[29] The other approach was modeled by Hillel. In his teachings he emphasized, "Be of the disciples of Aaron, loving peace and pursuing peace, loving humankind and drawing them to the Torah."[30] Hillel was willing to accept proselytes on questionable grounds. He labored to bring the un-

---

[26] It is interesting that the term "and sinners" (καὶ ἁμαρτωλῶν) is missing in manuscripts C and D (see Luke 5:30). Quite likely it is an early scribal addition.

[27] See the words of Jose ben Yoezer in *Abot* 2:4: "Let thy house be a meeting-house for the wise; and powder thyself in the dust of their feet; and drink their words with thirstiness" (Taylor, *Sayings,* 1:28).

[28] See *Abot* 3:4: "R. Simeon said, If three have eaten at a table and have spoken there no words of Torah, it is as if they had eaten of sacrifices to dead idols" (Hertz, *Daily Prayer Book,* 649).

[29] See *Abot R. Nat.*, version A, ch. 9 (Goldin, *Rabbi Nathan,* 53) for the text and a discussion on this saying from *Abot* 1:7.

[30] See *Abot R. Nat.*, version A, ch. 12, on *Abot* 1:12–14 (Goldin, *Rabbi Nathan,* 63).

observant into religious faith. His desire was to draw others to the teachings of Torah.[31]

The suggestion that Jesus was not offending all Pharisees in advocating a caring outreach for the lost may at first seem unfounded. Listening to the Gospel story without the prejudices based on the tragic history of Jewish and Christian relations is not easy. If, however, one views Jesus as a teacher among his people rather than the founder of a completely new religion, the authenticity of the situation becomes clear. Naturally, some religious teachers would frown upon this type of open fellowship with wrongdoers, which might call into question Jesus' integrity. But when Jesus explained the meaning of the effort, finding the lost and calling the sinner to training in Torah learning, the whole process was justified. The reign of God is for everyone. He is calling the wrongdoer to accept the yoke of the kingdom of heaven. In fact, most Pharisees would feel that such a worthy cause should be encouraged. Flusser, who is perhaps the foremost authority in this area of research, has commented:

> Many modern theologians increasingly attempt to define the message of Jesus over against Judaism. Jesus is said to have taught something quite different, something original, unacceptable to the other Jews. The strong Jewish opposition to Jesus' proclamation is emphasized. To deal with such views is not the task of New Testament scholarship but belongs to modern research of ideology; yet Jewish parallels to the words of Jesus and the manner in which he revised the inherited material clearly refute the above assumptions. Even though he gave his own personal bent to Jewish ideas, selected from among them, purged and reinterpreted them, I cannot honestly find a single word of Jesus that could seriously exasperate a well intentioned Jew.[32]

Those "Jewish parallels to the words of Jesus and the manner in which he revised the inherited material" make it difficult to accept the view that first-century Jewish people would have rejected Jesus' intensive outreach to people in need. His teachings concerning the search for the lost and having fellowship with people in need would by no means "exasperate a well intentioned Jew" from the period. Jesus sought to strengthen Judaism, not undermine the religious piety of his people.

LEARNING OR DOING

In the original context of Jesus' ministry, the parables of the Lost Sheep and the Lost Coin probably gave greater emphasis to the approach that stressed doing good deeds over and above the study of Torah. This issue was

---

[31] See ibid. (Goldin, *Rabbi Nathan*, 68): "This teaches that one should bend men to and lead them under the wings of the Shekinah the way Abraham our father used to bend men and lead them under the wings of the Shekinah."

[32] Flusser, "Reflections of a Jew," 16.

hotly debated among the religious leaders and Torah scholars. Leading sages such as Rabbi Tarfon believed that action took precedence over learning. Rabbi Akiva, on the other hand, argued that learning must precede doing. After all, the study of Torah leads to practice.[33] His approach became recognized as the more correct method of fulfilling the demands of Torah. One must acquire an understanding of the teachings of Scripture and then apply them in daily life. Although the distinction for moderns may seem somewhat trivial, the discussions in rabbinic literature indicate that the issue was a matter of intense soul-searching and agonizing discussion.[34]

Is it possible that these parables preserve some of this sharp friction among various factions during the time of Jesus? The seeking of a lost sheep or the intensive search for the misplaced silver drachma are descriptions of social involvement. Such deeds of loving-kindness must be given top priority for Jesus. They would give precedence to good works over study. On the other hand, no one should doubt the stress given to Torah learning in the circle of Jesus' disciples. The Sermon on the Mount as well as the high ethical and moral message of his parables reach for the best of academic learning. Yet the practical daily application that must be lived in strict obedience to Torah is found at the core of so much of what is taken from these Gospel teachings. The essence of Jesus' teachings is "hear and obey." Deeds of loving-kindness that reach out to help others take precedence over study for the sake of learning.

The parables of the Lost Sheep and the Lost Coin challenge the listeners to seek the lost, bear the burden of restoration, and share the joy of finding the sinner with the community of faith. The lost are found through active involvement and social interaction. Jesus modeled the approach by his fellowship with the irreligious and the wrongdoers of his day. He pursued an energetic outreach to the disreputable tax collectors and sinners. He encouraged them to become his disciples. Decisive action is the essence of these parables. The search requires diligence. Seeking the lost involves laborious effort. The strenuous work, however, is accompanied by sheer joy when the lost is found.

---

[33] *Sifre Deut.* 41 (*Sifre Devarim*, ed. Finkelstein, 85); j. *Pesach* 30b, ch. 3, halakah 7; j. *Chag.* 76c, ch. 1, halakah 7; b. *Kidd.* 40b. Cf. G. Alon, *The Jews in Their Land in the Talmudic Age* (2 vols.; Jerusalem: Magnes, 1984) 2:499. Cf. also Young, *Jewish Parables*, 96–100, 256–58.

[34] Cf. *Abot* 1:17: "Simeon, his son, said, 'All my days I have grown up among the wise, and I have found nothing of greater benefit than silence; not learning but doing is the chief thing.' "

11 The Find

FOCUS

The parables of the Hidden Treasure and the Pearl of Great Price (Matt 13:44–46) have puzzled interpreters, who have asked whether these straightforward illustrations emphasize more the cost of discipleship or the value of the kingdom. What price must the disciple be willing to pay? When he or she decides to answer the challenging call of Jesus, the cost involves everything he or she owns, as well as all relationships with other people. How is it possible, on the other hand, to measure the worth of God's reign? The kingdom is infinitely beyond human value, but these parables teach that the kingdom is within one's grasp if one is willing to sacrifice all to obtain it.[1]

The major significance of these seemingly straightforward illustrations, therefore, has been the subject of intense debate. Jeremias, for example, strongly rejects the idea that these parables merely call upon the disciple for "heroic action." The core message is not the cost of discipleship. Rather, the news of Jesus' preaching made the heart glad. Jeremias understands the parable as stressing above all else the great joy of discovering the kingdom.[2] The church fathers tended to identify the treasure and the pearl with Christ. He is the center of their theology and the focus of the parables. Do the

[1] See McNeile, *Matthew,* 203. McNeile emphasizes the value of the kingdom: "The parable, as a whole, illustrates an aspect of the Kingdom . . . its enormous worth, for which any sacrifice should be made." It should be remembered that in the first century pearls were very precious gems, which the ancients probably prized much more highly than diamonds.

[2] See Jeremias, *Parables of Jesus,* 200–201. He observes (quoting Gulin), "In reality, it is 'completely misunderstood if it is interpreted as an imperious call to heroic action.' The key-words are rather ἀπὸ τῆς χαρᾶς. . . . Thus it is with the Kingdom of God. The effect of the joyful news is overpowering; it fills the heart with gladness."

parables teach Christology or the inner gladness one experiences at hearing Jesus' preaching of grace?

Matthew's version of these illustrations, however, is more concise and to the point. They are kingdom parables. Overwhelming joy accompanies the man who sells all to obtain the treasure in a field. The diligent seeker finds a pearl beyond all expectations. The man and the merchant must risk everything for the treasure and the pearl. In the study of the Jewish roots of Jesus' parabolic teachings, these partner illustrations would fall within the domain of learning Torah and of making disciples to serve in the work of God's kingdom. In fact, the introductions that speak about the kingdom of heaven are almost certainly original.[3] These parables speak about the reign of God. The disciple must be willing to surrender all for training in the kingdom of heaven. Jesus is grooming disciples who will transmit his teachings to others. The goal of this educational training is the fear of God. Heschel has perceptively noted the distinctive role of education in Jewish culture: "The Greeks learned in order to comprehend. The Hebrews learned in order to revere."[4] Reverence for God required a commitment to education so that individuals would understand and ultimately obey God's teachings in the Torah. They revere God and seek to interpret his will from Torah. Jesus wanted his followers to understand the proper meaning of the Scriptures in order that they could obey God as sovereign. The central role of Torah education and the close relationship between the disciple and his chosen master have been stressed by Safrai.[5] Jesus' teachings concerning the kingdom of heaven exalted the divine purpose for living as set forth in the message of Torah.

The essence of the twin parables is this: the kingdom is worth all a person has—and so very much more! The kingdom is expensive. It costs everything the disciple possesses. The joy of discipleship, however, overpowers every worldly hindrance.

CHRISTIAN INTERPRETATION

Christian interpretations of the parables of the Hidden Treasure and the Pearl of Great Price show a strong christological interest. Irenaeus taught that the treasure is Christ. Such an allegorical approach has been rejected, however, by the consensus of modern scholars. Irenaeus proclaims, "For

---

[3] While the introductions to the parables may show more how the evangelists understood them rather than the original context, one should note that both *Thomas* and Matthew introduce these parables with the kingdom theme. The content of the parables, moreover, must be understood in light of Jesus' kingdom teachings.

[4] Abraham Joshua Heschel, *The Insecurity of Freedom* (New York: Schocken, 1972) 41.

[5] See S. Safrai, "The Jewish Cultural Nature of Galilee in the First Century," *Immanuel* 24/25 (1990): 147–86; and "Education and the Study of Torah," in Safrai, et al., *Jewish People,* 2:945–70. See also E. E. Urbach, *Class-Status and Leadership in the World of Palestinian Sages* (Jerusalem: Israel Academy of Sciences and Humanities, 1966).

Christ is the treasure which was hid in the field, that is, in this world (for 'the field is the world'); but the treasure hid in the Scriptures is Christ."[6] While Irenaeus read the Gospels from his own historical perspective, which was based on his experience in the church and his understanding of the divine redemptive plan, interpreters should refrain from imposing such later theological presuppositions on the parables of Jesus.

Everything that is known about Jesus and the technique he used to teach the people about his special mission opposes this type of christological interpretation. To imagine that the historical Jesus told a parable in which he himself appears as the great treasure accidentally discovered, or the diligently sought pearl of great price, is nonsense. Even though Matthew suggests that these parables were taught to the disciples in private, the Jesus of history did not ordinarily speak about his person in such a way, although he certainly had an acute self-awareness of his purpose and unique calling. He was overwhelmed with the passion to call the people into the kingdom, where they could experience spiritual renewal through the power of God. The force of God's reign is much closer to the essence of these parables, as their introductions indicate. Moreover, Jesus, in an effort to suppress any sort of personality cult, warned against people calling him "Lord, Lord." Would this same man then tell a story about himself as the treasure and the pearl?

Origen, too, understood the treasure and the pearl as referring to Christ, but took the allegorical method one step further when he discussed the meaning of the field in light of salvation history. The field represents the Scriptures and the treasure is Christ. The Jews rejected him, hence the treasure has been passed on to the Christians. Origen's approach not only erects a barrier between Jesus and his people but strips the Jews of their inheritance.

Origen's Allegorical Interpretation

And, having hidden it, he goes away, working and devising how he shall buy the field, or the Scriptures, that he may make them his own possession, receiving from the people of God the oracles of God with which the Jews were first entrusted. And when the man taught by Christ has bought the field, the kingdom of God which, according to another parable, is a vineyard, "is taken from them and is given to a nation bringing forth the fruits thereof,"—and to him who in faith has bought the field, as the fruit of his having sold all that he had, and no longer keeping by him anything that was formerly his; for they were a source of evil to him. And, you will give the same application, if the field containing the hidden treasure be Christ, for those who give up all things and follow Him, have, as it were in another way, sold their possessions, in order that, by having sold and surrendered them, and having received in their place from God—their helper—a noble resolution, they may purchase, at great cost worthy of the field, the field containing the treasure hidden in itself.[7]

[6] Irenaeus, *Against Heresies* 4.26.1 (ANF, 1:496).
[7] Origen, *Commentary on Matthew* 10.6 (ANF, 10:416).

No doubt, the major figure in the parable for Origen is Christ. His Christology is based in part upon divine wisdom, which is revealed in Christ. Origen explains, "The treasure hidden in the field is the thoughts concealed and lying under that which is manifest, 'of wisdom hidden in a mystery,' 'even Christ, in whom are all treasures of wisdom and knowledge hidden.' "[8] Like Irenaeus, Origen was a great church leader who has had a lasting impact upon theology,[9] but his allegorical approach robs the parable of its original meaning. The context ties the parable to the kingdom teachings of Jesus, not Christ himself.[10] Jesus never intended his parable to teach that the Jewish people had been disinherited, as Origen thought.

As a kingdom parable, its message is closely tied to other teachings of Jesus in the Gospels. For instance, Flusser properly understands "selling all" as an allusion to "seeking first the kingdom," which means that these illustrations are connected to Jesus' teachings concerning the reign of God.[11] By seeking first the kingdom, other physical needs of the disciple will be provided for. Thus, selling everything to enter the sovereignty of God is worth the risk. In the same way that the man sells everything to acquire the treasure or the merchant gambles all he owns to buy the pearl, the kingdom demands all. Willingness to surrender everything for the reign of God is the proper action. In any case, Origen's approach undermines the force of the kingdom's challenge. The allegorical features of his interpretation totally obscure the powerful call to discipleship. The parable is not about Jewish failure and Christian success but the essence of God's rule as a challenge to hear and obey!

GOSPEL OF THOMAS 109; 76: THE FIND

Jesus said: The Kingdom is like a man who had a treasure [hidden] in his field, without knowing it. And [after] he died, he left it to his [son. The] son did not know (about it), he accepted that field, he sold [it]. And he who bought it, he went, while he was plowing [he found] the treasure. He began (ἄρχεσθαι) to lend money to whom ever he wished. (*Gos. Thom.* 109)

Jesus said: The Kingdom of the Father is like a man, a merchant, who possessed merchandise (φορτίον) (and) found a pearl (μαργαρίτης). That merchant was prudent. He sold the merchandise (φορτίον), he bought the one pearl (μαργαρίτης) for himself. Do you also seek for the treasure which fails

[8] Ibid., 10.5 (ANF, 10:416).

[9] Cf. Joseph W. Trigg, *Origen* (Atlanta: John Knox, 1983) 244–60.

[10] Bultmann questioned the introduction, but the core message of the text is the cost of discipleship in the kingdom. Cf. Rudolf Bultmann, *The History of the Synoptic Tradition* (ET; rev. ed.; New York: Harper & Row, 1968; repr., Peabody, Mass.: Hendrickson, 1993) 173.

[11] Flusser, *Gleichnisse*, 129–33.

> not, which endures, there where no moth comes near to devour and (where) no (οὐδέ) worm destroys. (*Gos. Thom.* 76)

In the *Gospel of Thomas*, as in Matthew, both parables are introduced as kingdom illustrations.[12] Unlike Matthew, where the parables follow one another as partner illustrations, in *Thomas* they appear in different contexts, although after the pearl parable *Thomas* does speak about the "treasure which does not fail." The mention of a treasure here could allude to a version of the hidden treasure parable that may have been positioned after the story of the one pearl in *Thomas'* source.[13] The versions of the parables in *Thomas* also have strikingly distinctive features, such as finding the treasure with the plow and the ultimate image of financial success portrayed in the profession of a moneylender. The pearl merchant, moreover, is described as being prudent or shrewd. Did *Thomas* view the kingdom in this way? Perhaps it is saying that the kingdom is gained through wisdom or shrewdness. *Thomas* may also betray a distinctive perspective relating to the treasure and the pearl that is rooted in its theological system. Could the treasure and the pearl have a different meaning? *Thomas'* theology is not the same as that of the Synoptic Gospels. While the meager evidence does not allow much speculation, the image of a pearl sometimes has a different meaning in Gnosticism. These parallels in *Thomas* may have been attempts to depict the finding of the treasure and pearl as the discovery of the inner soul or the true self, i.e., the divine spark that sets a person free to enjoy a meaningful life. Other evidence for understanding *Thomas* would point to the pearl and the treasure as representing Christ.

In addition, like the later embellished version of a rabbinic parable that first appears in the *Mekilta*, the *Gospel of Thomas* describes the field as an inheritance and the one who has discovered the treasure as flaunting his newfound wealth. But the parable in *Thomas* is more complex. In it the son who inherits the land sells it to the one who locates the treasure. The original owner of the field was ignorant of the treasure, and he gave the field to his son, who then sold it. These elaborate transactions rob the illustration of its sharp focus. With such a treasure, furthermore, the finder in the *Gospel of*

---

[12] The parable of the Treasure in *Gos. Thom.* 109 appears in a series of kingdom sayings that climax in the conclusion of the gospel, "For every woman who makes herself male will enter the Kingdom of Heaven." The apparent underlying ideal of the androgynous state, known in some gnostic circles, is foreign to the Jesus of the canonical Gospels.

[13] The "treasure which does not fail" saying is paralleled in Matt 6:19–21 and Luke 12:33–34. While the parable of the Hidden Treasure precedes the Pearl of Great Price in Matthew, the fact that one pearl and the unfailing treasure come together in *Thomas* may be significant. See John Dominic Crossan, *Finding Is the First Act: Trove Folktales and Jesus' Treasure Parable* (Missoula, Mont.: Scholars, 1979) 104–6. Crossan suggests "that Thomas (1) replaced the treasure parable with the treasure aphorism because (2) he intended a very different version of that treasure story which was no longer in parallel with that of The Pearl."

Thomas begins to loan money. This is surely a shock for the readers, because the moneylender is not viewed as a particularly righteous individual. The successful moneylender, however, becomes the picture of great wealth and prosperity. The rabbinic story, on the other hand, describes the lucky fellow who has discovered the treasure as showing off his wealth by building a palace and parading through the market with his retinue of many servants.[14] When studying Matthew's accounts of the Hidden Treasure and the Pearl of Great Price, we see the earlier source of these rabbinic parables, found in the *Mekilta.* Compare the series of rabbinic parables that are quoted below to *Thomas* and note the similar embellishments.

The Treasure Find and Israel

R. Simeon b. Yochai taught: [The Egyptians were] like a man who inherited a piece of ground used as a dunghill. Being an indolent man, he went and sold it for a trifling sum. The purchaser began working and digging it up, and he found a treasure there, out of which he built himself a fine palace, and he began going about in public followed by a retinue of servants—all out of the treasure he found in it. When the seller saw it he was ready to choke, and he exclaimed, "Alas, what have I thrown away." So when Israel were in Egypt they were set to work at bricks and mortar, and they were despised in the eyes of the Egyptians. But when the Egyptians saw them encamped under their standards by the sea in military array, they were deeply mortified and exclaimed, "Alas, what have we sent forth from our land!" as it says, *And it came to pass* (wayyehi), *when Pharaoh had let the people go,* etc. (Ex. XIII,17). R. Jonathan said: They were like a man who had a field the size of a *beth kor*, and went and sold it for a trifle. The purchaser went and dug wells in it and planted gardens and orchards. When the seller saw it, he was deeply mortified and exclaimed, "Alas, what have I thrown away!" So when the Israelites were in Egypt they were set to work at bricks and mortar, and were despised in the eyes of the Egyptians. But when they saw them encamped under their standards by the sea in military array, they were deeply mortified and exclaimed, "Alas, what have we let go from our land!" as it says, "*And it came to pass, when Pharaoh had let the people go.*" R. Jose said: They were like a man who had a thicket of cedars that he sold for a trifle. The purchaser went and made from the wood boxes and towers and carriages. When the seller saw it he was deeply mortified and said, "Alas, what have I thrown away!" So when the Israelites were in Egypt they were set to work at bricks and mortar, and were despised in the eyes of the Egyptians. But when they saw them encamped under their standards in military array by the sea, they were deeply mortified and exclaimed, "Alas, what have we let go from our land!" as it says, "*And it came to pass, when Pharaoh had let the people go.*"[15]

---

[14] *Song Rab.* 4.12.1 (Freedman, *Midrash Rabbah,* 219) and the parallel in *Pesik. Rab Kah.* 11:7 (*Pesikta Derav Kahana,* ed. Mandelbaum, 1:183; English trans., Braude and Kapstein, *Kahana,* 206–7). See the discussion below, "Israel as a Precious Treasure." The version of the parables in the *Mekilta* is more concise and earlier.

[15] Ibid.

The three rabbinic parables serve to reinforce each other. They are told by different rabbis almost as if each one is trying to top the other's story. In reality the rabbis are pondering the significance of Exod 14:5. Why did the heart of Pharaoh change? What caused him to pursue the Israelites? How did he feel when he saw the people of Israel gathered at the sea? The parables show that it was like a man who found a treasure. The motifs are very similar to *Thomas;* the message and application are entirely different.

The pearl merchant in *Thomas*'s second parable is described as a prudent businessman who will take the risk of selling his merchandise to buy the one pearl for himself. This description is lacking in Matthew's more concise version. In gnostic thought, the pearl may represent Christ, or, as in the *Acts of Thomas,* the soul or the true self.[16] By knowledge the gnostic believer can discover the true self and appear before the King of kings. In this respect, the gnostic interpretations of the parables would lead in quite a different direction. Does the pearl refer to the soul? It is possible that for the *Gospel of Thomas* the two parables have different meanings, which may account for the separation of them? For *Thomas* the treasure could be Christ or the kingdom of the Father, while the pearl is the soul. In any case, originally the two parables were together.[17] The relationship between *Thomas* and the Synoptics will continue to occupy the interests of NT scholars.[18] These parables are remarkable for their similarity to Matthew's version, and yet they are so distinctive. They have been broken apart, placed in separate contexts, and expanded in a manner characteristic of folklore.

The colorful details in *Thomas*' parables are best explained as additions that were incorporated for more effect. The added elements may be derived

---

[16] See F. Hauck, μαργαρίτης, *TDNT* 4:473 n. 13; and *Acts Thom.* 113:104–105: "And he promised me that to the gate/Of the king of kings I should journey with him again/And with my gift and my pearl/With him appear before our king" (W. Schneemelcher and E. Hennecke, *New Testament Apocrypha* [trans. R. McL. Wilson; 2 vols.; rev. ed.; Louisville: Westminster/John Knox, 1991–1992] 2:385); see also the discussion by Han J. W. Drijvers, 2:335. It is not certain that the *Acts of Thomas* sheds light on the meaning of the pearl in the *Gospel of Thomas*'s version of the parable. Cf. also *Acts Pet.* 20 (Schneemelcher and Hennecke, *NT Apocrypha,* 2:304): "this Jesus you have, brethren, the door, the light, the way, the bread, the water, the life, the resurrection, the refreshment, the pearl, the treasure, the seed, the abundance, the mustard-seed, the vine, the plough, the grace, the faith, the word: He is all things, and there is no other greater than he." Cf. *Acts John* 109.

[17] While this claim may be debated, the method of telling two parables to illustrate a message was a favorite way of teaching that must have been used by the historical Jesus. Groups of two or more similar parables to illustrate the same point are not infrequent in rabbinic literature.

[18] See the discussion by John H. Sieber, "The Gospel of Thomas and the New Testament," in *Gospel Origins and Christian Beginnings* (Sonoma: Polebridge, 1990) 64–73. Sieber argues for the independence of *Thomas,* but W. Schrage, *Das Verhältnis des Thomas Evangeliums zur synoptischen Tradition und zu den koptischen Evangelienübersetzungen* (Berlin: Töpelmann, 1964) still offers much convincing evidence to the contrary.

from oral tradition or from similar Jewish stories, that were circulating independently of the Gospel sources. Many of these folklore traditions crossed religious and ethnic borders. If the *Gospel of Thomas* circulated as an oral tradition in Egypt, these colorful additions eventually influenced the final written form. These secondary aggrandizements in *Thomas* detract from the shorter and more poignant form of the parables in Matthew.[19] The element of joy, moreover, is completely absent.[20]

THE PARABLES IN THE LIGHT OF JEWISH TRADITION

The parables of the Hidden Treasure and the Pearl of Great Price have a rich background in Jewish tradition when viewed in the context of Torah learning. Accepting the kingdom meant entering into obedience to God and searching the deeper meaning of his revelation in Torah. The Gospels portray Jesus as a dynamic teacher, who raises up disciples for total commitment in the kingdom of heaven.[21] In Jewish thought, the recital of the Shema was the acceptance of the yoke of the kingdom, because one was making a declaration that one has chosen the LORD to the exclusion of all other gods, and God's way for living life. Praying the Shema opened up communion with the one true God. Disciples training under a master teacher were required to dedicate themselves to the task. Such devotion to God and God's revelation in Torah was not without sacrifices.

John Dominic Crossan has observed elements of folklore related to the parable of the Hidden Treasure. He has discussed the popular theme of treasure troves, from pirate figures such as Edward Teach (Blackbeard) and William (Captain) Kidd to the Jewish parallels related to the *Gospel of Thomas.*[22] He recognizes the distinctive nature of the theological and cultural context of ancient Judaism: "There are not very many Jewish tales of hidden treasure in its standard earthly form and those that exist usually evince the expected international motifs and types but adopted and adapted to the moral and monotheistic vision of Judaism."[23] It is this "vision of Judaism" in the *nimshal,* or the reality behind the word-picture, that makes one of the major differences. While some folklore motifs are shared, the vision of God and God's will are distinctive. In the teachings

[19] On the Treasure parable, Funk, Scott, and Butts (*Parables,* 37) conclude: "The short, tight structure of the Treasure in Matthew is characteristic of oral tradition. The form in Thomas is more elaborate and therefore a developed version of the parable."

[20] Joy is often viewed as the major theme of the parable (e.g., Jeremias, *Parables of Jesus,* 200–201).

[21] Compare m. *Ber.* 2:2 and parallels. "Receiving the kingdom" became an idiomatic way of referring to the recital of the Shema. See the story of Rabban Gamaliel in m. *Ber.* 1 and parallels.

[22] Crossan, *Finding,* 20.

[23] Ibid., 60.

of Jesus, much like the world of Jewish learning, attention is directed toward the reign of God and following the instruction of Torah in daily life. Here one begins to appreciate what Petuchowski calls the theological significance of Gospel and rabbinic parables.[24] This background is essential for a proper appreciation of the message.

Jesus asked his disciples to surrender all for the kingdom of heaven. Such was the case of the rich man, who had observed the teachings of the law from his youth but had failed to become concerned about the needs of the poor. Observing Torah, in the mind of Jesus, demanded radical action. To love his neighbor in fulfillment of the laws pertaining to relationships among people, the rich man would be required to give of his abundance to help suffering humanity. Jesus called him to the inner circle of disciples by asking him to sell all and give the money to the poor. The other disciples had left homes and businesses to devote themselves to the kingdom teachings of Jesus. He illustrated this in these parables, describing a treasure and a pearl. To acquire the treasure or to buy this special pearl, one must sell all. The rich man walked away sorrowfully, but the disciples of Jesus experienced joy like those in the parable.

These parables portray the reality of the kingdom in human experience. Like Jesus, the rabbis speak about the kingdom in daily life. The great rabbinic scholar Solomon Schechter speaks about a visible and an invisible kingdom that he discerns in ancient Jewish thought. The visible rule of God is universal and national. The invisible aspect of the kingdom he describes as "less expressive of an accomplished fact than of an undefined and indefinable ideal, and hence capable of a wider interpretation of varying aspects."[25] Jesus never defines the kingdom but, rather, describes what it is like in an associative method that looks to a higher reality. These varying aspects of God's rule are grasped by seeing the abstract concepts in theological clusters. The parables portray the spiritual reality in concrete word-pictures. The rabbis felt this spiritual reality in prayer. By reciting the Shema, they experienced the spiritual force of God's reign in words of prayer. Because of the inward realization of the divine presence of the sovereign Creator, saying the Shema becomes an act in which the person receives the kingdom.[26] If one is on a journey when the time comes to recite the Shema, one must stop and direct one's heart to God in awe, trembling, and complete devotion.[27] Schechter's understanding of this ancient Jewish idea of receiving the kingdom when reciting the Shema is worth noting.

---

[24] Petuchowski, "Significance," 76–88.

[25] Solomon Schechter, *Aspects of Rabbinic Theology* (New York: Schocken, 1961) 65–66; see also notes 26, 27.

[26] See m. *Ber.* 2:2 and parallels.

[27] Schechter, *Aspects,* 66.

Receiving the Kingdom

> Communion with God by means of prayer through the removal of all intruding elements between man and his Maker, and through the implicit acceptance of God's unity as well as an unconditional surrender of mind and heart to his holy will, which the love of God expressed in the *Shema* implies, this is what is understood by the receiving of the kingdom of God.[28]

The powerful images in the word-pictures of treasure and pearl refer back to the reality of God's kingdom. The sovereignty of God is what every person really wants. God's rule is worthy of the cost. When we examine the background of the Gospels within Jewish culture, the relationship between the master and the disciple takes on deep significance. The disciple becomes completely devoted to his master. By serving him and learning words of Torah from his lips, the disciple discovers the deeper meaning of God's will in daily life. The kingdom is realized in everyday experience.

In this regard, the story of R. Johanan is of interest, even though it first appears in sources from the Amoraic period[29] Rabbi Johanan and R. Chaya bar Abba were traveling from Tiberias to Sepphoris. As they passed through some of the most fertile land in the entire country, R. Johanan began to recall how he sold certain plots of land in order to finance his studies. The talmudic legend stresses R. Johanan's sacrifice for Torah. Rabbi Chaya bar Abba is concerned that his friend will not have the resources necessary for his old age. But R. Johanan is filled with joy because he learned Torah. The exchange was well worth the sacrifice.

Cost of Torah Learning

> R. Johanan was once going on foot from Tiberias to Sepphoris, accompanied by R. Hiyya b. Abba. As they passed a certain field, R. Johanan said: "This field used to belong to me, and I sold it so that I could devote myself to the study of the Torah." They came to a vineyard and R. Johanan said: "This vineyard used to belong to me, and I sold it in order to devote myself to the study of the Torah." They passed an olive press and he said the same thing. R. Hiyya began to weep. "Why are you weeping?" he asked. He replied: "I am weeping because you have not left yourself anything for your old age." He said to him: "Hiyya my son, think you so little of what I have done in selling a thing which was presented after six days, as it says, *For in six days the Lord made heaven and earth* (Ex. XX,II)? But the Torah was given after forty days, as it says, *And he was there with the Lord forty days (ib.* XXXIV, 28), and it is also written, *Then I abode in the mount forty days*" (Deut. IX, 9). When R. Johanan was laid to rest,

---

[28] Ibid., 66–67. Compare Kurt Hruby, "The Proclamation of the Unity of God as Actualization of the Kingdom," in *Standing before God* (ed. A. Finkel and L. Frizzell; New York: KTAV, 1981) 189: "The acceptance of God's sovereignty and the commitment to observe the commandments of the Torah as expressed by the *Shema* are the prototype of all Jewish prayer."

[29] Cf. Str-B 1:817; and Oesterley, *Parables*, 82.

> his generation applied to him the verse, IF A MAN WOULD GIVE ALL THE SUBSTANCE OF HIS HOUSE FOR LOVE—for the love which R. Johanan bore to the Torah—HE WOULD UTTERLY BE CONTEMNED.[30]

Rabbi Johanan had counted the cost and dedicated himself to Torah learning. The entire story is an example for others who would seek to study and learn as disciples of the wise. Was it common for the disciple to make sacrifices for learning? In rabbinic teaching, the disciple of Torah is required to minimize his or her efforts in business, go on little sleep, and develop the kind of strong character qualities that will lead to a better understanding of the Scriptures.[31]

Finding a center of learning with the proper spiritual leaders was very important. Jewish learning involved discussion and active interchange among the sages. The disciples would learn how to ask the right questions, to which their teachers could respond. This atmosphere of learning and free interaction was highly valued. The story is told about how R. Jose ben Kisma refused to abandon a center of Torah learning even though he was offered much gold, pearls, and precious stones as an incentive to relocate. While it is possible that the man wanted to learn Torah at the feet of R. Jose

---

[30] See *Song Rab.* 8.7.1 (Freedman, *Midrash Rabbah,* 310) and the parallels: *Pesik. Rab Kah.* 27:1 (*Pesikta Derav Kahana,* ed. Mandelbaum, 402–3; English trans., Braude and Kapstein, *Kahana,* 411–12); *Lev. Rab.* 30, beginning (*Vayikra Rabbah,* ed. Margulies, 4:688f.; Freedman, *Midrash Rabbah,* 380); *Yal. Shimeoni on Sol.*, vol. 2, Remez, 994; *Yal. Shimeoni on Exod.*, vol. 1, Remez, 363; *Tanchuma Ki Tisa* 29 (*Tanchuma,* ed. Buber); *Exod. Rab.* 47:5; discussed by W. Bacher, *Die Agada der paläestinensischen Amoräer* (5 vols.; Strassburg: Karl Tübner, 1892–99) 1:221–22.

[31] See *Abot* 6:6 (Hertz, *Daily Prayer Book,* 711): "The Torah is greater than the priesthood and than royalty, seeing that royalty demands thirty qualifications, the priesthood twenty-four, while the Torah is acquired by forty-eight. And these are they: By audible study; by distinct pronunciation; by understanding and discernment of the heart; by awe, reverence, meekness, cheerfulness; by ministering to the sages, by attaching oneself to colleagues, by discussion with pupils; by sedateness; by knowledge of the Scripture and of the Mishna; by moderation in business, in intercourse with the world, in pleasure, in sleep, in conversation, in laughter; by patience; by a good heart; by faith in the wise; by resignation under affliction; by recognising one's place, rejoicing in one's portion, putting a fence to one's words, claiming no merit for oneself; by being beloved, loving the All-present, loving mankind, loving just courses, rectitude and reproof; by keeping oneself far from honour; not boasting of one's learning, nor delighting in giving decisions; by bearing the yoke with one's fellow, judging him favourable, and leading him to truth and peace; by being composed in one's study; by asking and answering, hearing and adding thereto; by learning with the object of teaching, and by learning with the object of practising; by making one's master wiser, fixing attention upon his discourse, and reporting a thing in the name of him who said it. So thou hast learnt, Whosoever reports a thing in the name of him that said it brings deliverance into the world; as it is said, And Esther told the king in the name of Mordecai." See also the chapter here concerning the parable of the Sower.

ben Kisma, it is just as likely that R. Jose was being offered a better job or career advancement. Most of the rabbis were professionals who studied Torah after working hours. Whatever the situation, R. Jose could not learn enough Torah from the sages and refused to leave his own study environment.

No Price for Torah Learning

R. Jose, the son of Kisma, said, I was once walking by the way, when a man met me and greeted me, and I returned his greeting. He said to me, Rabbi, from what place are you? I said to him, I come from a great city of sages and scribes. He said to me, If you are willing to dwell with us in our place, I will give you a thousand golden dinars and precious stones and pearls. I said to him, Even if you were to give me all the silver and gold and precious stones and pearls in the world, I would not dwell anywhere but in a home of the Torah.[32]

The legend focuses on R. Jose ben Kisma's dedication. He would not give up his occupation with Torah for any price. He was determined to stay in a place where study was a way of life.

C. G. Montefiore understands the Gospel parables of the Treasure and the Pearl as portraying the kingdom in Jesus' teachings, which he links with the learning of Torah. Hence the kingdom must be compared to the intense occupation with Torah in the lives of the rabbis. For the rabbis, studying Torah was a way of drawing closer to God and communing with him. As they learned Torah, the sages reached beyond for God. In a similar way, Jesus demanded complete dedication for his kingdom teachings. Montefiore explains the similarity between the spirituality of the rabbis and Jesus' teaching concerning the kingdom:

The Torah and the Kingdom

The Torah was to the Rabbis the pearl of great price. It contained, as it were, the Kingdom of God within itself. By studying and serving the Torah, by practising it and fulfilling its laws, the Israelite both accepted and took upon himself the glad yoke of the Kingdom; he widened the range of the Kingdom, and in the eschatological sense he brought the advent of the Kingdom nearer.[33]

Montefiore has portrayed a living spirituality in the life spent learning Torah as practiced among some sectors of Jewish scholars, those who first and foremost sought the kingdom. The word-pictures of the Gospels that stress willingness to sell everything are closely related to the type of devotion required among the early followers of Jesus, a devotion also prevalent among other Jewish teachers and their disciples.

---

[32] *Abot* 6:9 (Hertz, *Daily Prayer Book,* 717). See the discussion by Safrai, "Cultural Nature," 159–61. Safrai suggests that the center of Torah learning was the city of Tiberias.

[33] Montefiore, *Rabbinic Literature and Gospel Teachings*, 254.

THE POWER OF A PICTURE

These word-pictures have tremendous power to convey the kingdom's value and the cost of discipleship in concrete motifs. The contrast between a poor man and a rich merchant are probably portrayed here. At least the merchant who traveled in search of pearls is wealthy. The man who accidentally discovered the treasure would probably be considered poor because he had to sell everything to buy the land. He was not on the bottom of the economic ladder, because he owned enough assets to raise sufficient funds to buy the property, but he would have been viewed as a lower-income earner who stumbled onto a real bonus without even looking for it. This type of contrast was an effective technique for involving the audience in the plot of the story. The joy of discovery associated with the type of find that a normal person probably would never experience in real life catches the imagination of the rich and poor alike.

THE MOTIFS IN RABBINIC LITERATURE

The motifs of finding a treasure or obtaining a valuable pearl are not uncommon in rabbinic literature. Depending on the context, the treasure may have more than one meaning. The anecdotes may serve to teach a lesson from biblical history or the way that righteous living will bear fruit by bestowing a blessing according to the divine plan. In fact, the rabbis sometimes use twin illustrations based on the theme of treasure in order to drive home the point.

In expounding upon the theme of the miraculous deliverance from Egypt during the exodus, two rabbis give parables that illustrate the way that Pharaoh failed to recognize the glory of the people of Israel until they were released from captivity. Rabbi Jose the Galilean and Rabbi Simeon bar Yochai each tell a story to illustrate the meaning of the biblical verse "When the king of Egypt was told that the people had fled, the mind of Pharaoh and his servants was changed toward the people, and they said, 'What is this we have done, that we have let Israel go from serving us?' " (Exod 14:5). These two parables would have been quite appropriate for a Passover Seder meal, although we are not told the occasion during which they were told. It should be remembered that discussing the intricacies of the exodus into the wee hours of the morning during the celebration of Passover was considered very meritorious. Quite likely on such occasions many parables and thought-provoking illustrations were used to teach those present, especially the young children, the significance of the exodus for the Jewish people. These parables would serve as fine sermon illustrations in the oral tradition.

The parables tell about Israel, which is like a hidden treasure. Rabbi Jose the Galilean tells about a man who inherited a sizable field and sold it for a trifle. Rabbi Simeon bar Yochai (celebrated in talmudic literature for his extensive knowledge of parable lore)[34] tells a parable designed to describe the beauty of the Jewish people as God's cherished treasure and using the theme of finding a lost treasure. In the embellished parallel to the same parable, the man inherits a trash heap instead of a residence.[35] When the heap is sold, the new owner begins to dig, discovers the treasure, and becomes very wealthy. He becomes the envy of the original owner, which in Middle Eastern culture accentuates the sense of honor or shame. The newly rich man has honor showered upon him because of the treasure, while the original owner suffers shame. The whole series of word-pictures portrays God redeeming the people of Israel from Egypt.

Israel as a Precious Treasure

> R. Jose the Galilean, giving a parable, says: To what can this be compared? To a man to whom there has fallen as an inheritance a *bet-kor* of land which he sold for a trifle. The buyer, however, went and opened up wells in it, and planted gardens and trees and orchards in it. The seller, seeing this, began to choke with grief.[36] So it happened to the Egyptians who let go without realizing what they let go. Of them it is stated in the traditional sacred writings: "Thy shoots are a park of pomegranates" (Cant. 4:13).
>
> Another interpretation: R. Simon the son of Yohai, giving a parable, says: To what can this be compared? To a man to whom there had fallen as an inheritance a residence in a far off country which he sold for a trifle. The buyer, however, went and discovered in it hidden treasures and stores of silver and of gold, of precious stones and pearls. The seller, seeing this, began to choke with grief. So also did the Egyptians, who let go without realizing what they let go. For it is written: "And they said: 'What is this we have done that we have let Israel go' (Exodus 14:5)" etc.[37]

Clearly these two parables have a different reality behind their word-pictures than the Gospel parables of the Hidden Treasure and the Pearl of Great Price. Nevertheless, the images used in the colorful dramas as well as the action of

---

[34] See the fine examination of Rabbi Simeon bar Yochai's parabolic teaching by Dov Noy, "Mishle Melechim shel Rashbi," *Machanayim* 56 (1961) 73–87.

[35] See the discussion "The Treasure Find and Israel" above, where the later rabbinic parables are examined in relation to the embellished form of the parables of Jesus in *Gospel of Thomas*.

[36] The choking is a fine Hebraic way of speaking that also brings a colorful touch of artistry to the parable of the Sower.

[37] *Mekilta Derabbi Yishmael* on Exod 14:5 (*Mekhilta Derabbi Ishmael*, ed. Horovitz and Rabin, 87; cf. *Mekhilta Derabbi Ishmael*, ed. and trans. Jacob Lauterbach [3 vols.; Philadelphia: Jewish Publication Society, 1976] 1:197–98) and parallels, esp. *Pesik. Rab Kah.* 11:7; *Song Rab.* 4.12.1; and *Yal. Shimeoni*, vol. 2, Remez 988. The parallel in *Song of Solomon Rabbah* betrays evidence of embellishment. Did the *Pesikta* know an earlier version of the parable than that in *Song of Solomon Rabbah*? In any case, these midrashim show how an illustration from an exegetical midrash like the *Mekilta* can be adapted and recycled in a homiletical midrash like the *Pesikta*, which seems to be based upon *Song of Solomon Rabbah* or its source.

the plot in each story are quite similar. The rabbinic parables illustrate the undiscovered treasure of the people of Israel, while the Gospel texts portray the intrinsic value of the kingdom and the cost associated with obtaining it. Like the Gospel of Matthew, the *Mekilta* uses two illustrations to drive home the same point. The partner parables are basically identical twins with only minor changes in the motifs pulled together from a vast storehouse of folklore. The people of Israel became the precious treasure of God while the pharaoh of Egypt failed to comprehend the intrinsic value of the great nation he had released. By the same token, the disciple should recognize the intrinsic worth of the incomparable kingdom of God as he or she surrenders all to obtain it.

The exciting find of a lost treasure is a powerful theme when calling to mind divine blessing and recompense for a righteous lifestyle. The rabbis tell the story of Abba Judan and his saintly wife, who were genuinely pious and righteous people.[38] Abba Judan loved to give money to the poor as well as generous assistance to rabbis studying Torah. In fact, he had impoverished himself by giving more than he was able. When he saw R. Eliezer, R. Joshua, and R. Akiva collecting money for the worthy cause of disciples learning Torah, he was overcome with a desire to give. His face turned white because he had nothing left. His wife, who was even more pious than her husband, realized his desire to give. She seemed to be more aware of the financial value of the family's assets and urged Abba Judan to sell half of their last tract of land in order to donate the money to these outstanding rabbis who were raising funds for Torah study. He sold the land and gladly contributed the money for the worthy cause. After experiencing the joy of giving, he went to plow the other half of the tract of land, which is all he had left. His cow fell into a hole in the ground and broke a leg. As he labored to help his cow, God enlightened his eyes to discover a buried treasure. The hidden treasure made him much wealthier than ever before. He and his wife could do even more for charity while enjoying the fine life of the well-to-do.

In a similar story that illustrates the value of a single pearl and the divine favor given to a pious man, God works a miracle to bless financially a saintly man named Joseph who always honored the Sabbath.[39] Joseph was well known in the city as one who observed the Sabbath in the best way he was able. In the district lived a pagan who owned a great deal of property. The pagan discovered through a soothsayer that Joseph was going to receive all

---

[38] *Lev. Rab.* 5:4 (Freedman, *Midrash Rabbah,* 66–67; *Vayikra Rabbah,* ed. Margulies, 1:110–13) and parallels in j. *Hor.* 48a, ch. 3, halakah 7; also an edited Hebrew version in *Deut. Rab.* 4:8 (Freedman, *Midrash Rabbah,* 97–98). The story is deleted in *Midrash Devarim Rabbah,* ed. S. Liebermann (Jerusalem: Wahrmann, 1974); see note there on p. 94. See also the discussions by Billerbeck, Str-B 1:674; and more recently Crossan, *Finding,* 62–63; Scott, *Hear,* 396.

[39] See b. *Shabb.* 119a (Epstein, *Babylonian Talmud,* 586); and the fine commentary in A. Steinsaltz, *The Talmud* (New York: Random House, 1989) 522.

his land and enjoy the fruit of his labors. The pagan, of course, desired to foil fate and prevent any financial loss to himself. He therefore sold all his property and bought a pearl of exceptional value. (This element of the talmudic legend is very much like the parable of the Pearl of Great Price.) The pagan fastened the exquisite pearl securely to his turban, where he felt it would be safe. While travelling over a bridge, however, a great gust of wind knocked the pearl into the river, where it was eaten by a great fish. This fish was then caught on the eve of the Sabbath. The fishermen knew that only one person would buy such a great fish. Ordinarily, a person would spare such expense, but Joseph, one who honored the Sabbath, would buy it eagerly because of the sanctity of the day. They sold Joseph the fish. When he prepared the Sabbath dinner, he discovered the pearl that would make him very wealthy. He sold it for thirteen roomfuls of gold denarii. The whole elaborate and entertaining story focuses on the unanticipated blessings that come from honoring the Sabbath day and how God blesses the righteous, sometimes at the expense of the wicked. While the date of the story is uncertain, its folkloric color from Jewish life illustrates the theme of finding lost treasure. One is reminded of Peter, who caught a fish with the temple tax payment in its mouth. Here, however, the prize pearl is discovered and is sold at the unbelievable cost of thirteen roomfuls of gold denarii. Certainly the joy of discovery surrounds the story of Joseph, a man who honored the Sabbath.

Finding a costly pearl in the belly of a fish may seem somewhat far-fetched (though many anglers do have their stories to tell), but finding buried treasure in the Middle East was probably not unusual. In fact, the procedure was discussed by Josephus in his description of the destruction of Jerusalem by the Romans, who knew that the Jews had buried many valuables before the city fell.

Josephus on Buried Treasure

> Of the vast wealth of the city no small portion was still being discovered among the ruins. Much of this the Romans dug up, but the greater part they became possessed of through the information of the prisoners, gold and silver and other most precious articles, which the owners in view of the uncertain fortunes of war had stored underground.[40]

Thus the Romans were among those who dug for buried treasure, discovered through the interrogation of Jewish prisoners. The situation was typical of the turbulent Middle East. People about to flee for their lives would bury their most treasured possessions, hoping that someday they would return and recover them. Because of the unpredictability of events in history and politics, return was not always possible. For biblical scholars, the Dead Sea Scrolls will always be the foremost example of hidden treasure. The main

[40] Josephus, *War* 7.113–115. The passage is often discussed in commentaries.

treasure trove of scrolls remained hidden for nearly two thousand years. So when a parable of Jesus speaks about buried treasure, the historical situation made the exciting story of discovery much more plausible than it would be for our culture.

THE ACTION-PACKED DRAMAS

Finding hidden treasure is an exciting plot for any drama. No doubt, the quick-paced action of these two concise illustrations captured the attention of the audience. Stories of buried treasure are created to excite the imagination. Jesus used these common motifs to stir up thoughts concerning the joy of discovering untold riches. The catch to these finds is the serious risk necessary to obtain the treasure and the pearl. Acquisition involves total sacrifice. Four major scenes compose these action-packed mini-dramas. The major distinction between the parables of the Hidden Treasure and the Pearl of Great Price is found in scene 1. The last three scenes develop the plot by stressing the same action in both parables. The only other real difference is the description of joy for the common man who finds the treasure and decides to take the risk of acquiring it. The joy in the first illustration carries over into the second one, even though it is not redundantly repeated verbatim. But joy is not the main subject of the parables.[41] The stress of the stories is on the decision, which must be prompt and resolute.

The first scene introduces the cast and orients the listener for the ultimate decision. The different settings invite involvement by more than one type of listener. Who is the leading actor in each of the dramas? The leading man in parable one is poor compared with the merchant in parable two, who is quite well off. The first man could be an ordinary field worker, a sharecropper, the foreman, a steward, or someone merely walking by who notices something in the field. Such an ordinary person is like so many listening to the story. He goes about his work without a sense of expectancy. In his daily routine, he would never dream of discovering a treasure. On the other hand, the wealthy merchant who travels far and wide in search of choice merchandise is the type of intriguing character who would be found in the fantasy world of many a farm boy. He is a fascinating figure who adds a touch of mystery to the fiction of the parable. The wealthy would love to own such a pearl, but the dream of travel and exploration that results in unrivaled financial success is an alluring theme in the making of a good story. The listeners can identify with at least one of these two characters. So the parables produce two very different leading men for the dramatic portrayal of the kingdom and the cost of discipleship.

The most significant difference, however, is found in the main characters' orientation to life. While the merchant is a seeker of fine pearls, the man

[41] Contrary to the conclusion of Jeremias, *Parables of Jesus,* 200–201.

in the first parable is an ordinary laborer who makes a chance find. He is an average guy with common roots. He represents every John and Jane Doe who has long since stopped expecting to discover. Perhaps he should be called an ordinary person, while the wealthy businessman should be cast as the extraordinary merchant. The businessman longs for very special kinds of pearls. In the world of finance, he yearns for success. This merchant's longing to find pearls of exceptional quality forces him to travel from place to place in his intensive search. Among the listeners in the audience were both types of seekers, people like the well-to-do merchant and the ordinary person who had forgotten the wonder of discovering something completely extraordinary such as God's kingly power.

The plot of the drama should be followed like the successive scenes in a play. Surprisingly, the average guy and the wealthy businessman have a lot in common. Both of them discover, sell, and buy. These three actions determine the outcome of the story. They form individual scenes in the dramatic presentation of each parable.

Ordinary Person		
Scene 1	1. Not seeking	1. Ordinary person
Scene 2	2. Finds treasure	2. Confrontation
Scene 3	3. Joyfully sells all	3. Decision
Scene 4	4. Buys treasure	4. Risk

Extraordinary Merchant		
Scene 1	1. Seeking	1. Extraordinary Merchant
Scene 2	2. Finds pearl	2. Confrontation
Scene 3	3. (Joyfully) sells all	3. Decision
Scene 4	4. Buys pearl	4. Risk

In scene 1 the characters are introduced and the action is begun. Ricoeur has described the action of parables as fitting into a three-part scheme: orientation, disorientation, and reorientation.[42] Scene 1 fits well into his description of "orientation." The common man is not seeking a treasure; he is simply going about his normal routine. The merchant is searching for fine pearls, but he is not prepared for his discovery. This orientation in scene 1 involves what is familiar. In the present parable, the words "disorientation" and "reorientation" are probably not quite strong enough. Disorientation may occur during a strange circumstance, but usually one finds a special item, buys it, and after a time decides to sell it. But in the parable the one who finds must devise a plan to acquire the treasure or the pearl. He must sell what he owns and then buy the item. The ordinary person is overwhelmed with joy. The listeners to the parable, moreover, are reoriented with joy when the treasure in the field and the pearl of great price have been acquired. While orientation fits scene 1 of the story, perhaps the terms

[42] See Ricoeur, "Hermeneutics," 75.

"confrontation" and "redirection" would be more fitting for what follows. The words "disorientation" and "reorientation" are not strong enough.[43] The introduction of the story that orients the listener to the character types involved is not designed to surprise.

In scene 2 the listeners are surprised when they are confronted with a hidden treasure and the pearl of great price. The word-pictures set up the listeners for a sudden shift, which demands an action. The one who discovers the treasure is sometimes portrayed as a dishonest man who took unfair advantage of the owner of the field. Here it is not necessary to reexamine the questions relating to the legality of his actions.[44] The legal evidence as well as the silence of the parable indicate that the man obtained the field along with everything in it without breaking the law.[45] The process required significant risk because he was forced to sell everything he owned in order to buy the property. The self-sacrifice and risk involved in his decision to embark on a real-estate venture in which he could lose all is the fundamental plot of the story. If he found the treasure, someone else could also do so. In the world of parable lore and the experience of real life, many complications could suddenly appear that would cause the man to lose what he had. But he was within all legal standing to purchase the land with the treasure.

In recent discussion of this parable, Crossan, and Scott after him, have questioned the moral, ethical. and legal aspects of the man's action. Crossan concludes, "If the treasure belongs to the finder, buying the land is unnecessary. But, if the treasure does not belong to the finder, buying the land is unjust."[46] Scott goes further in stressing that buying the land to obtain the treasure is an unjust act and probably prevented the man from enjoying his newly discovered wealth. In the first place, Scott believes that finding the treasure is pure narcissism because one escapes "to a lawless world where we are rewarded for not working."[47] Was Jesus a modern philosopher intensely concerned about the narcissistic character of treasure and being rewarded for not working? While some of Scott's insights may be helpful, here he has found a complicated modern Jesus in his quest for the historical one.

---

[43] Crossan (*In Parables,* 34) has described "Advent, Reversal, and Action" for the drama. The advent of the kingdom brings unforeseen possibilities that reverse one's past by selling all and fosters action in a "new world of life."

[44] Everything depends on the terms of the bill of sale and whether the treasure has an owner. Since we must assume that the abandoned treasure in the field has no owner, the legal question is connected to the sale. Does the purchase of the property include all the movables (המטלטלין)? No doubt the man buying the property made certain that these possible legal entanglements were treated properly. See m. *B. Bat.* 4:4; *Mishnah,* ed. Albeck, 130–31; Danby, *Mishnah,* 371. He bought the field and everything in it.

[45] See the insightful study of J. Duncan M. Derrett, "The Treasure in the Field," in *Law,* 1–16.

[46] Crossan, *Finding,* 91–92.

[47] Scott, *Hear,* 402.

In Scott's final analysis, the man who finds the hidden treasure should be pitied because he winds up impoverished by the circumstance of losing everything but not being able to use his costly treasure. He pines away because he is afraid to make use of the tremendous find he acquired. Scott claims, "So now the man has sold all, is impoverished, yet possesses a treasure he dare not dig up unless he wants to face the rather embarrassing question of whence it came."[48] While these novel ideas stir up the curiosity of twentieth-century moderns, it is highly doubtful that such thoughts would ever have crossed the minds of oriental Jews in the first century. We may certainly err when we impose our own cultural perspective upon Jewish stories from the Middle East. Just as acquisition of Torah learning or experiencing the power of God's rule is a positive redirecting of one's life, so also is obtaining the hidden treasure. The treasure provided new possibilities. Scott misinterprets this parable when he claims the story portrays a corrupting aspect of the scandal of God's kingdom. Scott asserts that this is the clear indication of the parable's authenticity: "This corrupting aspect of the kingdom is part of the scandalous, hidden aspect of the kingdom that Jesus' parables reveal—his distinctive voice which we frequently overlook or ignore."[49] In order to arrive at a conclusion that the lust for the treasure ruined the man who succeeded in obtaining it, one must first accept Scott's unproven presuppositions. The parable is a tale of success, not failure.

In this cultural setting the treasure, like the pearl, was a blessing and not a curse. God's rule is not a scandal or corrupt. The parables tell us what the kingdom is like. In the minds of Middle Easterners, the discovery of the treasure would be a sign of divine favor rather than a narcissism that defies order. While it is true that the discoverer had information about the hidden treasure that he apparently did not reveal to the original owner of the property, in Middle Eastern culture he acted shrewdly. Jesus' audience would have praised his astute foresight and sharp-witted business sense. If the main character of the parable had acted differently, he would have been considered foolish at worst and peculiar at best. Perhaps he was on the verge of lying when he did not tell the owner about the treasure. But unless he was asked, technically he did not tell a lie by remaining silent. In Middle Eastern culture, he plays the role of a clever underdog. He improves his situation by cleverly devising a plan and acting upon it. The treasure is the focus of the story. While not everyone finds a treasure, the kingdom is accessible to all. But in order to win the kingdom, one must act decisively in the same way as one who discovers a treasure must prudently seek to obtain it through high-risk investment. The wealthy landowner should be pleased to sell his property at a profit. In his privileged position as a wealthy property owner he is well able to forfeit the treasure magnanimously to the clever man who devises a plan and acts decisively.

---

[48] Ibid.

[49] Ibid.

An ordinary person found a treasure and purchased the land, including all that was on it, at the property's fair market value. Did he lie? Was he unjust? Did he cross the line by practicing deceit? The man who buys the field is neither immoral nor amoral. He is proven to be shrewd, sharp-witted, and willing to take risks in order to achieve results. He is a character in the drama. He is a man of decisive action. The stipulations of the law were on his side. The law did not require the buyer to give an account of all the movables on a piece of property he wished to purchase. The action of the buyer in the parable may not be considered doing right in everyone's estimation of ethical business procedure, but his actions were not illegal. While he could have given the treasure to the owner of the field and hoped for a reward, this is not the plot for our parable. No matter what judgment is pronounced upon his conduct, which is an issue, we must look to the core of the parable in its original cultural setting. He made a decision to obtain the treasure legally by acting shrewdly and risking everything. He is the little guy who gets a break at the expense of the wealthy landed aristocracy. The nobleman who owns much property can afford to lose a small parcel of land with a hidden treasure to one of the little people. To ask more from a stock character in a parable is too much. He astutely gambles everything and wins by using his quick thinking and bold action. Deep psychological analysis of such stock characters is unnecessary and counterproductive. The main point, very much like the second illustration about the pearl, focuses attention on the risk and self-sacrifice involved in making the decision to sell all.

In fact, the parallel story concerning the Pearl of Great Price reinforces the first illustration.[50] The action of the merchant is not considered illegal. When he finds the pearl, he makes the decision to sell everything and to buy it. Nothing he owns is worth missing the unique opportunity to buy the pearl. When viewed together, these parables complement and reinforce one another's message. The ordinary man and the extraordinary merchant have been confronted with a unique opportunity that calls for decisive action. A firm and resolute decision is needed or the opportunity will be lost forever.

The confrontation leads to redirection. Only unrelenting determination that willingly risks everything will obtain results. The selling of everything is very much like the account of the rich man and Jesus. Jesus asked him to sell everything, give to the poor, and follow him. In rabbinic literature, the saintly Yeshevav sold everything he owned to give alms to the needy. The rabbis were afraid that such generosity would impoverish pious people and make them dependent upon charity. They decreed that no one should give all but limited such generous charity to one-third of one's assets. In any case,

---

[50] Scott and Crossan study the two parables individually. The *Gospel of Thomas* separates them. They really must be viewed as a unit in which one parable complements the other. Even if the idea that Jesus used dual parables in this way is rejected, Matthew certainly saw them as partner illustrations. Cf. W. D. Davies and D. Allison, *The Gospel according to St. Matthew* (3 vols.; ICC; Edinburgh: T. & T. Clark, 1988–1995) 2:437 n. 16.

the idea of giving all is paralleled in Jewish literature. "Giving all" meant a complete redirection. The same expression is used in regard to a man who is pulling together the family assets in his efforts to raise the funds for a dowry. The rabbis give wise counsel: "Our rabbis taught: Let a man always sell all he has and marry the daughter of a scholar, and marry his daughter to a scholar."[51] In this way, the child who loses a parent will be raised in the awe and reverence of God. A virtuous woman who is the daughter of a scholar is worth all a man possesses.

The ordinary person and the extraordinary merchant realize—by way of confrontation with the treasure in the field and the pearl of great price—that the benefit is worth the deliberate risk and the hazardous measures they must take to buy what they want. Obtaining the treasure and the pearl will redirect their lives with new and exciting possibilities.

Three action verbs capture the attention of the listener: find, sell, and buy. Finding is confrontation. Selling is decision. Buying is risk. Giving all one has for something of inestimable value is the plot of the parable. The risk involves the unknown and the unknowable God. The action is so urgent that risk is completely forgotten. The find puts one on a new path.

A treasure in the field will change everything forever. The pearl is beyond everything the wealthy merchant hoped and dreamed to find. But with the discovery comes the confrontation with a new reality. The discovery brings the ultimate confrontation. If the ordinary man is going to obtain the treasure or the wealthy merchant buy the pearl, a decision is required. This decision is scene 3 of the parable. Scene 4 involves the risk that costs everything a person has. The average guy and the ambitious merchant must pursue a course of decisive action to acquire what they really want. The sacrifice demands all. The complete redirection comes for the ordinary person and the extraordinary merchant when they are willing to make a decision to risk everything in order to buy what they desperately desire to own.

The parable involves everyone in the audience. One person will identify with the man who finds the treasure, and another with the merchant who finds the pearl. The wide appeal of the illustrations reaches out to involve all people—the poor and the rich as well as those who find without a search and those who seek diligently to get what they want. In both illustrations, the actor finds, sells all, and buys.

THE VALUE OF THE KINGDOM OR THE COST OF DISCIPLESHIP?

Are the parables concerned about the cost of discipleship or the value of the kingdom? This is one of the most complex and difficult questions of

[51] See b. *Pesach* 49a; and cf. the metaphorical language of *Seder Elijah* 30. See Fiebig, *Gleichnisreden*, 96–97.

Gospel scholarship. It is a crucial issue that must be resolved in order to understand the teachings of Jesus. Since the parables function to communicate one message, such a question is difficult to resolve, because the kingdom and discipleship are closely related and seem almost inseparable in this context. So much in the action of the parables focuses on the immediate response on the part of their characters. They must set a course of action by making the decision to acquire the treasure or the pearl. On the one hand, the cost of discipleship screams from every action verb in the stories. On the other hand, it is the kingdom that brings confrontation and conflict. The kingdom is in a realm beyond. Jesus teaches his disciples to seek first the kingdom, and all the other things associated with human need will be provided. The disciple must not worry about food, clothing, or shelter. God's reign overtakes all concerns relating to money and success. The disciple must make a decision about the kingdom. He or she must be willing to give all and may well lose everything to enter the kingly power of God.

The cost of discipleship is actually a secondary theme supporting the theme of overriding passion for God's reign. Jesus is consumed with a passion to see God's rule realized. The kingdom is above all. Its intrinsic value cannot be measured in worldly possessions. It is far more valuable than property, pearls, or treasures. The idea of a costly pearl or a hidden treasure is like the kingdom. A person would give anything to obtain them if he or she had such a chance. While almost no one will ever be able to obtain a treasure or the pearl of great price, all may enter into the kingdom of heaven and experience God's power. Each one is invited to joyfully give up everything to enter the kingdom. These parables are pictures of the kingdom's unimaginable worth—a value beyond all human comprehension. The kingdom takes precedence over the supporting theme of the cost demanded from disciples following Jesus. Joyfully seeking the kingdom will provide for every need. For Jesus, the kingdom is everything.

12 *The Decision: The Tower Builder and the King Going to War*

FOCUS

The twin parables of the Tower Builder and the King Going to War (Luke 14:28–33) focus on the self-examination necessary to make a decision for surrendering to the call of Jesus. The ultimate commitment is demanded of every disciple. No one should make such a decision rashly. Just as cost estimation is needed to build a tower in a field and intense strategic planning is required to wage war, the one considering discipleship must weigh the cost. To complete the task successfully, one must consider each demand in Jesus' teachings concerning the kingdom of heaven. Only after intensive self-testing should the decision be made to follow Jesus in his call to radical discipleship.

These parables depart sharply from the message found in the parables of the Hidden Treasure and the Pearl of Great Price. The man who discovered the treasure tossed caution to the wind and sold all he owned. The merchant forgot about finding fine pearls for his business ventures when he discovered the pearl of exquisite quality. He took a deliberate risk when he sold everything to buy a single pearl. The Tower Builder and the King Going to War stress the wisdom of careful consideration. One must estimate the cost and the available resources to complete any project.

No disciple should begin training in the kingdom of God unless he or she has recognized fully the insistent demands of total commitment and has determined to shoulder the responsibilities with unrelenting resolve. By way of comparison, anyone who begins a simple building project first contemplates the costs of labor and construction materials. But it is far easier to build a tower in a field than it is to wage a war against another king. In contrast to the building of a tower, warfare was considered the most serious of all undertakings. The king must first know the strength of the forces coming to fight him. He must carefully consider the might of his own armies and whether he will be able to win the battle or suffer defeat. Such a battle is a life-or-death situation, which will change the lives of everyone the king loves—not to mention the annals of history, where wise kings and strong generals are always remembered. An ignominious defeat will ruin the king, destroy his kingdom, and cost him everything. The disciple's defeat can be just as devastating. While few would compare a religious decision such as becoming a disciple with a king's preparation for battle, in Luke Jesus stresses the similarities between the word-picture of a king planning for war and the reality of an individual deciding to follow Jesus' teachings. Would-be followers must enter the kingdom with open eyes, being fully aware of the demands.

The focus of these two parables is the cost of discipleship. No one who begins the job and quits is worthy. Do not put your hand on the plow unless you are ready for hard work![1] The challenge of the kingdom will demand a complete redirection. One must carefully contemplate the cost before making a decision. But once the decision has been made, one should never look back. A firm and resolute decision must be made, but only after all the costs have been given every consideration. Learning to follow the teachings of Jesus in complete obedience demands total commitment.

CHRISTIAN INTERPRETATION

For Luke these parables form a complex of teachings focusing on radical discipleship. Hating one's parents or dying for one's beliefs are concepts that perplex and challenge. The hard sayings about abandoning family ties and taking up one's cross lead into these two parables. They raise ominous questions about the teachings of Jesus. Here the sayings are collected in a block, Luke 14:25–35, which forms a whole complex of teaching materials. These materials are positioned in the framework of Luke after a semiformal dinner in the home of a ruler of the Pharisees, an occasion that includes a series of sayings about eating, humility, banquet etiquette, and the open invitation to the kingdom, concluding with the parable of the Great Supper. Now a transition occurs in Luke when he reports that great multitudes are accompanying Jesus.

The mention of the multitudes is Luke's way of stressing the popularity of Jesus. Such popularity, however, must be tempered by his travel plans. The direction they have taken leads to Jerusalem, where Jesus will suffer and die. In many ways, the impending danger in Luke's context weakens the moral and ethical fiber of Jesus' teaching. The theological ramifications of the passion of Jesus somewhat undermine the call to radical discipleship. In actuality, the example of Jesus should urge complete dedication even as it

[1] Luke 9:57–62.

leads to the way of the cross. For Christianity, the cross has become more a symbol of salvation than a call to radical discipleship. In fact, sometimes it may even serve as the excuse for not following the teachings of Jesus. Grace is freely given to the sinners who keep on sinning. Such an approach may be the fruit more of Reformation theology than of traditional Christianity.[2]

But the danger of diluting Jesus' radical call to action by spiritualizing his practical teachings is never very far removed from the preaching of salvation through the cross. In the teachings of Jesus, in contrast, the image of the cross was a call to radical discipleship.[3] One must hear and obey. The stress was not on salvation but on obedience. The fear of God is rooted in the wisdom obtained through Torah learning and active involvement in fulfilling wisdom's teachings. Radical discipleship meant social action in the highest sense of the term. The force of the kingdom is demonstrated by people working together, empowered by God, to bring healing to a hurting world in the midst of a society that often has abandoned God and his ways.

The setting in Luke is the evangelist's emphasis on Jesus' popularity and the journey to Jerusalem. The message on discipleship is rooted in Jesus' radical call. C. H. Dodd has noted, "These [parables] are associated by the evangelist with the call of Jesus to men to take great risks with open eyes; and although the actual connection in which he has placed them may be artificial, the general reference is no doubt right. . . . Possible followers are reminded in stern terms of the cost which they must be prepared to pay."[4] J. Jeremias echoes the element of "self-testing" found in these two parables. Because of the challenge of the hour, "to be near Jesus is dangerous." One must be prepared to give all for the call. "Only through fire may the Kingdom be attained."[5]

Luke involves the whole audience when he introduces the parables with "Which of you . . . ?"[6] These double parables are deeply embedded in Luke's Gospel and represent a realized discipleship that comes from Jesus' authentic teachings.[7] In Christian interpretation, the message of radical discipleship as

---

[2] See Harold W. Attridge, "Christianity from the Destruction of Jerusalem to Constantine's Adoption of the New Religion: 70–312 C.E.," in *Christianity and Rabbinic Judaism* (H. Shanks, ed.; Washington, D.C.: Biblical Archaeology Society, 1992) 151–94. Moral and ethical issues were important as well as the theological struggle against powerful teachers such as Marcion and Valentinus. Works such as *Didache* demonstrate a concern for discipleship and commitment to ethical teachings. This is due in part to the earlier Jewish source that is the basis of *Didache*.

[3] See my article "The Cross, Jesus, and the Jewish People," *Immanuel* 24/25 (1990): 23–34.

[4] C. H. Dodd, *The Parables of the Kingdom* (rev. ed.; Glasgow: Collins, 1961) 86.

[5] Jeremias, *Parables of Jesus,* 196.

[6] See Flusser, *Gleichnisse,* 55, 105.

[7] For a different view, see Funk, Scott, and Butts, *Parables*, 68–69. The authenticity of these parables is totally rejected on the basis of dissimilarity. In this regard, I find no clear and complete parallel to these parabolic examples. See, e.g., Lachs, *Commentary*, 305:

learning Jesus' teachings and putting them into practice in a pragmatic way has frequently been overshadowed by abstract theological discussion.

JEWISH TRADITION

In Jewish tradition, the stress on learning and doing plays a prominent role in the life of the community that forms a setting in life for these parables. The motifs of a tower in a field and a king going to battle appear in other rabbinic parables, but usually they illustrate a different message.

In fact, the Bible itself attests to the Hebrew imagery of these parables of self-examination. At least Prov 24:3–6 provides visible associations with Luke's parables, whether there is a direct link or not. This biblical text in praise of wisdom has images of building a house and seeking wise counsel to plan for war: "By wisdom a house is built, and by understanding it is established; by knowledge the rooms are filled with all precious and pleasant riches. A wise man is mightier than a strong man, and a man of knowledge than he who has strength; for by wise guidance you can wage your war, and in abundance of counselors there is victory." Derrett has observed the importance of this text for the parables in Luke. The house is not a tower and wisdom is not the same as radical discipleship. Nonetheless, one observes the clear association between building a house and going to war, similar to the association of preparation for tower and war in Luke's double parables. Derrett notes, "The actual problem, as we have seen, is intrinsically about prudence and *risk.* Has one the strength to complete an enterprise?"[8] Could the verse have been in the mind of Jesus? Did Luke know the text in Proverbs? I believe that an affirmative answer to either of these two questions would refer more to the subconscious mind than to a conscious effort to allude to the biblical text. On the other hand, Jesus makes many veiled allusions to the Hebrew Bible. But construction of a tower is different from that of a house.

In the parable of the Wise and Foolish Builders, the first man constructed his home on the rock and the second used sand as a foundation. Thus a parable of Jesus did use the word-picture of house building. In fact, Mark, Matthew, and the church fathers attest to the tradition that by trade Jesus was a τέκτων, which is usually translated "carpenter" but could refer to a stone mason or even one who made plows and yokes.[9] He may have known from firsthand experience what it was like to get sawdust in his eye while

---

"There are no rabbinic parallels to these illustrations." Lindsey's work has proved, in my view, the importance of Luke's witness to Jesus' teaching. See Lindsey, *Translation;* and Flusser, *Yahadut,* 28–49.

[8] J. Duncan M. Derrett, *Studies in the New Testament* (Leiden: Brill, 1982) 93.

[9] Mark 6:3; Matt 13:55; also *Prot. Jas.* 9:2; 13:1; Justin, *Dial.* 88: "He was in the habit of working as a carpenter when among men, making plows and yokes." See G. Dalman, *Sacred Sites and Ways* (London: SPCK, 1935) 68–70; Mann, *Mark,* 289.

laying down a crossbeam, or how to construct a solid foundation for a building. But such illustrations were part of a common treasury of story images.[10] Even so, the tower is an interesting departure from a more common motif of building a house. If Proverbs was in mind, I believe a reference to the house would be more direct. The construction of a simple tower in a field is intended as a sharp contrast to the directing of a war effort. Derrett, however, perceptively points to the issue of prudence and risk. The parables of Jesus, like the wisdom saying from Proverbs, stress the need for careful planning.

These double parables should be viewed in light of parallel images used in Jewish literature. The close imagery in Prov 24:3–6 already shows part of the rich background. A rabbinic parable attributed to R. Jose the Galilean also uses the motif of the construction of a tower in an orchard. Clearly the building of a tower in a field was common. These stone towers, some of which were quite elaborate, served numerous functions. Sometimes, especially during harvest season, they were occupied by guards to make certain that thieves would not steal the produce. Even when unoccupied, a tower was somewhat like a scarecrow because it provided the semblance of a human presence guarding a field that might be some distance from the village. Thick-walled stone towers also provided shade and a cool place for the foreman and other workers to rest in the hot afternoons. Sometimes field tools as well as other valuables were stored in these towers. Finally, the foreman in charge of the field labor could sit in the tower and supervise the workers' activities.

The King's High Tower

> Rabbi Jose the Galilean told a parable. To what may the matter be compared? To a human king who owned an orchard and built a high tower within it. [There happened] to be in the midst of it laborers and stewards who were going about their work. The king would rise high above to the top of the tower from which he could observe them [and how well they performed their duties.] But they could not see him. Thus it is said, "But the LORD is in his holy temple; let all the earth keep silence before him (Hab. 2:20)."[11]

---

[10] Cf. b. *Arak.* 16b; b. *B. Bat.* 15b; *Abot R. Nat.*, version A, ch. 24.

[11] *Midr. Prov.* 16 (*Midrash Mishle,* ed. S. Buber [Wilna: Wittwa & Gebrüder Romm, 1891] 41b); and *Sem. R. Chiyah* 3:6 (*Masekhet Semachot,* ed. Higger, 222–23). See the excellent Hebrew edition by Burton Visotzky, *Midrash Mishle* (New York: Jewish Theological Seminary, 1990) 129. The parallel to R. Jose the Galilean's parable in *Semachot* is attributed to Rabbi. It is much more elaborate and stresses the judgment at the close of the day somewhat like Matt 20:1–16, while the parable in *Midrash Proverbs* may well be abbreviated. Both rabbinic parables are probably related to an earlier version in a common fund of tower illustrations. Cf. also the translation of Burton Visotzky, *The Midrash on Proverbs* (New Haven: Yale University Press 1992) 82: "R. Jose the Galilean said: [Let me tell you a] parable: To what may this be likened? To a king of flesh and blood who had a garden in which he built a tall tower. He showed affection for the garden by

Stern has stressed that the rabbinic parable is the greatest attempt by the rabbis to imagine God.[12] In R. Jose the Galilean's example, the listener is reminded that an agricultural process parallels God's way of supervision. Like a foreman who watches his laborers, God is the king of the universe enthroned on high, observing carefully each person's activities. God is the unseen presence who sees all.

The parable uses the experience of the people in daily life. They were familiar with building a tower for work in the fields. As another rabbinic parable illustrates, the figure of a king may also be portrayed in anger, poised to wage war against a city. The king in Jesus' parable represents a man or a woman struggling with self-examination, considering whether to become a disciple of Jesus. In rabbinic parables, the king is always God.[13] Here is a major difference between the parable of Jesus and its rabbinic counterparts. The use of the king to represent a disciple making a difficult decision is surely an indication of the authenticity of this parable. At least it is an early example of parabolic teaching where a king may represent a figure other than God.

Rabbi Jonathan tells a parable to illustrate Isa 55:6, "Seek the LORD while he may be found, call upon him while he is near." The parable, a stern warning, uses the motif of a king going to war, but the king represents God, and the war refers to divine judgment. One must prepare oneself through repentance during the ten days of awe. A heartfelt turning to God at the proper time will prevent disaster when judgment is pronounced. Rabbi Jonathan illustrates the urgency of the moment—it is as when an angry king prepares for a battle.

The Angry King

R. Samuel bar Nahman said in the name of R. Jonathan: By what parable may the verse just above be explained? By that of a king who lived in a certain principality. When the people of the principality provoked him, the king was angered [and would not abide in their midst]. He removed himself some ten miles from the city before he stopped. A man who saw him went to the people in the city and said: Know that the king is angry at you and may well send legions against the city to destroy it. Go out and appease him before he removes himself still further away from you. Thereupon a wise man who was standing by said to the people: Fools, while he was in your midst, you did not seek him. Now, before he moves further away, seek him out. He may receive you. Hence it is said *Seek ye the Lord while He may be found* (Isa. 55:6)—that is, seek Him during the Ten Days of Repentance while He is abiding in Israel's midst. [At other times], as Ezekiel said in His name, *There*

---

assigning workmen to it, and ordered them to busy themselves with its cultivation. The king thereupon ascended to the top of the tower, from which he could see them but they could not see him, as it is said, *But the Lord in His holy temple; be silent before Him all the earth* (Hab. 2:20)."

[12] Stern, *Parables in Midrash*, 93–94.

[13] There may be rare exceptions of which I am unaware.

may be a wall between Me and you (Ezek. 43:8). Therefore, *Call upon Him while He is near; let the wicked forsake his way and the man of iniquity his thoughts; and let him return unto the Lord, and He will have compassion upon him, and to our God, for He will abundantly pardon* (Isa. 55: 6–7).[14]

The later example of R. Jonathan illustrates an entirely different theme in the preaching of the synagogue. The king is God himself, who is abundant in mercy for all who seek him in repentance. Now is the time to ask for compassion and to seek him. The same merciful monarch can also come in angry judgment. The king in the Gospel parable refers to a potential disciple. The word-picture is somewhat similar in the sense that both are preparing for war. The images of kings and their royal activities provided a rich resource for craftsmen developing dramatic illustrations. [15]

The Gospel parables focus on the self-testing of the person contemplating discipleship. The rabbinic parables focus on the divine character and the human response needed. Because God is in his tower, everyone must recognize God's unseen supervision and respond by maintaining high moral conduct pleasing to God. He is a king of compassion and full of mercy when people seek him for forgiveness; but when the king is angered, he will seek judgment with legions of soldiers. The theme of repentance is stressed in a word-picture that portrays the king going to war.

While it is certainly true that the rabbinic parables, though similar in motif, illustrate a message different from the Gospel parables, one should not forget the common theological foundation for all these stories. They tell us about God. They teach human responsibility. For Jesus, the disciples must consider the all-encompassing demands of his call, and for the rabbis, people must live holy lives pleasing to God. A common heritage links these colorful parables, as each story illustrates some aspect of how men and women approach a holy God in proper service.

CULTURAL HUMOR AND DRY WIT

In a shame-and-honor culture, these double parables of the Tower Builder and the King Going to War issue forth keen humor and striking wit. The greatest virtue in such a culture is the avoidance of shame. One seeks honor while avoiding shame.[16] While humor is difficult to define because of

[14] See *Pesik. Rab Kah.*, suppl. 7:3 (*Pesikta Derav Kahana*, ed. Mandelbaum, 2:472; English trans., Braude and Kapstein, *Kahana*, 491). Cf. the discussion of McArthur and Johnston, *Parables*, 194.

[15] Of course, the classic treatment of this area of study is found in Ziegler, *Königsgleichnisse.*

[16] See Bruce J. Malina and Jerome H. Neyrey, "Honor and Shame in Luke-Acts: Pivotal Values of the Mediterranean World," in *The Social World of Luke-Acts* (ed. Jerome H. Neyrey; Peabody, Mass: Hendrickson, 1991) 25–66. As Bailey noted (*Cross*, 22), "In

its cultural orientation, the present examples exude an authentic flavor of a Middle Eastern situation comedy.[17] Even a farmer who may not be able to finance construction of a field tower and a king who commands his empire have one thing in common: neither of them wants to be mocked.

The man who starts to build and finishes only the foundation would be the laughingstock of village life.[18] After all, such a tower is not a major construction project. The shame of failure to complete it would be comparable, for many Middle Eastern people, to a king losing a war. The shame would be unbearable. The situation produces a comical scene that effectively communicates the theme of self-testing. One must carefully weigh the demands of discipleship in the same way that one plans a construction project based on a realistic estimation of the cost of labor and materials.

The tower builder is of modest financial means and little political influence in comparison with the king who commands an army. The king is willing to accept shame by seeking terms of peace if it becomes clear that he will be defeated in battle, which would be the ultimate shame and result not only in humiliation but also quite probably in death. The comedy of these two situations and the characters involved would not escape a first-century audience. They probably laughed. The laughter would lead them to a point of decision concerning the challenging message of Jesus.

COMEDY AND PURPOSE

The comedy from the original cultural setting serves a powerful purpose. It communicates the depth of Jesus' message. Although the authenticity of the parables has been questioned by some scholars, much evidence supports a fresh evaluation. While Luke's style is revealed both in his introduction ("For which of you," which moves from the second person to the third person of the language of the parables[19]) and in the forceful conclusion that stresses that one must renounce all (v. 33), the core text of these parables reflects an

the Middle East a man *never blames himself for anything.* He does not say, 'I missed the train,' but rather 'the train left me!' "

[17] See Jónsson, *Humour,* 173: "It may be seen from the examples mentioned above that much of the humour of the synoptic Gospels is the humour of action and situation. This shows the close relationship between the methods used by Jesus and the rabbis in general."

[18] See ibid., 112: "Those who start work or begin a war, without thinking out their plans, become ridiculous, because they suddenly have to give up. 'All that behold it, begin to mock him.' Both the examples may have been known in practical life and in history."

[19] The introductory phrase, τίς γὰρ ἐξ ὑμῶν, can be translated into fine Hebrew, מי מכם. It could have been used as an introduction to the parables, but the transition from second to third person is difficult. This partitive genitive is used in other Gospel contexts, e.g., Luke 11:5. The natural response to such an introduction would be, "What would I do?" or, "He is talking to me."

earlier Semitic source. For instance, the description of the man and the king who sit in order to count the cost and to take counsel is a redundant use of the participle characteristic of Hebrew.[20] The use of the participle λέγοντες ("saying," v. 30) is well known in Semitic languages, which introduce quotations with לאמר. The ὅτι phrase (v. 30) as well as the syntax of the sentence with the use of infinitives most probably are evidence of a Hebrew undertext: ὅτι οὗτος ὁ ἄνθρωπος ἤρξατο οἰκοδομεῖν καὶ οὐκ ἴσχυσεν ἐκτελέσαι, which may be rendered כי האיש הוא התחיל לבנות ולא יכול לשלם. The dramatic flair of the local color in the story brings out the mocking derision that will be heaped upon the man who fails to complete the project he started.

The comedy of a king with his finger in the wind, making war and seeking peace with concern not for moral principle but rather for the expediency of the moment, satirizes the demise of courageous leadership. No doubt examples of such meandering royal policy would be well known. The high priest Jonathan, for instance, waged war on the Macedonian garrison in Jerusalem while sending an envoy of peace to King Demetrius with bribes of silver and gold.[21] He could lay siege to the garrison in Jerusalem successfully but could not win in the battlefield against the superior forces of Demetrius. In any case, the parable of Jesus unmasks the lack of justice in many a king's war effort, which produces a humorous anecdote. The cynical commonsense wisdom of the parable makes a parody of the fact that most despots will go to battle only if they are certain of victory, regardless of the just political cause for the war. But if his ten thousand soldiers face twenty thousand, the king will lose no time in securing a peaceful solution, which usually means paying costly tribute money.

The two mini-dramas flow from one scene to another. The action involves the listener in the culturally conditioned concern of avoiding shame. The humor of the illustrations is situated well within the setting of Jesus' teaching. The purpose is the teaching of self-inventory and personal assessment as a precondition of discipleship. The sharp focus of the parables is in strong accord with the overall message of Jesus in the Gospels.

---

[20] Cf. the discussion by N. Turner in J. H. Moulton, *A Grammar of New Testament Greek*, 4:51.

[21] Jonathan gathered an army from all Judea. Then he assaulted and attacked the citadel in Jerusalem, which contained a "Macedonian garrison and some of the godless Jews who had abandoned their native customs." Demetrius became very angry when he heard about it. He took forces and started from Antioch to attack Jerusalem. "Thereupon Jonathan, although he did not stop the siege, took with him the elders of the people and the priests and came to Demetrius, bringing gold, silver and garments and a multitude of presents" (Josephus, *Ant.* 13.4.9 [120–24]; 1 Macc 11:23–24). While this is a similar example, not all the facts fit the parable of Jesus. See also the satire of Fable 93 in Babrius, which warns against peace by a negotiated surrender (*Babrius and Phaedrus*, ed. Perry, 114–15).

The double parables of the Tower Builder and the King Going to War preserve the authentic voice of Jesus. Choosing the vocation of disciple to a learned master teacher in first-century Jewish community life involved tremendous sacrifices. The warning is clear: no one should accept the challenge unadvisedly, without due consideration. Only after serious reflection and soul-searching should the person finalize the decision.

13 *The Unjust Steward*

FOCUS

The parable of the Unjust Steward (Luke 16:1–13) is regarded as one of the most, if not the most, perplexing of the parables of Jesus. The complex problems of interpretation have invited numerous approaches. The lack of consensus concerning the meaning and message of the parable exposes the paucity of convincing explanations. Most interpreters, however, agree that here is an authentic echo from the teaching of Jesus, one that shocks the listener by glorifying the actions of a shady business character. At the expense of his master's trust, money, and time, the steward watches out for himself. Could the historical Jesus have promoted dishonesty by telling a parable with such a rogue as its hero? Why would the master (Jesus?) praise the steward for his unethical wheeling and dealing, which costs the master dearly? The steward pursued his self-interest without concern for his own integrity. In spite of all this, he receives praise from his lord.

While the story was designed to excite the imagination with the irony of the master's response, the parable was probably better understood by the listeners in the original cultural situation. A first reading of the text shows a very rich man, who seems to be the master of a large estate, discovering that a trusted steward is squandering his wealth. Although described as wasteful, the steward has a more grievous shortcoming. He lacks probity. He is not merely inefficient; he is downright dishonest. For this reason the rich man tells the estate manager to turn in the records and dismisses him. The stinging realization of imminent destitution compels the clever steward to devise a scheme to save his own neck. After all, no one else has learned that he has been fired. The brief period between his fateful meeting with his master and his final departure creates an opportunity for the crafty steward to implement his plan for self-preservation. He quickly calls in his master's debtors and ingratiates himself to them by reducing their debt.

Giving a generous discount to his master's debtors, the unjust steward helped someone other than himself. To be sure, his actions were motivated by self-interest. Nonetheless, by reducing the debt he was helping someone else. Moreover, if the application of the parable, which stresses faithfulness in money matters, is properly placed and authentic, the terms "sons of light" and "mammon of unrighteousness" may have special significance. While many have divorced vv. 10–13 from the parable, besides sometimes casting suspicion on v. 9 and/or 8b, these references to the "sons of light," "mammon of unrighteousness," and being faithful with a trust appear to be in place. Flusser believes that Jesus used these terms in reference to the Dead Sea community. The policy of the Essenes was to confiscate all the financial holdings and personal belongings of their members. The covenanters of the Dead Sea Scrolls, which the consensus of scholars tends to identify with the Essenes, referred to themselves as the "sons of light."[1] Money belonging to those outside their community was deemed the "mammon of unrighteousness."

When read in the light of Flusser's insightful suggestions, the parable reveals Jesus' opinion about the Essenes. The steward is like the sons of light, i.e., the Essenes, who are taking unfair advantage of the people. The children of this age are wiser than these Essenes, who require total financial investment in the community, cutting each member off from the outside world. Money of outsiders is unrighteous mammon, whereas the currency of the community is viewed quite differently. When the unjust steward reverses his actions and starts helping the people he has been cheating, he should be praised. He has made a career out of exploiting his master's wealth and profiteering from overcharging his clients. With his own financial ruin on the horizon, and the unbearable shame it will bring, he takes drastic measures to control the damage. In fact, although he is portrayed as the steward of unrighteousness from the beginning, because he was squandering his master's assets, his final action may actually have been legitimate in the eyes of the debtors, even if it was unethical and unjust. Quite probably he was canceling his own sizable commission, which had been calculated into the amounts owed his master. In such a case, what he did was shrewd and perfectly legitimate, because he was taking his percentage of the profits and returning it to those whom he had been overcharging. The window of opportunity between the announcement of his dismissal and his departure from his post enabled him to exercise one last time the power vested in him as an agent of his wealthy master. The steward's bold initiative displayed a new approach for the excessive goods he had squandered. At least the scattering of his master's goods most likely refers to dishonest business dealings rather than ineffectual management. He probably took a cut at both ends, first by overcharging clients and second by embezzling his master's goods.

[1] On the identification of the Dead Sea community with the Essenes, see James C. VanderKam, *The Dead Sea Scrolls Today* (Grand Rapids: Eerdmans, 1994) 71–98.

The master could have had him imprisoned, but instead mercifully fired him. Now the steward was giving his cut to others. He no longer sought only to enrich himself. Instead he sought to help someone else who had been wronged. In the end, the gracious master praises the dishonest steward's shrewd conduct.

The main focus of the parable is money and stewardship. While the riddle of the parable of the Unjust Steward defies simplistic solutions, the Dead Sea Scrolls and the cultural background of the story do provide some valuable insight. Jesus valued people much more than money. In the pursuit of God's kingdom, people must come before money. Proper stewardship of resources would bring help to others. When one makes God one's master, money becomes a tool for assisting those in need. The Essene community was the antithesis of active social reform, and would have been exclusive rather than inclusive. The steward had been raking money in for himself instead of pouring it out for others. The sons of this age are more faithful stewards because of their commercial and social interaction with one another. The application of the parable not only reveals a negative parody against the communal wealth of the Essenes but also calls for social interaction. Faithful stewardship of financial resources can take place only with and among people. Active involvement with the needs of others is essential. The Essenes kept their money in their own bank and harbored a sectarian hatred for outsiders and their unrighteous mammon. Jesus' parable ridicules their approach to financial resources. Money must be used to help people. Financial resources should be put to work for social reform that benefits all.

THE PARABLE IN CHRISTIAN INTERPRETATION

The riddle of the parable of the Unjust Steward has largely defied Christian interpretation. As Derrett observed, "Much as commentators disagree as to the meaning of the parable of the Steward, all are agreed as to the embarrassment it has caused."[2] Appearing only in the Third Gospel, the parable is hardly Luke's creation in a later reflection on Jesus, even though the soliloquy of the steward is sometimes thought to be the result of Lukan redaction.[3] In fact, soliloquy is not unusual in rabbinic parables. The scandalous nature of the plot has persuaded most scholars to attribute the Lukan parable to the religious genius of Jesus himself. Luke's record of Jesus' life must be carefully considered. An overemphasis on Markan priority has

[2] J. Duncan M. Derrett, *Law in the New Testament* (London: Darton, Longman & Todd, 1974) 48.

[3] While the issue must be studied in the context of synoptic parables, it should be noted that monologue and soliloquy have often been used as effective means of character development in ancient storytelling. Cf. M. Niehoff, "Do Biblical Characters Talk to Themselves? Narrative Modes of Representing Inner Speech in Early Biblical Fiction," *JBL* 111 (1992): 577–95.

tended to undermine the value of Luke and Matthew. This colorful story, which is difficult to understand apart from its original context, is carefully preserved in Luke. It reveals rich Semitic imagery in a colorful setting. The characters of a wealthy, magnanimous landowner and the rascal, who plays the leading role of the drama, are quite typical of Gospel and rabbinic parables. Matthew and Mark, moreover, may well have been acquainted with the illustration but considered it too scandalous or puzzling to be incorporated into their portrayals of Jesus.

In the days of the Reformation, John Calvin proclaimed the Bible the sole authority for the life of the church. He searched for a proper understanding of this perplexing Gospel story. In his commentaries on the Scriptures he recognized some of the problems surrounding the interpretation of parables. On the parable of the Unjust Steward, Calvin observed that, on the one hand, it "seems hard and far-fetched" but, on the other, the illustration teaches that "we must treat our neighbors humanely and kindly, so that when we come before God's judgment seat, we may receive the fruit of our liberality."[4] Calvin obviously accepted the application of the parable in Luke 16:9, "And I tell you, make friends for yourselves by means of unrighteous mammon, so that when it fails they may receive you into the eternal habitations." Modern interpreters have tended to view this verse and vv. 10–13 as additions to the parable. The editors of the twenty-seventh edition of the Nestle-Aland *Greek New Testament* considered v. 9 an original part of the parable,[5] but Fitzmyer has argued that the parable ended with v .8. In all events, Calvin's noble attempt to make sense of the parable by stressing proper conduct, liberality, and the reverent concern of a future judgment is very much like that of other Christians who were troubled by the master's praise of the steward's behavior. More modern interpreters have also struggled with the bewildering issues surrounding this parable.[6]

Morton Smith suggested that the key to understanding the parable was interpreting more accurately the major figures in the story. If the master is evil, then the steward's behavior is justified, since he is fighting against wrong. In one of his early works Smith suggested, "The rich man is Satan,

[4] See *Calvin's Commentaries: A Harmony of the Gospels of Matthew and Luke*, 22 vols.; trans. A. W. Morrison and ed. David W. Torrance and Thomas F. Torrance (Edinburgh: Saint Andrew Press, 1972) 2:111–12. Cited by Kissinger, *Parables*, 49.

[5] E. Nestle and K. Aland, *Novum Testamentum Graece* (27th ed.; Stuttgart: Deutsche Bibelstiftung, 1981), 213.

[6] In an engaging study of the parable ("The Riddle of the Unjust Steward: Is Irony the Key?" *JBL* 82 (1963): 15–30), Donald R. Fletcher interpreted it as irony. He saw irony in the use of the term "shrewd" (φρόνιμος): "The sons of this world are shrewd; they are sharp and clever in a way which those who are sons of light are not to envy, and even less to try to emulate. You cannot keep pace with the cleverness, the kind of astutely self-interested dealing admired in the present world, and still be a citizen of the kingdom of God. The two do not mix."

the lord of this world; the steward is everyman. . . . Therefore he must deal deceitfully with the mammon of unrighteousness in order to receive 'true riches.' "[7] If the rich master of the parable is Satan, the actions of the "dishonest" steward are acceptable and even praiseworthy.[8]

More recently, in a similar approach, though without such clear movement toward allegory as Smith's suggestion, Mary Ann Beavis has argued that the master is a rogue taking unfair advantage of an accused slave.[9] In her view, the servant was "falsely" accused (διαβάλλω). The victim of the parable is better understood as a slave than as a privileged steward. As a slave, he is wrongly treated but succeeds in overcoming his difficulties through shrewd actions. The master is faulted for accepting a false report and determining to dismiss a faithful slave without sufficient cause. In the end, however, the slave proves himself in his master's eyes. The slave plays the role of a trickster clever enough to meet the challenge of his master. Her study is fraught with problems. Her rendering of διαβάλλω as "falsely accused" in this context is not convincing. The unrighteous steward was involved in wrongdoing and was not falsely accused. Moreover, he seems to occupy a high position as a financial manager. While some slaves were entrusted with major responsibilities, attaining high levels, the man's status as one who was commissioned to keep records of accounts and collect payment suggests that he was a high-ranking steward rather than a slave who was wronged by an evil master, no matter how many examples from Greco-Roman literature may be turned up where ancient slaves were mistreated. Slavery was a horrific injustice in antiquity, and historical sources describe the shocking realities of mistreatment, but the parable of the Unjust Steward comes from a different milieu, which focuses attention on another set of issues.

---

[7] Morton Smith, *Tannaitic Parallels to the Gospels* (JBLMS 6; Philadelphia: Society of Biblical Literature, 1951) 140.

[8] Scott (*Hear*, 260) also sees the parable as attacking the rich man: "Since the master is rich—a redundant marker if he has a steward to look after his property—he may well play the role of antagonist. In the world of Galilean peasants, rich masters play the expected role of despots, and the master in this story may be an absentee landlord, a common phenomenon in Galilee." On the contrary, while some Gospel stories, such as the Rich Man and Lazarus or the parable of the Rich Fool, portray the temptations and the excesses of the wealthy, parables of stewardship in Christian and Jewish literatures without exception view the master as the ideal character of common goodness. His kind and generous character is a picture of God's nature. In the present parable, rather than playing the role of a penny-pinching despot, the kind master cares not about his financial loss when the steward reduces the amount owed by the debtors.

[9] Mary Ann Beavis, "Ancient Slavery as an Interpretive Context for the New Testament Servant Parables with Special Reference to the Unjust Steward (Luke 16:1–8)" *JBL* 111 (1992): 37–54. Her valuable study embraces the larger Greco-Roman world of fable lore but is decidedly weak in the area of Jewish sources. She is not acquainted with Flusser's strong arguments concerning the parable of the Unjust Steward and the Dead Sea Scrolls nor with Flusser's unparalleled contributions in *Gleichnisse.*

In all events, the major fallacy of Smith's and Beavis's proposals is in their suggestion that the master was an evil character, victimizing others. In rabbinic literature, and indeed in all the servant parables of the Gospels, the master is a magnanimous, noble personality who is kind, generous, and just, even though he must be revered because of his awesome authority.

The parable does not address the inhumanity of ancient slavery. It is a story about a rich man and his estate manager. The master's justice in such stories reaches a higher standard than that of the common person. His generosity is prized in a community that receives his benevolence. The theme of stewardship focuses on the proper use of another's trust. The steward should make good use of the master's resources. The master is noble and just. The steward is dishonest. The master could have thrown such a wasteful estate manager into prison. Instead, he dismisses him. When the steward shrewdly gives away discounts and exploits his position to win favor from his master's debtors, the rich man again displays magnanimity and nobility by praising his astute business practice.

Smith was right in focusing on the task of more accurately interpreting the major figures of the story, especially the rich master. Properly interpreting this figure is a prerequisite for unlocking the parable's meaning. Here, as in rabbinic parables, the master is benevolent and honorable, even to the point of lauding his steward when the steward causes him financial loss. While the steward's first concern is self-preservation, the master's response reveals his kind and generous nature. As lord of the estate, he is all-powerful and demanding. When he learns that his steward has wasted his goods, an investigation of the matter is pursued and a judgment is determined. The surprise twists to the story—the clever actions of the shrewd, double-dealing steward and the magnanimous master's reaction—would have strongly impacted a first-century Jewish audience.

THE PARABLE IN THE LIGHT OF ITS JEWISH BACKGROUND

The parable of the Unjust Steward is best understood in its first-century Jewish context. The reality behind the story is discovered in the agrarian financial world of Israel during the Second Temple period. Agriculture was big business. The elements of country living and the economics of farm management were well known to the common people. Quite probably the steward reduced the debts of tenant farmers, who were required to pay a portion of the harvest in exchange for use of good farming land. The steward supervised the deals involving land leasing, collecting produce, keeping records, receiving income, and paying out disbursements. As an agent of a wealthy landowner, the steward received a salary and quite possibly a commission as well as kickbacks from grateful renters who recognized his authority and appreciated his favors. While some gratuities for helpful services would be honorable and acceptable business practice, the dishonest steward is described as squandering the assets of his master. When called to give an account, he is surprisingly silent. The audience would anticipate a vociferous defense, an attempt to save his job. By remaining silent he is acknowledging his wrongdoing and recognizing that the master probably has irrefutable evidence against him.[10]

J. Jeremias identified the realistic setting portrayed in the parable as a lease agreement with tenant farmers or promissory notes given to merchants marketing the produce. In either case, the financial arrangements described in the parable involved vast sums of money or equivalents in goods and produce. The landowner is very rich, and the business people with whom he deals are not poor either. The trusted steward is the middleman who acts as a broker for the super rich, the go-between for the wealthy master and his clients. While the exact economic factors are difficult to calculate with accuracy, Jeremias estimated the amounts involved in the transactions of these debtors:

> The debtors (χρεοφειλέτης) are either tenants who have to deliver a specified portion (a half, a third, or a quarter) of the yield of their land in lieu of rent, or wholesale merchants, who have given promissory notes for goods received. One hundred baths (=c. 800 gals.) of oil corresponds to the yield of about 146 olive-trees, and a debt of about 1,000 denarii; 100 cors (=c. 120 quarters) of wheat equals 550 cwt. and corresponds to the yield of about 100 acres, and a debt of about 2,500 denarii. Hence heavy obligations were involved. The remission (400 gals. of the oil and 24 quarters of the wheat) is approximately equal in the two cases, since oil is much dearer than wheat; its value in currency would be about 500 denarii. In our parable Jesus betrays the oriental story-teller's love for large numbers.[11]

---

[10]This point has been made strongly by Bailey, *Poet and Peasant*, 97: "The listener/reader of the parable expects the steward to be silent after the first question. But after the steward is told, 'You're fired; turn in the books!' the listener/reader expects a classic debate in which the steward loudly and insistently protests his innocence." Instead, "he walks out having offered no defense. This silence is supremely significant in the Oriental context. The man is indirectly affirming by his silence at least the following: 1. I am guilty. 2. The master knows the truth; he knows I am guilty. 3. This master expects obedience; disobedience brings judgment. 4. I cannot get my job back by offering a series of excuses."

[11]Jeremias, *Parables of Jesus*, 181. The exact amounts are difficult to determine. Cf. also Nolland, *Luke*, 2:799: "Both the quantity of olive oil and of wheat mentioned here are found identically in the list that specifies the extravagant release of resources authorized by Artaxerxes for Ezra (Ezra 7:22). The quantities involved are quite huge. The oil involved would represent the annual yield of a very large olive grove. Similarly the wheat debt 'would represent a half-share rent for almost 200 acres, which is perhaps twenty times the size of an average family plot' (Kloppenborg, *Bib* 70 [1989] 482)." Jeremias relied largely on Dalman for his calculations. In such matters Dalman and Jeremias are generally more reliable.

So while the parable does not state whether the debtors are tenant farmers or merchants, clearly very significant amounts of money are involved in each transaction. I tend to think that the original audience would have pictured tenant farmers of large and profitable tracts making a deal with the landowner's real estate agent, who serves as a business manager. Since they have done business with him in the past, they do not begin to imagine that he has been dismissed. If Jeremias is correct, both debtors receive similar amounts in discounts of goods, equaling about 500 denarii in monetary value.

The steward himself therefore occupies a respectable position of authority, invested with the power of his wealthy master. According to the law, as the official representative of his lord, the steward's word has the same force. In modern terms, the steward has been entrusted with the power of attorney. When he loses his position, he will lose prestige and honor, the most highly prized possession he will ever enjoy. The fear of being unemployed and the problem of finding another position after he has been fired for mismanagement are also very weighty concerns. He is "ashamed" to be a beggar.

The prospect of disgrace is overwhelming in oriental culture. Shame must always be avoided, no matter what the cost. The words "I am too weak to dig" may even have been humorous to the original audience. The sharp contrast between a sun-scorched manual laborer digging in the dirt and this highly placed financial manager must have been amusing for the listeners. Poverty and wealth are portrayed as a revolving door—one minute the steward is affluent and the next he is among the poor. As a homeless outcast he will join the most vulnerable of all people in the social setting of oriental culture. Derrett has tried to describe his plight:

> Our steward was an agent possessing the most comprehensive authority. . . . Our steward would leave with as little as he first brought with him, save items which might pass his master's scrutiny. His social equals, other stewards, would not welcome him; those who had dealt with him as steward in the past would either scorn him or rejoice at his fall; and re-employment in a similar capacity would be possible only far enough away for news of his dismissal not to have been heard. That would require capital, and good fortune. His situation and predicament are clear. Good will, on a generous scale, he must try to win.[12]

The steward, finding himself in a desperate situation, had to devise a plan and act quickly. The legality of his action would be upheld by his position as agent of his master as long as he could conceal the fact of his dismissal. Legally, his authority to represent his master had been canceled (ἀπόδος τὸν λόγον τῆς οἰκονομίας σου, οὐ γὰρ δύνῃ ἔτι οἰκονομεῖν, "Turn in the account of your stewardship, for you can no longer be steward"). The wording makes it clear that he has been fired. But the master's clients are uninformed about that. If they knew that he has been released, they would never join in the scheme that would make them partners in the crime. They

[12] Derrett, *Law in the New Testament*, 55.

need a credible business relationship with the noble master of the estate. But they believe the steward is acting with full authority of his master.

The ethical question regarding the steward's action is a major issue in the interpretation of the story. Did he act legally? Was his scheme ethical? Derrett has suggested that the steward was trying to circumvent interest payments owed to the master. Since usury was in reality forbidden, although in the cause of economic advancement efforts were made to overcome its complete prohibition, the action of the master's agent would be praised by all. In fact, although the rich man would be deprived of the interest payments, he would gain prestige as a generous benefactor. While Derrett has carefully studied the issues in Jewish law and oriental thought, the parable does not mention interest, and it is impossible to know whether the original audience would have considered the issue of usury. I am not convinced that the parable deals with interest on loans. More precisely, the story fits the land-leasing agreements of agricultural operations.

Fitzmyer has defended the view that the steward was giving up his own commission.[13] The amounts of his commission, however, are difficult to determine. In the parable, the rebate is 50 percent in the case of the oil and 20 percent in the case of the wheat. In monetary equivalents they would be roughly the same. The first example of 50 percent is a high profit margin for a steward. The wasteful manager, however, may well have been overcharging his master's clients for his own enrichment. A 20 percent markup for the transaction seems more realistic. Would five hundred denarii be the price of a good deal?[14] The dishonest steward shows imagination and creativity in any way he can get ahead. The olive oil business was very profitable. A 50 percent cut on about 150 trees is a significant payoff. Twenty percent income on around 100 acres of wheat is a lucrative kickback for a steward who merely sets up the deal. After all, the tenant farmers do all the labor, and the master controls the capital and owns the land. In the case of merchants, they must transport and market the goods and produce. The steward is the middleman who does not have to endure hard manual labor or take the risks of the landowner.

In all events, the whole procedure of discounting the debts would not be considered entirely ethical. Such income opportunity was negotiated in the master's name and would be designated for whoever served as his manager or for the landowner himself. There is no evidence suggesting that the steward would enjoy a residual income from negotiated contracts after he had been dismissed. The loss of revenue would directly impact the wealthy master, regardless of whether it was the agent's commission or not. While it

[13] Fitzmyer is probably the most notable scholar associated with this innovative approach (*Luke*, 2:1097–98). The theory has a history all its own. See Bailey, *Poet and Peasant*, 88, who mentions the study by Margaret Gibson, "On the Parable of the Unjust Steward," *ExpT* 14 (1902): 334.

[14] Cf. Jeremias, *Parables of Jesus*, 181.

may not have been ethical or legal in the strict order of business, in the eyes of the clients it would have been legitimate because they believed that the steward is acting with the full authority of his master. They did not know that he had been dismissed.

The intense language of the parable emphasizes the urgency of the steward's action. All must be done "quickly" (ταχέως) if his plan is to succeed. He assumes his former position by asking, "How much do you owe *my master?*" (italics added). In normal Western business procedures, such a person would be prosecuted and his unethical actions declared void until a proper investigation could uncover what agreements had been reached under false pretenses. The unjust steward had ceased to represent his master. These new contracts would be annulled and/or renegotiated. But in the shame-and-honor culture of the East, as Bailey has pointed out, the entire story makes perfect sense.[15] Both the master and his steward want to avoid shame. Such unprecedented generosity in the name of the rich man would be received with gratitude. He is a wealthy and magnanimous man who can afford the loss and is also willing to demonstrate his benevolence. Because of his generosity, everyone will praise him as a hero. His steward will also be esteemed because of his actions in the name of his wealthy master. The listeners in the cultural environment will put the pieces of the puzzle together and relish the entertaining plot of the story. The pretense is already set in motion. After the fact, the master must play along with the unjust steward. Reneging on these benevolent acts carried out in his name would ravage his reputation. The master cannot change the agreements and retain the respect of his community. Bailey's insights into the cultural setting make the drama come alive.

> The master knows full well that in the local village there has already started a great round of celebration in praise of him, the master, as the most noble and most generous man that ever rented land in their district. He has two alternatives.
>
> He can go back to the debtors and explain that it was all a mistake, that the steward had been dismissed, and thus his actions were null and void. But if the master does this *now*, the villagers' joy will turn to anger, and he will be cursed for his stinginess.

---

[15] See Bailey, *Poet and Peasant*, 86–118. For the most part, I believe that Bailey (p. 94) has properly understood the life setting of the parable:
In summary, clearly the most probable cultural setting for the parable is that of a landed estate with a manager who had authority to carry out the business of the estate. The debtors were most likely renters, *chakirin*, who had agreed to pay a fixed amount of produce for the yearly rent. The steward was no doubt making extras "under the table," but these amounts were not reflected in the signed bills. He was a salaried official who, in addition, was paid a specific fee by the renter for each contract. The master was a man of noble character respected in the community who cared enough about his own wealth to fire a wasteful manager.

> Second, he can keep silent, accept the praise that is even now being showered on him, and allow the clever steward to ride high on the wave of popular enthusiasm. This master *is* a generous man. He did not jail the steward earlier. To be generous is a primary quality of a nobleman in the East. He reflects for a moment and then turns to the steward and says, "You are a very wise fellow." One of the Old Testament definitions of "wisdom" is an instinct for self preservation.[16]

In light of Bailey's oriental exegesis, the plot of the parable is intriguing and convincing. The parable captures the imagination of the people and leads them on a journey filled with interesting twists. The mashal therefore opens a window through which moderns may view the Middle Eastern cultural setting behind the folklore elements in the parables of Jesus. The wealthy master is cheated by the unjust steward. But the shrewd steward swindles his master in such a way as to make it extremely counterproductive to seek restitution. The master is generous, noble, and magnanimous. He loves the people in his community, with whom he does business. In fact, he is so rich that he does not seem to care about the loss.

While vv. 10–12 often have been considered later additions to the parable, there is ample reason to reevaluate the evidence. First, it should be recognized that the mashal of rabbinic literature often includes a *nimshal* that elucidates and applies the word-picture. This practical application is often introduced with the Hebrew term כך, "Thus," or "So it is with." As entertaining stories, both rabbinic and Gospel parables are designed to make a comparison and to illustrate a teaching.

Flusser has convincingly argued that the cultural setting of the *nimshal* in vv. 10–12 is discovered in the communal life and economic structure of the Dead Sea sect.[17] The scrolls sometimes provide remarkable linguistic parallels to the words of Jesus in the Gospels. On the one hand, the term "sons of light" is understood as referring to the early Christians in Johannine and Pauline writings. On the other, the "sons of light" refers to the members of the Dead Sea sect in the scrolls. Verse 8 has the only reference to the "sons of light" in the Synoptic Gospels.

Flusser discovered the parody of the parable in the scrolls, where the sons of light are exalted and the sons of darkness, all outsiders, are condemned. Not only are they condemned in the eschatological future; their money is called the "wealth of unrighteousness." The questionable financial practices of the dishonest steward in Jesus' parable recall the policies of the Dead Sea community. They collect the money of all their members and reject

---

[16] Ibid., 101–2.

[17] David Flusser, "Jesus' Opinion about the Essenes," in *Origins;* see Flusser's popularization of this study, "The Parable of the Unjust Steward: Jesus' Criticism of the Essenes," in *Judaism and the Dead Sea Scrolls* (ed. J. Charlesworth; New York: Doubleday, 1993) 176–97. Cf. also David Flusser, *Das essenische Abenteuer* (Winterthur, Switzerland: Cardun, 1994) 30–40, 101–20.

all business ties with outsiders. As religious isolationists, they kept their money within their sect. This closed community of wealth is a serious matter. In contrast, like the Pharisees and the rabbis after them, Jesus emphasized almsgiving to alleviate human suffering.

In a study entitled "Jesus' Opinion about the Essenes," Flusser observed the sect's hatred for all people outside their group. The *Manual of Discipline*, the Hebrew document written for new members of the sect, stresses the relationship between the Essenes and outsiders. They must love the sons of light and hate the sons of darkness: "Everyone who wishes to join the community must pledge . . . to love all the children of light [members of the Essene sect] . . . and to hate all the children of darkness [everyone outside the Essene sect] . . ." (1QS 1:1–11).[18]

The strict separatism of the community was all-encompassing. Financial involvement with outsiders was forbidden, except for simple cash purchases.

> So no member shall be united with him (the outsider) in his work or in his wealth, lest he defile the member with guilty iniquity, but distance shall be kept from him in every matter . . . no member shall eat from their property nor drink from it, nor take anything from their hands except by payment. . . . For all who are not accounted as in his covenant keep them separate and all that belongs to them . . . and all their deeds filthiness before him and uncleanness is in all their wealth.[19]

> And let no person of the covenant of God [member of Essene sect] trade with the sons of perdition [all other people] except for cash. And let no person make a partnership for trade unless he informs the overseer in the camp and makes a written agreement.[20]

> And the wealth belonging to men of holiness [members of the Essene sect] who walk in perfection—their wealth shall not be mingled with the wealth belonging to men of deceit [all other people] who have not cleansed their way to be separated from iniquity and to walk in perfection of way.[21]

Of special interest is the terminology used here for money belonging to those outside the Essene fold. It is הון רשעה, "wealth of unrighteousness," which is a dynamic equivalent to "unrighteous mammon" (μαμωνᾶ τῆς ἀδικίας) in Luke 16:9. Would it exasperate an ardent Essene to suggest that he could win a friend by the use of unrighteous mammon? For Jesus,

[18] Matt 5:43, "Love your enemies," also well may have been directed against the Essenes.

[19] See 1QS 5:14–20, Vermes, p. 68. See esp. Flusser, "Opinion."

[20] CD 13:14–16, Vermes, p. 98. See Flusser, "Opinion."

[21] 1QS 9:8–10, Vermes, pp. 74–75. The Hebrew words הון אנשי קודש, "wealth belonging to men of holiness," are contrasted with הון אנשי הרמיה, "wealth belonging to men of deceit." See Licht, *Megilat Haserachim*, 190.

the test of one's faithfulness is found in the way one uses "unrighteous mammon" (Luke 16:11).

The sharp dualism between light and darkness, holiness and deceit is an expression of sectarian hatred, which also reveals itself in the economic structure of the community. Josephus tells us that for members of the community even "presents to relatives are prohibited without leave from the managers."[22] They guarded their community of wealth through strict laws and rigorous supervision. Borrowing language belonging to the Dead Sea sect, Jesus cleverly ridiculed their attitude toward money. The Essenes confiscated money from new members and then hoarded it for the needs of their own sect. Jesus advocated giving money away to benefit those who need it.

MONEY, JESUS, AND THE RABBIS

Regarding the proper use of money, Jesus and many rabbis seem to have much in common. At least powerful streams of thought in Judaism from the Second Temple period stressed giving money to the downtrodden. Money should be used to alleviate human need. Genuine religious piety must be characterized by generous contributions to those who are less fortunate. In this respect, the Essene laws creating a closed community of wealth portray a sharp antithesis to the teachings of Jesus and the rabbis. Not only did the Essenes keep their money in the bank; they owned the bank. The Dead Sea community owned their bank's deposits and regulated the lives of its depositors. Having all the finances of members controlled in a communal treasury profoundly influenced the Essene sectarians and their relationship with others. Such a view of wealth left no room for acts of piety, which entailed giving liberally to needy people irrespective of group affiliation. Giving of *tzedakah* (צדקה) is cherished in traditional Jewish teachings, which are rooted in Second Temple period Judaism.

Both Jesus and the rabbis speak about mammon.[23] A person of faith should be characterized by charity and good deeds, which will be rewarded in the world to come. Like Jesus, the rabbis taught that the proper use of money includes providing assistance for others. For example, "Acquire for yourselves this world and the world to come by your mammon [that is, give money to help the needy and you will acquire both this world and the world to come]."[24]

Traditional Jewish themes concerning money and stewardship provide the glue that bonds the various pieces of the dramatic plot of the parable of

[22] Josephus, *War* 2.134.

[23] The word mammon, ממון (Greek equivalent μαμωνᾶς) is used frequently in Tannaitic and Amoraic writings (cf. Levy, *Wörterbuch*, 3:138–39).

[24] *Der. Er. Zut.* 4 (see *Derekh Eretz*, ed. M. Higger, 99–100). Cf. Matt 6:19–21.

the Unjust Steward. The estate manager is wasting his master's goods by seeking to enrich himself at the expense of others. The master is displeased with the steward's normal practice. The steward is wasteful because he keeps the profits for himself. But when he breaks with this type of conduct and gives away his master's wealth to the clients, he is praised. Hoarding money is viewed as wasting God's resources. But when the money is given to the master's clients, the master is not upset but pleased. This is the perfect caricature of the sectarian "children of light" and the way the Essenes were frustrating the divine purpose. The theme of stewardship is then picked up and developed in the application to the parable.

Jesus teaches, "He who is faithful in a very little is faithful also in much; and he who is dishonest in a very little is dishonest also in much" (Luke 16:10). The steward fits this picture. A somewhat parallel saying appears in the Mishnah in a context that deals with tithing. The idiom was probably a floating expression that appeared in various contexts. It stresses the virtue of "faithfulness," that is, one who proves to be "trustworthy," נאמן. It could be applied to tithing or almsgiving or any other duty in which a person is called to be steadfast in proper observance. In a discussion concerning who is reliable in the area of tithing, the rabbis tell R. Judah, "He who would not be faithful in what concerns himself, how then could he be faithful in what concerns others?"[25] In the Gospel text, Jesus was addressing issues of charity and almsgiving when he challenged his audience, "If then you have not been faithful in the unrighteous mammon, who will entrust to you the true riches? And if you have not been faithful in that which is another's, who will give you that which is your own?" (Luke 16:11).[26]

In the larger context of the teachings of Jesus the great value of almsgiving is stressed.[27] He not only praises generous giving but also speaks about the proper way to provide assistance to those in need. One should give with liberality and in a way that does not seek recognition. Here the hero of the parable is a rogue estate manager, who winds up giving away money even if it comes out of the pockets of his rich master and is given for the wrong motive. The children of this world are wiser than the "children of light," i.e., Essenes. Like other Gospel parables, such as a wicked judge who cares nothing about

[25] See m. *Demai* 2:2; and cf. the notes on Matt 25:21 by Paul Billerbeck, Str-B 1:972, also citing *Exod. Rab.* 2:3 (cf. Shinan's edition, 106). See also L. Ginzberg, *Genizah Studies* (New York: Hermon, 1969) 1:46–37; and cf. *Tanchuma*, ed. Buber, Shemot 10.

[26] Compare here also the discussion of the parable of the Pounds in Matt 25:14–30 and Luke 19:11–27. See also Flusser, "Aesop's Fable."

[27] On almsgiving in the Gospels, see Matt 6:1–4; 6:19–21 (Luke 12:33–34); Matt 6:22–23 (Luke 11:34–36); Matt 6:24 (Luke 16:13); Matt 25:35. Compare in rabbinic literature the story of Monaboz, the Jewish convert king, whose generosity is celebrated in words that closely parallel Matt 6:19–21 and Luke 12:33–34. The king's legendary benevolence is praised in t. *Peah* 4:18; b. *B. Bat.* 11a; j. *Peah* 15b, ch. 1, halakah 1, and parallels.

a widow, a contemptible friend who will not help his neighbor with a simple request, or a terrible publican who goes to the temple for prayer, the villain of the story may surprise and delight the listener. The ungodly person may shock the listener by breaking the mold of expected conduct. In the case of the unjust steward, giving away money is a favorite theme in the folklore of Jewish piety. A modern equivalent might be the story of a greedy, unscrupulous bank president who loves money more than people. He is the criminal type who will do anything for the dollar. The members of the bank's board decide to fire him. They summon him to a meeting, expose his wrongdoing, and ask him to prepare his final report. After the shock of this personal tragedy, the dishonest bank president has a change of heart. He calls in all the hard-working wage earners struggling to make those exorbitant mortgage payments. In a sweeping action of charity, using the resources of the financial empire under his supervision, he eliminates all the loan payments. In his final act, the greedy criminal does good for other people.

JESUS' CRITICISM OF THE ESSENES: A CALL FOR FINANCIAL RESPONSIBILITY

Jesus and the rabbis rejected Essene separatism and bigotry. In the parable of the Unjust Steward and its application Jesus blasts the Essenes' sectarian hatred and their highly regulated, stringent, self-serving, closed economic policies. Unlike Jesus and the Pharisees, the Essenes preached double predestination to indoctrinate those who joined their covenant community. That is, the sectarians believed that God had already determined or predestined both the individuals who would be saved and also those who would be eternally damned. In contrast to the teachings of the Pharisees and Jesus, who urged making a decision to serve God in his kingdom, the Dead Sea sect taught that the children of darkness had already been predetermined. They narrowly identified members of their sect as the sons of light, who had been preordained to obtain victory in the eschatological war that would end all wars.[28] Hence, long before Paul or John would call the early Christians the "children of light" with a different meaning, the Essenes claimed that they were the true sons of light.

As Flusser has shown, the technical term "sons of light" in the parable of the Unjust Steward refers to the Essenes and not to the disciples of Jesus. Jesus called his disciples the poor in spirit, the peacemakers, the merci-

[28] See Flusser, *Origins*, 156: "According to a famous rabbinic concept, God concealed the light which he created on the first day from the present world, 'but in the world to come it will appear to the pious in all its pristine glory.' This explanation of the sons of light is absent from the Dead Sea Scrolls where it is only said that, 'in the spring of light are generations of truth and from the well of darkness come the generation of perversity' (1QS 3:19)."

ful—but he never referred to them as the sons of light in the first three Gospels. Later, in the next wave of Christianity, in the Pauline and Johannine communities, the term "sons of light" became recognized as another name for members of the church.[29] But when the original audience of Jesus' parable heard the term "sons of light," one can be certain that they did not think of the early Christians. People in first-century Israel knew that members of the community living in the desert a half day's walk from Jerusalem thought of themselves as the sons of light, and it is these sectarians who most likely would have entered the minds of Jesus' listeners.

The Essene attitude toward money was a corollary of their notion of double predestination and enmity for outsiders. The Essenes called money belonging to outsiders unrighteous mammon.[30] Of great significance for our parable is the fact that the Essenes were forbidden—except under special circumstances—to buy from or sell to someone from among the children of darkness. If business transactions involving nonsectarians were unavoidable, they were permitted if one paid cash, thereby minimizing contact with outsiders. The Essene hatred for all outsiders and their claim on the finances of the members of the sect would have been known in many circles. Their sect was secretive, but even the historian Josephus seems to have had information about the inner functioning of their community.

In many ways the parable of the Unjust Steward is a parable of conflict. It lashes at the Essenes, exposing their approach to money and people. Unlike the Essenes, Jesus emphasized God's love for the outsider. When the steward reduces the debts of the outsiders, his master's clients, whom he has been cheating in order to enrich himself, they become the grateful recipients of his grace. One should not unduly push the limits of the parable's imagery, but it is possible that Jesus alludes to the grace of God in commending the steward for what seemed to be a dishonest act.

The original hearer of the parable knew that the primary characteristic of the wealthy master is generosity. The householder in the story must be magnanimous. The parable is somewhat humorous because the dishonest steward outwits the generous landowner. But, because the landowner is wealthy and magnanimous, he forgives the debts and commends the steward. All the people are blessed by the steward's cleverness. The master will be praised throughout the land for his noble generosity. The landowner is full of grace. He shows compassion. The village is alive with the praise of the generous landowner. He will not try to punish the dishonest steward. Instead he acknowledges the steward's cleverness.

The parable teaches that God's grace is unlimited. The master is like God when he allows the release of debts to stand and praises the dishonest steward. The separatism of the Essene community of wealth, therefore, must

---

[29] Compare Flusser, "The Dead Sea Sect and Pre-Pauline Christianity," in *Origins*, 23–74.

[30] The Hebrew word הון, "wealth," is the dynamic equivalent for mammon.

be completely rejected. Clearly Jesus wanted his followers to have contact with the people outside his movement. In fact, he was well known for his association with individuals of ill repute. Jesus loved them. Characteristic of Jesus in the Gospels, he invited himself to dine with the notorious tax collector Zacchaeus, who was known for dishonesty.[31] In a dramatic act of kindness, Jesus associated himself with an outsider who desperately desired love and acceptance. After meeting Jesus, Zacchaeus gave half of all he owned to the poor and restored fourfold all that he had stolen from others. In the parable of the Great Banquet, Jesus seems to make a point that the outcasts of society, who would not be welcome as members in the Essene community, are invited to feast at the rich man's table.[32]

The children of this world are not like the Essenes. They try to do business with everyone. In like manner, Jesus is teaching his disciples to reach out to all people, just as the children of this world buy and sell with everyone. The "sons of light," the Essenes, will trade only with their own closed group. They reject all others as the children of darkness, who, in their opinion, already have been predestined to burn on the day of judgment no matter what they do. They have no hope. For the Essenes, double predestination was a fact. But for Jesus, everyone has hope. He would urge his followers to trade with the unbeliever and to have free association with the outcasts of society. For it is only through unfettered personal interaction with people that their needs can be identified and met. By loving others more than money, almsgiving will become a way of life. A generous heart will win friends and enable others to see the grace in the divine character.

In fact, in the context of Jesus' other teachings the final interpretation of the parable calls for earnest financial responsibility. People and their needs must come before money. By seeing God's abundant grace as a fund accessible to all, the followers of Jesus must reach beyond group affiliation and self-righteous prejudice. In contrast to the Essene exclusive community of wealth, Jesus and his disciples must pursue a different course of action. Social reform and humanitarian aid must be sought to bring help to others in need on a universal level.

[31] Luke 19:1–10.

[32] See the discussion of the parable of the Great Banquet above, ch. 9.

Part 6

Torah Learning and God's Reign

14 *Four Types of Hearers*

FOCUS

The traditional name, parable of the Sower, focuses attention on the farmer. The whole story, however, revolves around the reality illustrated by sowing seed into four different types of land, and its title should reflect the essence of its message (Matt 13:1–23; Mark 4:1–20; Luke 8:4–15). The parable should be called "the Hearers," because Jesus, in a word-picture describing seeds' growth in various soils, portrays four different types of disciples who hear his teaching. Their response to the message is the primary focus of the parable, rather than the sower, who represents the preacher, or the seed, which refers to the word of God. The condition of the soil determines the growth of the seed and the success or failure of the harvest. The good soil produces a hundredfold return.

When one looks at a field, one sees the different types of disciple in the land itself. The path, the rock, the thorns, all portray the conditions of the soil. The good soil will produce abundantly. The productivity of the seed in this story has little to do with the sower or the seed itself, but rather with the nutrients and growth-producing conditions of the ground in which the seed has been sown. Farmers are much concerned about the soil. The preparation of the soil for planting often is considered the major determining factor in the success of the harvest. Seed that falls on the path as the farmer scatters it in the field will not produce any crop. Rocks and thorns will prevent the seed's growth.

The parable of the Sower (Hearers) has created numerous problems for interpreters throughout the centuries. Would the people who first heard it have understood the meaning of the parable? A study of Jewish parallels that also use numerous analogies with four types shows that the answer to the question must be affirmative. In a context of Jewish learning and Torah study, four different soil conditions would be viewed as various types of disciples absorbing the words taught by their master. The field tells the story. The good earth that provides food for the people with its harvest corresponds to disciples devoted to Torah learning. In the Synoptic Gospels, the reason for speaking in parables must be viewed as blessing the followers of Jesus who hear his teachings and obey them. The interpretation of the parable of the Sower, which is often rejected as an allegory of the church, should be examined more closely. Its Semitic linguistic background as well as numerous rabbinic parables that have interpretations call into question a cavalier approach that deems every biblical explanation of a parable a late allegory of the church. Why is it so unlikely that Jesus explained the parable when so many Jewish parallels have such applications? These word-pictures sometimes needed further elucidation, even though the basic meaning would be clear to the original audience.

Why did Jesus tell parables? This question is entertained by the evangelists Matthew, Mark, and Luke, who creatively deal with the issues surrounding Jesus' teaching method in their sources.[1] The setting in life and the roots of Jesus' teachings in Jewish culture demonstrate the purpose of the parables. Jesus used parables to illustrate his message. The parables made it easier for the audience to understand. Although this simple statement seems clear enough, many church fathers and a number of NT scholars find it extremely controversial because of the parable of the Sower and its explanation in the Gospels.[2] In fact, the church fathers, some leading scholars, and popular Bible teachers have tended to think that Jesus wanted to hide his message from the common people by cleverly concealing spiritual truth in perplexing parables. They view each element of the parables as a brainteaser. Sometimes they treat a parable like a crossword puzzle.[3] The interpreters search for clues to uncover the symbolic meaning of each word in the story. Once they write a new word in the box, they are one step closer to solving the entire puzzle. Thus the mystery is revealed to insiders only.[4]

---

[1] See Matt 13:10–17; Mark 4:10–12; Luke 8:9–10.

[2] According to Clement of Alexandria (*Miscellanies* 5.12) the parables contain secret mysteries that are sealed by Christ to those outside. Scott views the parable in Mark as being difficult for the original audience to understand: "That parables are simple, clearly understandable stories is not supported by the evidence of mashal" (*Hear*, 24). Some church fathers and NT scholars argue that the parables were even more difficult for the Jewish people to comprehend because of their spiritual blindness. On the contrary, the meaning of the Gospel parables may be better appreciated in light of their relationship to Jewish parallels and even by corroboration with Jewish scholarship.

[3] Adolf Jülicher effectively challenged this approach in his monumental study of the parables (*Die Gleichnisreden Jesu* [1888; repr. Darmstadt: Wissenschaftliche, 1963]), which attacked the allegorical method. But his strict application of his method must be critically evaluated. After all, Jesus himself as the storyteller, or the context of the situation, may introduce multiple points of comparison between the *Bild* (picture) and the *Sache* (thing), even if, as Jülicher insisted, the parable teaches only one essential message.

[4] Some leading NT scholars, such a Hunter, Dodd, Jeremias, and Manson, have challenged this view. They have argued that the parables were designed to teach. See, e.g., the discussion by Hunter, *Parables*, 110–12, with a foundational summary.

Unfortunately, this "secret meaning" approach often invites special interpretation of a parable based on newly revealed knowledge that is completely removed from the historical setting of Jesus' life and ministry. Some Christian interpreters have boldly claimed that, although Jews contemporary with Jesus were blind to a proper understanding of the parables, they themselves discern the meaning. But in all honesty, are Christians from another day better able to understand Jewish parabolic teachings than first-century Jews? The parable of the Hearers should be studied in light of Jewish culture. The setting in life is to be found in the context of Torah learning and practical discipleship. It describes the healthy tension between learning and doing when the attitude of the heart determines the disciple's ability to take the message and put it into action.

THE PARABLE IN CHRISTIAN INTERPRETATION

In Christian interpretation, this parable has been allegorized to teach different messages. Already in the Apostolic Fathers, *1 Clement* refers to the parable in a proof of the reality of a future resurrection: Clement introduces his treatment of the parable by explaining, "Let us consider, beloved, how the Master continually proves to us that there will be a future resurrection." His point is that the produce from the seed in this parable clearly teaches the doctrine of the future resurrection. The seed is planted and comes up in a crop that is like the Last Judgment at the resurrection of the dead, when each person is judged. The good crop is rewarded and the others receive punishment.

> Let us observe, beloved, the resurrection that occurs in the regularity of the seasons. Day and night manifest resurrection: night falls asleep, and day arises; day departs night returns. Or take for example the crops: how in what way is the sowing done? The sower goes out and sows each seed in the ground, and they fall to the earth dry and bare, and decay. Then from their decay the wondrous providence of the Master raises them, and from each one more grow and bear fruit.[5]

First Clement uses some analogies from Stoic thought that show the renewal of the world in the cycle of day and night, which produces the seed time and harvest.[6] It is parallel to the Christian doctrine of the resurrection, which certainly is rooted in the teachings of the Pharisees. Of course, the context in the Gospels does not mention the resurrection. *First Clement* has adapted the parable to a new setting and focused attention on another doctrine. Funk, Scott, and Butts have correctly observed, "The version in 1 Clement is a good

---

[5] *1 Clem.* 24:2–5 (R. M. Grant and H. H. Graham, *The Apostolic Fathers a New Translation and Commentary* [New York: Thomas Nelson, 1965] 50).

[6] See Grant and Graham, *Apostolic Fathers,* note on 24:1–5; and R. M. Grant, *Miracle and Natural Law in Graeco-Roman and Early Christian Thought* (Amsterdam: North Holland Publishing Company, 1952) 235–45.

example of the editorial modification of a parable to support a special theological point."[7] While the images of the Gospel parable may be used to illustrate different themes, such as the resurrection, the problem with *1 Clement* is its lack of interest in the original message of Jesus. Allegory may completely undermine the teachings of Jesus in the parables. The storyteller in the Gospels is addressing an entirely different issue.

A similar problem is seen in Clement of Alexandria, who views the parables as concealing the hidden mysteries of God. When speaking about the Gospel text that explains the purpose of the parables, Clement of Alexandria interprets the message as referring to the secrets that have been sealed by Jesus. Instead of teaching clearly about the mysterious nature of God in concrete images easy to comprehend, the parables are designed to conceal the truth of God from the common people. The divine nature is beyond comprehension, and the parables contain hidden meanings.

> These things the Saviour himself seals when He says: 'To you it is given to know the mysteries of the kingdom of heaven.' And again the Gospel says that the Saviour spake to the apostles the word in a mystery. For prophecy says of Him: 'He will open His mouth in parables, and will utter things kept secret from the foundation of the world.' And now, by the parable of the leaven, the Lord shows concealment.[8]

Clement does not view the parables as illustrations that make the teachings of Jesus easier to understand. Rather, the parables speak of concealment, such as the parable of the leaven and the mysteries of the kingdom of heaven that have been sealed by Jesus. The implication is that the inside community may understand the hidden secrets through proper discernment of the allegorical meaning, while the outsiders can never grasp the message. The original setting of the purpose for speaking in parables may suggest another approach—that the attitude of the heart and one's willingness to obey Jesus' teachings are the core issue.

The *Gospel of Thomas* preserves another form of this parable. The members of the Jesus Seminar have recognized the secondary Christian interpretations in all versions of the parable. In their color-coded results of voting on the authenticity of each Gospel parable, the version in the *Gospel of Thomas* was printed in pink, which means, "Jesus probably said something like this," while the version in Luke appeared in gray, one step lower, signifying, "Jesus did not say this, but the ideas contained in it are close to his own."[9] Matthew's

---

[7] Funk, Scott, and Butts, *Parables*, 59.

[8] Clement of Alexandria, *Miscellanies* 5.12 (ANF, 2:463).

[9] See Funk, Scott and Butts, *Parables*, 21 for an explanation of the voting procedures. The pink may also be interpreted as meaning, "I would include this item with reservations (or modifications) in the data base for determining who Jesus was." The gray could also mean, "I would not include this item in the primary data base, but I might make use of some of the content in determining who Jesus was."

and Mark's versions were also printed in pink.[10] The consensus of the Jesus Seminar is that the version in *Thomas* is superior to that in Luke.

GOSPEL OF THOMAS 8–9: THE SEED AND THE WORM

> Whoever has ears to hear let him hear. Jesus said, See, the sower went out, he filled his hand, he threw. Some (seeds) (μέν) fell on the road; the birds came, they gathered them. Others fell on the rock (πέτρα) and did not strike root in the earth and did not produce ears. And others fell on the thorns; they choked the seed and the worm ate them. And others fell on the good earth; and it brought forth good fruit (καρπός); it bore sixty per measure and one hundred twenty per measure.

The *Gospel of Thomas* version, however, betrays clear evidence of editorial modification. It adds the secondary details of worms eating the seed and the more precise measurement of the seed for each amount produced in the harvest. While it does not give the purpose for speaking in parables or the interpretation, one should not assume that these teachings did not appear in *Thomas*'s source. The extended version would not fit into *Thomas*'s context of collected aphorisms. Nonetheless, *Thomas* also stresses the idea of mystery and in another context emphasizes the dualism of light and darkness. In 91:34 Jesus says, "I tell My mysteries (μυστήριον) to those [who are worthy of my] mysteries (μυστήριον)." Does this saying indicate that *Thomas*'s source contained a form of the saying concerning the mystery of the kingdom of heaven (Luke 8:9–10 and parallels)? The concept of mystery in *Thomas* receives a meaning over and beyond perplexing images in a parable. These mysteries may well be related to some type of esoteric knowledge or secret religious doctrine of *Thomas*'s community. *Thomas*'s version, however, must always be studied carefully, and each individual case must be considered.

In this case, the reference in *Thomas* to a farmer who filled his hand with seed could be the faint memory of a Semitism:[11] Hebrew and Aramaic love idioms that mention the hand. An exact Semitic equivalent for this particular expression in *Thomas*, however, is not known. The overall linguistic analysis of *Thomas* reveals a secondary reworking of an earlier version of the parable. For *Thomas* it is as if the thorns are not a powerful enough motif. The image of thorns "choking" the young plants is very good Hebrew idiom. Hebrew often uses the colorful action verb "choke" (חנק).[12] The *Gospel of Thomas* is compelled to introduce the worms into the parable. Not only do the thorns

[10] Ibid., 57–59.

[11] See H. J. Thackery, *A Grammar of the Old Testament in Greek* (Cambridge: Cambridge University Press, 1909) 42: "Hebrew is fond of what may be called *physiognomical expressions*, that is to say phrases referring to parts of the human body, ear, eye, face, hand, mouth."

[12] Cf. Eliezer Ben Yehuda, *Milon Halashon Haevrit* (17 vols.; Jerusalem: General Federation of Jewish Labor in Eretz Israel, 1959), 3:1659–61.

choke the sprouts of the good seed; the worms eat it as well. Why are worms among the thorns? In good storytelling technique, the worms would introduce yet another type. This would break the flow of the story around four types, three negative and the final positive one. The picture of the seed that fell among the worms seems to be another indication for the secondary character of *Thomas'* version.

The version in Luke, moreover, must be considered the most authentic in regard to the actual words of Jesus, for that version preserves the original balance of a Hebrew parallelism. While Semitic parallelism is a subject of debate, the correspondence between the positive action of sowing the seed, the three negative results due to the condition of the soil, and the astounding positive return because of the good earth form a strong parallel structure.[13] The seed sown is a positive action that is brought into conflict with either productive or counterproductive physical elements. The correspondence between the positive action and the productive or counterproductive elements forms a parallel structure that builds like steps in a staircase. The climax is reached after the threesome of negative elements that have undermined the positive action have run their course. For a first-century farmer, nothing would be more positive than sowing the seed. Each farmer, however, is aware that proper soil preparation as well as good soil are required for a fruitful harvest. The parallelism could be simply illustrated:

A: positive—sowing the seed	B: negative—path soil
A: positive—sowing the seed	B: negative—rock soil
A: positive—sowing the seed	B: negative—thorn soil
A: positive—sowing the seed	A: REVERSAL—good soil

The basic structure of A:B, A:B, A:B, A:A builds a dynamic parallelism based on a three-part correspondence that leads to a grand reversal. The seed along the path may be trodden underfoot and exposed to birds, which can easily spot the seed from the air. The seed that fell on the rock sprouts but withers because of little moisture and no room for root expansion.[14] The seed

---

[13] On the difficulties of defining parallelisms, see W. F. Howard, "Semitisms in the New Testament," in *A Grammar of New Testament Greek* (ed. J. H. Moulton; 4 vols.; Edinburgh: T. & T. Clark, 1930) 2:418–19. For a delightful and insightful discussion of parallelisms in biblical literature see Adele Berlin, *The Dynamics of Biblical Parallelism* (Bloomingdale: Indiana University Press, 1992). Berlin notes (p. 2), "Parallelism promotes the perception of a relationship between the elements of which parallelism is composed, and this relationship is one of correspondence. The nature of correspondence varies, but in general it involves repetition or substitution of things which are equivalent on one or more linguistic levels."

[14] In this case, Luke's wording is secondary to that of Mark and Matthew. The plant withers because it has no root. Luke is one step ahead, because the lack of root makes it vulnerable to the sun; hence it dries up and withers away. Luke 8:13 mentions the root.

that fell among the thorns grows up with the thorns, which choke the surrounding plants. The Semitic background of the parable may be seen in the way it develops the action.

The Semitic structure and language of the parable are best preserved in Luke's version. The Christian interpretation in the transmission of the parable in three different versions is seen by a study of the linguistic background. At least two elements in Luke are less Semitic, the reference to lack of moisture rather than deficiency in the root structure, and the mention of believing to be saved in the interpretation of the parable (8:12). Matthew and Mark betray more decisive stylistic editing in Greek. Luke, for instance, preserves the mention of "his seed" (τὸν σπόρον αὐτοῦ, 8:5), which forms a more complete Hebrew sentence that would be considered cumbersome to a Greek editor. Semitic languages love to add possessive pronouns to nouns. Hebrew is fond of the repetition of the same root word: "a sower went out to sow his seed," יצא הזורע לזרוע את זרעו. The Greek text keeps what seems to be the original syntax of a Hebrew parable with the predicate preceding the subject, literally, "He went out, the sower, to sow his seed" (Ἐξῆλθεν ὁ σπείρων τοῦ σπεῖραι τὸν σπόρον αὐτοῦ).

While all three of the Synoptics preserve the fine Semitic idiom of the infinitive construct with the pronominal suffix, "And in his sowing" (καὶ ἐν τῷ σπείρειν αὐτόν, ובזרעו), only Luke speaks of the "birds of the heaven [RSV: air]," an idiom often used in the Hebrew Bible. The Greek words τὰ πετεινὰ τοῦ οὐρανοῦ find a Hebrew equivalent in עוף השמים, "birds of the heavens." Matthew and Mark only refer to the birds without an allusion to the common Hebrew construct phrase preserved by Luke.[15] "Birds of the heaven" does not sound quite right to the Greek listener. Luke 8:6 also preserves a better Semitic text in describing the seed that falls "on the rock" (ἐπὶ τὴν πέτραν, על הסלע, or, less likely, בסלע. The wording in Mark (πετρώδες) and Matthew (πετρώδη), "rocky ground," shows greater concern for Greek stylistic considerations.

Matthew and Mark also show the tendency to expand the shorter and more direct version of Luke. They go into detail concerning the depth of the soil and the seed's sudden growth. They use one of Mark's favorite words, "immediately," to stress the sudden growth of the seed.[16] Why would Luke omit the word if he is copying Mark? Why is the immediate growth of the seed so important for Mark? It tends to break the parallelism. In fact, the embellishment seems to introduce a distracting aside in comparison with the precision of Luke's language. Matthew and Mark even describe the sunrise.

---

[15] In the Sermon on the Mount, Matthew preserves this phrase and Luke omits it (Matt 6:26, "birds of the heaven [RSV: air]"; Luke 12:24, "ravens"). In any event, it is difficult to call this a Lukan imitation of the LXX.

[16] This is a fine example of what Lindsey called the "Markan Cross Factor." See his crucial observation, which cannot be ignored in the discussions of the synoptic problem, in *Translation*, 19–22.

Did the farmer sow the seed at night? Probably Mark and Matthew intend to portray a farmer who sowed seed that sprouted during the very same night. But the sprouts were killed the next day as the sun rose and produced a scorching heat. They elaborate details such as the rising sun and scorching heat.[17] The version of Luke is more direct and fits the parabolic style of a Hebrew parallelism. The four different types of soil are better described in the Semitic structure and parallelism in the Gospel of Luke.

The clincher for Luke is his hundredfold return bombshell, which is seriously undermined in both Matthew and Mark. The hundredfold is the climax of the story because it is unusually high. What an abundant harvest for the seed sown in good soil! Though not a total impossibility, depending on how the farmer calculates the ratio between the seed and the crop produced, it is nonetheless a dynamic shock because such an abundant harvest would be more like an unattainable dream than common experience for most of the farmers listening to the story.[18] The climax is weakened in Matthew and Mark. They make the parable more believable, "yielding thirtyfold and sixtyfold and a hundredfold" (Mark 4:8) or "some a hundredfold, some sixty, some thirty" (Matt 13:8).[19] Because of the prevailing theory of Markan priority, it is difficult to visualize the strengths of Luke's version. It is shorter. It is more direct. It has the strength of a shock technique in telling a good story. If Luke was copying Mark, why would he abbreviate? Luke's "hundredfold" clincher seems far more authentic, whether one attributes it to his special source or to some other possibility.[20] *Thomas'* version, in

[17] Why would Luke delete these colorful details if he is copying Mark? His version is much more concise.

[18] Discussions of the hundredfold return are not always in agreement. See the noteworthy nineteenth-century reference to farming procedures by Thomson, *Land and the Book*, 1:116; cf. also Jeremias, *Parables of Jesus*, 150. In Thomson's experience, the farmers would calculate loss of seed to crows and insects as they determined the amount of return. Such cultural references from the nineteenth century are of great value because many methods of farming may not have changed over the centuries. But caution must be exercised because it is impossible to know what adaptations have been made.

[19] Jeremias, *Parables of Jesus*, 150, discovers an eschatological thrust to the harvest theme: "The abnormal tripling, presented in true oriental fashion, of the harvest's yield (thirty, sixty, a hundredfold) symbolizes the eschatological overflowing of the divine fullness, surpassing all human measure (v. 8)." While harvest is sometimes associated with the Last Judgment, this is not the case in the context of the parable of the Sower. Jeremias seems to allegorize the story in a way not unlike *1 Clement*. Is it a parable of eschatology or the resurrection? More to the point, the parable focuses on discipleship and the different types of hearers. The heart makes the disciple.

[20] No matter what one's approach to the synoptic problem, source criticism must prevent servitude or outright bondage to a particular text. Luke's text is often superior to Mark or Matthew. Matthew and Mark may better preserve their common source(s) with Luke and thus prove superior at other times. The Semitic flavor of the source(s) makes linguistic analysis of major importance.

contrast, seems clearly to be the last stage in these developments, with its precise explanation of "sixty per measure and one hundred twenty per measure." *Thomas* doubles its second amount. Matthew keeps the hundredfold return at the beginning of his text, which reverses the order of Mark. This may indicate the first evangelist's acquaintance with Luke or Luke's source. Mentioning the hundredfold return first, Matthew preserves the shock element more effectively than Mark or *Thomas.* Mark starts out on the low end of the scale, which softens the blow. The bolt from the blue so characteristic of Jesus' parables is forcefully and skillfully administered in Luke's version.[21]

All things considered, Luke's version is closer to the Semitic undertext of the Gospels. Christian interpretations of the parable of the Hearers have tended to allegorize it for new purposes, such as teaching the resurrection of the dead in *1 Clement,* or to theorize a hidden mystery behind the story, as in Clement of Alexandria. The traditional approach of the church fathers invited more unfounded allegories that depart from the life setting of Jesus' teachings. The versions of Matthew and Mark betray evidence of stylistic modifications to assist a Greek audience, probably partly from a pastoral concern. They tame the parable and make it easier to understand. The stark parallelism of the positive action—sowing the seed—which corresponds to a counterproductive result in three scenarios, thereby gaining momentum for a dynamic reversal in the fourth case, seems to reflect an earlier Semitic undertext. The version of Luke best preserves this aspect of the parable. Luke's language and style give evidence for the influence of Hebrew idiomatic expressions such as "birds of the heaven." The Semitic flavor of the whole story, as well as its agricultural setting in the fields of first-century Jewish farmers, invites a serious examination of the parable's background. The historical context of Torah learning and discipleship suggests a realistic setting for the story in the cultural experiences prevailing among the Jewish people in Jesus' day.

THE JEWISH BACKGROUND OF THE PARABLE

The Hearers as Four Types of Soil

The images of farming in first-century Israel are foreign to the modern world, and sometimes the word-pictures from another culture will invite very wrong interpretations. Moreover, the conceptual world of Jewish learning is even more remote to many Western thinkers. This conceptual world

[21] Cf. b. *Pesach.* 87b: "surely a man sows a *se'ah* in order to harvest many *kor!*" (Epstein, *Babylonian Talmud,* 463). There are thirty seahs in a kor (cf. discussion of Talmudic units of volume in Steinsaltz, *Talmud,* 286–87). If the farmer reaped three kors for one seah of seed sown in the field, he harvested nearly a hundredfold return.

highly valued Torah education and discipleship, and the message behind the word-picture created by the story has deep roots in it.

The parable creates mental images of the sower, the seed, and the soils. The sower scatters his seed in a field, which has pathways, rocky places, and thorn patches, besides the good soil. Farming the land of Israel was a very special and highly esteemed calling. While the work was hard, the farmer recognized the miracle of seed time and harvest. For successful farming, everything depended upon divine favor. Ben Sira said, "Do not hate toilsome labor, or farm work, which were created by the Most High" (Sir 7:15). In fact, among the earliest Hebrew inscriptions known is the Gezer calendar, which describes the yearly cycle of seed time and harvest.[22] The Torah guides the farmer in the labor on the land and promises divine favor for obedience to God's law.[23] In fact, the learned rabbis of the talmudic period were deeply involved in agricultural labor, as were Jewish religious leaders during the time of Jesus.[24]

The major grain crops were wheat and barley. The soil was softened by the heavy first rains in October and November, which made plowing possible. (One prayer in the Talmud makes the petition, "Lord do not hear the prayers of the travellers!" Only a farmer would pray such a prayer, for he would not want the travellers' prayers for sunshine to stop the much needed rains.) Barley could be planted later in the season. The winter grains could be sown from October through December.[25] The farmer would walk through the fields scattering his seed. Sometimes the fields were planted at the same time they were being plowed. In all events, the parable's description of the scattering of the seed by hand and of the physical limitations of paths, stones, and thorns composes a visual image familiar to farmers in the land of Israel and well known to the common folk.

The farmer's greatest concern is the condition of the soil. The soil's fertility determines how productive each seed will be. In the parable, the sower is doing his job well and the seed is of high quality, capable of an excellent return. But what captures the attention of the farmer—and is the central focus of the story—is the condition of the soil. Farmers in every culture are very concerned about their soil. They till it, water it, fertilize it, and do all in their power to increase its potential for productivity. Soil preparation is essential for a bountiful harvest. In the parable of the Hearers four different soil types are described, building a strong foundation for the message of Jesus in the application of the parable. Teaching analogies that use four types appear in Jewish sources that parallel the teachings of Jesus. Hence

---

[22] See Ruth Hestrin and Yael Israeli, eds., *Inscriptions Reveal: Documents from the Time of the Bible, the Mishna, and the Talmud* (Jerusalem: Israel Museum, 1972) 13, 18.

[23] See, e.g., Deut 22:9–11; 28:8–14.

[24] See, e.g., the descriptions in t. *Kil.* 1:15–16 (*Tosefta*, ed. Lieberman, 205f., *Tosefta Kifshutah*, p. 604).

[25] See t. *Taan.* 1:7 (*Tosefta*, ed. Lieberman, 325).

a large part of the problem for modern interpreters is not only cultural but religious. While farmers everywhere recognize the value of fertile soil, not everyone is acquainted with the Jewish method of teaching that speaks about four types of disciples.

Through Jewish Eyes

Viewing the story through first-century Jewish eyes clears up many difficulties. When the parable is placed in the context of Jewish learning, the emphasis of the story is seen as the good soil. It corresponds to the good heart (Luke 8:15) in the interpretation of the parable, and it communicates the deeper message of Jesus concerning discipleship in the kingdom.[26] Here the story parable as characteristic of parallel Jewish sources will be explored for a proper understanding of the parable in its cultural setting.

Why did Jesus tell parables? He wanted the people to understand his message and follow his teaching as disciples. First, the parables illustrate his teaching. Second, they challenge his listeners to make a decision. Although the parable of the Hearers is frequently viewed as containing secret truths, it really calls upon people to put Jesus' dynamic teaching into practice. The message of Jesus is for living. It is simple but profound. Jesus was a practical teacher. He wanted his followers to understand his message and to experience the fullness of a life dedicated to the principles of God's reign. The parable must be viewed as parallel to an emphasis in the rich religious life of first-century Judaism: one must hear *and obey* the words of Torah; hearing alone is not enough.

Buy Life—Study Torah!

Torah learning was highly valued in Jewish faith and practice. Rabbi Alexandri taught that anyone who desires to find life should acquire Torah. The study of Torah and the commitment to follow its teachings by corresponding actions will give life to everyone who becomes a disciple. When the importance of discipleship in the kingdom is fully appreciated, the Jewish worldview that study of Torah will give life becomes closely related to the parables of Jesus. While at times in some Christian traditions the law has been viewed very negatively, the colorful story of a distinguished rabbi shouting in the marketplace illustrates the positive way that Torah learning is treasured in Judaism.

> Once Rabbi Alexandri was shouting out, "Who wants life, who wants life?" All the people came and gathered around him saying: "Give us life!" He then

[26] While the interpretation of the parable has been edited by the evangelists, it is like so many interpretations given to rabbinic parables that it must be viewed as an authentic part of Jesus' original teachings. Jesus would have told the interpretation to make the point even clearer. The call for decision, namely, to receive the word of his teaching and live by it, would have been understood without the deeper explanation.

> quoted to them, "Who is the person who desires life and covets many days that he may enjoy good therein? Keep your tongue from evil, and your lips from speaking deceit. Depart from evil and do good, seek peace and pursue it" (Psalm 34:13–15). . . . The Bible teaches "Depart from evil and do good!" There is none good except Torah, as it is written, "For I have given you a good doctrine, my Torah, do not forsake it" (Proverbs 4:2).[27]

The story invites the listener to imagine a learned rabbi behaving like a loud-mouthed merchant in the marketplace. A merchant creates a scene by calling out his special bargains to advertise his business. But the learned rabbi draws a crowd to encourage the people to live their lives dedicated to the spiritual values taught in Torah learning.

This story about R. Alexandri, the popular haggadic teacher from Israel in the third century, is somewhat similar to an action associated with the outstanding figure of Hillel the Elder, an older contemporary of Jesus. The life of the Jewish community as portrayed in these vivid anecdotes revolves around Torah study as a way of life. In such an environment, the parable of the Hearers takes on refreshing significance as a description of four kinds of disciples who hear the teaching of the sacred word. Somewhat like Rabbi Alexandri, Hillel would stand in the gate of Jerusalem and encourage the people to put less emphasis on gainful employment and to study Torah.

> A story is told about Hillel the Elder, how he used to stand at the gate of Jerusalem as people were going to work. He asked them: "For how much are you working today?" This one said to him: "For a denarius." Another one replied: "For two denarii." He asked them, "What do you do with this money?" They answered, "We will provide for the necessities of life." He said to them, "Why do you not come with me and gain knowledge of Torah so that you may gain life in this world and life in the world to come." In this way Hillel used to act during all his life until he brought them under the wings of heaven.[28]

The center of Jewish life in many circles was Torah learning and making disciples. Hillel encouraged greater participation in Torah scholarship by meeting people as they were going to work. He is famous for his saying "The more Torah the more life."[29]

The original context of the parable of the Hearers would naturally be the teaching of Torah. Perhaps the words of Isa 55:11 were not far from the minds of the people: "so shall my word be that goes forth from my mouth; it shall not return to me empty, but it shall accomplish that which I purpose." In v. 10 the prophet makes a comparison between the blessings of rain for seed time and harvest and the inspired word of God spoken by his prophets. The

[27] b. *Abod. Zar.* 19b.

[28] *Abot R. Nat.*, version B, ch. 26 (trans. Saldarini, *Rabbi Nathan*, 156). See also Nahum Glatzer, *Hillel the Elder: The Emergence of Classical Judaism* (New York: B'nai B'rith Hillel Foundations, 1956) 50–51.

[29] *Abot* 2:8.

water from rain and snow causes the seed to grow. In the same way that God gives his word to the people for their benefit, so also he gives seed to the sower and the rain that causes it to grow. Not surprisingly, in Jewish thought Isa 55 was viewed as describing the study of Torah. The word of God will not return to him void. It will accomplish his purpose. When disciples put it into practice, it gives life.

THE PURPOSE OF PARABLES: ISAIAH AND JESUS

One must understand the purpose of the parables. They illustrate. They teach. They drive home a point. They never obscure the message of Jesus. Why then does Jesus cite Isa 6:9–10, which seems at first to suggest that both Jesus and Isaiah wanted their listeners to stumble? In the Gospel, Jesus compares the parables to the words of Isaiah, "Go, and say to this people: 'Hear and hear, but do not understand; see and see, but do not perceive.' Make the heart of this people fat, and their ears heavy, and shut their eyes; lest they see with their eyes, and hear with their ears, and understand with their hearts, and turn and be healed." Was Isaiah's mission designed to prevent the people from being healed? Like Jesus, Isaiah wanted the people to be healed. He did not want one person to stumble through a lack of understanding. Like Isaiah, Jesus was a prophet whose message was not accepted by everyone who heard it. In the same way that Isaiah wanted his listeners to accept his prophetic message, Jesus wanted the multitudes to put his message into practice. But not everyone was willing to listen and obey. The parables made the message of Jesus clear. Isaiah explained his prophetic word so much that the people's ears became heavy. They heard Isaiah and understood him but they did not all want to change their ways. They comprehended the message, but they were not willing to accept by a change in their behavior what was taught. Even in English, sometimes, when a person says, "He did not understand me," he or she really means, "He did not agree with what I had to say." Jesus wanted his hearers to become genuine disciples by putting his message into practice.

Lindsey describes these words of Isaiah as prophetic irony. He emphasizes the deep desire in the prophetic ministry of Jesus to reach out to hurting people. They needed to change their ways and experience God's goodness. Lindsey observes, "They knew Isaiah had spoken to his generation in supreme irony, much as a mother might to a rebellious child. Her hope—and the hope of Isaiah under God—is to shock the rebel into a right perception of his erroneous ways."[30] The primary concern is for the healing and well-being of the people. The prophet longs for the people to return to the Lord with a full heart. In the first century, some of the people of the land (*am*

[30] See the comments of Lindsey as well as Flusser in "A Panel Discussion of the Parable," esp. 149.

haaretz in Hebrew), who were ignorant and unlearned in the way of life taught in Torah, would listen to the message but would not respond with an open heart. They rejected God's rule in their lives. Jesus' teaching concerning discipleship in the kingdom of heaven challenged them to receive the word with a good heart. Both Jesus and Isaiah desired the best for God's people. As prophets, they longed for healing and restoration for all.

In short, the parables were like the prophecies of Isaiah. While parables were not hard for the original audience to understand, they did demand a decision. The challenge to decide was the issue. The meaning of the saying of Jesus is similar to that of the words of Isaiah. Isaiah wanted the people to repent. Jesus wanted the people to receive his message, follow him, and serve God with all their hearts. They needed to experience the reign of God in their personal lives. But not everyone was ready to hear what Isaiah had to say. Though all the men of Nineveh repented at the preaching of Jonah, not everyone received the message of Jesus.

The text of Isaiah speaks about how the people hear but do not understand. A closer look at the wording of Isaiah shows that the people did understand but they did not want to obey. They listened to the words and comprehended the message, but they were not willing to repent. Jesus wanted everyone to accept his message concerning God's reign. The people heard and understood Jesus, but not all were willing to accept his message concerning God's kingship. Many followed Jesus. He raised up many disciples from beyond the inner circle, as one sees clearly from the book of Acts and the history of his early band of followers. Nonetheless, not all received the word with a good heart.

The Soil and the Harvest

The parable of the Hearers is a parable of harvest. Calling it the parable of the Sower focuses attention on the preacher. If it is named the parable of the Seed, attention is shifted to the word preached. But the parable is concerned with the response of the people. It is about the productivity of the soil types. The physical conditions of the soil, such as the impenetrable path, the hard rock, and the thorns that choke the crop, may ruin the harvest. The reality behind the word-pictures in the story deals with the importance of discipleship, in the sense that one who receives the word with a good heart and puts it into practice will bear much fruit in the kingdom. If one devotes oneself to the study of Torah, one will receive life in this world and the world to come. The disciple with a good heart will be blessed with divine favor of inestimable value. The parable of the Sower is really concerned with the response of the individual to the message of Jesus. Hence, as has been seen, a better title would be the parable of the Hearers. As Jesus explained and applied the meaning of Torah in everyday living, each disciple is encouraged to practice the teachings concerning God's reign in his or her individual life.

The parable of the Hearers focuses upon the miracle of seed time and harvest. The fact is that a seed planted always grows. When seeds grow, they bring forth fruit. Some will produce a hundredfold. All that a person is asked to do is to receive the teachings of Jesus with a good heart. The miracle occurs as they become disciples and the seed takes root in their lives. Nonetheless, the miracle of growth is beyond one's human comprehension. A seed planted grows. When the conditions are right, the planting of the seed will bring forth an abundant harvest that far exceeds human finite understanding. The listeners' attention is drawn to the four types of soil described in the story.

The Four Types in Jewish Thought

In parallel to the teachings of Jesus, four types of disciples are often mentioned in early Jewish teachings. They form quadripartite parallelisms. Flusser was the first to call my attention to the relationship between these Jewish sayings and the parable of the Sower.[31] The four types weigh against each other like the different sides of a balance scale. They are frequently compared and contrasted with one another. For example, compare the parable with the following humorous saying from the Jewish literature.[32]

Four characteristics of a disciple:
1. Quick to learn and quick to lose,
   his gain is canceled by his loss.
2. Slow to learn and slow to lose,
   his loss is canceled by his gain.
3. Quick to learn and slow to lose,
   this is a good portion.
4. Slow to learn and quick to lose,
   this is an evil portion.

Each of the four types of disciple is weighed in the balance in order to determine his positive qualities compared with less desirable characteristics. The rich humor of the rabbis emerges in the colorful comparisons. The strong characteristics are weighed against the weaker qualities in four parts. In the world of Jewish learning and Torah scholarship, each person can evaluate his or her strengths and weaknesses. What will happen when one is weighed in the balance? Will one be considered quick to learn but quick to forget? Then one's gain is canceled by the loss. The best characteristic of a

---

[31] The most valuable discussion of this parable is found in Flusser, *Gleichnisse*, 235–63. Flusser has demonstrated the direct connection between the blessing of the disciples (Luke 10:21–24; Matt 11:25–27) and the reason for speaking in parables (Matt 13:11–16; Luke 8:10). The theory of Markan priority has greatly influenced the interpretation of the parable of the Sower. In modern NT scholarship, Mark's version has frequently been overemphasized to the neglect of Luke's text (see Lindsey, *Translation*).

[32] *Abot* 5:15. A similar saying concerning four types of people who go to study Torah is found in *Abot* 5:17. There the importance of going to the house of study is balanced against the virtue of putting Torah study into practice. The highest value is placed on the one who both goes to study and practices what he learns. See Flusser's remarks in "A Panel Discussion of the Parable," esp. 147.

disciple is one who is quick to learn and slow to forget! The form and structure of the rabbinic saying is very similar to the four types of soil in the parable of the Sower.

The rabbis also use rich humor in comparing students of Torah to four common utensils: "There are four qualities among those who sit at the feet of the sages: they are like a sponge, a funnel, a strainer, or a sieve." Is it more complimentary to be compared to a sponge or a sieve? "A sponge soaks up everything; a funnel takes it in at one end and lets it out at the other; a strainer lets the wine pass through but retains the lees; a sieve lets out the bran and retains the fine flour" (*Abot* 5:18). The worst characteristic is the disciple who lets the teaching go in one ear and out the other. He is like a funnel. The most desirable type of disciple is like a sieve who retains only the best of the teaching. The famous Rabbi Meir compared study to eating sweet dates. You eat the fruit of the date and spit out the large pit. One must see the strengths and weaknesses of every position and seek to break fresh ground in the analysis of an old problem of Bible wisdom.

Rabban Gamaliel the Elder compared the disciples in the academy to four different types of fish: the unclean fish, the clean fish, the Jordan River fish, and the Mediterranean Sea fish. The best type comes from the Mediterranean Sea and is like a disciple who becomes proficient in all the disciplines of Torah learning and can also enter into critical and dialectical discussion. Others master the subject but are unable to interact with real-life problems and issues. Somewhat like Shammai, Gamaliel viewed the potential scholars from well-established homes of prominent families as more likely to attain distinction in Torah learning than disadvantaged students without the benefits of adequate finances. Hillel, as can be seen from the story about his life cited above, did not accept these class distinctions. Hillel went to the gates of Jerusalem and tried to enlist potential Torah scholars from among all, including the poor day laborers. Hillel taught, "One ought to teach every man, for there were many sinners in Israel who were drawn to the study of Torah, and from them descended righteous pious, and worthy folk."[33] Here, in contrast to Hillel, Gamaliel portrays the better students as coming from families of higher class and wealth.

> "On the subject of disciples Rabban Gamaliel the Elder spoke of FOUR kinds: An unclean fish, a clean fish, a fish from the Jordan, a fish from the Great Sea.
>
> An unclean fish: who is that? A poor youth who studies Scripture and Mishnah, Halakha and Agada, and is without understanding.
>
> A clean fish: who is that? That's a rich youth who studies Scripture and Mishnah, Halakah and Agada, and has understanding.

[33] See *Abot R. Nat.*, version A, ch. 3 (trans. Goldin, *Rabbi Nathan*, 26). Shammai, in contrast, wanted only talented students from the best families who were somewhat wealthy.

A fish from the Jordan: who is that? That's a scholar who studies Scripture and Mishnah, Halakha and Agada, and is without talent for using it in argument.

A fish from the Great Sea: who is that? That's a scholar who studies Scripture and Mishnah, Midrash, Halakha, and Agada and has the talent for using it for argument."[34]

In all events, the correspondence that Gamaliel draws between the four types of fish and the disciples of the wise who study Torah in the academy is based on the motif of fours, which also appears in the parable of the Hearers. Jesus would be closer to the school of Hillel on issues of wealth and poverty. In fact, for Jesus wealth may even be a hindrance to devoting oneself to the higher principles of the kingdom of heaven. The structure of four as a teaching device that captures the listeners' attention and aids in retaining the message is very much a part of the teaching of both Gamaliel and Jesus. The dry wit and cynical humor of Gamaliel's illustration effectively communicated the point of his argument.

Philo of Alexandria also used the motif of four types of disciples. The famous Jewish thinker used the figures of the father for the perfect right reason and of the mother for the lower learning of the schools that forms the basis of all education.

These parents have four classes of children. The first is obedient to both; the second is the direct opposite, and gives heed to neither, while each of the other two lacks its half. One of them is heartily devoted to the father and gives ear to him, but disregards the mother and her injunctions. The other, on the contrary, appears devoted to the mother, and serves her in every way, but pays no heed to the words of the father. Of these four the first will carry off the palm of victory over all comers, while the second its opposite will receive defeat accompanied by destruction. Each of the others will claim a prize, one the second, the other the third; the second belongs to the class which obeys the father, the third to the class which obeys the mother.[35]

Philo uses the family to illustrate four different types of students. The best type absorbs wisdom from both parents, the practical reason from the father and the foundational knowledge from the mother. The child who is obedient to both will "carry off the palm of victory over all comers." Philo praised

---

[34] *Abot R.Nat.*, version A, ch. 40 (trans. Goldin, *Rabbi Nathan,* 166). See Finkelstein, *Akiba,* 114, and the views of the school of Shammai concerning the poor in *Abot R. Nat.*, version A, ch. 3. Shammai opposed admitting the poor into the academy of learning. In regard to the comparison of disciples to the four fish, Finkelstein notes, "The coarseness of the similes betrays the prejudice of the patrician." Is this Gamaliel II or Gamaiel I? Finkelstein discusses the intensity of the class struggle. In the end, even R. Akiva, a common shepherd with a background of poverty, achieves prominence in Jewish religious life as one of the outstanding leaders.

[35] Philo, *Sobr.* 35 (Colson and Whitaker, LCL). I am grateful to Flusser for pointing out this important parallel to me.

practical reason and foundational education. Like the parable of Jesus, which speaks about four different types of soil, Philo illustrates his point using four classes of children.

The Jewish setting of the parable should be viewed as an approach to learning Torah and putting it into practice. A rabbinic parallel describes the difficulty of acquiring Torah learning and the danger of losing the benefit of one's study.

> The words of Torah are difficult to acquire as vessels of pure gold and they are easily lost and broken like vessels of fragile glass. What will happen if vessels of gold or glass are broken? Who will be able to restore them as they were? So it is also with a disciple of the sages who forgets his learning. How will he be able to return and study it again as before?[36]

The study of Torah is a sacred task that requires concentrated effort. In the same way that thorns can choke the life out of young plants that sprout from good seed, a fragile vessel of glass is easily broken. Torah learning demands steadfast devotion.

The ever popular allegorical method that seeks to discover secret symbolic meanings in the parables actually only conceals the original purpose of Jesus. The parable of the Sower becomes clouded in mystery. People cannot hear its message because the interpreter is forcing his own meaning on each detail of the parable, like *1 Clement*, which imposed a teaching about the future resurrection on the parable. One must listen to Jesus as he tells the parable and see the story in light of rabbinic literature and the rich heritage of the first-century Jewish people. The focus therefore is on Torah learning and discipleship.

THE SECRETS OF GOD

Within this world of learning and discovery, the words of Jesus concerning a mystery that is given to his disciples makes perfect sense. The idea is not that his teachings have secret messages that can be decoded only by his inner circle of disciples. Rather, his followers are devoted to the practice of Jesus' teaching. They hear the word and do it. They can understand the mystery because of their decision to obey. But for the others the message is heard only in simple parables, so easy to understand but so difficult to put into practice. They hear but do not understand. In reality, they understand the parables perfectly well but are unwilling to decide to practice the teaching. For the disciples, the mysteries of God are plain because they are practicing what they have learned.

In Luke 8:10 Jesus affirms his disciples by saying, "To you it has been given to know the secrets of [the kingdom of] God; but for others they are in

[36] j. *Chag.* 77b.

parables." Those who obey God grasp the divine mysteries while those who refuse to follow the teachings of Torah hear the message in easy-to-understand parabolic stories. They see but do not see, and hear but do not understand, in the sense that no one sees and understands unless without obeying fully the demands of the Torah. In fact, in characteristic genius and perceptive intuition, Flusser suggested that the words τῆς βασιλείας (of the kingdom) in Luke 8:10 were added later by a scribe who was well acquainted with the Gospel references to the kingdom of God. The words τῆς βασιλείας are missing from the manuscripts W, 579, 716, *l*253, *l*1761, as well as Lvt, (ff2), PET-C, and Eusebius.[37] While these are not major external witnesses for the text of the NT, when combined with the internal evidence, the case for accepting the more difficult reading, "To you has been given to know the mysteries [RSV: secrets] of God," merits serious consideration. No scribe would purposely delete "the kingdom" from this crucial text, but the tendency to add the "the kingdom" in an effort to harmonize the saying with other teachings of Jesus concerning the kingdom of heaven might well have proved irresistible for a pious scribe. Once the addition was made, it would achieve scribal preference because of the pervasive use of the term "kingdom of God" in the Gospels.

The difference in meaning is monumental.[38] The parables are all about God. First and foremost, they teach the way of the Lord as a path of obedient surrender to the divine will. They are designed to teach the people about God and God's nature. The theme of the kingdom of God is one aspect of the divine character. But the parables reach beyond every other religious idea or sacred doctrine. They portray God in dynamic, full-of-life pictures that show the natural affinity between the supernatural realm and the physical world of daily experience. The parables are full of God and God's mysterious ways. The seed nurtured in the good soil produces a hundredfold harvest. It is among the mysteries of God that are grasped by the disciples.[39] The one who obeys understands the mysteries of God.

---

[37] Cf. the text of *The New Testament in Greek: The Gospel according to St. Luke,* ed. American and British Committees of the International Greek New Testament Project (2 vols.; Oxford: Clarendon, 1984–87) 167.

[38] Admittedly, for many the distinction between "mysteries of the kingdom of God" and "mysteries of God" will seem insignificant. But Jesus' parables focused on the character of God and his ways among people. While similar to the idea of the kingdom, the shorter text is much more dynamic. In that regard it is much more like the language of the Dead Sea Scrolls. The mystery of God is understood in the action of doing. One comprehends the divine through godliness and obedience to Jesus' call.

[39] Flusser has suggested that the blessing for the disciples from Matt 11:25–27 and Luke 10:21–24 belongs here, after the saying about the mysteries of God. This is a powerful argument in light of his linguistic analysis of the blessings. See Flusser, *Gleichnisse*, 265–81; and Brad H. Young and David Flusser, "Messianic Blessings in Jewish and Christian Texts," in David Flusser, *Judaism and the Origins of Christianity* (Jerusalem: Magnes, 1989) 280–300.

The shorter text of Luke, τὰ μυστήρια τοῦ θεοῦ, "the mysteries of God," is a dynamic equivalent for the Hebrew idiom from the Dead Sea Scrolls, רזי אל or רזי אלוהים.[40] The language of the scrolls has cast light on the study of the words of Jesus. Some crucial idioms, such as "poor in spirit," have been paralleled in the language of the scrolls.[41] "Poor in spirit" became a technical term for the members of the Dead Sea sect, who were devoted disciples of the Scriptures and the religious teachings of their community. Now, the expression "mysteries of God" finds a dynamic equivalent in the Gospel tradition. Discipleship was strictly practiced in the Dead Sea community. The members of the community gave up everything to live the life of discipleship. They spoke about dedication to God and used words similar to the teachings of Jesus.[42] Jesus told his disciples, "To you it has been given to know the mysteries of God" (Luke 8:10); in the Dead Sea sect it was taught, "And now my children, hearken unto me and I will reveal for your eyes to see and to understand the works of God."[43]

This beautiful Hebrew text from Jewish life during the Second Temple period refers to "my children," which is like the disciples of Jesus. Its mention of "the works of God" is near to the concept of "the mysteries of God" in the saying of Jesus, as well as in other scrolls. Also, the controlling idea of the scroll views the followers of the Dead Sea sect's teaching as having experienced an inward revealing. Their eyes have been opened, which enables them to see and to understand. The opening of their eyes echoes the words of Jesus, "To you it has been given to know the mysteries of God." The members of the community are living the life of disciples. This text from the Dead Sea Scrolls both affirms the Hebrew language background for the teachings of Jesus and illustrates the concept of discipleship to Torah learning. In the Gospel parable, Jesus' disciples are compared to the good soil because they receive the word and act upon it in obedience.

THE INTERPRETATION OF THE SOWER

In the interpretation of the parable of the Sower, Jesus explains to the disciples the meaning of each of the four types of soil that receive the seed. The fertility of four soil types with regard to their outward circumstances is compared to the difference of levels of receptivity among the people.

The allegorical approach tends to distort the original message of Jesus. The parables are word-pictures. A strong reality stands behind the world pictured in the parables, but the picture is not identical with the reality. When one begins to ascribe specialized meaning to the word-picture, the reality

[40] Cf., e.g., 1QpHab 7:8; 1QM 3:9; 1QS 3:23; 4Q511 2 2:6.

[41] See esp. Flusser, *Origins*, 102–25.

[42] Cf. Flusser, *Gleichnisse*, 235–63.

[43] CD 2:14. As noted above, most translations of Luke 8:10 read, "secrets of the kingdom of God" instead of "secrets of God."

behind the images is forgotten. The reality is the heart of the matter. While a parable has one message, making a point and calling for a decision, it may have several points of contact between the word-picture and the reality it portrays. The seed (picture) is the word of God (reality).[44] The fertile soil that produced a harvest with a hundredfold return is compared to the disciple with a good heart. The one message is clear: be like the disciple who receives the word of Jesus' teaching with a good heart. The word sown will produce an abundant return. The word-picture communicates the force of Jesus' teaching in the form of a graphic illustration.

Although several points of contact between the word-picture of a parable and the reality it illustrates may emerge from the plot of the story, as is seen in the interpretation of the Sower, parables themselves should never be viewed as allegories. Actually parables should be placed in a separate and distinct category. The allegorical approach to the parables pursues the intuitive effort to solve the cryptogram by arbitrarily ascribing meaning to the word-picture. Parables, however, must be studied to hear the message of the storyteller in the context of the situation. Only meaning ascribed by the storyteller may be accepted as showing a correspondence between the picture (mashal) and the reality *(nimshal)*. In fact, allegory often misrepresents the original intention of Jesus. If an interpretation is called for, Jesus the master teller of parables gives additional clarity to his example. Such is the case with the parable of the Sower. He describes its application with greater force in the parable's interpretation.[45] While the interpretation does contain phrases from Luke or the pre-Lukan redactor's reworking of the text (e.g., ἵνα μὴ πιστεύσαντες σωθῶσιν, "that they may not believe and be saved," in Luke 8:12), the meaning of the reality behind the word-picture can be discovered only by listening to the parable teacher.

The parables of Jesus, like their counterparts in rabbinic literature, are unique. Some teaching forms, such as fables or allegories, are somewhat similar to Gospel and rabbinic parables, but the classic form of story parables, such as those in the Gospels and rabbinic literature, is a distinct type of teaching technique that has no parallel. They do not appear in the Dead Sea Scrolls, the Apocrypha, or the Pseudepigrapha. They do appear frequently in talmudic texts. In rabbinic literature, they are always told in Hebrew and not Aramaic.[46]

[44] Jeremias, *Parables of Jesus*, 77–79, argues at length that the interpretation appended to this parable "must be ascribed to the primitive Church." None of Jeremias's arguments is strong, especially not his underlying presupposition concerning eschatology (pp. 149–50). On the linguistic issues, compare the fine Hebrew translation in Lindsey, *Translation*, 99. Flusser has often argued for the originality of the interpretation (in many private conversations in which he championed the Semitic flavor of the text in Luke's version).

[45] Rabbinic parables often have interpretations. See McArthur and Johnston, *Parables*, 139–43.

[46] See my treatment of this matter in Young, *Jewish Parables*, 40ff.

The parables are not allegory. They do portray a reality in word-pictures. They demonstrate the natural affinity between the physical realm and the higher ethical and spiritual meaning in life. Like the parable of the Sower with its interpretation, many rabbinic parables also give explanation and application. They make the implicit points of comparison between the picture and the reality explicit. Two rules should always be followed to avoid the wrong allegorical approach. First, the parable teller is the only one who imposes meaning on the elements of his illustration. He is the one who communicates a message in parable form. Listen to him. The significance for each point of comparison between the picture and the reality must be made clear by the storyteller himself or herself. Second, the immediate context may grant insight into the meaning of the word-picture. The storyteller is giving an illustration to communicate his or her message. How does the parable fit into the context of his or her teaching? In Gospel parables, Jesus often calls upon the individual to make a decision. Frequently he is concerned about discipleship in the kingdom. The close affinity between the Gospel parables and their rabbinic counterparts should caution against a quick decision to delete an application of Jesus' parabolic teachings such as the interpretation that follows the parable of the Sower.

Other evidence must be examined and carefully considered. From a linguistic standpoint, Mark's text is much longer than Matthew's or Luke's. Both Mark and Matthew betray evidence of embellishment. Luke's version, in contrast, is much closer to a Semitic original. The major focus is on the seed as the word of God and the productive soil as the good heart. In fact, Luke does not even mention the sower at all. Mark has elaborated much about the sower who sows the word like a Christian preacher. He introduces the interpretation of the parable with an artificial conversation between Jesus and his disciples. These fine and colorful details are absent in Luke and seem to have been added by Mark. One should ask why Luke would have omitted these details. Mark 4:15 and 17, as well as the Matthean parallels, introduce the word "immediately," which is non-Semitic and seems to be a Markan aggrandizement. These two evangelists also mention classic Christian terms such as "tribulation" and "persecution," which seem to reflect concerns of the primitive church. Luke's text seems much closer to the actual words of Jesus on this score. The reworking of Matthew and Mark, moreover, fails to mention the "good heart" that appears in Luke's version. As will be seen, the "good heart" is a direct parallel to the teachings of Johanan ben Zachai, which was filled with meaning in the Jewish environment of early Christianity. Mark's version of the interpretation of the parable of the Sower is the most lengthy and elaborate. His innovations are more appropriate to a Greek style. He seems to have influenced Matthew, whose wording is much closer to Mark than to Luke.

In any case, the language of Luke is more forceful and closer to a Semitic background, although evidence of editing in Greek is also seen. It may aid in linguistic analysis to recast these powerful words into a possible Hebrew setting. Many of the arguments for the authenticity of the interpretation of the Sower based on Hebrew would also be true for Aramaic. In all events, the text has a striking Semitic flavor when it is seen through Hebrew eyes and is reconstructed into a hypothetical source text. What appears to be Greek editing will be enclosed in square brackets and translated accordingly in Hebrew.

A Hebrew Interpretation of the Hearers
Luke 8:11–15

Ἔστιν δὲ αὕτη ἡ παραβολή· Ὁ σπόρος ἐστὶν ὁ λόγοω τοῦ θεοῦ.

זה המשל: הזרע הוא דבר אלוהים

οἱ δὲ παρὰ τὴν ὁδόν εἰσιν οἱ ἀκούσαντες, εἶτα ἔρχεται ὁ διάβολος καὶ αἴρει [τὸν λόγον] ἀπὸ τῆς καρδίας αὐτῶν, [ἵνα μὴ πιστεύσαντες σωθῶσιν.]

אלה שבדרך המה השומעים ואז בא השטן ונוטל מלביהם

οἱ δὲ ἐπὶ τῆς πέτρας οἳ ὅταν ἀκούσωσιν ματὰ χαρᾶς δέχονται [τὸν λόγον], καὶ οὗτοι ῥίζαν οὐκ ἔχουσιν, [οἳ πρὸς καιρὸν πιστεύουσιν καὶ ἐν καιρῷ πειρασμοῦ ἀφίστανται.]

אלה שבסלע המה השומעים ומשמחה מקבלים אף אין לאלה [להם] שורש

[τὸ] δὲ εἰς τὰς ἀκάνθας [πεσόν], οὗτοί εἰσιν οἱ ἀκούσαντες, καὶ ὑπὸ μεριμνῶν καὶ πλούτου [καὶ ἡδονῶν τοῦ βίου] πορευόμενοι συμπνίγονται καὶ οὐ τελεσφοροῦσιν.

אלה שבקוצים המה השומעים ומדאגות ועושר הולכים ונתנחקים ולא יעשו פרי

[τὸ] δε ἐν τῇ καλῇ γῇ, οὗτοί εἰσιν οἵτινες ἐν καρδίᾳ καλῇ καὶ ἀγαθῇ ἀκούσαντες [τὸν λόγον] κατέχουσιν καὶ καρποφοροῦσιν [ἐν ὑπομονῇ].

אלה שבאדמה הטובה המה השומעים בלב טוב ומקבלים ונושאים פרי

English Translation of Hebrew Text

This is the parable: The seed is the word of God.

Those [which fell] on the path are those who hear [the word] and then Satan comes and takes [it] from their hearts.

Those [which fell] upon the stone are those who hear [the word] and receive [it] with joy but have no root.

Those [which fell] among the thorns are those who hear [the word] but because of concerns and riches, go and are choked and do not bear fruit.

Those [which fell] in the good soil are those who hear with a good heart, receiving and bearing fruit.

The linguistic analysis of Luke's Greek text highlights a possible Semitic source underlying his carefully crafted story and reveals a strong tradition that sounds much like Jesus of the Gospels.[47] The interpretation of the parable of the Hearers is rooted in the best sources available for reconstructing the life and teachings of Jesus.

Of major significance for the interpretation of the parable is the correspondence drawn between the good soil and the good heart in Luke 8:15, τὸ δὲ ἐν τῇ καλῇ γῇ, οὗτοί εἰσιν οἵτινες ἐν καρδίᾳ καλῇ καὶ ἀγαθῇ ἀκούσαντες τὸν λόγον κατέχουσιν καὶ καρποφοροῦσιν ἐν ὑπομονῇ, "And as for that in the good soil, they are those who, hearing the word, hold it fast in an honest and good heart, and bring forth fruit with patience." The phrase "honest and good heart" has an important variant reading in Codex Beza Cantabrigiensis. The words καλῇ καὶ, "honest and," are omitted.[48] It must be observed that the preceding description of the soil as "good" uses the same word, καλῇ, and it was natural for scribes to make an addition that sought to describe the meaning of the good heart more precisely. The theme of the good heart probably was understood more readily among Jewish readers but needed further qualification and interpretation for others. The phrase in Hebrew, לב טוב, "good heart," has parallels in Jewish thought, especially in the teachings of Johanan ben Zachai.[49]

Luke's text draws upon Hebrew thought, Semitic parallelism, and poetic balance while it makes the basic message of the parable clearer. While most of the listeners would have readily grasped the major focus of the parable and its call for decision, the interpretation stressed the main point. Receive the word with a good heart. Hear the teachings of Torah and obey them with the proper attitude. In many ways, the wording of the interpretation recalls Isa 55:10–11, "giving seed to the sower . . . so shall my word be that goes forth from my mouth; it shall not return to me empty." The word of God is received into good soil and produces a hundredfold harvest.

THE GOOD SOIL

In Luke's interpretation of the parable of the Hearers, the good soil is related to the motif of the good heart (Luke 8:15). The term "good heart" was filled with meaning in circles of Jewish learning during the period. In at least one major episode in Jewish literature, the famous teacher Johanan ben Zachai asked his disciples a question, "Go and see which is the good way to which a person should cleave?" As in the Gospels, where Jesus teaches his

[47] I am grateful for outstanding colleagues who have aided greatly in this reconstruction. Lindsey and Flusser have offered insightful suggestions. The strengths of such a reconstruction should be attributed to their thoughts, and the weaknesses to my own deficiency. In any case, I believe that the beautiful Hebrew behind Luke's fine text precludes the prevalent approach that views the interpretation as an allegory of the primitive church.

[48] See *New Testament in Greek: Luke*, 169.

[49] See the discussion below.

disciples through question-and-answer sessions, one encounters lively discussion and free exchange between the master teacher, Johanan ben Zachai, and his followers. The story helps refine the meaning of the good heart.

The Good Heart

> He [Johanan ben Zachai] used to say to them: Go and see which is the good way to which a person should cleave? R. Eliezer [b. Horkenos] said, A good eye. R. Joshua [ben Hananiah] said, A good associate. R. Jose [the Priest] said, A good neighbor. R. Simeon [b. Nathanel] said, One who sees the event. R. Eleazar b. Arach said, A good heart. He said to them I approve of Eleazar ben Arach more than your words, for in his words are included yours.[50]

According to Johanan ben Zachai, a person who has a good heart will be generous and kind. That one has a good eye and is a good companion. A person with a good heart also is helpful, is perceptive, and embodies all the noble characteristics so desirable in Torah scholarship. The ideal disciple has a good heart. According to Jesus, the person with a good heart will allow the miracle of growth to take place. He or she receives the word, which is like a seed planted in fertile soil. Such a disciple allows the seed to grow. He or she hears the message with keen receptivity and obeys the teaching by putting it into practice. The disciple with a good heart seeks first the kingdom of God and his righteousness. This is the path for a full and meaningful life.

THE PARABLES IN THEIR JEWISH CONTEXT

Jesus was an integral part of Jewish life and thought during the time of the Second Temple. In culture and religion, Jesus was Jewish, and he spoke to other Jews. The parables demonstrate the strong solidarity he shared with other Jewish sages and rabbis who flourished during the period. Jesus spoke Hebrew. The language of the parables is always Hebrew. On the one hand, the Gentile church was not in a position to comprehend the cultural background of the parables. On the other hand, the Jewish people from the time of Jesus identified with and understood his teachings.

The parable of the Hearers makes the message of Jesus clear, as it calls upon each person to make a life-changing decision. No one should seek special symbolic meaning for each detail of a parable and allegorize it to suit his or her own purposes. But Jesus as the master parable teacher may impose his meaning on the word-picture by the context and by his own interpretation. One must study the context and listen to the parable teacher. The parable of the Sower should be studied in its original Jewish setting of Torah learning and discipleship.

Jesus taught about a lifestyle that seeks the divine reign in all aspects of personal relationships. Jesus demonstrated the way of life by his own

---

[50] *Abot* 2:13.

example. As Master, he is the model for his disciples to follow. A good heart is all that is needed for a miraculous harvest. The miracle develops from a tiny seed, which is planted in productive soil. The kingdom of heaven means that people can acknowledge his reign and receive the power to dedicate their lives to God. If the people receive the teaching of Jesus with a good heart, they receive God's kingdom with joy and do not allow anything or anyone to discourage them. They hear the words of Jesus and put them into operation.

Torah learning is highly esteemed in the message of Jesus. But each person must make the decision. In the interpretation of the parable, one sees that Satan takes the word away from some listeners. Others do not allow the seed to take root in their hearts. Others become entangled with the cares of this world and miss Jesus' message. The determining factor is the condition of the soil. It is easy to see ourselves in the four different types of soil. Everyone is able to receive the teaching of Jesus in the same way that fertile soil provides the necessary nutrients for a seed to grow. The love of Jesus the master teacher emerges from his challenge for each person to receive the word with a good heart. Surely each person who hears and acts upon the word of his teaching with a good heart will produce much fruit.

15 Death and Eschatology: The Theology of Imminence

FOCUS

Eschatology and the old Pharisaic belief in reward and punishment following death are prominent themes in the parables of both Jesus and the rabbis. Foundational in Jesus' teachings is the future coming of a deliverer called the Son of man. Following death, moreover, each individual must face judgment before the Creator. Both Jesus and the Pharisees believed in an impending divine retribution. Until the destruction of the temple in 70 C.E. the belief in the imminent judgment of God that would end the present world and its corruption gained greater currency in Jewish thought. (After the catastrophe of the first revolt [66–70 C.E.] and the trampled messianic hopes of the second [132–135 C.E.], eschatological themes and apocalyptic fervor waned in the teachings of the Pharisees.[1] Leaders such as Johanan ben Zachai stressed the study of Torah and preservation of the oral tradition more than the apocalyptic hopes of the world beyond.)

Reward and punishment may be given in the eschatological Day of the Lord or after a person dies. Jesus' parables translated the lofty ideas of a final judgment and retribution in life after death into an awesome reality. A sense of imminence pervaded the teachings of Jesus. The parables reveal the urgency of decision in view of the facts that the human soul will endure after death and God will pronounce judgment. Like the Pharisees, Jesus emphasized reward and punishment.

---

[1]See the important study by W. D. Davies, "Apocalyptic and Pharisaism," in *Christian Origins and Judaism* (Philadelphia: Westminster, 1962; repr., New York: Arno, 1977) 19–30.

The parables of Jesus as well as their rabbinic counterparts emerge from Pharisaic Judaism of the late Second Temple period. The Pharisees, according to Josephus, passionately "believe that souls have power to survive death and that there are rewards and punishments under the earth for those who have led lives of virtue or vice: eternal imprisonment is the lot of the evil souls, while the good souls receive an easy passage to a new life."[2] Such a strong belief in the immortality of the soul, combined with a sense of divine recompense for actions in the present life, laid the foundation for holy living. It gave priority to arduous preparation.

ON DEATH AND MONEY

The parable of the Rich Fool (Luke 12:16–20; *Gos. Thom.* 63) focuses on human mortality and the divine imperative to use money to alleviate the woes of the disadvantaged. The wealthy man's fields have produced so much that his barns are insufficient to hold the bountiful harvest. He devises a plan to build more spacious barns to expand his storage capacity. For the rich fool, enough is never enough. He wants more for himself without thinking of others. He says to himself, "Soul, you have ample goods laid up for many years; take your ease, eat, drink, be merry" (Luke 12:19).

In the parable, God changes the man's attitude. Even those who are rich and powerful in this world must face the agony of death and the judgment of God. God pays an unexpected visit to the successful man, perhaps sending the angel of death,[3] with the stinging message, "Fool! This night your soul is required of you." The wealth he hoarded for himself in this life will be of no use to him in the hereafter. In many ways, the wealthy man's attitude reflects the beliefs of the Sadducees, who denied the soul's existence after death. Concerned only about the pleasures of this world, without thought for the hereafter, the rich farmer denies the belief in the resurrection by his actions. He does not respond to human suffering. Like the fool who says in his heart, "There is no God" (Ps 14:1), the wealthy farmer maps out his life as if God does not exist. In contrast to the fool of Ps 14:1, who lives as if God does not exist, most Jewish farmers in the first century recognized their need for God's blessing to ensure a bountiful harvest.[4] As mentioned, one famous prayer in the Talmud petitioned God

---

[2] Josephus, *Ant.* 18.14. Cf. L. Ginzberg, "The Religion of the Pharisees," *Students, Scholars and Saints* (Philadelphia: Jewish Publication Society, 1928) 88–108. See also Flusser, *Origins*, 469–93.

[3] Though the angel of death does not appear in a direct reference, Jeremias (*Parables of Jesus*, 165) is probably correct when he suggests that the people thought of his role when they heard the parable. See also Marshall, *Luke*, 524.

[4] Consider, e.g., m. *Ber.* 6:1f. Whenever someone says a blessing over food, he or she recognizes that it is God who brings forth the produce from the earth and who creates the fruit of the vine.

not to listen to the prayers of travelers,[5] since travelers pray for sunshine, and the rabbis, many of whom were farmers, wanted rain.

In current Christian interpretation, J. Jeremias sought to make the parable into a warning of the eschatological crisis, i.e., the soon-to-come πειρασμός as the culmination of human history.

> We are not to think that Jesus intended to impress upon his audience the ancient maxim, "Death comes suddenly upon man." Rather do all the appeals and parables of warning taken together show that Jesus is not thinking of the inevitable death of the individual as the impending danger, but of the approaching eschatological catastrophe, and the coming Judgement. Thus here too in Luke 12.16–20 we have an eschatological parable.[6]

On the one hand, Jeremias rightly corrected a neglect of eschatology in parable research. On the other hand, he overemphasized the eschatological crisis to the neglect of other foundational Jewish concerns. The theme of preparation in the face of death's inevitability is prevalent in ancient Judaism. Jeremias is greatly mistaken when he discounts the fear of death. The end of the world was merely one of many concerns in the message of Jesus and the teachings of the sages of ancient Judaism. The fear of death overrides the eschatological idea in this parable.

Death and money are significant themes in the writings of Ben Sira. When a person dies, the money the person earned goes to others. But death ushers the individual into a new realm of existence where God judges all that was accomplished for good or evil. "There is a man who is rich through his diligence and self-denial," Ben Sira declares, "and this is the reward allotted to him: when he says, 'I have found rest, and now I shall enjoy my goods!' he does not know how much time will pass until he leaves them to others and dies" (Sir 11:18–19).[7] No man knows when death will come.

In the Talmud, the rabbis encourage active involvement in community needs. The self-reliant individual seeking personal gratification ultimately will stand unprepared to face divine retribution that follows death. Everyone must prepare for the unknown time of death.

> When the community is in trouble let not a man say, "I will go to my house and I will eat and drink and all will be well with me." For of him who does so Scripture says, *And behold joy and gladness, slaying oxen and killing sheep, eating flesh and drinking wine—"Let us eat and drink, for to-morrow we shall die"* (Isa. 22:13). What follows after this [verse]?—*And the Lord of Hosts revealed Himself in mine ears; surely this iniquity shall not be expiated by you till ye die* (verse 14). This is the conduct of the ordinary man, but what does Scripture say of the conduct of the wicked? *Come ye, I will fetch wine, and we will fill ourselves with strong drink; and*

---

[5] B. *Yoma* 53b; b. *Taan.* 24b.
[6] Jeremias, *Parables of Jesus,* 165.
[7] Cf. also Eccl. 2:1–23; Job 31:24–28.

> *to-morrow shall be as this day* (Isa. 56:12). . . . But rather a man should share in the distress of the community.[8]

The distress of the community calls for action. What community is not in distress? The attitude "Let us eat and drink for tomorrow we die" is that of apathy and indifference. Although the Gospel parable about the prosperous farmer does not mention the poor, its companion illustration in theme and content, the Rich Man and Lazarus, makes direct mention of the poor who suffer from the indifference of the wealthy. The rich man in the parable feasts on the best foods while poor Lazarus eats the crumbs from his table. The thorny issue of injustice in a world where the wicked prosper and the righteous suffer is tackled in this parable concerning life and death. Though the rich man enjoys the finest pleasures of life in this world, he will suffer in the afterlife. The postmortem existence of the poor man Lazarus, in contrast, is one of great joy. He enjoys the blessing of Abraham's bosom while the rich man is tormented. The greatest sin of the rich man is apathy. He did nothing in his great wealth and power to alleviate the sufferings of the poor.

The priority of the kingdom calls for decisive action. The time of death is not known. The certainty of death, however, is arguably the greatest fear of each human being. For living, wealth may provide some security and pleasure, but when the time of dying arrives, money matters little.[9] Only what is accomplished to help others and what is done to please God will merit reward. Jesus directs attention to the kingdom of heaven in daily living. The kingdom is experienced by the humble person who seeks to help others. The wealthy characters in these parables are preoccupied with self-gratification. They care little about the anguish of the poor.

Rabbi Jacob taught that this life is a time of preparation for the world to come. Every individual must repent of wrong and serve God in a life of good deeds.

> R. Jacob said, This world is like an ante-chamber to the world to come; prepare thyself in the ante-chamber, that thou mayest enter into the hall. He used to say, Better is one hour of repentance and good deeds in this world than the whole life of the world to come; yet better is one hour of blissfulness of spirit in the world to come than the whole life of this world.[10]

Rabbi Akiva also stressed the final judgment of God. In living life, he had a strong awareness of the divine retribution for good and evil.

> He used to say, Everything is given on pledge, and a net is spread for all the living: the shop is open; and the dealer gives credit; and the ledger lies open; and the hand writes; and whosoever wishes to borrow may come and borrow; but the collectors regularly make their daily round; and exact payment from man, whether he be content or not; and they have that where on they can rely

---

[8] b. *Taan.* 11a; see also Str-B 2:190.

[9] Compare Matt 6:19–21 and parallels; as well as 1 Tim 6:6–10.

[10] *Abot* 4:21–22 (Hertz, *Daily Prayer Book*, 677).

in their demand; and the judgment is a judgment of truth; and everything is ready for the feast.[11]

The notion that all is given on pledge and that God will require accountability is rooted in the doctrines of the Pharisees. The language of Luke's parable, moreover, "your soul is required of you" (τὴν ψυχήν σου ἀπαιτοῦσιν ἀπὸ σοῦ, Luke 12:20), recalls the concept that life is a gift from God that is given to a person on loan.[12] On the day of reckoning, the person must return the pledge to God and give an account of everything. The sense of imminent death and constant preparation is carried over into the teachings of Eleazar HaKappar: "He used to say, They that are born are destined to die; and the dead to be brought to life again; and the living to be judged."[13] Like Jesus, the ancient rabbis emphasized repentance and good works as a preparation for the day of judgment. Grace and mercy are extended to everyone who repents. The portrayal of the afterlife in the parable of the Rich Man and Lazarus particularly communicates the urgency of the time.

Ruth Rabbah, a later rabbinic text, preserves a lucid parallel to this theme in a moving story illustrating the urgency of time.

Two Wicked Men

In this world, he who is crooked can be made straight, and he who is straight can become crooked, but in the hereafter he who is crooked cannot be made straight, nor he who is straight crooked. *"And that which is wanting cannot be numbered."* Consider two wicked men who associated with one another in this world. One of them repented of his evil deeds before his death while the other did not, with the result that the former stands in the company of the righteous while his fellow stands in the company of the wicked! And beholding him he says, "Woe is me, is there then favour shown here? We both of us committed robberies, we both of us committed murders together, yet he stands in the company of the righteous and I in the company of the wicked." And they [the angels] reply to him and say, "You fool! you were despicable after your death and lay for three days, and did not they drag you to your grave with ropes? *The maggot is spread under thee, and the worms cover thee* (Isa. XIV, 11). And your associate understood and repented of his evil ways, and you, you also had the opportunity of repenting and you did not take it."

He thereupon says to them, "Permit me to go and repent!" And they answer him and say, "You fool! Do you know that this world is like the Sabbath and the world whence you have come is like the eve of the Sabbath? If a man does

[11] Ibid., 3:20 (Hertz, *Daily Prayer Book,* 660–63).

[12] See also Marshall, *Luke* 524; Nolland, *Luke,* 2:687.

[13] *Abot* 4:29 (Hertz, *Daily Prayer Book,* 681–82). See the saying of Akavaya, a contemporary of Hillel, in *Abot* 3:1: "Reflect upon three things, and thou wilt not come within the power of sin: know whence thou camest, whither thou art going; and before whom thou wilt in the future have to give account and reckoning."

not prepare his meal on the eve of the Sabbath, what shall he eat on the Sabbath?"[14]

The Pharisees' beliefs in resurrection and divine retribution made their view of death distinctive. Their doctrines shaped the teachings of Jesus and the later rabbis. This fear of death, which can come at any moment, is not far removed from the fear of the eschatological judgment. A parable of Johanan ben Zachai about wise and foolish servants, dealing with the unknown time of death, is very similar in content and motif to Jesus' parable of the Wise and Foolish Maidens (Matt 25:1–13). The rabbinic parable contrasts the actions of the wise servants, who were always prepared, with those of the foolish, who made excuses.

The Wise and Foolish Servants

R. Johanan ben Zachai said: This may be compared to a king who summoned his servants to a banquet without appointing a time. The wise ones adorned themselves and sat at the door of the palace, ["for"] said they, "is anything lacking in a royal palace?" The fools went about their work, saying, "can there be a banquet without preparations?" Suddenly the king desired [the presence of] his servants: the wise entered adorned, while the fools entered soiled. The king rejoiced at the wise but was angry with the fools. "Those who adorned themselves for the banquet," ordered he, "let them sit, eat and drink. But those who did not adorn themselves for the banquet, let them stand and watch."[15]

The similarity to Jesus' parable is striking. Jesus warns against the unknown time of the coming of the Son of man in eschatological judgment by telling a story of a wedding feast. The ten bridesmaids were divided into two types. Five were foolish (μωραί), like the foolish servants (טפשים) in the rabbinic parable, and five were wise (φρόνιμοι), comparable to the wise king's servants (פקחים).

ON THE IMMINENCE OF JUDGMENT

The Gospel parable of the Ten Maidens is eschatological. It addresses the awesome prospect of God meting out retribution when the eschatological judge suddenly appears. In contrast, Rabban Johanan ben Zachai's parable of the Wise and Foolish Servants deals with the suddenness of death. In fact,

---

[14] *Ruth Rab.* 3:3 (Freedman, *Midrash Rabbah*, 44–45). See the fine critical edition by M. Lerner, "Midrash Rut Rabbah" (diss., Hebrew University, Jerusalem, 1971) 86–87; and the parallel in *Eccl. Rab.* 1:15,1 (Freedman, *Midrash Rabbah*, 42). Cf. the discussion by McArthur and Johnston, *Parables*, 195.

[15] b. *Shabb.* 153a. See esp. Flusser, *Gleichnisse*, 170–71; and cf. *Sem. R. Chiya* 2:1 (*Masekhet Semachot*, ed. Higger, 216). Cf. also the similar rabbinic parable in *Midrash Mishle*, ed. Visotzky, 131.

the Talmud places it in the context of Rabbi Eleazer's famous saying, "Repent one day before your death." His disciples were perplexed, and asked, "How is a person able to know the day of death, in order to repent before dying?" "All the more reason to repent today!" exclaimed Rabbi Eleazer, "lest he die tomorrow, and hence his whole life should be spent in repentance."[16] Jesus, however, is warning against the unknown time of the final judgment: "Watch therefore, for you know neither the day nor the hour" (γρηγορεῖτε οὖν, ὅτι οὐκ οἴδατε τὴν ἡμέραν οὐδὲ τὴν ὥραν, Matt 25:13). The urgency of the time and proper preparation are stressed in the forceful command γρηγορεῖτε, "Watch." Impending judgment, whether at the unknown time of death or the sudden appearance of the eschatological judge, gives these two parables common cause. The response of the listener to both should be identical: repentance and good works. The urgent need to always be prepared for the unknown time of death or last judgment is deeply connected to Jewish thought. Though death is certain, the actual moment in which a person will die is not known. Since this is not the case, the religious person must be prepared through repentance and righteous conduct.

Death and Repentance

> We learned elsewhere, R. Eliezer said: Repent one day before your death. His disciples asked him, Does then one know on what day he will die? Then all the more reason that he repent to-day, he replied, lest he die to-morrow, and thus his whole life is spent in repentance. And Solomon too said in his wisdom, "Let thy garments be always white; and let not thy head lack ointment" (Eccl 9:8)[17]

While J. Jeremias overemphasized the coming of the eschatological catastrophe to the neglect of the fear of death in the teachings of Jesus, the reality of a final judgment in both cases serves to unify the two themes. Gospel parables taught about the imminence of death and the need for preparation. The message is very similar to the teachings of the rabbis, which are based upon the doctrines of the Pharisees. Jewish eschatology and apocalyptic greatly impacted the teachings of Jesus in certain parables.

The clear eschatological message of Jesus emerges from the parables of the final judgment. The apocalyptic coming of the Son of man will bring divine recompense. Dodd and Jeremias wrongly linked the appearance of the Son of man with the coming of the kingdom. In its most fundamental meaning, the kingdom of heaven in the teachings of Jesus denotes the reign of God, which is experienced as a present force for healing, wholeness, and salvation in people's lives. The kingdom is never defined as identical with the coming of the Son of man. The final judgment, of course, is another display of divine sovereignty, which rewards the righteous and punishes the wicked.

---

[16] See b. *Shabb.* 153a and parallels.
[17] Ibid.

Though the judgment may be an expression of God's kingly power, it should not be equated with the definition of the kingdom of heaven. Jesus experienced God's sovereign power in his ministry (Luke 11:20).[18] For him, the kingdom is manifest in full force each time a person experiences and obeys God. Similarly, the rabbis believed that people received the kingdom when they acknowledged God's lordship by reciting the Shema.[19]

Prominent in the Gospel figure of the Son of man are the traditions of Daniel and Enoch. Flusser has also shown the significance of *Melchizedek*, a Dead Sea document in which the eschatological judge is Melchizedek. Flusser links the imagery of the Melchizedek judge to the figure of the Son of man in the Gospels.[20] Though initially A. S. van der Woude identified the figure of Melchizedek with the archangel Michael,[21] Flusser compellingly argues for viewing the text as a part of a stream in early Jewish teachings concerning an eschatological judge like the Son of man in the Gospel texts. Like the Epistle to the Hebrews in the NT, the Dead Sea scroll text *Melchizedek* has an incredible role for Melchizedek. The mysterious figure from the Hebrew Bible is described as liberating the righteous and punishing the wicked.

> [*To proclaim liberty to the captives* (Isa. lxi,1). Its interpretation is that He] will assign them to the Sons of Heaven and to the inheritance of Melchizedek; f[or He will cast] their [lot] amid the po[rtions of Melchize]dek, who will return them there and will proclaim to them liberty, forgiving them [the wrong-doings] of all their iniquities.
>
> . . . And Melchizedek will avenge the vengeance of the judgements of God . . . and he will drag [them from the hand of] Satan and from the hand of all the sp[irits of] his [lot].[22]

---

[18] See Young, *Jewish Parables*, 189–235.

[19] Compare L. Ginzberg, "The Religion of the Jews at the Time of Jesus," *HUCA* 1 (1924): 305–21. I am grateful to Joseph Frankovic, who called my attention to this important article. Ginzberg discusses how the rabbis linked the saying of the Shema with the acceptance of God's kingdom. He affirms, "The idea of the Kingdom of Heaven was accordingly for the Pharisees, neither eschatological nor political but that of the rule of God in the heart of the individual" (p. 312). Ginzberg stresses, "The implicit acceptance of God's unity as well as unconditional surrender of mind and heart to His holy will which the love of God expressed in the '*Shema*' implies, this is what is understood by the receiving of the Kingdom of God" (ibid.).

[20] See Flusser, "Melchizedek and the Son of Man," in *Origins*, 186–92.

[21] See A. S. van der Woude, "Melchisedek als himmlische Erlösergestalt in den neugefundenen eschatologischen Midraschim aus Qumran Höhle XI," *Oudtestamentische Studiën* 14 (1965): 354–73. This view continues to be dominant. See VanderKam, *Scrolls*, 53–54.

[22] 11QMelch, trans. Vermes, *Scrolls*, 300–301. Cf. the very important work by P. J. Kobelski, *Melchizedek and Mechireshâ* (CBQMS 10; Washington D.C.: Catholic Biblical Association, 1981).

Many questions are left unanswered because of the fragmentary nature of this scroll. The eschatological scene of judgment is not that far removed from the imagery of texts such as Dan 7:13 and related literature of the period.[23] W. Horbury has demonstrated conclusively the pervasive theme of the Son of man as eschatological judge in ancient Judaism during the time of Jesus.[24] While scholars will continue to debate the Son of man theme, some of them maintaining that it arose from Christian soil rather than the seedbed of pre-70 C.E. Judaism, most agree that the eschatological scene of the judge separating the righteous from the wicked permeated the religious thought of the Pharisees and related groups.[25] In Matthew, Jesus tells the parables of the Tares among the Wheat and the Bad Fish among the Good, which vividly portray the theme of a final separation. The tares, which look so much like wheat, can be removed only at harvest time. The dragnet brings in fish of every kind, both those permitted and those prohibited by Jewish law. The prohibited must be thrown aside so that the good fish may be eaten or sold in the market. The eschatological message of these parables is rooted in the vision of the end that guided the historical Jesus in his ministry of teaching. Properly understood, Jesus' approach to eschatology has much more to do with conduct pleasing to God in the present world than with attaining reward in the afterlife.

The metaphor of the wheat harvest was also used by the rabbis to illustrate the divine judgment of the nations. The removal of the wicked from the company of the righteous is the chief concern of the Jewish teachers telling these parables. The nations of the world may appear like the people of Israel and claim their divine promises, but in the end the harvest will determine the fate of all peoples. While the tares look genuine, the threshing of the grains will cause the good wheat to be separated from the worthless tares.

The Argument of the Wheat and the Tares

The tares said to the wheat, "We are more (as) beautiful than (as) you are. The rain falls for us and for you; and the sun shines on both of us." The wheat said to the tares, "It is not important what you say, nor is it important what we

[23] Cf. S. Mowinckel, *He That Cometh* (New York: Abingdon, 1954) 336.

[24] See the important article and primary sources cited by W. Horbury, "The Messianic Associations of the Son of Man," *JTS* 36 (1985): 34–55.

[25] See David Flusser, "Jewish Messianic Figures in Primitive Christianity," in *Messianism and Eschatology* (in Hebrew) (Jerusalem: Zalman Shazar Center, 1983) 103–34. Cf. also esp. David Flusser, "Jesus and the Sign of the Son of Man," in *Origins,* 526–34, discussing the high self-awareness of Jesus referring to himself as a sign (אות): "We will become aware that when Jesus spoke about the son of man who will be the sign to this generation in the final judgment, he was referring to himself and could not possibly have had another in mind" (p. 533). Luke 11:29–32 must be viewed in light of *Jub.* 4:14, 17, 23 and Sir 44:16. Flusser links the Son of man with the eschatological judge.

say; but rather the winnowing fan because it comes and separates us for the storehouse, and you for the birds to eat." Thus the nations of the world and Israel are mixed together in this world.[26]

The tares argue that they are more becoming than the wheat. The wheat will not resort to worthless talk but confidently awaits the day of harvest, when it will be separated from the tares. The same theme of judgment drives another illustration using the metaphors of a royal consort and a Cushite maidservant. The two argue over which is more beloved by the king. The racy story of the king's lovers and their arguments will not be settled until the morning, which functions as the harvest in the rabbinic story of the wheat and the tares.

The Argument between the Consort and the Maidservant

It is like a consort who had a Cushite maidservant. The consort's husband went off to a foreign province. All night the maidservant said to the consort: I am more beautiful than you. The king loves me more than he loves you. The consort replied: Let morning come, and we will know who is more beautiful and whom the kings loves.

Similarly, the nations of the world say to Israel: Our deeds are more beautiful, and we are the ones whom the Holy One, blessed be He, desires. Therefore Israel says: Let morning come, and we will know whom the Holy One, blessed be He, desires—as it is said, "The watchman replied, Morning comes" (Isa. 21:12): Let the world to come, which is called morning, arrive, "and you shall come to see the difference between the righteous and the wicked" (Mal. 3:18).[27]

The harvest motif is used in yet another rabbinic illustration. The separation of the wheat from the straw, chaff, and stubble during the threshing process was a familiar part of the agricultural landscape. Middle Eastern wheat farmers knew the importance of separating the wheat. Even modern wheat farmers in Oklahoma have explained to me how what they call "cheat," namely, chaff, stubble, and tares, can rob a crop of its true value when mixed into the harvested grain. In antiquity as well as in many villages in the Middle East today, the wheat farmers winnow their crop on a spacious threshing floor.[28] The wheat is thrown into the air, and the wind removes the straw, chaff, and stubble. The waste is burned and the precious wheat is stored away.

---

[26] My translation; texts used: *Agadat Bershit* 23, *Bet Hamidrash*, ed. Jellinek 4:36, see also *Yalkut Shimeoni* I, 140; C. Bialik and J. Rabnitzki, *Sefer Haagadah* (Tel Aviv: Davir, 1973). See Flusser, *Gleichnisse*, 134.

[27] See *Midrash Tanchuma*, ed. Buber (*Num. Rab.* 16:23); trans. Stern, *Parables in Midrash*, 116.

[28] Cf. E. Masterman, *Studies in Galilee* (Chicago: University of Chicago, 1909) 138.

The Argument of the Wheat, Straw, Chaff, and Stubble

> The following parable will illustrate this. The straw, the chaff and the stubble were arguing with one another, each claiming that for its sake the ground had been sown. Said the wheat to them: "Wait till the threshing time comes, and we shall see for whose sake the field has been sown." When the time came and they were all brought into the threshing-floor, the farmer went out to winnow it. The chaff was scattered to the winds; the straw he took and threw on the ground; the stubble he cast into the fire; the wheat he took and piled in a heap, and all the passers-by when they saw it kissed it, as it says, *Kiss ye the corn* (Ps. II, 12). So the nations some say, "We are Israel, and for our sake the world was created," and others say, "We are Israel and for our sake the world was created." Says Israel to them: "Wait till the day the Holy One, blessed be He, comes, and we shall see for whose sake the world was created; and so it is written, *For, behold, the day cometh, it burneth as a furnace,* etc. (Mal. III, 1a); and it is written, *Thou shalt fan them and the wind will carry them away* (Isa. XLI, 16). But of Israel it is said, *And thou shalt rejoice in the Lord, thou shalt glory in the Holy One of Israel* (ib.)."[29]

The metaphors of divine justice arise from the colorful imagery of harvest time. The division occurs on the threshing floor. The wheat is separated from the chaff, stubble, and straw. The fire burns the excess.

The motif of consuming fire and cataclysmic judgment that it conveys is a prominent part of the early Gospel tradition. John the Baptist proclaims concerning the coming one, "he will baptize you with the Holy Spirit and with fire. His winnowing fork is in his hand, to clear his threshing floor, and to gather the wheat into his granary, but the chaff he will burn with unquenchable fire" (Luke 3:16–17; cf. parallels).[30] The idea of judgment by fire probably originates from the biblical account of the Noachic deluge. After the flood, God promised Noah that he would never again destroy the world by water (Gen 9:11). Moreover, God annihilated the Sodomites by raining down fire from heaven (Gen 19:24). This may have given rise to the popular concept of fire as the agent of divine judgment. Perhaps the prophet Jonah would have expected a similar fate to befall Nineveh. At least the sacred writer of the story conjures up the images of Sodom and Gomorrah in the warning Jonah gave the Ninevites.[31] The psalmist also echoes the idea of a fiery judgment: "On the wicked he will rain coals of fire and brimstone" (Ps 11:6).

---

[29] *Song Rab.* 7.3.3 (trans. Freedman, *Midrash Rabbah,* 282–84); cf. the parallel in *Pesik. Rab.* 10 (*Pesikta Rabbati,* ed. Friedmann, 35b); Braude, *Pesikta Rabbati,* 1:175ff.; Fiebig, *Rabbinische Gleichnisse,* 40, 43; cf. Feldman, *Parables and Similes,* 66f. Cf. Bacher on Rabbi Levi, *Amoräer,* 2:322–24 (Heb. ed., 2, part 2, 30–32).

[30] John apparently believed that these events would follow one after the other in rapid sequence.

[31] Compare Jonah 3:4 with Gen 19:25.

The writers of the Dead Sea Scrolls were also familiar with this concept. The *Pesher on Habakkuk* expressed a similar idea when charging that the wicked priest will be condemned to the judgment fire: "He [God] will bring him thence for judgement and will declare him guilty in the midst of them, and will chastise him with fire of brimstone."[32] The Hebrew expression "fire of brimstone" recalls the destruction of Sodom and Gomorrah (Gen 19:24). In the continuation of this passage the writer returns to that theme: "that they might be punished with fire who vilified and outraged the elect of God."[33] The *Manual of Discipline* contains a Levitical curse for the followers of Belial: "Be cursed without mercy because of the darkness of your deeds! Be damned in the shadowy place of everlasting fire!"[34] The idiom "everlasting fire" also appears in Matt 25:41: "Then he will say to those at his left hand, 'Depart from me, you cursed, into the eternal fire prepared for the devil and his angels.'" The *Manual of Discipline* warns the neophytes to the community of the disastrous end for those who are overcome by sin: "eternal torment and endless disgrace together with shameful extinction in the fire of the dark region."[35] The judgment of the sinner is connected with the fire, which probably was not considered a mere metaphor but an accurate portrayal of the intense agony and suffering of the condemned.

This motif is used by the authors of pseudepigraphic texts also. In the *Testament of the Twelve Patriarchs* Zebulun concludes his final discourse with the hope of resurrection and also the punishment of the wicked: "But the Lord shall bring down fire on the impious and will destroy them to all generations" (*T. Zeb.* 10:3).[36] Judah foretells that Beliar "will be thrown into eternal fire" (*T. Jud.* 25:3).[37] *First Enoch* 67:13; 103:7; *4 Macc.* 9:9; and *Apoc. Ab.* 31:2–3, 5 also mention punishment by fire.[38] In *Testament of Abraham* (longer recension 12–13), the fiery angel purifies a man's soul while Abel officiates as judge.[39] In *4 Ezra* 13:5–11 a messianic figure wipes out a legion

[32] 1QpHab 10:5; trans. Vermes, *Scrolls,* 288.

[33] 1QpHab 10:13; trans. Vermes, *Scrolls,* 288.

[34] 1QS 2:12; trans. Vermes, *Scrolls,* 63. See the critical edition of Licht, *Megilat Haserachim,* 98.

[35] 1QS 4:13; trans. Vermes, *Scrolls,* 66.

[36] Trans. H. C. Kee, in Charlesworth, *OT Pseudepigrapha,* 1:807. Cf. also the important notes by H. W. Hollander and M. de Jonge, *The Testaments of the Twelve Patriarchs* (Leiden: Brill, 1985) 274–75.

[37] Trans. H. C. Kee, in Charlesworth, *OT Pseudepigrapha,* 1:802. See the translation of Hollander and de Jonge, *Testaments,* 229: "it will be cast into the fire for ever and ever."

[38] See also M. Black, "The Messianism of the Parables of Enoch: Their Date and Contributions to Christological Origins," 145–68; and A. Yarbro Collins, "The 'Son of Man' Tradition and the Book of Revelation," 536–68, both in Charlesworth, *Messiah.*

[39] See the critical edition by Francis Schmidt, *Le Testament grec d'Abraham* (Tübingen: J. C. B. Mohr, 1986) 134–35; cf. also M. Stone, trans., *The Testament of Abraham* (Missoula, Mont.: Society of Biblical Literature, 1972) 31. Abel is described as the wondrous man

of men with a fiery blast that pours forth from his mouth. The book of Revelation describes the lake of fire that punishes the ungodly. While these exemplary texts may not necessarily be directly related to the Gospel narratives, they do show a popular conception of an eschatological judgment.

In rabbinic literature, the description of the unrepentant sinner's punishment by fire appears, but the substance of the motif is not identical with the views listed above, which are found throughout the literature of the Second Temple period. Moreover, one must keep in mind that it is difficult, if not impossible, to find a view concerning the afterlife that would be embraced by all religious leaders of the ancient synagogue.[40] Perhaps the basic rabbinic idea of justice in terms of reward and punishment could be summarized by the expression "measure for measure."[41] For instance, the enemies of Israel will be recompensed for their wrongdoings with the torment that they caused Israel. In contrast to the writers of the Dead Sea Scrolls, who seemed quite happy about the everlasting fiery punishment their enemies eventually would receive, Rabbi Akiva maintains that the punishment of the wicked in Gehenna lasts for only twelve months.[42]

The rabbis emphasize that God always provides opportunity for repentance. If the wicked do not take advantage of this opportunity, then their punishment is justified. The *Mekilta* (on Exod 15:5–6) relates how God gave "an extension of time to the generation of the Flood, that they might repent—but they did not repent."[43] Likewise, the men who built the Tower of Babel and the wicked inhabitants of Sodom and Gomorrah did not repent when given opportunity. Punishment for their wrongs came upon them. But a final annihilation by fire was not accepted doctrine for all of Israel's sages.[44] The *Mekilta* (on Exod 18:1) describes the reaction of the kings of the earth when Israel received the Torah. They feared a flood of fire similar to the deluge in Noah's time. Then Balaam calmed their anxieties: "He is not going to bring a flood of water or a flood of fire. He is just going to give the Torah to his people!"[45] Furthermore, the Torah is sometimes compared to a purifying fire.[46] In reality, the giving of the Torah provided people with an opportunity to respond to the divine message. Nevertheless, these passages indicate that judgment by fire was indeed a widespread idea.

(ἀνὴρ ὁ θαυμάσιος) who sits upon the throne of judgment. He is the son of man, namely, the literal son of Adam, who is worthy as the righteous martyr.

[40] Cf. E. E. Urbach, *The Sages: Their Concepts and Beliefs* (2 vols.; Jerusalem: Magnes, 1975) 1:4.

[41] Compare the earlier and later development of the concept. Cf. Martha Himmelfarb, *Tours of Hell* (Philadelphia: Fortress, 1983) 68–168.

[42] See m. *Ed.* 2:10 and parallels.

[43] Trans. *Mekhilta*, ed. Lauterbach, 2:40.

[44] Cf. S. Raphael, *Jewish Views of the Afterlife* (London: Jason Aronson, 1994).

[45] Trans. *Mekhilta*, ed. Lauterbach, 2:162–63.

[46] Cf. M. Gross, *Otzar Haggadah* (3 vols.; Jerusalem: Mosad Harav Kook, 1977), 1:82ff.

In the discussions of the afterlife, moreover, the above text from the *Mekilta* reveals some hesitation to attribute a final conflagration to a merciful God. In *Gen. Rab.* 51:3 the third-generation Palestinian Amora Rabbi Chanina ben Pazzi objected to the doctrine that a rain of fire and brimstone would fall upon the wicked. Other sages, however, felt compelled to reject his view.

Brimstone and Fire

Thus it is written, *Upon the wicked he will cause to rain "coals"* (פחים)—this means coals and snares—*Fire and brimstone* (Psalm 11:6). Rabbi Judan said: Why does a man instinctively recoil when he smells brimstone? Because his soul knows that it will be punished therewith in the future.[47]

In rejecting the view of Rabbi Chanina ben Pazzi, Rabbi Judan noted humankind's natural fear of fire. Instinctively the human soul knows that it will be tried by fire in the future, and so fire ignites a strong fear of being burned in the present. Moreover, the wicked have been punished by fire in the past, and this will be their future punishment. This whole complex of ideas finds expression in several midrashim.[48] Though it has been preserved in later sources, there is little doubt that it originates from earlier traditions. The Dead Sea Scrolls and the Pseudepigrapha indicate that the motif of a fiery judgment circulated widely during the Second Temple period. It was rooted in several biblical passages, and such interpretations for these Scriptures could have arisen at any time. In all events, the fire used for burning the tares in the Gospel parable portrayed a fearful end in the final judgment of the human soul.

The parable of the Tares among the Wheat (Matt 13:24–30) as well as its companion illustration, the Bad Fish among the Good (Matt 13:47–50), reach a climax in a judgment by fire.[49] In scene 1 of the parable of the Tares the landowner sows good seed into his field. While the field workers slept, an enemy of the landowner comes and sows tares into the soil in a plan to destroy the harvest. The tares resemble the wheat in appearance but have

[47] See *Gen. Rab.* 51:3 and the parallel in *Midr. Pss.* 11:5–6. For parallels and further discussion see *Midrash Bereshit Rabbah*, ed. Albeck and Theodor, 2:534f.

[48] See *Midrash Bereshit Rabbah,* ed. Albeck and Theodor, 2:536f.; cf. *Lev. Rab.* 7:6 (*Vayikra Rabbah*, ed. Margulies, 1:161–63). One of the finest studies of these questions was conducted by Chaim Milikowsky, "Gehenna and 'Sinners of Israel' in the Light of Seder Olam" (in Hebrew) *Tarbiz* 51 (1986): 311–43.

[49] See also Flusser's fine discussion, *Gleichnisse,* 63–64. Some have justifiably questioned the ending of the seine net parable. Although there is reason to view it as a redactional addition, this application of the parable, as in so many rabbinic parallels, is fitting and most probably an original part of Matthew's source. The parable of the Tares among the Wheat also betrays the redactional tendencies of the first evangelist with its introductory formula and use of the word τότε, "then." Matthew uses the term some ninety times in his Gospel, while Luke uses τότε fifteen times and Mark only six. See Lindsey and dos Santos, *Concordance,* 3:244–47.

no marketable or nutritional value.[50] The plant itself, *Lolium temulentum*, is well known in rabbinic literature by the designation זונין.[51] In *Genesis Rabbah* this pseudo-wheat is described as a type of prostituted wheat.[52] The tares appear in a rabbinic parable in another midrash. A king has many granaries filled with this worthless pseudo-wheat; these granaries are compared to the Gentile nations. The king also has another granary that corresponds to the nation of Israel. This granary is filled with wheat and considered very valuable.[53]

This pseudowheat of Jesus' parable was well known and considered a great nuisance. A farmer faced a serious crisis when he discovered tares growing in his wheat. Jesus' illustration depicts a true-to-life situation. Occasionally someone would sow bad seed in his adversary's field in order to cause his misfortune. W. O. E. Oesterley noted, "He [Jesus] was referring to a nefarious act that many of His hearers must have known to have been perpetrated from time to time."[54] Interestingly, Roman law has treated a similar crime in Justin's *Corpus juris civilis: Digesta*.[55] Gustaf Dalman has noted additional attestation for such a crime, though from a much later period, "from a Palestinian folk-tale, where reeds were sown in field."[56] In

---

[50] Cf. m. *Ter.* 2:6; *Num. Rab.* 4:1. For a discussion and drawing of tares, see J. T. Durward, *Holy Land and Holy Writ* (Baraboo, Wisc.: Pilgrim, 1913) 50, 593.

[51] See, e.g., m. *Kil.* 1:1; *Ter.* 2:6; t. *Ter.* 6:10 (*Tosefta*, ed. Liebermann, 139; *Tosefta Ki-fshutah*, part 1, 387). Cf. also Ben Yehuda, *Dictionary*, 3:1313; also Str-B 1:667. See M. Jastrow, *A Dictionary of the Targumim, the Talmud Babli and Yerushalmi, and the Midrashic Literature* (2 vols.; repr.; New York: Judaica, 1975), 388, who identifies the root זנה with a "degenerate wheat."

[52] *Gen. Rab.* 28:8 (*Midrash Bereshit Rabbah*, ed. Albeck and Theodor, 1:266f.). Cf. the English translation of Freedman, *Midrash Rabbah*, 229: "R. Julian [Lulianus] b. Tiberius said in R. Isaac's name: Even the earth acted lewdly; wheat was sown and it produced pseudo-wheat [זונין], for the pseudo-wheat we now find came from the age of the deluge."

[53] *Num. Rab.* 4:1. See Str-B 1:667. Cf. also *Pesik. Rab.* 10:4, where Rabbi Levi says, "wheat is the life of the world."

[54] Oesterley, *Parables*, 60f.

[55] P. Krueger and T. Mommsen, eds., *Corpus juris civilis* (2 vols.; Berlin: Weidmann, 1908) 1:159 (*Digesta*, lib. 9, tit. 2, lege 27, 14, ad legem Aquiliam): "Et ideo Celsus quaerit, si lolium aut avenam in segetem alienam inieceris, quo eam tu inquinares, non solum quod vi aut clam dominum posse agere vel, si locatus fundus sit, colonum, sed et in factum agendum . . ." "Therefore Celsus asks, if you have thrown tares or oats into another's field so that you might damage its productivity, not only that the master can act with force or covertly but if the estate has been leased to a tenant farmer, he can act with force or covertly but also he can sue for damages. . . ." My thanks to Dr. Tom Benediktson for his assistance in translating and interpreting this text. In this passage from Justin's legal writings, Celsus (106 or 107 C.E.) is discussing the third B.C.E. law of Aquila which deals with the violation of agricultural interests. See *The Oxford Classical Dictionary*, edited by N. G. L. Hammond and H. H. Scullard (Oxford: Clarendon Press, 1970), 218 and 311. The parable of Jesus portrays a realistic setting.

[56] Dalman, *Sites*, 187.

modern India an opponent may threaten a farmer by saying that he will plant a poor-quality seed in the farmer's field, causing disaster for the produce.[57] Even though these sources are derived from testimonies that are far removed from first-century Israel, all of the evidence indicates that Jesus is using a known criminal act in his illustration.

In the second scene of the parable the crisis develops. The tares are discovered growing among the wheat. The workers find in abundance the sprouts of the dreaded tares. They report the situation to the landowner. He recognizes that an enemy has planned to destroy his crop. The dilemma must be faced: should the tares be uprooted immediately, or should the workers wait until the time of harvest to separate the crop? If the tares are not uprooted at once, they will consume many of the soil's nutrients that could make the wheat stronger and healthier. The tares will choke the wheat as they compete for room to grow. But because the roots of the tares are mixed together with the roots of the wheat, the removal of the tares would destroy both plants. The only way to salvage some of the crop is to wait for the harvest. Hence the wise landowner decides to delay the removal of the tares from among the wheat. The damage has already been inflicted, and nothing can be done to remedy the problem until the proper time arrives.

The third and final act of Jesus' dramatic illustration concentrates on the harvest. The separation of the tares and the wheat reaches its climax when the waste is burned.[58] The reapers are sent out. After gathering and burning the tares, the reapers harvest the wheat and place it in the storehouse. The vivid metaphor of fire drives home the message.

Like its partner illustration, the parable of the Dragnet, better named the parable of the Bad Fish among the Good, focuses attention on preparation for the eschatological end of the ages. They are companion parables. The second illustration is not an exact replica of the first, but their use of different motifs teaches a similar lesson. The scenes of the play have different settings, but the plot of the drama is basically the same. True, the dramatic features of the Tares among the Wheat are more developed than the individual elements of the Bad Fish among the Good. The various word-pictures in each parable may be easily recognized as corresponding with one another. The net is cast into the sea as the seed was sown in the field. The sea gives forth good and bad fish in much the same way as the field yielded both wheat and tares. The fishermen separate the fish just as the farm workers separated the tares from the wheat. By way of contrast, the dramatic element of the enemy is missing in the fishing illustration, and the flaming furnace appears only in the brief explanatory remarks in its conclusion.

---

[57] Joseph Roberts, *Oriental Illustrations* (London: Thomas Tegg, 1844) 530. This has been confirmed to me by a friend of Indian origin, who told me that farmers have been known to threaten one another with acts of agricultural reprisal.

[58] Cf. also Flusser, *Gleichnisse*, 134–36.

The evangelist's editorial work may be seen in the parable's introductory formula, "Again, the kingdom of heaven is like." The standard introduction relates the theme of the last judgment to the sovereignty of God in the teachings of Jesus. In Matt 13, the evangelist relates his collection of parables to the kingdom message. The eschatological parable warns of the coming judgment of God. The bad fish in the parable probably refer to those without fins or scales, thus not meeting the requirements of *kashrut* (Lev 11:10).[59] The Sea of Galilee does contain *Clarias macracanthus*, a forbidden variety of fish that resembles what is popularly called the catfish in America.[60] This kind of fish swims close to the bottom. The seine net drags the bottom of the lake, catching all kinds of fish, including this kind. After dragging the net onto the pebbly shore, the fishermen sort their catch for market. In the process, they also would clean the nets of stones and snakes.[61] For metaphoric representation of the last judgment, only two types of fish are mentioned. Here the illustration has been adapted for the theme of the parable. The subject of the story is the eschatological judgment. The good and the bad fish are like the righteous and the wicked, who will be divided from one another at God's awesome final judgment.

The conclusion and explanation of the word-picture of the Bad Fish among the Good has been flatly rejected by many NT critics as a free expansion by the evangelist. For example, Manson, Kingsbury, and Davies and Allison have all denied that these interpretative elements could be the original conclusion for the parable.[62] The phrase "close of the age" makes the entire section suspect. This idiom appears only in Matthew's Gospel.[63] The fact that this phrase is unparalleled in Mark and Luke makes it look secondary in the various Matthean narratives where it occurs. In the so-called Synoptic Apocalypse, Mark parallels this unique Matthean phrase with the words "when these things are all to be accomplished" (Mark 13:4; Matt 24:3). Luke parallels the expression with the words "when this is about to take place" (Luke 21:7). Mark retains συντελέω, which is the basis for the verbal noun συντέλεια. No doubt, several instances of the idiom "the close of the age" in Matthew's Gospel appear as a result of the evangelist's own redactional tendencies, but to claim that the phrase is *always* due to redaction is oversimplified.

---

[59] Jeremias, *Parables of Jesus,* 226.

[60] See Dalman, *Sites,* 134.

[61] See Mendel Nun, *Ancient Stone Anchors and Net Sinkers from the Sea of Galilee* (Israel: Kibbutz Ein Gev, 1993) 39–62. Nun has described the ancient method of fishing with the dragnet in his work *The Sea of Galilee and Its Fishermen,* 16–22. See also the similar motif in fable lore, Babrius, Fable 4 (*Babrius and Phaedrus,* ed. Perry, 8–11).

[62] Manson, *Sayings,* 198; J. D. Kingsbury, *The Parables of Jesus in Matthew 13* (London: SPCK, 1969) 121–25; Davies and Allison, *Matthew,* 2:442.

[63] Matt 13:39, 40, 49; 24:3; 28:30. The expression appears once in Heb 9:26. Cf. LXX Dan 9:27; 11:6, 13, 25, 27, 40; 12:4, 7, 13.

The evangelist was capable of proliferating the phrase "the kingdom of heaven is like" as a standard introductory formula for the parables. By doing so, Matthew has forced the modern critical reader to consider each parable in light of Jesus' other teachings concerning the kingdom of heaven. A similar question arises in regard to the Matthean use of the words "in the end of the age" (ἐν τῇ συντελείᾳ τοῦ αἰῶνος). This phrase may be reconstructed into excellent Hebrew, which well may reveal its Semitic background. Although Dalman did not regard the statement as original with Jesus, he did point to several early texts in which the phrase is used.[64] The expression itself appears in *T. Benj.* 11:3, and similar idioms can be found in the book of Daniel and the Dead Sea Scrolls. The text represents the Semitic idiom בקץ העולם. No philological problem, therefore, should exclude this idiom concerning the eschatological judgment from the early Hebrew story of Jesus' life, a primary hypothetical source behind the Synoptic tradition.

In all events, both the imminence of the end of the age and a healthy fear regarding divine retribution of the soul at the time of death fuel the metaphoric presentation of these Gospel parables. On the one hand, Jesus' parables are filled with the mystery of God's plan for final redemption. On the other hand, each person must be prepared at all times for the final recompense or the unknown time of death. In the parable about the Unfruitful Fig Tree (Luke 13:6–9), the urgency of being productive is emphasized because death may come at any moment. The tragic collapse of the tower of Siloam killed eighteen. Pilate murdered pious Jewish pilgrims from Galilee who were offering sacrifice. Luke describes how the Roman governor mingled the blood of the dead worshiper with his or her offering. In the Lukan context for the parable, Jesus used the sudden and unexpected death of these people to stress the urgency of the time. The owner of the fig tree wanted fruit. Being disappointed with the unproductive tree, he commanded the vinedresser to cut it down. Quite possibly, such a tree would be burned for firewood. But the vinedresser pleaded with his master for more time. Perhaps some fertilizer and additional care would cause the tree to bear fruit. Jesus sternly warned, "I tell you, No; but unless you repent you will all likewise perish" (Luke 13:5). The urgency of the time and the suddenness of death demand constant preparation through repentance and good works.

AN ESCHATOLOGY OF IMMINENCE

The eschatology of Jesus as portrayed in the parables is not so unlike major streams of Second Temple Jewish thought concerning the final judgment. While the theme of the end times was very important, the people's experience of faith and profound sense of divine sovereignty placed ultimate authority in the hands of God. In the Gospels, Jesus strongly rejects setting

[64] G. Dalman, *The Words of Jesus* (Edinburgh: T. & T. Clark, 1909) 155.

the date for the end times. He in no way encouraged preoccupation with eschatological speculations. Weiss, Schweitzer, Dodd, and Jeremias seem to have missed the significance of Jewish theology regarding the end times. Jesus' eschatology is one of imminence, stressing present action over against anticipating the final result.

In Matt 25:31–46, a text unique to the first evangelist, Jesus describes the coming of the Son of man and the eschatological judgment of the nations. The suddenness of the event, rather than the time of his coming, is emphasized, in what is undoubtedly the most eschatological and apocalyptic description in the teachings of Jesus, and arguably in the entire NT. Those who mistakenly have tried to determine the season of the Parousia fail to recognize the words of Jesus, "But of that day and hour no one knows, not even the angels of heaven, nor the Son, but the Father only" (Matt 24:36; Mark 13:32). The timing of the event is not a concern. Constant preparation for the suddenness of his coming, however, is paramount. The imminence of the end demands decisive measures. Ultimately Jesus viewed the future judgment through the prism of present action. God determines the future. People determine the present. The time has come to make a decision. Now is the time to act. In his most eschatological teaching, the master from Galilee stresses above all else the alleviation of human suffering. The Son of man, whom God appoints to sit on a glorious throne as judge and coming king, declares to the righteous (in Matt 25:34b–36),

> "Come, O blessed of my Father, inherit the kingdom prepared for you from the foundation of the world; for I was hungry and you gave me food, I was thirsty and you gave me drink, I was a stranger and you welcomed me, I was naked and you clothed me, I was sick and you visited me, I was in prison and you came to me."

The righteous never saw the king in desperate need. But according to the Gospel text, even if one helps another human being, no matter how insignificant in the eyes of the world, it is as if one had helped the Lord himself. The high moral and ethical nature of this teaching must be studied within the context of the last judgment. The reality of the judgment is vividly portrayed in the conversation between the judge and the accused. The righteous are known for their good deeds. They gave assistance to the disadvantaged, while the wicked only cared for themselves. Here one meets a theology of imminence. Awareness of the reality of a final judgment is profoundly felt. The suddenness of the future event is stressed. But the exalted judge renders his decisions based on one criterion, humble service directed toward those in need. Hence the call of the kingdom is to respond to people with love in a way characterized by indefatigable determination and practical humanitarian action.

Ideally, the eschatology of imminence should engender a profound conviction that the climax of all human history could come at any moment, when the supernatural realm of God almighty overwhelms the present world order and the final judgment commences. The eschatological judge will come transforming the present world and fulfilling the divine plan of redemption. In the Gospel tradition, the judge is the Son of man, who will separate the sheep from the goats, rewarding the righteous with eternal blessing and punishing the wrongdoer severely. The day will come as a sudden, shocking revelation because most people do not, and seemingly cannot, believe in such a radical transformation of the present world. They will not be prepared. Their daily conduct is not governed by the conviction that God's final judgment rewarding the righteous and punishing the unjust is an approaching reality. The eschatology of imminence believes with total faith that at any time God's realm of glory and transcendence can eclipse the domain of all humanity, transform a corrupt world, and usher in a new age guided by divine justice. The individual must decide to act now, because what is done in this life is preparation for the future world. A delay in acting upon one's decision will prove to be deadly.

Social involvement is elevated to the level of faith and piety. Prayer must go beyond the words of the liturgy and take the form of action. Practical religion becomes the ultimate concern during the end-times judgment. A person's spirituality is measured in terms of humanitarian relief efforts and societal reform. It is a clear echo of the classical prophetic message: help the poor and underprivileged.[65] Good works prepare the nations to face the eschatological judgment of God at the climactic end of the ages.

[65] In some respects, this view of Jewish eschatology was championed by Ginzberg: "The development of the religious thought of the Jew shows the marked tendency to fix the center of gravity of religion not in the thought of a world beyond but rather to fasten and establish it in the actual life of man on earth. In this respect the scribes and Rabbis were the true successors to the prophets. For the latter, morality was the most essential feature of religion and there is an ethically weak point in even the purest and loftiest ideas concerning the bliss of future life" ("Religion of the Jews," 314).

Epilogue: Jesus, the Parables, and the Jewish People

In 1922 the highly respected Jewish scholar Joseph Klausner claimed that any sound methodology critically examining the historical Jesus must meet at least two requirements.[1] First, critical research must place Jesus believably among the Jewish people in first-century Israel. Second, the historical analysis should explain how the church and the synagogue parted ways, resulting in the formation of the new Christian religion. In 1985 Sanders upheld the validity of these foundational principles in his widely acclaimed book, *Jesus and Judaism*.[2] Since one-third of the recorded sayings of Jesus appear in parables, these Gospel illustrations have the potential to solve a number of mysteries surrounding the nascent faith. Who is Jesus of Nazareth and how did Christianity originate? How has the presence of Jewish traditions in the parables of Jesus influenced Christianity?

Both Jesus and the rabbis loved to tell parables in order to capture the attention of their listeners and drive home the meaning of their teachings about God and people. The parables vividly portray the Jewish concept of God and what that God expects from every human being, each of whom was created in the divine image.

The Gospel parables' practical advice concerning prayer, faith, forgiveness, good works, Torah learning, and developing healthy interpersonal

---

[1] This was the first book about Jesus written originally in Hebrew by a respected Jewish scholar for Jewish readers. It was subsequently translated into English and German. On these issues see Joseph Klausner, *Jesus of Nazareth* (New York: Macmillan, 1945) 9–12.

[2] See Sanders, *Jesus and Judaism,* 18: a good hypothesis "should situate Jesus believably in Judaism and yet explain why the movement initiated by him eventually broke with Judaism."

relationships should never become overshadowed by a preoccupation with eschatology. The reality of the last judgment is not to be questioned, but the moral and ethical teachings of Torah must be implemented. Belief in God's justice and mercy is the foundation for the concept of final redemption. There is a sense of imminence in this type of theology. Discipleship in the kingdom means hearing the message of Jesus and responding decisively with obedience. Within the parameters of God's plan of redemption, Jesus urges a decision through his parables. Proper conduct and good works must characterize the life of his followers.

In many ways, the Gospel parables belong to the rich cultural heritage and folklore traditions of the Jewish people. No one will grasp the meaning of Jesus' parables without an extensive knowledge of ancient Judaism. Christian interpretations have tended to sever the parables from their cultural roots and apply them to new situations. In the destiny of humankind, the transcendence of the colorful illustrations goes beyond a single interpretation at one time and place in history. As Bultmann has taught us, the human predicament and our own experiences connect us with the traditions of the Bible.[3] These traditions do have a universal meaning that touches each listener's existence and personal experience.

The historical setting of the parables, however, attest to the Jewish roots of Jesus' message. The Jesus of the parables would blend in much more harmoniously with a band of Pharisees arguing matters of Torah learning than with a symposium of modern Christian theologians. In faith and prayer, Jesus shares much in common with the old Jewish *chasidim* like Choni the Circle Drawer or Chanina ben Dosa. In Torah learning, he is not far from the teachings of Hillel, Shammai, or Johanan ben Zachai. In telling parables, he joins with numerous Jewish preachers, such as Rabbi Akiva and Rabbi Meir. Through the pens of church fathers and later interpreters, the Gospel parables have been recast into theological treatises dealing with Christology and ecclesiastical doctrine. Allegory has served the church theologians well, while muffling the voice of the Jewish theologian Jesus. Christian interpretation of the parables frequently distorted the meaning of the illustration and undermined the original intent. Often Jesus spoke of Torah and its proper interpretation for living a life pleasing to God, but his words became too distorted to be comprehended in that way. In the light of Jewish traditions, the Gospel parables form an inextricable link between Jesus and the Jewish people, a bridge of solidarity that cannot be collapsed by time and history, nor by prejudice and tendentious theology.

---

[3]Cf., e.g., R. Bultmann, *Jesus and the Word* (ET; New York: Scribner, 1958) 3–4: "Therefore, if this book is to be anything more than information on interesting occurrences in the past, more than a walk through a museum of antiquities, if it is really to lead to our seeing Jesus as a part of the history in which we have our being, or in which by critical conflict we achieve being, then this book must be in the nature of a continuous *dialogue with history*."

Bibliography

Studies on the Parables

Bailey, Kenneth E. *Poet and Peasant*. Grand Rapids: Eerdmans, 1976.
———. *Through Peasant Eyes*. Grand Rapids: Eerdmans, 1980.
Beavis, Mary Ann. "Ancient Slavery as an Interpretive Context of the New Testament Servant Parables with Special Reference to the Unjust Steward (Luke 16:1–8)." *JBL* 111 (1992): 37–54.
Blomberg, Craig. *Interpreting the Parables*. Downers Grove, Ill.: InterVarsity, 1990.
Buttrick, George. *The Parables of Jesus*. New York: Doubleday, 1928.
Caird, G. B. *The Language and Imagery of the Bible*. Philadelphia: Westminster, 1980.
Crossan, John. *Finding Is the First Act: Trove Folktales and Jesus' Treasure Parable*. Missoula, Mont.: Scholars, 1979.
———. *In Parables: The Challenge of the Historical Jesus*. Sonoma, Calif: Polebridge, 1992.
———. "The Parable of the Wicked Husbandmen." *JBL* 90 (1971): 451–65.
Daube, David. "Inheritance in Two Lukan Pericopes." *ZSRG.R* 72 (1955): 326–34.
———. "Nathan's Parable." *NovT* 24 (1982): 275–88.
Davies, W. D. "Apocalyptic and Pharisaism." In *Christian Origins and Judaism*. Pages 19–30. Philadelphia: Westminster, 1962. Reprint. New York: Arno, 1977.
Derrett, J. Duncan M. "Law in the New Testament: The Parable of the Prodigal Son." *NTS* 14 (1967): 56–74.
Dodd, C. H. *The Parables of the Kingdom*. Rev. ed. Glasgow: Collins, 1961.
Donahue, John R. *The Gospel in Parable, Metaphor, Narrative, and Theology in the Synoptic Gospels.* Philadelphia: Fortress, 1988.

Feldman, A. *The Parables and Similes of the Rabbis, Agricultural and Pastoral.* Cambridge: Cambridge University Press, 1927.

Fiebig, Paul. *Altjüdische Gleichnisse und die Gleichnisse Jesu.* Tübingen: J. C. B. Mohr, 1904.

______. *Die Gleichnisreden Jesu.* Tübingen: J. C. B. Mohr, 1912.

______. *Rabbinische Gleichnisse.* Leipzig: J. C. Hinrichs, 1929.

Fletcher, D. R. "The Riddle of the Unjust Steward: Is Irony the Key?" *JBL* 82 (1963): 15–30.

Flusser, David. "Aesop's Fable and the Parable of the Talents." In *Parable and Story in Judaism and Christianity.* Pages 9–25. Edited by C. Thoma and M. Wyschogrod. Mahwah, N.J.: Paulist, 1989.

______. *Die rabbinischen Gleichnisse und der Gleichniserzähler Jesus.* Bern: Peter Lang, 1981.

Funk, R. W. "Poll on the Parables." *Forum* 2 (1, 1986): 54–80.

Funk, R. W., B. Scott, and J. R. Butts. *The Parables of Jesus.* Sonoma, Calif.: Polebridge, 1988.

Gibson, Margaret. "On the Parable of the Unjust Steward." *ExpT* 14 (1902): 334ff.

Goebel, Siegfried. *The Parables of Jesus.* Edinburgh: T. & T. Clark, 1894.

Guttmann, T. *Hamashal Batekufat Hatannaim.* Jerusalem: Abir Yaakov, 1940.

Hendrickx, Herman. *The Parables of Jesus.* San Francisco: Harper, 1986.

Hengel, M. "Das Gleichnis von den Weingärtnern Mc 12:1–12." *ZNW* 59 (1968): 1–39.

Hunter, A. M. *Interpreting the Parables.* London: SCM, 1972.

Jacobs, J. "Aesop's Fables among the Jews." In *The Jewish Encyclopedia.* Jerusalem: Keter, 1972. 1.221f.

Jeremias, J. *The Parables of Jesus.* Translated by S. H. Hooke. 2d rev. ed. New York: Scribner's, 1972.

______. "Zum Gleichnis vom verlorenen Sohn, Luk. 15, 11–32." *TZ* 5 (1949): 228–331.

Johnston, R. M. "Parables among the Pharisees and Early Rabbis." In *A History of Mishnaic Law of Purities Part XIII: Miqvaot.* Pages 224ff. Edited by J. Neusner. Leiden: Brill, 1976.

______. "Parabolic Interpretations Attributed to Tannaim." Dissertation. Hartford Seminary Foundation. 1977.

Jones, G. V. *The Art and Truth of the Parables.* London: SPCK, 1964.

Jülicher, Adolf. *Die Gleichnisreden Jesu.* 1888. Reprint. Darmstadt: Wissenschaftliche, 1963.

Kingsbury, J. D. *The Parables of Jesus in Matthew 13.* London: SPCK, 1969.

Kissinger, W. *The Parables of Jesus: A History of Interpretation and Bibliography.* London: Scarecrow, 1979.

Kümmel, W. G. "Das Gleichnis von den bösen Weingärtnern (Mark 12:1–12)." In *Aux sources de la tradition chrétienne.* Pages 120–31. FS Maurice Goguel. Neuchâtel: Delachaux & Niestlé, 1950.

Linnemann, Eta. *The Parables of Jesus.* London: SPCK, 1977.

Linton, Olof. "Coordinated Sayings and Parables in the Synoptic Gospels." *NTS* 26 (1980): 139–63.

Little, James. "Parable Research in the Twentieth Century: I. The Predecessors of J. Jeremias." *ExpT* 87 (1975): 356–60.

______. "Parable Research in the Twentieth Century: II. The Contribution of J. Jeremias." *ExpT* 88 (1976): 40–43.

______. "Parable Research in the Twentieth Century: III. Developments since J. Jeremias." *ExpT* 88 (1977): 71–75.

Lowe, M. "From the Parable of the Vineyard to a Pre-synoptic Source." *NTS* 28 (1982): 257–63.

Maisonneuve, D. de la. "Parables of Jesus and Rabbinic Parables." *Sidic* 19 (1987): 8–15.

McArthur, H. K., and R. M. Johnston. *They Also Taught in Parables.* Grand Rapids: Zondervan, 1990.

Newell, Jane E., and Raymond R. Newell. "The Parable of the Wicked Tenants." *NovT* 14 (1972): 226–37.

Noy, Dov. "Mishle Melechim shel Rashbi." *Machanayim* 56 (1961): 73–87.

Oesterley, W. O. E. *The Gospel Parables in the Light of Their Jewish Background.* New York: Macmillan, 1936.

Pearl, Chaim. *Theology in Rabbinic Stories.* Peabody: Hendrickson, 1997.

Perkins, Pheme. *Hearing the Parables of Jesus.* New York: Paulist, 1981.

Perrin, Norman. "The Modern Interpretation of the Parables of Jesus and the Problem of Hermeneutics." *Int* 25 (1971): 131–48.

Petuchowski, Jakob. "The Theological Significance of the Parable in Rabbinic Literature and the New Testament." *Christian News from Israel* 23 (1972–1973): 76–86.

Sanders, J. T. "The Parable of the Pounds and Lucan Anti-Semitism." *TS* 42 (1981): 550–668.

Schwarzbaum, Haim. *The Mishle Shualim (Fox Fables) of Rabbi Berechiah Ha-Nakdan: A Study in Comparative Folklore and Fable Lore.* Kiron, Israel: Institute for Jewish and Arab Folklore Research, 1979.

Scott, B. B. "Essaying the Rock: The Authenticity of the Jesus Parable Tradition." *Forum* 2 (1, 1986): 3ff.

______. *Hear Then the Parable: A Commentary on the Parables of Jesus.* Minneapolis: Fortress, 1989.

Stein, R. H. *An Introduction to the Parables of Jesus.* Philadelphia: Westminster, 1981.

Stern, David. "Interpreting Parables: The *Mashal* in Midrash with Special Reference to *Lamentations Rabba.*" Dissertation. Harvard University. Cambridge, Mass. 1980.

______. "Jesus' Parables from the Perspective of Rabbinic Literature: The Example of the Wicked Husbandmen." In *Parable and Story in Judaism and Christianity.* Edited by C. Thoma and M. Wyschogrod. Pages 42–80. Mahwah, N.J.: Paulist, 1989.

______. *Parables in Midrash: Narrative and Exegesis in Rabbinic Literature.* Cambridge: Harvard University Press, 1991.

Thoma, C. "Prolegomena zu einer Übersetzung und Kommentierung der rabbinischen Gleichnisse." *TZ* (1982): 518–31.

Thoma, C., and S. Lauer. *Die Gleichnisse der Rabbinen.* Bern: Peter Lang, 1986.

Thoma, C., and M. Wyschogrod, eds. *Parable and Story in Judaism and Christianity.* Mahwah, N.J.: Paulist, 1989.

Tolbert, Mary Ann. *Perspectives on the Parables: An Approach to Multiple Interpretations.* Philadelphia: Fortress, 1979.

Via, Dan O., Jr. *The Parables: Their Literary and Existential Dimension.* Philadelphia: Fortress, 1967.

Wallach, L. "The Parable of the Blind and the Lame." *JBL* 65 (1943): 333–39.

Wenham, David. *The Parables of Jesus.* Downers Grove, Ill.: InterVarsity, 1989.

Westermann, Claus. *The Parables of Jesus in the Light of the Old Testament.* Minneapolis: Fortress, 1990.

Wilder, Amos. *Jesus' Parables and the War of Myths.* London: SPCK, 1982.

Winterbotham, Rayner. "Christ or Archaelus?" *Expositor* 8th series, 4 (1912) 338–47.

Ziegler, Ignaz. *Die Königsgleichnisse des Midrasch beleuchtet durch die römische Kaiserzeit.* Breslau: Schlesische Verlags-Anstalt v. S. Schottlaender, 1903.

General Bibliography

Primary Sources, Editions, and Translations

The Ante-Nicene Fathers. Edited by A. Roberts and J. Donaldson. 1885–1887. Reprint. Peabody, Mass.: Hendrickson, 1994.

Aboth de Rabbi Nathan. Edited by S. Schechter. Vienna: Lippe, 1887.

Babrius and Phaedrus. Edited and translated by Ben Edwin Perry. Loeb Classical Library. Cambridge: Harvard University Press, 1965. Reprint 1984.

Bede the Venerable: Homilies on the Gospels. Translated by L. Martin and D. Hurst. 2 volumes. Kalamazoo, Mich.: Cisterican, 1991.

Batei Midrashot. Edited by S. A. Wertheimer. Jerusalem: Ketav Vesefer, 1980.

Bet Hamidrash. Edited by A. Jellinek. Jerusalem: Wahrmann, 1967.

Black, M. *The Book of Enoch.* Leiden: Brill, 1985.

Braude, W. G. *The Midrash on Psalms.* 2 volumes. New Haven: Yale University Press, 1958.

______. *Pesikta Rabbati.* 2 volumes. New Haven: Yale University Press, 1968.

______. *Tanna Debe Eliyyahu.* Philadelphia: Jewish Publication Society, 1981.

Braude, W. G., and I. Kapstein. *Pesikta de Rab Kahana.* Philadelphia: Jewish Publication Society, 1975.

Charles, R. H., ed. *The Apocrypha and Pseudepigrapha of the Old Testament.* 2 volumes. Oxford: Clarendon, 1977.

Charlesworth, J. H., ed. *The Old Testament Pseudepigrapha.* 2 volumes. New York: Doubleday, 1983–1985.

Clark, E. G. *Targum Pseudo-Jonathan of the Prophets.* Hoboken, N.J.: KTAV, 1984.
Cohen, A., and Israel Brodie, eds. *The Minor Tractates of the Talmud.* 2 volumes. London: Soncino, 1971.
Danby, Herbert. *The Mishnah.* New York: Oxford University Press, 1977.
The Dead Sea Scrolls on Microfiche. Edited by S. Reed, M. Lundberg, E. Tov, and Stephen J. Pfann. Leiden: Brill, 1993.
Delitzsch. F., trans. *Haberit Hechadashah.* Tel Aviv: Bible Society, 1976.
Díez Macho, A. *Neophyti I.* 6 volumes. Text and translations into Spanish, French, and English. Madrid: Consejo Superior de Investigaciones Científicas, 1968–1979.
Epstein, I., ed. *The Babylonian Talmud.* 35 volumes. London: Soncino, 1935–1978.
Freedman, H., ed. *Midrash Rabbah.* 9 volumes. London: Soncino, 1951.
Friedlander, G. *Pirke de Rabbi Eliezer.* New York: Hermon, 1981.
Gaster, Theodor H. *The Dead Sea Scriptures.* New York: Anchor, 1976.
Goldin, J. *The Fathers according to Rabbi Nathan.* New York: Schocken, 1974.
Goldschmidt, S. *Seder Haselichot.* Jerusalem: Mosad Derav Kook, 1975.
Grant, R. M. *Miracle and Natural Law in Graeco-Roman and Early Christian Thought.* Amsterdam: North Holland Publishing Company, 1952.
Grant, R. M., and H. H. Graham. *The Apostolic Fathers: A New Translation and Commentary.* New York: Thomas Nelson, 1965.
Haberman, A. *Megillot Midbar Yehuda.* Tel Aviv: Machbarot Lesifrut, 1959.
Hammer, Reuven. *Sifre: A Tannaitic Commentary on the Book of Deuteronomy.* New Haven: Yale University Press, 1986.
Hertz, J. H. *The Authorised Daily Prayer Book.* Hebrew text, English translation with commentary and notes. New York: Bloch, 1959.
Herford, T. *Pirke Aboth: The Ethics of the Talmud—Sayings of the Fathers.* New York: Schocken, 1975.
Hollander, H. W., and M. de Jonge. *The Testaments of the Twelve Patriarchs.* Leiden: Brill, 1985.
Horst, P. W. van der. *The Sentences of Pseudo-Phocylides.* Leiden: Brill, 1978.
Hyman, A. *Torah Haketubah Vehamasurah.* 3 volumes. Tel Aviv: Davir, 1979.
______. *Toldot Tannaim Veamoraim.* 3 volumes. Jerusalem: Boys Town, 1964.
James, M. R. *The Apocryphal New Testament.* Oxford: Clarendon, 1924.
Josephus. Edited and translated by H. St. J. Thackeray, R. Marcus, and L. H. Feldman. 10 volumes. Loeb Classical Library. Cambridge: Harvard University Press, 1978.
Klein, M. L. *The Fragment-Targums of the Pentatech.* 2 volumes. Rome: Pontifical Biblical Institute, 1980.
______. *The Geniza Manuscript of the Palestinian Targum to the Pentateuch.* 2 volumes. Jeruslaem: Hebrew Union College Press, 1986.
Licht, J. *Megilat Hahodayot.* Jerusalem: Bialik Institute, 1957.
______. *Megilat Haserachim.* Jerusalem: Bialik Institute, 1965.
Masekhet Semachot. Edited by M. Higger. Jerusalem: Makor, 1970.

Masekhtot Derekh Eretz. Edited by M. Higger. 2 volumes. Jerusalem: Makor, 1970.

Mekhilta Derabbi Ishmael. Edited by H. S. Horovitz and Ch. Rabin. Jerusalem: Wahrmann, 1970.

Mekhilta Derabbi Ishmael. Edited by M. Friedmann. 1870. Reprint. Jerusalem: Old City, 1978.

Mekhilta Derabbi Ishmael. Edited and translated by Jacob Lauterbach. 3 volumes. Philadelphia: Jewish Publication Society, 1976.

Mekilta Derabbi Shimeon Bar Yochai. Edited by Y. N. Epstein and E. Z. Melamed. Jerusalem: Hillel, 1980.

Midrash Bereshit Rabbah. Edited by C. Albeck and J. Theodor. 3 volumes. Jerusalem: Wahrmann, 1980.

Midrash Devarim Rabbah. Edited by S. Liebermann. Jerusalem: Wahrmann, 1974.

Midrash Ekha Rabbah. Edited by S. Buber. Wilna: Wittwa & Gebrüder Romm, 1899.

Midrash Hagadol. 5 volumes. Jerusalem: Mosad Harav Kook, 1975.

Midrash Lekach Tov. Edited by S. Buber. Wilna: Wittwa & Gebrüder Romm, 1880.

Midrash Mishle. Edited by S. Buber. Wilna: Wittwa & Gebrüder Romm, 1891.

Midrash Mishle. Edited by Burton Visotzky. New York: Jewish Theological Seminary, 1990.

Midrash Rabbah. 2 volumes. Wilna: Wittwa & Gebrüder Romm, 1887.

Midrash Rabbah. Edited with commentary by Moshe Mirkin. 11 volumes. Tel Aviv: Yavneh, 1977.

Midrash Rabbah Hamevuar. Edited by A. Steinberger. Jerusalem: Hanachal, 1983.

"Midrash *Rut Rabbah.*" Edited by M. Lerner. Dissertation. Hebrew University. Jerusalem. 1971.

Midrash Seder Olam. Edited by D. Ratner. New York: Talmudic Research Institute, 1966.

Midrash Shemuel. Edited by S. Buber. Cracow: Joseph Fischer, 1893.

Midrash Shir Hashirim. Edited by Eliezer Halevi Grunhut. Jerusalem: n.p., 1897.

Midrash Shir Hashirim Rabbah. Edited by Shimshon Donski. Tel Aviv: Davir, 1980.

Midrash Tanchuma. 1879. Reprint. Jerusalem: Lewin-Epstein, 1975.

Midrash Tanchuma. Edited by S. Buber. Wilna: Wittwa und Gebrüder Romm, 1885.

Midrash Tannaim. Edited by D. Hoffmann. 1908. Reprint. Jerusalem: Books Export, n.d.

Midrash Tehilim. Edited by S. Buber. Wilna: Wittwa & Gebrüder Romm, 1891.

Midrash Vayikra Rabbah. Edited by Mordecai Margulies. 5 volumes. Jerusalem: Wahrmann, 1970.

Mishnah. Edited by C. Albeck. 6 volumes. Jerusalem: Bialik Institute, 1978.

Mishnayoth. Edited and translated by Philip Blackman. 7 volumes. New York: Judaica, 1990.

Neusner, J., ed. *The Talmud of the Land of Israel Sanhedrin and Makkot.* Chicago: University of Chicago Press, 1984.

———, trans. *The Tosefta.* New York: KTAV, 1981.

New Testament Apocrypha. Edited by W. Schneemelcher and E. Hennecke. Translated by R. McL. Wilson. 2 volumes. Rev. ed. Louisville: Westminster/John Knox, 1991–1992.

The New Testament in Greek: The Gospel according to St. Luke. Edited by the American and British Committees of the International Greek New Testament Project. 2 volumes. Oxford: Clarendon, 1984–1987.

Novum Testamentum Graece. Edited by S. C. E. Legg. 2 volumes. Oxford: Clarendon, 1935–1940.

Otzav Midrashim. Edited by J. D. Eisenstein. 2 volumes. Jerusalem: Hillel, 1969.

Pesikta Derav Kahana. Edited by S. Buber. Ełk, Poland: L. Silbermann, 1868.

Pesikta Derav Kahana. Edited by B. Mandelbaum. New York: Jewish Theological Seminary, 1962.

Pesikta Rabbati. Edited by M. Friedmann. Vienna: Josef Kaiser, 1880.

Philo. Edited and translated by F.H. Colson and G. H. Whitaker. 10 volumes. and 2 supplementary volumes. Loeb Classical Library. Cambridge: Harvard University Press, 1981.

Pirke Derabbi Eliezer. Edited by David Luria. Warsaw: Bomberg, 1852.

Rieder, D. *Targum Jonathan ben Uzziel.* 2 volumes. Jerusalem: Naveh Simchah, 1984–1985.

Saldarini, A. *The Fathers according to Rabbi Nathan.* Leiden: Brill, 1975.

Salkinson, J., trans. *Haberit Hechadashah.* London: Trinitarian Bible Society, 1957.

Schmidt, Francis. *Le Testament grec d'Abraham.* Tübingen: J. C. B. Mohr, 1986.

Seder Eliyahu Rabbah. Edited by M. Friedmann. Jerusalem: Wahrmann, 1969.

Segal, M. *Sefer Ben Sira Hashalem.* Jerusalem: Bialik Institute, 1972.

Shinan, A. *Midrash Shemot Rabbah.* Jerusalem: Dvir, 1984.

Sifra. Edited by L. Finkelstein. 5 volumes. New York: Jewish Theological Seminary, 1984.

Sifra (incomplete). Edited by M. Friedmann. 1915. Reprint. Jerusalem: Old City, 1978.

Sifra. Edited by J. H. Weiss. Vienna: J. Salsberg, 1862.

Sifra: An Analytical Translation. Translated by J. Neusner. 3 volumes. Atlanta: Scholars, 1985.

Sifre Al Bemidbar Vesifre Zuta. Edited by H. S. Horovitz. Jerusalem: Wahrmann, 1966.

Sifre Debe Rav. Edited by M. Friedmann. 1864. Reprint. Jerusalem: Old City, 1978.

Sifre Devarim. Edited by L. Finkelstein. New York: Jewish Theological Seminary, 1969.

Sifre to Numbers. Translated by J. Neusner. 2 volumes. Atlanta: Scholars, 1986.
Sperber, A. *The Bible in Aramaic*. 5 volumes. Leiden: Brill, 1959–1968.
Steinsaltz, A. *The Talmud*. New York: Random House, 1989.
Stone, M., trans. *The Testament of Abraham*. Missoula, Mont: Society of Biblical Literature, 1972.
Stroker, William D. *The Extracanonical Sayings of Jesus*. Atlanta: Scholars, 1989.
Tal, A. *The Samaritan Targum of the Pentateuch*. Tel Aviv: Tel Aviv University, 1980.
Talmud Babli. Wilna: Wittwa & Gebrüder Romm, 1835.
Talmud Jerushalmi. Krotoshin: Dov Baer Monash, 1866.
Taylor, C. *Sayings of the Fathers*. 2 volumes. Cambridge: Cambridge University Press, 1877.
Torah Shelemah. Edited by M. Kasher. 43 volumes. New York: Talmud Institute, 1951–1983.
Tosefta. Edited with commentary by S. Liebermann. 15 volumes. New York: Jewish Theological Seminary, 1955–1977.
Tosefta. Edited by M. Zuckermandel. Jerusalem: Wahrmann, 1937.
Vermes, G. *The Dead Sea Scrolls in English*. 3d ed. Baltimore: Penguin, 1988.
Visotzky, Burton. *The Midrash on Proverbs*. New Haven: Yale University Press, 1992.
Wacholder, B., and M. Abegg. *A Preliminary Edition of the Unpublished Dead Sea Scrolls*. Washington, D.C.: Biblical Archaeological Society, 1991–1995.
Wengst, K. *Schriften des Urchristentums*. Munich: Köstel, 1984.
Wertheimer, A. J. *Batei Midrashot*. 2 volumes. Jerusalem: Ketav Vesefer, 1980.
Yalkut Hamakiri. Edited by S. Buber. Berdyczew: Ch. J. Schefftel, 1899.
Yalkut Hamakiri. Edited by A. W. Greenup. Jerusalem: Hameitar, 1968.
Yalkut Hamakiri. Edited by Y. Shapiro. Jerusalem, 1964.
Yalkut Shimoni. Wilna: Wittwa & Gebrüder Romm, 1898.
Zlotnick, Z. *The Tractate Mourning*. New Haven: Yale University Press, 1966.

Secondary Literature

Abbott, Edwin. *Clue: A Guide through Greek to Hebrew Scripture*. London: Adam and Charles Black, 1900.
Abel, E. L. "Who Wrote Matthew?" *NTS* 17 (1971): 138–52.
Abrahams, Israel. *Studies in Pharisaism and the Gospels*. New York: KTAV, 1967.
Aland, Kurt, and Barbara Aland. *The Text of the New Testament*. Grand Rapids: Eerdmans, 1989.
Albright, W. F., and C. S. Mann. *The Gospel according to Matthew*. AB 26. New York: Doubleday, 1981.
Alon, G. *The Jews in Their Land in the Talmudic Age*. Jerusalem: Magnes, 1984.
Amidon, P. *The Panarion of St. Epiphanius*. New York: Oxford University Press, 1990.
Amiry, S., and V. Tamari. *The Palestinian Village Home*. London: British Museum, 1989.

Attridge, Harold. "Christianity from the Destruction of Jerusalem to Constantine's Adoption of the New Religion, 70–312 C.E." In *Christianity and Rabbinic Judaism.* Washington, D.C.: Biblical Archaeology Society, 1992.

Avi-Yonah, Michael, *Views of the Biblical World.* 5 volumes. Jerusalem: International, 1961.

Ayali, M. *Poalim Veomanim.* Jerusalem: Yad Letalmud, 1987.

Baarda, T. A., G. P. Hilhorst Luttikhuizen, and A. S. van der Woude, eds. *Text and Testimony.* Kampen, Netherlands: Kok, 1988.

Bacher, W. *Die Agada der palästinischen Amoräer.* Strassburg: Karl Tübner, 1892–1899. Translated into Hebrew by A. Rabinovitz. *Agadot Amore Eretz Israel.* Jerusalem: Davir, 1926.

______. *Die Agada der Tannaiten.* Strassburg: Karl Tübner, 1890. Translated into Hebrew by A. Rabinovitz. *Agadot Hatannaim.* Jerusalem: Davir, 1919.

______. *Die Exegetische Terminologie der jüdischen Traditionsliteratur.* Leipzig: Hinrich, 1905. Translated into Hebrew by A. Rabinovitz. *Erche Midrash.* Jerusalem: Carmiel, 1970.

______. *Tradition und Tradenten.* Leipzig: Gustav Fock, 1914.

Baeck, Leo. *Judaism and Christianity.* New York: Leo Baeck Institute, 1958.

Bailey, Kenneth E. *Finding the Lost.* St. Louis: Concordia, 1992.

Barth, Karl. *Church Dogmatics.* Translated by G. W. Bromiley. 4 volumes. Edinburgh: T. & T. Clark, 1936–1962.

Beall, Todd. *Josephus' Description of the Essenes Illustrated by the Dead Sea Scrolls.* Cambridge: Cambridge University Press, 1988.

Beasley-Murray, G. R. *Jesus and the Kingdom of God.* Grand Rapids: Eerdmans, 1986.

Bell, G. K. A., and Adolf Deissmann. *Mysterium Christi.* London: Longmans, Green, 1930.

Bengel, J. A. *Gnomon of the New Testament.* Philadelphia: Perkinpine & Higgins, 1860.

Berlin, Adele. *The Dynamics of Biblical Parallelism.* Bloomington: Indiana University Press, 1992.

Betz, H. D. *The Sermon on the Mount.* Minneapolis: Augsburg Fortress, 1995.

Bialik, C., and J. Rabnitzki. *Sefer Haagadah.* Tel Aviv: Davir, 1973.

Bickerman, Elias. *The Jews in the Greek Age.* New York: Jewish Theological Seminary, 1988.

Billerbeck, P. *Kommentar zum Neuen Testament aus Talmud und Midrasch.* 6 volumes. Munich: C. H. Beck, 1978.

Birdsall, J. N. "The New Testament Text." In *Cambridge History of the Bible.* 3 volumes. Cambridge: Cambridge University Press, 1970. 1.308–77.

Bishop, Eric F. F. *Jesus of Palestine.* London: Lutterworth, 1955.

Bivin, David, and Roy Blizzard. *Understanding the Difficult Words of Jesus,* Arcadia, Calif.: Makor Foundation, 1983.

Black, M. *An Aramaic Approach to the Gospels and Acts.* Oxford: Clarendon, 1977.

Blizzard, Roy B., Jr. *Let Judah Go Up First.* Austin, Tex.: Center for Judaic-Christian Studies, 1984.

Boismard, M., and A. Lamouille. *Synopsis Graeca quattuor Evangeliorum.* Paris: Peeters, 1986.

Boring, M. Eugene, Klaus Berger, and Carsten Colpe. *Hellenistic Commentary to the New Testament.* Nashville: Abingdon, 1995.

Bowker, John. *Jesus and the Pharisees.* Cambridge: Cambridge University Press, 1973.

Brown, Raymond E. *The Birth of the Messiah.* New York: Doubleday, 1977. Rev. ed. 1993.

______. *The Death of the Messiah.* 2 volumes. New York: Doubleday, 1994.

______. *New Testament Essays.* Milwaukee: Bruce, 1965. Reprint. New York: Doubleday Image, 1968.

Buber, Martin, *Two Types of Faith.* New York: Macmillan, 1961.

Büchler, A. "Learning and Teaching in the Open Air in Palestine," *JQR* 4 (1914): 485ff.

______. *Die Priester und der Cultus im letzten Jahrzehnt des jerusalemischen Tempels.* Vienna: Hölder, 1895.

______. *Types of Jewish-Palestinian Piety.* London: Jews' College Press, 1922.

Bultmann, Rudolf. *History of the Synoptic Tradition.* ET. Rev. ed. New York: Harper & Row, 1968. Reprint. Peabody, Mass.: Hendrickson, 1993.

______. *Jesus and the Word.* ET. New York: Scribner, 1958.

Chajes, Z. H. *The Student's Guide through the Talmud.* Translated and annotated by J. Schachter. New York: Feldheim, 1960.

Charlesworth, James H. *Jesus within Judaism.* Garden City, N.Y.: Doubleday, 1988.

______, ed. *Jesus and the Dead Sea Scrolls.* New York: Doubleday, 1993.

______. , ed. *The Messiah.* Minneapolis: Fortress, 1992.

Cohen, B. *Everyman's Talmud.* New York: Schocken, 1975.

Cornfeld, G., ed. *The Historical Jesus: A Scholarly View of the Man and His World.* New York: Macmillan, 1982.

Cohn, Haim. *The Trial and Death of Jesus.* New York: KTAV, 1977.

Craddock, Fred. *Luke.* Interpretation. Louisville: John Knox Press, 1990.

Crossan, John. *The Historical Jesus.* San Francisco: Harper, 1991.

______. *Raid on the Articulate: Cosmic Eschatology in Jesus and Borges.* New York: Harper, 1976.

Dalman, G. *Jesus-Jeshua.* London: SPCK, 1929.

______. *Sacred Sites and Sacred Ways.* London: SPCK, 1935.

______. *The Words of Jesus.* Edinburgh: T. & T. Clark, 1909.

Daniélou, Jean. *The Infancy Narratives.* ET. New York: Herder & Herder, 1968.

Daniel-Rops, Henri. *Daily Life in Palestine at the Time of Christ.* ET. London: Weidenfeld & Nicholson, 1961.

Daube, David. *The New Testament and Rabbinic Judaism.* 1956. Reprint. Peabody, Mass.: Hendrickson, 1994.
Davies, W. D. *The Setting of the Sermon on the Mount.* Atlanta: Scholars, 1989.
Davies, W. D., and D. Allison. *The Gospel according to St. Matthew.* ICC. Edinburgh: T. & T. Clark, 1988–1991.
Derrett, J. Duncan M. *Law in the New Testament.* London: Darton, Longman & Todd, 1970.
______. *Studies in the New Testament.* Leiden: Brill, 1982.
Deissmann, Adolf. *Bible Studies.* Edinburgh: T. & T. Clark, 1901.
______. *Light from the Ancient East.* ET 1927. Reprint. Grand Rapids: Baker, 1980.
Dibelius, Martin. *From Tradition to Gospel.* ET. New York: Scribners, 1933.
Diels, H., and W. Kranz, *Die Fragmente der Vorsokratiker.* 3 vols. Weidmann, 1968.
Doeve, J. W. *Jewish Hermeneutics in the Synoptic Gospels and Acts.* Assen: Van Gorcum, 1954.
Downing, F. Gerald. *Cynics and Christian Origins.* Edinburgh: T. & T. Clark, 1992.
Durward, J. T. *Holy Land and Holy Writ.* Baraboo, Wisc.: Pilgrim, 1913.
Elbogen, I. *Jewish Liturgy.* Philadelphia: Jewish Publication Society, 1993.
Encyclopaedia Judaica. Edited by Cecil Roth. 16 volumes. Jerusalem: Keter, 1978.
Epstein, J. N. *Mevoot Lesifrut Hatannaim.* Jerusalem: Magnes, 1957.
Finkelstein, L. *Akiba, Scholar, Saint, and Martyr.* New York: Atheneum, 1975.
______. *Haperushim Veanshe Keneset Hagedolah.* New York: Jewish Theological Seminary, 1950.
______. *Mevo Lemesechtot Avot Veavot Derabbi Natan.* New York: Jewish Theological Seminary, 1950.
______. *New Light from the Prophets.* New York: Basic, 1969.
______. *The Pharisees.* Philadelphia: Jewish Publication Society, 1940.
Fischel, Henry A. *Rabbinic Literature and Greco-Roman Philosophy.* Leiden: Brill, 1973.
Fitzmyer, J. A. *The Gospel according to Luke.* AB 28. 2 volumes. New York: Doubleday, 1981–1985.
______. *A Wandering Aramean.* Chico, Calif.: Scholars, 1979.
Flusser, David. "Blessed Are the Poor in Spirit." *IEJ* 10 (1960): 1–10.
______. "The Crucified One and the Jews." *Immanuel* 7 (1977): 25–37. Reprinted in *Judaism and the Origins of Christianity.* Pages 575–87. Jerusalem: Magnes, 1989. German original. "Der Gekreuzigte und die Juden." *Jahresbericht* 6 (1975) for the Lucerne Theological Faculty and Catechetical Institute.
______. *Das essenische Abenteuer.* Winterthur, Switzerland: Cardun, 1944.
______. *Jesus in Selbstzeugnissen und Bilddokumenten.* Hamburg: Rowohlt, 1968. (A poor English translation was published: New York: Herder & Herder, 1969.)

______. "Jesus' Opinion about the Essenes." In *Judaism and the Origins of Christianity.* Pages 150–168. Jerusalem: Magnes, 1989.

______. "Jewish Messianic Figures in Primitive Christianity." In *Messianism and Eschatology* (in Hebrew). Jerusalem: Zalman Shazar Center, 1983.

______. *Judaism and the Origins of Christianity.* Jerusalem: Magnes, 1989.

______. "Sanktus und Gloria." In *Abraham unser Vater.* Pages 9–152. FS Otto Michel zum 60. Geburtstag. Edited by O. Betz, M. Hengel, and P. Schmidt. Leiden: Brill, 1963.

______. "To Bury Caiaphas, Not to Praise Him." *Jerusalem Perspective* 33/34. 1991. Pages 23–28.

______. "Die Versuchung Jesu und ihr jüdische Hintergrund." *Judaica* 45 (1989): 110–28.

______. *Yahadut Umekorot Hanatzrut.* Tel Aviv: Sifriyat Poalim, 1979.

Fraade, Steven. *From Tradition to Commentary: Torah and Its Interpretation in the Midrash Sifre to Deuteronomy.* Albany: State University of New York Press, 1991.

Freeman, K. *Ancilla to the Pre-Socratic Philosophers.* Oxford: Clarendon, 1948.

Fridrichsen, A. "Exegetisches zum Neuen Testament," *Symbolae Osloeneses* 13 (1934): 28–46.

Gehardsson, Birger. *Memory and Manuscript: Oral Tradition and Written Transmission in Rabbinic Judaism and Early Christianity.* Lund, Sweden: Gleerup, 1964.

______. *The Testing of God's Son.* Lund, Sweden: Gleerup, 1966.

Gilat, Y. *R. Eliezer ben Hyrcanus, a Scholar Outcast.* Ramat Gan, Israel: Bar Ilan University Press, 1984.

Gilmore, A. *Christian Baptism.* London: Lutterworth, 1959.

Ginzberg, L. "The Religion of the Jews at the Time of Jesus." *HUCA* 1 (1924): 305–21.

Glatzer, Nahum. *Hillel the Elder: The Emergence of Classical Judaism.* New York: B'nai B'rith Hillel Foundations, 1956.

Goldin, J. "The Two Versions of *Abot de-Rabbi Nathan.*" *HUCA* 19 (1945): 97–120.

Graetz, H. *Popular History of the Jews.* 6 volumes. New York: Hebrew Publishing Co., 1949.

Grintz, J. "Hebrew as the Spoken and Written Language of the Second Temple." *JBL* 79 (1960): 32ff.

Gros, M. *Otzar Haagadah.* 3 volumes. Jerusalem: Mosad Harav Kook, 1977.

Hahn, C. *Corpus fabularum Aesopicarum.* 3 vols. Leipzig: Teubner, 1875.

Halperin, David. *The Merkabah in Rabbinic Literature.* New Haven: American Oriental Society, 1980.

Harnack, Adolf. *The Sayings of Jesus.* New York: Williams & Norgate, 1908.

Harrington, D. *The Gospel of Matthew.* Collegeville, Minn.: Liturgical, 1991.

Heinemann, I. *Darche Haagadah.* Jerusalem: Masada, 1970.

Heinemann, J. *Agadot Vetodotehen.* Jerusalem: Keter, 1974.

______. *Derashot Batzibor Batekufat Hatalmud.* Jerusalem: Bialik Institute, 1982.

Heinemann, J. and Dov Noy, eds. "Studies in Aggadah and Folk-Literature." *Scripta Hierosolymitana* 22. Jerusalem: Magnes, 1971.

Heintz, J. G. "Royal Traits and Messianic Figures: A Thematic and Iconographical Approach (Mesopotamian Elements)." In *The Messiah.* Pages 52–66. Edited by James H. Charlesworth. Minneapolis: Fortress, 1992.

Hengel, Martin. *Judaism and Hellenism.* London: SCM, 1974.

______. *Studies in the Gospel of Mark.* London: SCM, 1985.

______. *The Zealots.* Edinburgh: T. & T. Clark, 1989.

Heschel, Abraham Joshua. *God in Search of Man: A Philosophy of Judaism.* New York: Farrar, Strauss & Giroux, 1994.

______. *The Insecurity of Freedom.* New York: Schocken, 1972.

______. "Protestant Renewal: A Jewish View." In *Jewish Perspectives on Christianity.* Pages 301–8. Edited by F. Rothschild. New York: Crossroad, 1990.

______. *Torah Men Hashamayim.* 3 volumes. New York: Soncino, 1972–1990.

Hestrin, Ruth, and Yael Israeli, eds. *Inscriptions Reveal: Documents from the Time of the Bible, the Mishna, and the Talmud.* Jerusalem: Israel Museum, 1972.

Himmelfarb, Martha. *Tours of Hell.* Philadelphia: Fortress, 1983.

Horbury, W. "The Messianic Associations of 'the Son of Man.'" *JTS* 36 (1985): 34–55.

Horst, P. W. van der. *Ancient Jewish Epitaphs.* Kampen, Netherlands: Pharos, 1991.

Hruby, Kurt. "The Proclamation of the Unity of God as Actualization of the Kingdom." In *Standing before God.* Pages 183–93. Edited by A. Finkel and L. Frizzel. New York: KTAV, 1981.

Huck, Albert. *Synopse der ersten drei Evangelien.* Revised by Heinrich Greeven. Tübingen: J. C. B. Mohr, 1981.

Jeremias, J. *Jerusalem in the Time of Jesus.* London: SCM, 1969.

______. *New Testament Theology.* London: SCM, 1981.

______. *The Prayers of Jesus.* Philadelphia: Fortress, 1984.

Jónsson, Jakob. *Humour and Irony in the New Testament: Illuminated by Parallels in Talmud and Midrash.* Leiden: Brill, 1985.

Kadushim, Max. *The Rabbinic Mind.* New York: Bloch, 1972.

______. *The Theology of Seder Eliahu: A Study in Organic Thinking.* New York: Bloch, 1932.

Kensky, A. "Moses and Jesus: The Birth of a Savior." *Judaism* 42 (1993): 43–49.

Kenyon, Frederic. *Handbook to the Textual Criticism of the New Testament.* London: Macmillan, 1912.

Kilpatrick, G. D. *The Origins of the Gospel according to Matthew.* Oxford: Clarendon, 1946.

Kister, M. "Plucking on the Sabbath and Jewish-Christian Polemic." *Immanuel* 24/25 (1990): 35–51.

Klausner, Joseph. *From Jesus to Paul.* London: George Allen & Unwin, 1946.
______. *Jesus of Nazareth.* New York: Macmillan, 1945.
______. *The Messianic Idea in Israel.* New York: Macmillan, 1955.
Klostermann, E. *Das Lukasevangelium.* Tübingen: J. C. B. Mohr, 1950.
______. *Das Markusevangelium.* Tübingen: J. C. B. Mohr, 1950.
Kobelski, P. J. *Melchizedek and Melchireša̓.* CBQMS 10. Washington, D.C.: Catholic Biblical Association, 1981.
Lachs, S. T. *A Rabbinic Commentary on the New Testament.* Hoboken, N.J.: KTAV, 1987.
Ladd, G. E. *The Presence of the Future.* Grand Rapids: Eerdmans, 1980.
______. *A Theology of the New Testament.* Grand Rapids: Eerdmans, 1974.
Lagrange, P. *The Gospel of Jesus Christ.* Westminster, Md.: Newman, 1951.
Lapide, P. *The Sermon on the Mount.* New York: Orbis, 1986.
Lapide, P., and Ulrich Luz. *Jesus in Two Perspectives.* Minneapolis: Augsburg, 1971.
Lauterbach, Jacob. *Rabbinic Essays.* Cincinnati: Hebrew Union College Press, 1951.
Lessing, Gotthold. *Lessing's Theological Writings.* Selected and translated by Henry Chadwick. Stanford: Stanford University Press, 1956.
Levine, Lee. *Ancient Synagogues Revealed.* Jerusalem: Israel Exploration Society, 1981.
______. *The Galilee in Late Antiquity.* New York: Jewish Theological Seminary, 1992.
______. *The Rabbinic Class of Roman Palestine in Late Antiquity.* New York: Jewish Theological Seminary, 1989.
Lieberman, Saul. *Greek in Jewish Palestine.* New York: Feldheim, 1965.
______. *Hellenism in Jewish Palestine.* New York: Jewish Theological Seminary, 1962.
______. *Mechkarim Betorat Eretz Yisrael.* Jerusalem: Magnes, 1991.
______. *Texts and Studies.* New York: KTAV, 1974.
Lindsey, Robert L. *A Hebrew Translation of the Gospel of Mark.* Jerusalem: Baptist House, 1973.
______. *Jesus Rabbi and Lord.* Oak Creek, Wisc.: Cornerstone, 1990.
______. *The Jesus Sources.* Tulsa: HaKesher, 1990.
Lindsey, Robert L., and E. dos Santos. *A Comparative Greek Concordance of the Synoptic Gospels.* 3 volumes. Jerusalem: Baptist House, 1985–1989.
Loewenstamm, S. "Beloved Is Man in That He Was Created in the Image." In *Comparative Studies in Biblical and Ancient Oriental Literature.* Pages 48–50. Vluyn: Neukirchener, 1980.
______. "Chaviv Adam Shnivra Betzelem." *Tarbiz* 27 (1957–1958): 1–2.
Lowe, M. "The Demise of Arguments from Order for Markan Priority." *NovT* 24 (1982): 27–32.
Lundström, G. *The Kingdom of God in the Teachings of Jesus.* Richmond: John Knox, 1963.
Mackin, T. *Divorce and Remarriage.* Mahwah, N.J.: Paulist, 1984.

Malina, Bruce J., and Jerome H. Neyrey. "Honor and Shame in Luke-Acts: Pivotal Values of the Mediterranean World." In *The Social World of Luke-Acts.* Pages 25–66. Edited by Jerome H. Neyrey. Peabody, Mass.: Hendrickson, 1991.

Mann, C. S. *The Gospel according to Mark*. AB 27. New York: Doubleday, 1986.

Mann, Jacob. "Jesus and the Sadducean Priests: Luke 10:25–37." *JQR* 6 (1914): 415–22.

Manson, T. W. *The Sayings of Jesus.* London: SCM, 1977.

______. *The Teachings of Jesus.* Cambridge: Cambridge University Press, 1951.

Marmonstein, A. "Das Motiv vom veruntreuten Depositum in der jüdischen Volkskunde." *MGWJ* 78 (1934): 183–95.

Marshall, I. Howard, *The Gospel of Luke.* NIGTC. Grand Rapids: Eerdmans, 1978.

Masterman, E. *Studies in Galilee.* Chicago: University of Chicago Press, 1909.

Mazar, Amihai. "Bronze Bull Found in Israelite 'High Place' from the Time of the Judges." *Biblical Archeology Review.* September/October 1983, 21–22.

McArthur, H., and R. Johnston. *They Also Taught in Parables.* Grand Rapids: Zondervan, 1990.

McGinley, L. *Form-Criticism of the Synoptic Healing Narratives.* Woodstock, Md.: Woodstock College Press, 1944.

McNamara, M. *The New Testament and the Palestinian Targum to the Pentateuch.* Rome: Pontifical Biblical Institute, 1966.

McNeile, A. H. *The Gospel according to St. Matthew.* London: Macmillan, 1949.

McRay, John. *Archaeology and the New Testament.* Grand Rapids: Baker, 1991.

Metzger, Bruce. *The Text of the New Testament: Transmission, Corruption, and Restoration.* New York: Oxford University Press, 1992.

______. *A Textual Commentary of the Greek New Testament.* New York: United Bible Societies, 1975.

Meyer, Ben. *Aims of Jesus.* London: SCM, 1979.

Milik, J. T. *Ten Years of Discovery in the Wilderness of Judaea.* London: SCM, 1959.

Milikowsky, Chaim. "Gehenna and 'Sinners of Israel' in the Light of Seder Olam" (in Hebrew). *Tarbiz* 51 (1986): 311–43.

Moore, G. F "Christian Writers on Judaism." *HTR* 14 (1921): 197–254.

______. *Judaism in the First Centuries of the Christian Era.* New York: Schocken, 1975.

Montefiore, C. G. *Rabbinic Literature and Gospel Teachings.* NewYork: KTAV, 1970.

______. *The Synoptic Gospels.* 2 volumes. New York: KTAV, 1968.

Montefiore, C. G., and H. Loewe. *A Rabbinic Anthology.* New York: Schocken, 1974.

Mowinckel, Sigmund. *He That Cometh.* New York: Abingdon, 1954.

Murphy, Frederick. *The Religious World of Jesus.* Nashville: Abingdon, 1991.

Niehoff, M. "Do Biblical Characters Talk to Themselves? Narrative Modes of Representing Inner Speech in Early Biblical Fiction." *JBL* 111 (1992): 577–95.

Newman, L., and S. Spitz. *The Talmudic Anthology.* New York: Behrman House, 1945.

Nolland, John. *Luke.* Word Biblical Commentary 35. 3 volumes. Dallas: Word, 1989–1993.

Nun, Mendel. *Ancient Stone Anchors and Net Sinkers from the Sea of Galilee.* Israel: Kibbutz Ein Gev, 1993.

______. *The Sea of Galilee and Its Fishermen in the New Testament.* Israel: Kibbutz Ein Gev, 1989.

Perrin, N. *Jesus and the Language of the Kingdom.* Philadelphia: Fortress, 1976.

Plummer, Alfred. *An Exegetical Commentary on the Gospel according to St. Matthew.* 5th ed. 1920. Reprint. Grand Rapids: Eerdmans, 1953.

______. *The Gospel according to St. Luke.* ICC. New York: Scribner, 1900.

Pococke, Edward. *A Commentary on the Prophecy of Micah.* Oxford: Oxford University Press, 1676.

Pritz, Ray. *Nazarene Jewish Christianity.* Jerusalem: Magnes, 1988.

Propp, V. *Theory and History of Folklore.* Minneapolis: University of Minnesota Press, 1985.

Raphael, S. *Jewish Views of the Afterlife.* London: Jason Aronson, 1994.

Resch, A. *Die Logia Jesu.* Leipzig: J. C. Hinrichs, 1898.

Riches, John. *Jesus and the Transformation of Judaism.* London: Darton, Longman & Todd, 1980.

Robinson, John A. T. *Redating the New Testament.* London: SCM, 1978.

Rothschild, F., ed. *Jewish Perspectives on Christianity.* New York: Crossroad, 1990.

Safrai, S. *Beyame Habayit Uveyame Hamishnah.* Jerusalem: Magnes, 1994.

______. "Chasididm Venashe Maaseh." *Tzion* 16 (1985): 134–54.

______. "The Jewish Cultural Nature of Galilee in the First Century." *Immanuel* 24/25 (1990): 147–86.

______. *Rabbi Akiva Ben Yosef Chayav Umishnato.* Jerusalem: Bialik Institute, 1970.

______. "Teaching of Pietists in Mishnaic Literature." *JJS* 16 (1965): 15–33.

Safrai, S., M. Stern, D. Flusser, and W. C. van Unnik, eds. *The Jewish People in the First Century.* 9 volumes. 10th in preparation. Amsterdam:Van Gorcum, 1974–1993.

Sanders, E. P. *The Historical Figure of Jesus.* London: Penguin, 1991.

______. *Jesus and Judaism.* London: SCM, 1985.

______. *Jewish Law from Jesus to the Mishnah.* Philadelphia: Trinity, 1990.

______. *Paul and Palestinian Judaism.* London: SCM, 1977.

Sanders, J. A. *Discoveries in the Judean Desert: The Psalms Scroll of Qumran Cave 11.* New York: Oxford University Press, 1965.

Sandmel, Samuel. *Judaism and Christian Beginnings.* New York: Oxford University Press, 1978.

______. "Parallelomania." *JBL* 81 (1962): 1–13.

Schechter, S. *Aspects of Rabbinic Theology.* New York: Schocken, 1961.

A. Schlatter. *Die Theologie des Judentums nach dem Bericht des Josefus.* Gütersloh: C. Bertelsmann, 1932.

Schnackenburg, R. *The Gospel according to St. John.* New York: Crossroad, 1975.

Schrage, W. *Das Verhältnis des Thomas Evangeliums zur synoptischen Tradition und zu den koptischen Evangelienübersetzungen.* Berlin: Töpelmann, 1964.

Schürer, E. *The History of the Jewish People in the Time of Jesus Christ.* 6 volumes. 1891. Reprint. Peabody, Mass.: Hendrickson, 1993.

______. *The History of the Jewish People in the Time of Jesus Christ.* Revised and edited by G. Vermes, F. Millar, and M. Black. 3 volumes. Edinburgh: T. & T. Clark, 1974–1987.

Schweizer, E. *Jesus.* London: SCM, 1971.

Sieber, John H. "The Gospel of Thomas and the New Testament." In *Gospel Origins and Christian Beginnings.* 2 volumes. Sonoma, Calif.: Polebridge, 1990. 1:64–73.

Sigal, Phillip. *The Halakah of Jesus of Nazareth.* Lanham, Md.: University Press of America, 1986.

Skehan, Patrick, and Alexander Di Lella. *Wisdom of Ben Sira.* AB 39. Garden City, N.Y.: Doubleday, 1987.

Smith, Morton. "A Comparison of Early Christian and Early Rabbinic Tradition." *JBL* 82 (1963): 169–76.

______. *Tannaitic Parallels to the Gospels.* JBLMS 6. Philadelphia: Society of Biblical Literature, 1951.

Soloveitchik, Joseph B. *Halakhic Man.* Philadelphia: Jewish Publication Society, 1983.

Stendahl, K. *The Scrolls and the New Testament.* New York: Harper, 1957.

Stein, S. "The Influence of Symposa Literature on the Literary Form of the *Pesah* Haggadah." *JJS* 8 (1957): 13–44.

Stern, M. "Aspects of Jewish Society: The Priesthood and Other Classes." In *The Jewish People in the First Century.* 2.561–603. Edited by S. Safrai, M. Stern, D. Flusser, and W. C. van Unnik. 9 volumes. Amsterdam: Van Gorcum, 1974–1993.

______. "The Greek and Latin Literary Sources." In *The Jewish People in the First Century.* 1:18–36. Edited by S. Safrai, M. Stern, D. Flusser, and W. C. van Unnik. 9 volumes. Amsterdam: Van Gorcum, 1974–1993.

______. *Mechkarim Betoldot Yisrael Beyame Bayit Sheni.* Jerusalem: Yad Izhak Ben Zvi, 1991.

Stoldt, Hans-Herbert. *History and Criticism of the Marcan Hypothesis.* Macon, Ga.: Mercer, 1980.

Strack, H. *Einleitung in Talmud und Midrasch.* Revised by G. Stemberger. Munich: C. H. Beck, 1981.

______. *Introduction to the Talmud and Midrash.* New York: Atheneum, 1978.

Strauss, David Friedrich. *The Life of Jesus Critically Examined.* 1892. Reprint. Philadelphia: Fortress, 1972.
Swete, H. B. *The Gospel according to St. Mark.* London: Macmillan, 1905.
Taylor, V. *The Gospel according to St. Mark.* London: Macmillan, 1941.
______. *The Text of the New Testament: A Short Introduction.* London: Macmillan, 1961.
Thoma, Clemens. *A Christian Theology of Judaism.* Mahwah, N.J.: Paulist, 1980.
Thomson, W. H. *The Land and the Book.* New York: Harper, 1859.
Tomson, Peter J. *Paul and the Jewish Law.* Assen: Van Gorcum, 1990.
Torrey, Charles C. *Our Translated Gospels.* London: Hodder & Stoughton, 1933.
Trigg, Joseph W. *Origen.* Atlanta: John Knox, 1983.
Tristram, H. B. *Eastern Customs in Bible Lands.* London: Hodder & Stoughton, 1894.
Urbach, E. E. *Class-Status and Leadership in the World of Palestinian Sages.* Jerusalem: Israel Academy of Sciences and Humanities, 1966.
______. *The Halakhah: Its Sources and Development.* Jerusalem: Yad Latalmud, 1986.
______. *The Sages: Their Concepts and Beliefs.* 2 volumes. Jerusalem: Magnes, 1975.
VanderKam, James. *The Dead Sea Scrolls Today.* Grand Rapids: Eerdmans, 1994.
Vermes, G. *Jesus and the World of Judaism.* London: SCM, 1983.
______. *Jesus the Jew.* London: Collins, 1973.
______. *The Religion of Jesus the Jew.* Minneapolis: Fortress, 1993.
______. "Sectarian Matrimonial Halakhah in the Damascus Rule." *JSS* 25 (1974): 197ff.
Weatherhead, L. *In Quest of a Kingdom.* New York: Abingdon, 1944.
Willis, W. *The Kingdom of God in 20th-Century Interpretation.* Peabody, Mass.: Hendrickson, 1987.
Wilson, Marvin. *Our Father Abraham.* Grand Rapids: Eerdmans, 1989.
Winter, Paul. *On the Trial of Jesus.* Berlin: Walter de Gruyter, 1961.
Wise, M., N. Golb, J. J. Collins, and D. Pardee. *Methods of Investigation of the Dead Sea Scrolls and the Khirbet Qumran Site.* New York: New York Academy of Sciences, 1994.
Wolpe, David. *Healer of Shattered Hearts: A Jewish View of God.* New York: Henry Holt, 1990.
______. *In Speech and Silence: The Jewish Quest for God.* New York: Henry Holt, 1992.
Woude, A. S. van der. "Melchisedek als himmlische Erlösergestalt in den neugefundenen eschatologischen Midraschim aus Qumran Höhle XI." *Oudtestementische Studiën* 14 (1965): 354–73.
Wünsche, A. *Erläuterung der Evangelien aus Talmud und Midrasch.* Göttingen: Vandenhoeck & Ruprecht, 1878.

Young, Brad H. "The Ascension Motif of 2 Corinthians in Jewish, Christian, and Gnostic Texts." *Grace Theological Journal* 9 (1, 1988): 73–103.

______. "The Cross, Jesus, and the Jewish People." *Immanuel* 24/25 (1990): 23–34.

______. *Jesus and His Jewish Parables.* Mahwah, N.J.: Paulist, 1989.

______. *Jesus the Jewish Theologian.* Peabody, Mass.: Hendrickson, 1995.

______. *The Jewish Background to the Lord's Prayer.* Austin, Tex.: Center for Judaic-Christian Studies, 1984.

______. *Paul the Jewish Theologian.* Peabody, Mass.: Hendrickson, 1997.

Young, Brad H., and David Flusser. "Messianic Blessings in Jewish and Christian Texts." In David Flusser, *Judaism and the Origins of Christianity.* Pages 280–300. Jerusalem: Magnes, 1989.

Grammatical and Lexical Aids

Bauer, W., W. Arndt, F. W. Gingrich, and F. W. Danker. *A Greek-English Lexicon of the New Testament and Other Early Christian Literature.* 2d ed. Chicago: University of Chicago Press, 1979.

Ben Yehuda, Eliezer. *Milon Halashon Haevrit.* 17 volumes. Jerusalem: General Federation of Jewish Labor in Eretz Israel, 1959.

Blass, F., and A. Debrunner. *A Greek Grammar of the New Testament and Other Early Christian Literature.* Translated and revised by R. Funk. Chicago: University of Chicago Press, 1961.

Brown, F. *The New Brown-Driver-Briggs-Gesenius Hebrew and English Lexicon.* 1906. Reprint. Peabody, Mass: Hendrickson, 1979.

Dalman, G. *Aramäisch-neuhebräisches Handwörterbuch.* Frankfurt am Main: J. Kaufmann, 1922.

______. *Grammatik des jüdisch-palästinischen Aramäisch.* 1905. Reprint. Darmstadt: Wissenschaftliche, 1960.

Golomb, D. *A Grammar of Targum Neofiti.* Chico, Calif: Scholars, 1985.

Howard, W. F. "Semitisms in the New Testament." In *A Grammar of New Testament Greek.* 2.418–19. Edited by J. H. Moulton. 4 volumes. Edinburgh: T. & T. Clark, 1930.

Jastrow, M. *A Dictionary of the Targumim, the Talmud Babli and Yerushalmi, and the Midrashic Literature.* 2 volumes. 1886–1903. Reprint. New York: Judaica, 1975.

Kittel, G., ed. *Theological Dictionary of the New Testament.* Translated by G. Bromiley. 10 volumes. Grand Rapids: Eerdmans, 1964–1976.

Koehler, L., and W. Baumgartner. *Lexicon in Veteris Testamentilibros.* 2d ed. Leiden: Brill, 1958.

Kosovsky, B. *Otzar Leshon Hatannaim Lasifra.* New York: Jewish Theological Seminary, 1967.

______. *Otzar Leshon Hatannaim Lasifre Bemidbar Vedevarim.* New York: Jewish Theological Seminary, 1971.

______. *Otzar Leshon Hatannaim Lemekilta Derabbi Ishmael.* New York: Jewish Theological Seminary, 1965.

Kosovsky, Ch. *Otzar Leshon Hamishnah.* Tel Aviv: Massadah, 1967.

______. *Otzar Leshon Hatalmud.* Jerusalem: Ministry of Education and Culture, Government of Israel, 1971.

______. *Otzar Leshon Hatosefta.* New York: Jewish Theological Seminary, 1961.

Kosovsky, M. *Otzar Leshon Talmud Yerushalmi.* Jerusalem: Israel Academy of Sciences and Humanities, 1979.

Kutscher, E.Y. "Aramaic." In *Encyclopaedia Judaica.* 3:260–87. Jerusalem: Keter, 1978.

______. *Studies in Galilean Aramaic.* Ramat Gan, Israel: Bar Ilan University Press, 1976.

Levias, C. *A Grammar of Galilean Aramaic* (in Hebrew). New York: Jewish Theological Seminary, 1986.

Levy, J. *Chaldäisches Wörterbuch über die Targumim und einen grossen Theil des rabbinischen Schriftthums.* 2 volumes. Leipzig: J. C. Hinrichs, 1867–1868.

______. *Wörterbuch über die Talmudim und Midraschim.* 4 volumes. Berlin: Benjamin Harz, 1924.

Liddell, H. G., and R. Scott, *A Greek-English Lexicon.* Oxford: Clarendon, 1976.

Moulton, J. H., ed. *A Grammar of New Testament Greek.* 4 volumes. Edinburgh: T. & T. Clark, 1930.

Nathan ben Zechiel. *Aruch Completum.* Edited by A. Kohut. 1878–1892. Reprint. Jerusalem, Israel: Books Export Enterprises, n.d.

Sokoloff, M. *A Dictionary of Jewish Palestinian Aramaic.* Ramat Gan, Israel: Bar Ilan University Press, 1990.

Spicq, Ceslas. *Theological Lexicon of the New Testament.* Translated and edited by J. Ernest. 3 volumes. Peabody, Mass.: Hendrickson, 1994.

Stevenson, W. B. *Grammar of Palestinian Jewish Aramaic.* Oxford: Clarendon, 1974.

Strack, H. L., and P. Billerbeck. *Kommentar zum Neuen Testament aus Talmud und Midrasch.* 6 volumes. Munich: C. H. Beck, 1922–1961.

Thackery, J. H. *A Grammar of the Old Testament in Greek.* Cambridge: Cambridge University Press, 1909.

Index of Parables and Illustrations

Introduction to Gospel and Rabbinic Parables

The Contemptible Friend and the Corrupt Judge (Luke 11:5–8 and 18:1–8)

The Fair Employer (Matthew 20:1–6)

The Talents: God's Gracious Gifts (Matthew 25:14–30; Luke 19:11–27; Mark 13:34)

The Samaritan: Love Your Enemies (Luke 10:25–37)

The Merciful Lord and His Unforgiving Servant (Matthew 18:23–35)

The Father of Two Lost Sons (Luke 15:11–32)

The Two Debtors (Luke 7:41–43)

The Urgent Invitation (Luke 14:15–24; Matthew 22:1–4; *Gospel of Thomas* 64)

The Search: The Lost Sheep and The Lost Coin (Luke 15:1–10; Matthew 18:12–14; *Gospel of Thomas* 107)

The Find (Matthew 13:44–46; *Gospel of Thomas* 76, 109)

The Decision
(Luke 14:28–33)

The Unjust Steward
(Luke 16:1–13)

Four Types of Hearers
(Matthew 13:1–13; Mark 4:1–20; Luke 8:4–15; *Gospel of Thomas* 8–9)

Death and Eschatology: A Theology of Imminence
(Luke 12:16–20; *Gospel of Thomas* 63)

Index of Names and Subjects

Index of Ancient Sources

RABBINIC LITERATURE

GREEK & LATIN AUTHORS

CHURCH TRADITION

Printed and bound by CPI Group (UK) Ltd, Croydon, CR0 4YY

07/02/2023

03189148-0001